THE
COLONIAL HISTORY
SERIES

General Editor
D. H. Simpson

Librarian of the Royal Commonwealth Society

CONSTITUTION OF THE BRITISH COLONIES IN NORTH AMERICA

A VIEW of the CONSTITUTION of the BRITISH COLONIES in North America and the West Indies

by

Anthony Stokes

1783

WITH A SUPPLEMENTARY INDEX

1969
DAWSONS OF PALL MALL
London

First published in London 1783
Reprinted with new index 1969

Dawsons of Pall Mall
16 Pall Mall, London, S.W.1

SBN: 7129 0346 1

PRINTED BY Unwin Brothers Limited
THE GRESHAM PRESS OLD WOKING SURREY ENGLAND
Produced by offset lithography

A member of the Staples Printing Group

A VIEW OF THE CONSTITUTION OF THE BRITISH COLONIES, IN NORTH-AMERICA AND THE WEST INDIES,

AT THE TIME

The CIVIL WAR broke out on the Continent of AMERICA.

IN WHICH

Notice is taken of ſuch Alterations as have happened ſince that Time, down to the preſent Period.

WITH

A Variety of COLONY PRECEDENTS, which are chiefly adapted to the BRITISH WEST INDIA ISLANDS; and may be uſeful to thoſe, who have any intercourſe with the COLONIES.

By ANTHONY STOKES,
Of the INNER TEMPLE, LONDON; BARRISTER AT LAW;
HIS MAJESTY'S CHIEF JUSTICE OF GEORGIA.

LONDON:
PRINTED FOR THE AUTHOR:
AND SOLD BY B. WHITE, IN FLEET-STREET.
MDCCLXXXIII.

PREFACE.

THE Editor of the following Sheets having resided several years on the Continent of America, and in different Islands in the West Indies, he flatters himself that he is not altogether unqualified for the present Undertaking.

When he had determined on going abroad in 1762, he in vain sought for some Book that would afford him an insight of the Constitution and Mode of Proceeding in the Colonies: he was equally unsuccessful in his search after Colony Precedents; for in all the English Law Books he met with, he does not remember to have found half a score Colony Forms. These disappointments early suggested to him the utility of a Compilation of this sort, and he soon began to collect Precedents for that purpose.

The Editor having taken a decided part in the cause of Great Britain against her Revolted Colonies, he was, on the breaking out of the Troubles in the Southern Provinces, made a Prisoner by the Americans; and after being confined some weeks, he was exchanged, with liberty to leave the Country; on which he returned to Great Britain, and then began to

digest

digeſt the Precedents he had collected, with an intention of making them public; but before that was done, he received an order to go abroad, and reſume the exerciſe of his office, in conſequence of the reduction, by his Majeſty's Forces, of the Province from whence he came. The King's ſhip in which he embarked having received ſome damage in an action with the enemy on the coaſt of France, ſhe returned to Great Britain to be refitted, which afforded the Editor an opportunity of reviſing his Work: and, on his ſecond embarkation, he left directions to have it printed; but a Bookſeller having declined to do ſo, the Editor is now enabled to notice ſuch alterations as have taken place between the year 1779, and May 1783.

The Province in which the Editor reſided being evacuated by the King's forces, he hurried home to his native Country, in hopes of ſpending the remainder of his days in the enjoyment of his family and friends, after eſcaping many dangers, and undergoing much ſickneſs, by a long reſidence in unwholeſome climates; but when he arrived at his own door, he was informed of the death of his only ſon, a young man of the moſt promiſing hopes, whoſe moral qualities ſo thoroughly kept pace with his literary acquirements, that it was doubtful in which he excelled. At the age of twenty-two, he died eſteemed and lamented by all that knew him; and he never occaſioned his parents any grief but what they experienced

at

at his death. The Reader will pardon this digreſſion, as a tribute due from a father to the memory of the beſt of ſons; in compariſon of whoſe death, all the Editor's other misfortunes are become trifles light as air.

The tears being wiped away, I reſume the ſubject.—During the ſiege of Savannah, the Editor's quarters were burned by a ſhell from the enemy's lines, and moſt of his papers were deſtroyed: but he has ſince met with other Precedents, ſome of which are inſerted herein.

The Editor is but too ſenſible of the numerous imperfections of this Eſſay; however he flatters himſelf, that as it is the firſt attempt of the kind, the Public will ſhew him ſome indulgence; ſince this feeble endeavour may induce an able hand to undertake the ſubject.

In this Work there are a few ſtrictures on the conduct of ſome Colony Officers; but the Editor could not prevail on himſelf to mention the names of thoſe Colony Officers, nor of the Countries where they reſided: Chriſtianity enjoins charity and benevolence towards all men; his reſentment, therefore, is levelled at the miſconduct, and not at the individual.

There are other Colony Officers whom the Editor wiſhes to notice with great reſpect; and particularly Sir James Wright (Governor of Georgia, from the ſecond year of his preſent Majeſty's reign, down to the Evacuation of that Province in the ſummer of 1782), whoſe whofe fidelity to the Crown, and unwearied attention to the welfare of the Colony in which he prefided, are too well known to need the Editor's mention of them. He alfo begs leave to exprefs his efteem for Sir Ralph Payne, formerly Governor of the Leeward Iflands; General Tonyn, Governor of Eaft Florida; and Colonel Martyn, Governor of North Carolina. The great humanity which Governor Tonyn fhewed to the loyal Refugees, who went from Georgia to St. Auguftine in 1776 and 1782, muft endear him to all thofe who feel for the virtuous under misfortunes: and it is defired that the Reader will not apply to either of the Governors above named, any inftance of mifconduct or miftake which this Work mentions to have been committed by Colony Officers. The character and conduct of moft of the Colony Governors, and other Officers, the Editor is unacquainted with, and he would be forry to give offence to any of them.

In order to confine the Publication to one Volume, it was found neceffary to omit feveral Conveyances, and other Colony Precedents. Some inaccuracies are difcovered to have efcaped the Editor, which it is hoped the Reader will excufe, when he reflects, that a polifhed ftyle, which is only to be derived from an intimate acquaintance with the Belles Lettres, cannot be expected from a man whofe profeffion leads him to the ftudy of Law-French Reports, and Law-Latin Entries, in the Black Letter.

Should

Should the Gentlemen of the Law from the Colonies discover any mistakes in this Production, the Editor will consider as a great favour their pointing out such mistakes, by a line directed to him at the Bookseller's: and the assisting him with any useful Colony Precedents, that might contribute to render this Performance more useful, in case a second Edition should be called for, would add to the obligation.

P. S. The Editor has just recollected his having mentioned, in page 138 of this Work, "That the King's cause in the Colonies was "greatly weakened by bestowing the lucrative "offices there on persons residing in Great "Britain:" he therefore thinks it necessary to observe, that he apprehends the nomination of Colony Officers was left to the American Minister for the time, with whom also the leave of absence originated. The Editor's attachment to the person and government of his Royal Master (the best of Kings), in whose service he has undergone many trying scenes, has induced him to say so much, to prevent misconstruction: and he flatters himself that no Gentleman who held the Department of American Minister, can take offence at the passage above quoted, as nothing more was done by those Ministers, than had been practised by their predecessors from the first Establishment of British Colonies.

A man

A man who has obſerved the miſery which the Americans brought on themſelves by ſubverting his Majeſty's Government, will put a true value on the ineſtimable bleſſings of a patriot King, and the beſt Conſtitution on earth; and will be particularly cautious of ſaying any thing that can be conſtrued into a diſreſpect of either.

TABLE

TABLE

OF

CONTENTS.

CHAP. XIII.

CHAP. XIV.

CHAP. XV.

CHAP. XVI.

CHAP. XVII.

CHAP. XVIII.

APPENDIX.

INTRODUCTION.

BEFORE I enter on the immediate ſubject of this Compilation, I muſt intreat the Reader's patience whilſt I take notice of the different European powers that have ſettlements in America, and amongſt whom ſuch parts of the New World as do not remain in the hands of the Indians, or in the poſſeſſion of the United States of America, are at preſent divided; which is the more neceſſary, on account of the change of property occaſioned by the late Peace. It may not be improper in the firſt place to premiſe, that America was diſcovered by Chriſtopher Columbus, a Genoeſe, in the ſervice of Spain, on the 16th day of October, 1492, and took its name from Americus Veſputius, a Florentine, who, in the year 1497, was employed by the Spaniards, or, as ſome ſay, by Emanuel king of Portugal, to make further diſcoveries. But the French pretend, that the Baſque fiſhermen frequented Newfoundland before Chriſtopher Columbus found out the New World.

The ſtory mentioned by Poſtlethwayt in his Dictionary, of a Welſh prince having diſcovered America in the year 1109, I take to be altogether fabulous.

On the diſcovery of America, Pope Alexander the Sixth, by Bull, gave the New World to Ferdinand and Iſabella, king and queen of Caſtile and Arragon, as if he had a right to diſpoſe thereof.

of. See an Extract from this Bull in Vattel's Law of Nations, fol. 90, *in notis*.

In the year 1497 or 1498, John Cabot was employed by Henry the Seventh, king of England, to find a North-weft paffage to China; but although he failed in that attempt, yet he difcovered the North-eaft Coafts of America, which compofe the greateft part of the Britifh Colonies in that quarter of the world. Sebaftian Cabot accompanied his father in that expedition; but was not the perfon employed by Henry the Seventh, as is commonly faid.

This great Weftern Continent, which is frequently called the New World, is faid to extend from the 80th degree of North Latitude to the 56th degree of South Latitude: And its greateft known breadth is from the 35th to the 136th degree of Weft Longitude from London. Its greateft length is faid to be between eight and nine thoufand miles; and its greateft breadth about three thoufand fix hundred and ninety. It is bounded on the Eaft by the Atlantic Ocean, which feparates it from Europe and Africa; and on the Weft by the Pacific Ocean, or South Sea, which feparates it from Afia. It is divided into North and South America; and both thefe great peninfulas are joined together by the Ifthmus of Panama, which, at Darien, is only fixty miles wide. The Englifh Spaniards, Portuguefe, French, Dutch, and Danes, are the only European nations that have Colonies in America, unlefs fome of the Iflands between America and Afia, which are claimed by the Ruffians, are nearer to the American than the Afiatic fhore. Soon after the difcovery of America, the Spaniards poffeffed themfelves of the largeft and beft parts of it. In North America they have all that part of Louifiana, which

which lies to the West of the river Miſſiſſippi, New Mexico, California, and Old Mexico; and by the treaty of Verſailles, Great Britain has ceded to Spain the two provinces of Eaſt and Weſt Florida. In South America the Spaniards poſſeſs Terra Firma, or Caſtilla del Ora, Peru, Chili, and Paraguay, or La Plata. They have alſo the Iſlands of Cuba, Porto Rico, Trinidada, Margarita, Juan Fernandez, and a great part of Hiſpaniola, or St. Domingo; beſides a great number of ſmall Iſlands, both on the Eaſt and Weſt-ſide of America, that are too inſignificant to be enumerated.

In South America the Portugueſe have Braſil, which was diſcovered by Americus Veſputius in 1498, and lies between the Equator and the 35th degree of South Latitude; and ſome ſmall Iſlands on the coaſt of Braſil, the principal of which are Fernando, St. Barbara, and St. Catharine's.

Since the ceſſion of Canada (or Quebec) to Great Britain, and of Louiſiana to Spain, the French have no ſettlement on the Continent except that at Cayenne, ſituate between the Equator and the 5th degree of North Latitude; but they have a great part of that large Iſland called Hiſpaniola, or St. Domingo, which is the moſt valuable of all their American Colonies. The French have alſo Guadaloupe, Martinique, St. Lucia, and ſeveral ſmall Iſlands, ſuch as Marigalante, Deſeada, the Saintes, Bartholomew or Barthelemi, Cayenne, and part of St. Martin's: And by the Preliminary Articles of 1783, Great Britain has ceded to France the Iſland of Tobago. St. Lucia was captured by the Engliſh in the laſt war, but was reſtored to the French on the late peace.

The Dutch have ſeveral Colonies on the Continent of America, ſituate a few degrees to the

north

north of the Equinoctial, which lie on large rivers. The principal of these settlements is at Surinam, which once belonged to the English; the others are Berbice, Demerara, and Essequibo; but these Colonies are not in a flourishing condition, owing to the land being low, and subject to floods; and Surinam and Demerara have suffered much from insurrections of the Negroes.— Some of these Dutch settlements (and in particular Demerara) are inhabited in a good measure by unfortunate planters from the English West India Islands. The Dutch have also the Islands of St. Eustatius, Saba, and part of St. Martin's to windward; and to leeward, near the Spanish main, they have the Islands of Curassou, Bonaire, and Aruba: but these Islands are small, and barren, and derive all their consequence from the contraband trade which the Dutch carry on with the Colonies belonging to other powers. In the last war, Demerara, Essequibo, St. Eustatius, Saba, and St. Martin's, were captured by the English, but retaken by the French. When I paid my respects to the Governor of St. Eustatius on my going to see that Island in 1763, he informed me, that in the former French war, before the English broke up the trade between St. Eustatius and the French Islands, he had seen upwards of two hundred and seventy sail of vessels in the Road of St. Eustatius at one time. I have lately been informed, by an acquaintance from the West Indies, that before Lord Rodney took St. Eustatius, there had been six hundred sail of vessels in the Road of St. Eustatius together. The Danes had no footing in America, until the English gave them St. Thomas's, one of the Virgin Islands; and after they had settled it, they took possession of St. John's, a small Island, which is

said

ſaid to have been the property of the Paynes of St. Chriſtopher's. Between thirty and forty years ago, the Danes purchaſed the Iſland of Santa Cruz, or St. Croix, from the French; and it at firſt belonged to a Daniſh Company, but has for ſeveral years paſt been a a Royal Government, and now produces almoſt as much ſugar as any Iſland the Engliſh have, except Jamaica and Grenada. The Danes owe the ſettlement of their Iſlands chiefly to the Refugee Debtors from the Britiſh Colonies, and by much the largeſt portion of the inhabitants of Santa Cruz are Engliſh. When I was in the Weſt Indies, I obſerved that ſeveral perſons in the Britiſh Iſlands, who owed more than they were worth, on being ſued for payment of their debts, they privately embarked in ſome out bay, and retired to a Dutch or Daniſh Iſland, carrying with them ſuch of their ſlaves and other property as they could conveniently remove. In thoſe foreign Iſlands they obtained the privileges of burghers for a ſmall ſum, and were conſidered as Dutch or Daniſh ſubjects by the Governors, who frequently protected them againſt the demands of their creditors, until remonſtrances were made againſt thoſe abuſes.

The Iſland of St. Thomas is conſiderable only for the goodneſs of its harbour, which the king of Denmark made a free port ſome years ago: and after the capture of St. Euſtatius, a vaſt commerce centered at St. Thomas's. The Thirteen United States of America, *viz.* New Hampſhire, Maſſachuſett's Bay, Rhode Iſland, and Providence Plantations, Connecticut, New York, New Jerſey, Pennſylvania, Delaware, Maryland, Virginia, North Carolina, South Carolina, and Georgia, are ſituate on the North-eaſt coaſts of America,

America, and extend from North Latitude 30 degrees and an half to 48 degrees; and from West Longitude 66 degrees and an half to 98 degrees and an half, having a sea-coast of 15 degrees of Latitude. But the particular boundaries of those States may be seen in the second article of the Provisional Treaty between Great Britain and the United States; and in Faden's Map of those States, published in 1783. Most of the lands within those boundaries are in the possession of the Indians.

A VIEW

A VIEW OF THE CONSTITUTION OF THE BRITISH COLONIES, &c. &c. &c.

CHAP. I.

Of the British Colonies in America.—The Nature of their Dependence on the Mother Country at the breaking out of the Civil War on the Continent of America—with such Alterations as have taken place down to the present Period.

COLONY (*Colonia*, from *Colonus*, a Farmer) signifies a Company of People sent to a remote place, to dwell there, and cultivate the land.

Plantation in the Sugar and Rice Colonies, denotes a piece, or tract of land, which is either granted to, or purchased by, a person to cultivate for his own use. But in the Northern British Colonies, where the produce is similar to that of England, the lands they cultivate are more frequently called Farms, than Plantations; as they informed

informed me, when I was at New York. In a more extended ſenſe, a Plantation is a place to which people emigrate, in order to dwell there, with an allowance of land for their tillage, and immunities for the good of themſelves, and the Metropolis, or Mother Country to which they belong; and in this acceptation, the word Plantation is uſed to denote a Britiſh Settlement in America. In ſtrict propriety of ſpeech, Colony denotes the people emigrated, and Plantation the place in which they are ſettled; but theſe words are often uſed in a ſynonymous ſenſe, both in Acts of Parliament, and on other occaſions. See Statutes 5 Geo. II. c. 7.—6 Geo. III. c. 12.—18 Geo. III. c. 12. ſ. 1.—22 Geo. III. c. 75.—Show. Parl. c. 31.

Colonies generally conſiſt of perſons who voluntarily offer themſelves, either upon the hopes of mending a broken and decayed fortune, or elſe of ſuch as are out of humour with the Government, and willing to be out of its ſight, when they find they are not to expect favours from it. See Puff. L. N. & N. l. viii. c. 11. ſ. 6. and l. viii c. 12. ſ. 5.

Province (*Provincia*) hath ſeveral different acceptations. Amongſt the Romans it was uſed for a country without the limits of Italy, gained to their ſubjection by conqueſt; but, in general, it is uſed to denote the diviſion of a kingdom or ſtate, as they are uſually diſtinguiſhed by the extent of their civil or eccleſiaſtical juriſdiction. With us, a Province ſignifies, 1ſt, An out-country, governed by a Deputy or Lieutenant: and 2dly, The circuit of an Archbiſhop's Juriſdiction. When the Britiſh Settlements in America are ſpoken of in general, they are called the Colonies or Plantations: If it is a Government

on

on the Continent, where the King appoints the Governor, it is uſually called a Province, as the Province of Quebec; the Province of Nova Scotia: but before the Civil War in America, a Plantation, in which the Governor was elected by the inhabitants, was uſually called a Colony, as the Colony of Connecticut. The word Province is never applied to an inſular Government, for it is not uſual to ſay, the Province of Jamaica; but the Iſland of Jamaica, the Iſland of Barbadoes, the Government of the Leeward Charribbee Iſlands, &c.

For ſome time before the Civil War broke out in America, the popular leaders there affected to call the Provincial Eſtabliſhments, or King's Governments on the Continent, "Colonies," inſtead of "Provinces;" from an opinion they had conceived, that the word Province meant a conquered country. It is ſaid in Show. Parl. c. 31. that Colony or Plantation does not import a conqueſt, but rather the contrary.

Colonies are of three ſorts: The firſt, are thoſe that ſerve to eaſe and diſcharge the inhabitants of a country, where the people are become too numerous; of this ſort were the Colonies of the Goths and Vandals, that over-ran the ſouthern parts of Europe. The ſecond ſort, are thoſe eſtabliſhed by victorious States, in the middle of vanquiſhed nations, to keep them in awe and obedience: ſuch were the bodies of men ſent by the Romans into the conquered Provinces. And the third ſort, are thoſe eſtabliſhed for the promotion of trade, called Colonies of Commerce; ſuch are the Colonies eſtabliſhed by Europeans in ſeveral parts of America.

Sir Walter Raleigh was the firſt that planted an Engliſh Colony in America, which he called

called Virginia, in honour of Queen Elizabeth.

Soon after the ſettlement of the Britiſh Colonies in America, King James the Firſt wanted to make the ſuperiority over them to be only of the King, and not of the Crown of England. Commons' Journal, 1620.—See alſo, Vaughan's Reports, 402.—It is ſaid, that King James did this with a view to make the Colonies a ſource of revenue for himſelf and his ſucceſſors, that they might not depend on the Parliament; but the Commons did not give up the matter, as appears by their Journals of 1624 and 1625.

The Britiſh Colonies are, in ſome reſpects, ſubject to the Engliſh laws. 1 Black. Com. 106.

It was holden by Lord Chief Juſtice Vaughan, in his Reports, 300. in the caſe of Crew *v.* Ramſay, that the Engliſh Plantations are dominions belonging to the realm of England, though not within the territorial dominion or realm of England, but follow it, and are a part of its royalty, and cannot be ſeparated from it but by Act of Parliament. See alſo 22 Geo. III. c. 46. and Show. Parl. c. 32, 33.

And in Vaughan's Reports, 400. under title, Proceſs into Wales, Lord Chief Juſtice Vaughan ſays, That the Colonies are of the dominions of England, and may be bound by laws made for them by an Engliſh Parliament.

Such was alſo the ſenſe of the Engliſh nation, ſoon after the ſettlement of the Colonies, even in the times of republicaniſm; for the Long Parliament, after the death of King Charles the Firſt, and when ſome of the Colonies had declared for King Charles the Second, againſt the then Commonwealth in England, paſſed an Act the 3d of October 1750; in which it is recited, "that in "Virginia,

"Virginia, and the Islands of Barbadoes, Antigua, "Saint Christopher's, Nevis, Montserrat, Bermu- "das, and divers other Islands and Places in "America, there have been and are Colonies "and Plantations which were planted at the cost, "and settled by the people, and by the authority "of this nation, which are and ought to be sub- "ordinate to, and dependent upon, England; "and have, ever since the planting thereof, been, "and ought to be, subject to such laws, orders, "and regulations as are or shall be made by the "Parliament of England." This Act having been made by the Long Parliament, when the King was unjustly kept from the throne, cannot be cited as an authority; but it shews what the opinion of that Parliament was, with respect to the right of the Mother Country over the Colonies; and New England, at that time, took the part of the Long Parliament.

With respect to the jurisdiction which the superior courts in Westminster Hall have over the Colonies, I shall cite a few cases.

And in the first place, it is held by Lord Mansfield, "That the court of King's Bench, in Eng- "land, can send a Writ of *Habeas Corpus* to the "Plantations, &c." 2 Burr. 856. Rex *v.* Cowle. "But notwithstanding the power which the court "of King's Bench in England has, yet where they "cannot judge of the cause, or give relief upon "it, they would not think proper to interpose. "Therefore upon imprisonments in the Planta- "tions, &c. Lord Mansfield said, he had known "complaints to the King in Council, and orders "to bail or discharge; but he did not remember "any application for a Writ of *Habeas Corpus*. Yet "cases have formerly happened of persons illegally "sent from hence, and detained there, where a

"Writ

" Writ of *Habeas Corpus* out of the court of King's
" Bench in England would be the most proper
" and effectual remedy." Ibid.

" Upon a proper Case, Writs not ministerially " directed (sometimes called Prerogative Writs, " because they are supposed to issue on the part of " the King), such as Writs of *Mandamus*, Prohibition, *Habeas Corpus*, *Certiorari*, may issue to " every dominion of the Crown of England.

" There is no doubt as to the power of the " Court of King's Bench in England, where the " place is under the subjection of the Crown of " England: the only question is, as to the propriety." Id. 855, 856.—See also 7 Co. Rep. 20. Calvin's Case. Vaughan's Rep. 290. 401, 402.

The respective Acts of Assembly, for establishing Courts of King's Bench and Common Pleas, in the Islands of Saint Christopher and Nevis, expressly reserve the jurisdiction of the court of King's Bench in England.

" Nothing concerning the Seigniory can be " tried in the place where the Seigniory is: and in " the Proprietary Governments in America, they " could not (before the Civil War there) try any " question concerning the Seigniory in their own " Courts; but it must have been tried in some " court in England." By Lord Mansfield, in the case of Fabrigas and Mostyn: " And whenever there is a question between two" (British) " Provinces in America, it must be tried in " England.

" The Judges in the Courts of England do " determine all cases that arise in the Plantations, " &c. and they must inform themselves, by " having the law stated to them. But there " may be some cases abroad, which may not be " fit to be tried here." Id.

" An

"An action was brought in the King's Bench "in England, against Captain Gambier, for "pulling down houses upon the coast of Nova "Scotia in North America, and it was holden "by Lord Mansfield that the action would lie, "as the reparation here was personal, and for "damages; otherwise there might be a failure "of justice, for there were no regular Courts of "Justice in that place; and if there had been "any, yet Captain Gambier might never go "there again; and the reason of locality in such "an action in England, did not hold in that "case." Id. See also Show. Parl. c. 30.

"A bill was brought in the High Court of "Chancery in England for the delivery of the "possession of a moiety of lands in Saint Christopher's, and likewise for an account of the "rents and profits. The defendant demurred "to the first part, for that the Court of Chancery in England had no jurisdiction over lands "in Saint Christopher's; and likewise to the account prayed of rents and profits, for that the "plaintiffs had not set forth a clear title to "them."

Lord Chancellor Hardwicke. "As to the "first part of the demurrer, I apprehend it is "very right, because the court has no jurisdiction, so as to put persons into possession, in a "place where they have their own methods, on "such occasions, to which the party may have "recourse; the present bill therefore, is carrying the jurisdiction of this court further than "it ever was before.

"Lands in the Plantations, are no more under "the jurisdiction of this court, than lands in "Scotland, for it only *agit in personam*.

"The

" The next queſtion is, whether an account of " rents and profits ought to be demanded before " the plaintiff has eſtabliſhed his right at law ?

" No impediment is ſhewn to prevent the " plaintiff from bringing his ejectment, for he " claims a moiety as tenant in common.

" As to the general equity, an infant here in " England may bring a bill for an account of " rents and profits againſt a perſon who keeps " poſſeſſion, after the death of the infant's an- " ceſtor; and as the demurrer is only to the bill, " I muſt take it for granted he is reſident here in " England.

" The defendant ſhould not have demurred " for want of juriſdiction, for a demurrer is al- " ways in bar, and goes to the merits of the " caſe; and therefore it is informal and im- " proper in that reſpect, for he ſhould have " pleaded to the juriſdiction.

" The delivery of the poſſeſſion, may be in- " forced in perſon, which was the old way; but " the writ of aſſiſtance to put perſons in poſ- " ſeſſion, as by way of injunction, is of more " modern date.

" Plantations were originally members of " England, and governed by the laws of Eng- " land; and perſons went out originally ſubject " to the laws of England, unleſs in ſome regu- " lations and cuſtoms, which they have a power " of making.

" There have been inſtances of Plantation " Eſtates being ſold in this court, and conſe- " quently, this court muſt have a power of in- " forcing a decree for a ſale, upon the perſon or- " dered to convey.

" His Lordſhip mentioned the caſe of the " Widow in Pennſylvania, and Hamilton; where " there was an order upon Hamilton to deliver

" poſſeſſion."

" possession."—1 Athyn's, 543, 544. Roberdeau and Rous. See also Show. Parl. c. 33. And in the case of Foster *v.* Vassal. 3 Athyns, 589. it was said by Lord Chancellor Hardwicke, " It is " certain where the provision is in England, let " the cause of suit arise in the Plantations, if the " bill be brought in England, as the defendant " is here, the Court" (of Chancery in England) " *agit in personam*, and may, by compulsion on " the person, and process of the Court, compel " him to do justice.

" Suppose different suits are brought there and " here, what is to be done? I take it to be clear, " if an action be brought in the Court of King's " Bench, or Common Pleas, and the defendant " pleads to it, an action in the Plantations they " could not take any notice of, nor would it " bar the jurisdiction of the Court here.

" The general rule of Courts of Equity, with " regard to Pleas, is the same as in Courts of " Law, but exercised with a liberal discretion.

" To be sure, two suits for the same matters in " the Plantations and here, may be attended with " inconvenience." And his Lordship said he would not, as Lord Cowper did in such a case, allow the plea to the discovery.

Sir William Blackstone says, the British Plantations are either such, where the lands are claimed by right of occupancy only, by finding them desart and uncultivated, and peopling them from the Mother Country; or where, when already cultivated, they have been gained by conquest, or ceded to us by treaties: and both these rights are founded upon the law of nature, or at least upon that of nations. 1 Black. Com. 107.—Show. Parl. c. 32. But there is a difference between these two species of Colonies; for it hath been held

held (Salk. 411. 666.—4 Mod. 222.) that if an uninhabited country be discovered and planted by English subjects, all the English laws then in being, which are the birthright of every subject, are immediately there in force. Show. Parl. c. 32.——2 P. Wms. 75. But this must be understood with very many, and very great restrictions. Such Colonists carry with them only so much of the English law as is applicable to their own situation, and the condition of an infant Colony; such, for instance, as the general rules of inheritance, and of protection from personal injuries. The artificial refinements and distinctions incident to the property of a great and commercial people; the laws of police and revenue (such especially as are inforced by penalties); the mode of maintenance for the established Clergy; the jurisdiction of Spiritual Courts, and a multitude of other provisions, are neither necessary nor convenient for them, and therefore are not in force. What shall be admitted, and what rejected; at what times, and under what restrictions; must, in cases of dispute, be decided, in the first instance, by their own provincial Judicature, subject to the revision of the King in Council; the whole of their Constitution being also liable to be new-modelled, and reformed, by the general superintending power of the Legislature in the Mother Country. 1 Black. Com. 107. Vaughan's Rep. 290. 402.—2 Lord Raymond, 1447, 1448. —2 P. Wms. 75.

But in conquered or ceded countries, that have already laws of their own, the King may indeed alter and change those laws; but till he does actually change them, the ancient laws of the country remain, unless such as are against the law of God; as in the case of an infidel country.

1 Black.

1 Black. Com. 107.—7 Rep. 17. Calvin's Case.—Shower's Parl. c. 31.—2 P. Wms. 75, 76. Trial of Fabrigas and Mostyn, 49. 58.

However, should Great Britain, either by conquest or cession, obtain possession of a country, in which the Government had been perfectly despotic; yet the Governor, or other Vicegerent of the Crown, is amenable for his conduct in the superior Courts of Common Law in Westminster Hall, if he acts unjustly or oppressively in his Government. For by Justice Gould, "Under such "a Constitution in which we live, if there is a "power that is not circumscribed by clear, posi-"tive, and precise rules, yet both natural justice "and equity are the principles that ought to go-"vern such a trust." Trial of Fabrigas and Mostyn, 49.

In Shower's Parliamentary Cases, 30, 31; in the case of Dutton *v.* Howell, and others, it was said by the counsel, *arguendo*, "Though a mat-"ter may justify a Governor for an act done in "his Government, which would not justify him "for the same act done in England, yet the Go-"vernor must shew that he hath pursued the "rules of law in that place; or, in case of no "positive laws, the rules of natural justice; for "either the common law, or new instituted laws, "or natural equity, must be the rule in those "places."

And if any country in which torture and banishment are the law, should come into the possession of Great Britain, these punishments fall of course; the Constitution of Great Britain puts an end to them. By Lord Justice de Grey, in the Trial of Fabrigas and Mostyn, 60.

The British American Plantations are principally conquered or ceded countries, having been obtained

obtained in the laſt century either by right of conqueſt, or driving out the natives (with what natural juſtice I ſhall not at preſent enquire), or by treaties: and therefore the common law of England, as ſuch, has no allowance or authority there, they being no part of the Mother Country, but diſtinct (though dependent) dominions. They are ſubject, however, to the control of Parliament, though not bound by any Acts of Parliament, unleſs particularly named. 1 Black. Com. 108.—2 P. Wms. 75.

The Engliſh Puritans who firſt ſettled in New England, notwithſtanding they were furniſhed with a charter from their Sovereign, purchaſed of the Indians the land they reſolved to cultivate. And this laudable example was followed by Mr. William Penn, who planted the Colony of Quakers in Pennſylvania. Vattel's Law of Nations, 91.—Hiſtoire et Commerce des Colonies Angloiſes, &c. 117, 118, 119.

Other ceſſions have been obtained from the Indians with the greateſt fairneſs; particularly that made in Georgia in the year 1774, when a Congreſs was held by Sir James Wright, Bart. Governor of Georgia, with a great number of the Kings and Headmen of the Creek and Cherokee nations; at which time theſe two nations ceded to the King of Great Britain ſeveral millions of acres of valuable land, in the moſt fertile and wholeſome part of the country, for the payment of the debts which they owed the Indian traders: but the breaking out of the Civil War prevented that ceſſion from producing the effects which were intended by it.

Vattel, in the place above mentioned, ſays, "That when a nation takes poſſeſſion of a diſtant "country, and ſettles a Colony there, that coun-

"try,

" try, though separated from the principal Esta-
" blishment, or Mother Country, naturally be-
" comes a part of the State, equally with its an-
" cient possessions. Whenever, therefore, the
" political laws or treaties make no distinction
" between them, every thing said of the territory
" of a nation ought also to extend to its Colo-
" nies." But this is not agreeable to the genius of the British Constitution. For in the passage above cited from Sir William Blackstone's Commentaries, it is said, That the British American Plantations are not part of the Mother Country, but distinct (though dependent) dominions; and that they are not bound by the acts of the British Parliament, unless particularly named. See also Vaughan's Rep. 300. 400.—2 P. Wms. 75.

And Vattel seems to be clearly mistaken, with respect to nations in general that have Colonies in a distant country, where he says, that "When-
" ever treaties make no distinction between the
" Mother Country and the Colonies, every thing
" said of the territory of a nation, ought also to
" extend to its Colonies." For a treaty permitting a nation, in general words, to trade with the Mother Country, does not permit that nation to trade to its Colonies. For it is acknowledged, That a commerce established between the Mother Countries, does not include a permission to trade in the Colonies, because these always continue in a state of prohibition; it being a fundamental law of Europe, that all commerce with a foreign Colony shall be regarded as a mere monopoly, punishable by the laws of the country. Spirit of Laws, Book 21. c. 17.

Before the Civil War in America, the British Colonies there were (with respect to their interior polity) divided by Sir William Blackstone into three

three sorts: 1. Provincial Establishments (commonly called King's Governments). 2. Proprietary Governments. 3. Charter Governments.

1. In the Provincial Establishments, their constitution depended on the respective commissions issued by the Crown to the Governors, and the instructions which usually accompanied these commissions; under the authority of which Provincial Assemblies were constituted, with the power of making local ordinances, not repugnant to the laws of England. 1 Black. Com. 108. And see the form of a Governor's Commission, chap. 4. *post.*

But it was usual for the General Assembly, in a new settled or ceded Colony, soon after they were first convened by the Governor, to pass an act for dividing the Colony into counties, districts, or other arbitrary divisions—to direct how many Representatives each district should send to the General Assembly—to regulate the mode of electing them, and to ascertain the qualifications of the Electors and Representatives: And in many Colonies the duration of the House of Representatives was limited; but in some of them, it continued until the Governor thought proper to dissolve the General Assembly.

In an island in the West Indies, where the House of Representatives continued until the Governor thought proper to dissolve the General Assembly, I once was retained by a candidate, to attend at an election, as counsel on his behalf. The Governor of the Island, and several of the Council, attended at the election, and offered to give their votes for the candidate that opposed my client. I objected, with some warmth, at the Governor's attempting to vote at the election of Representatives to the Assembly, as it was unconsti-

unconſtitutional, and tended to influence elections: and I alſo oppoſed the receiving the votes of the Members of the Council, as it was inconſiſtent for thoſe to vote for Repreſentatives, who had themſelves voices in the Legiſlature. But the Returning Officer (who was a gentleman of good character, and deſirous to do what was right) ſeemed unwilling to take on himſelf the deciſion of the matter; and propoſed to receive the votes of the Governor and Council, leaving the Houſe of Aſſembly to decide on the validity of thoſe votes. This propoſal was acquieſced in; and the queſtion afterwards came on before the Houſe of Aſſembly, when I urged every objection that occurred to me, againſt the votes of the Governor and Council; and the Houſe reſolved, "That "the Governor had no right to vote at the elec-"tion of Repreſentatives to the General Aſſem-"bly," or to that effect; but they admitted the votes of the Members of the Council. However I afterwards heard it ſaid, that the Governor gave the Members of the Aſſembly an intimation, that if the reſolution againſt his vote ſtood on their Journals, he would diſſolve them. And thereupon they razed the reſolutions from their Journals, to avoid the expence of a new election, as it is ſuppoſed. But the intimation of the Governor to the Aſſembly, and the raſure of the reſolution from their Journal, being only matters of common fame in the Iſland, I am not anſwerable for the authenticity of them; and I do not chuſe to aſſert any thing poſitively, that I am not clear in.

I was afterwards a Member of the Aſſembly in another Iſland; where, on a petition to the Houſe, it was carried by the majority, after a long and warm debate, that the Members of the Council had no right to vote at the election of Aſſembly-men.

bly-men. And on the Continent of America, they never attempted it in my time.

Before I enumerate the Provincial Eſtabliſhments, or King's Governments, it may be proper to obſerve, that all the Britiſh Colonies (except Falkland's Iſlands, which have been deſerted, as of no conſequence) are in North America: but as it is cuſtomary to diſtinguiſh the Colonies without the tropic of Cancer by the name of North America, and the Colonies between that tropic and the equinoctial by the name of the Weſt Indies, I ſhall comply with that diſtinction. See 18 Geo. III. c. 12. ſ. 1.—22 Geo. III. c. 75.

Before the Civil War in America, the Provincial Eſtabliſhments, or King's Governments there, were Canada, or Quebec (the boundaries of which were eſtabliſhed by the 14 Geo. III. c. 83, but great part of that Province hath been lately ceded to the United States of America); the Government of St. John's in the Gulf of St. Laurence (containing the Iſland of St. John, &c.); the Government of Newfoundland, which is partly inſular, and partly continental (containing the Iſland of Newfoundland, and that part of the continent which lies between the river St. John and Hudſon's Streights, with ſeveral Iſlands on that coaſt), Nova Scotia, or New Scotland, New Hampſhire, New York, New Jerſey or the Jerſeys, Virginia, North Carolina, South Carolina, Georgia, Eaſt Florida and Weſt Florida, the Government of the Bermuda or Summer Iſlands, and the Government of the Lucaya or Bahama Iſlands: but New Hampſhire, New York, New Jerſey, Virginia, North Carolina, South Carolina, and Georgia, are acknowledged by Great Britain to be Independent States; and Eaſt and Weſt Florida are ceded to Spain. The Bahama Iſlands

were

were captured by the Spaniards in the laſt War, but are now reſtored to Great Britain, by the Preliminary Articles of 1783, between Great Britain and Spain.

At the beginning of the laſt War, the Provincial Eſtabliſhments in the Weſt Indies were, the Iſland of Barbadoes, the Government of the Southern Charribbee Iſlands, (which comprehended Grenada, and the Grenadines, and Tobago,) St. Vincent's, Dominica, the Government of the Leeward Charribbee Iſlands, (which comprehended Antigua, Montſerrat, Nevis, St. Chriſtopher's, Barbuda, Anguilla, Tortola, Spaniſh Town, and many ſmall Iſlands near Tortola, being part of that cluſter called the Virgin Iſlands) and Jamaica.

There was alſo a ſmall ſettlement of Engliſh at the Muſquito ſhore, on the Continent, over which a King's Agent preſided, who was appointed by the Governor of Jamaica: and many Britiſh ſubjects were ſettled in the Bay of Honduras, where they were permitted to cut logwood and mahogany, &c. in conſequence of the treaty of Paris between Great Britain and Spain. They had a conſiderable town at St. George's Key in the Bay, where much trade was carried on, until the Spaniards drove away all the Britiſh ſettlers in the laſt war. Three of the principal merchants from the Bay of Honduras, that had been carried priſoners to the Havannah, arrived in Charleſtown Road in a flag of truce, in the Summer of 1782, and went from thence to New York with me, in one of the King's tranſports. Thoſe merchants gave me a particular account of the ſettlements at the Muſquito ſhore and the Bay of Honduras, and repreſented their commerce as very beneficial to Great Britain, until the Spaniards broke up those settlements in the last war. The Musquito shore was afterwards retaken by an armament sent from Jamaica: and the Preliminary Articles of 1783, between Great Britain and Spain, have made no express provision respecting it; but the 6th Article stipulates, "That all the countries and "and territories which may have been, or may "be, conquered in any part of the world what-"soever, by the arms of his Britannic Majesty, "or by those of his Catholic Majesty, and which "are not included in the present articles, shall "be restored without difficulty, and without re-"quiring compensations." Now, as the Musquito shore was always claimed by Spain, and the British settlement there was neither acknowledged by Spain, nor openly avowed by Great Britain in times of peace, I apprehend the Musquito shore will be restored to his Catholic Majesty. With respect to the Bay of Honduras, the Preliminary Articles say nothing of it by name; but the 4th Article stipulates, "That his Catholic Majesty "shall not, for the future, suffer the subjects of "his Britannic Majesty, or their workmen, to "be disturbed or molested, under any pretence "whatsoever, in their occupation of cutting, "loading, and carrying away logwood, in a di-"strict, of which the boundaries shall be fixed "by the definitive treaty, or within six months "after the ratification, &c. But this stipulation "is not to derogate from the rights of sovereignty "of the King of Spain."

In the last war Grenada and the Grenadines, Tobago, St. Vincent's, Dominica, Montserrat, Nevis, and St. Christopher's, were captured by the French; but all of them were restored to Great Britain on the late peace, except Tobago, which was ceded to France.

By

By the commiſſions to the Governors of Grenada and St. Vincent's, which have been made out ſince the late peace, a new arrangement has taken place with reſpect to the Grenadines: for General Matthews's commiſſion includes Grenada and all the Grenadines, to the ſouthward of the Iſland of Carriacou, incluſive of that Iſland. And Governor Lincoln's commiſſion comprehends St. Vincent's, Bequia, and all the Grenadines, to the northward of Carriacou.——I now come to

2. Proprietary Governments, granted out by the Crown to individuals, in the nature of feudatory principalities, with all the inferior regalities, and ſubordinate powers of Legiſlation which formerly belonged to the owners of counties palatine: yet ſtill with theſe expreſs conditions, that the end for which the grant was made be ſubſtantially purſued; and that nothing be attempted, which may derogate from the ſovereignty of the Mother Country. 1 Black. Com. 108.

Many of the Colonies which are contained in the above enumeration of Provincial Eſtabliſhments, or King's Governments, were formerly Proprietary Governments; but all the Proprietary Governments which remained at the breaking out of the Civil War, were the Government at the Hudſon's Bay, called New Britain, the Province of Pennſylvania, the three Counties of Newcaſtle, Kent, and Suſſex, on Delaware (now called the Delaware State) and Maryland.

The country called New Britain, was granted to the Hudſon's Bay Company, by a charter of King Charles II. of the 2d of May 1670, in the 22d year of his reign (which was confirmed by an act of Parliament made in the year 1690). The charter gives that Company an excluſive trade to all that country which lies round Hud-

ſon's

ſon's Bay: but I apprehend, that ſince 6 Ann. c. 37. (ſ. 15.) no charter can be granted to exclude or reſtrain any ſubject from a full and free trade to America. I have ranked the country called New Britain under this title of Proprietary Governments (in preference to that of Charter Governments), becauſe the trade is carried on ſolely for the benefit of the proprietors in England; and all the Britiſh ſubjects that reſide at Hudſon's Bay, or trade to that country, are ſervants to the Hudſon's Bay Company.

The Pennſylvania Charter was granted to William Penn, by King Charles II. in the 14th year of his reign, which was 1681-2: and the Charter of Maryland was granted to Lord Baltimore, by King Charles I. in the 8th year of his reign, which was 1632.

By the Charters, the proprietors had a right of appointing Governors; but by ſtatute 7 & 8 Wil. III. c. 22. ſ. 16. it was enacted, "That all "Governors nominated and appointed by any "perſons or proprietors who ſhould be entitled "to make ſuch nomination, ſhould be allowed "and approved of by his Majeſty, his heirs or "ſucceſſors; and ſhould take the oaths appointed by that, or any other act to be taken, "by the Governors or Commanders in Chief, "in other his Majeſty's Colonies or Plantations, "before their entering upon their reſpective Go"vernments, under the like penalties as his Ma"jeſty's Governors and Commanders in Chief "were, by the ſaid acts, liable to."

Pennſylvania, Delaware, and Maryland, are now acknowledged by Great Britain to be Independent States.—I come, laſtly, to

3. Charter Governments; in the nature of civil Corporations, with the power of making bye-laws

laws for their own interior regulation, not contrary to the laws of England, and with ſuch rights and authorities as are ſpecially given them in their ſeveral Charters of Incorporation. 1 Black. Com. 108.

The only Charter Governments that remained at the breaking out of the Civil War in America, were the Colonies of the Maſſachuſett's Bay, Rhode Iſland and Providence Plantations, and Connecticut.

The firſt Charter of the Maſſachuſett's Bay was granted by King James I. in the 18th year of his reign, and the people were thereby empowered to chuſe all their own Officers, except thoſe of the Admiralty and Cuſtoms: but that Charter was created by a judgment in Chancery, in the year 1684. However, in the 3d year of King William and Queen Mary, the people of the Maſſachuſett's Bay obtained another Charter, which reſerved to the Crown the appointment of the Governor, Lieutenant Governor, Secretary, the Officers of the Admiralty, and the Officers of the Cuſtoms. The Governor, with the conſent of the Council, appointed the Judges, Commiſſioners of Oyer and Terminer, Sheriffs, Provoſt Marſhals, Juſtices of the Peace, and the Officers belonging to the Council and Courts of Juſtice. The appointment of the other Civil Officers was veſted in the Council and Aſſembly, independent of the Governor. The Freeholders elected an Houſe of Repreſentatives, and that Houſe choſe a Speaker and Council, which was alſo the Upper Houſe of Legiſlature. The Governor, the Council, and the Houſe of Repreſentatives, conſtituted the General Court; which was, in the firſt place, the Legiſlature of the Colony; ſecondly, a Court of Equity; and, thirdly, a Court of Appeals (or Errors)

Errors) from Judgments given in the other Courts. See Hutchinson's and Chalmers's Histories of the Massachusett's Bay, and Political Reflections on the late Colonial Governments.

The Charter of Rhode Island, and Providence Plantations, was granted them by King Charles II. in the 15th year of his reign, which was 1663; and the Charter of Connecticut was granted them by King Charles II. in the 14th year of his reign, which was 1662. The respective Charters of these Colonies, empowered the people to elect all their Officers, except those of the Admiralty and Customs: and before the Civil War, the General Court in each of these Colonies, had the same powers within their respective Governments, as the General Court in the Massachusett's Bay had there. But all these Charter Governments are now acknowledged by Great Britain to be Independent States.

It is said, that the first Charter granted by the Crown of England, for the purpose of Colonization, was that granted by King James I. to the two Virginia Companies, bearing date the 10th of April 1606: and that the Charters which preceded it, were granted for the purpose of discovery only.

Before the Civil War in America, the form of Government in most of the Colonies was borrowed from that of England. 1 Black. Com. 108. And the commissions to the King's Governors expressly provided, "That all laws, statutes, and "ordinances in the Colonies, were not to be repugnant to, but as near as might be agreeable "to the laws and statutes of the kingdom of "Great Britain." The form of those commissions still continues to be the same, with respect

to

to ſuch Colonies as yet remain to Great Britain.

The Colony Charters alſo directed, "That the "bye-laws, conſtitutions, orders and ordinances, "pains and penalties there, ſhould be reaſonable, "and not contrary or repugnant to the laws and "ſtatutes of the realm."

In the Provincial Eſtabliſhments, or King's Governments, the Governor was always named by the King; and that is ſtill the caſe, with reſpect to ſuch Colonies as remain to Great Britain; for the Governor is the King's Repreſentative, or Deputy. 1 Black. Com. 108.

But I have already obſerved, that before the Civil War, the Governor in a Proprietary Government, was named by the Proprietor, ſubject to the reſtrictions contained in 7 and 8 Wil. III. c. 22. ſ. 16.

That in the Maſſachuſett's Bay, the Governor, Lieutenant Governor, Secretary, Officers of the Admiralty, and Officers of the Cuſtoms, were named by the Crown.

And that in the other two Charter Colonies, all the Officers, except thoſe of the Admiralty and Cuſtoms, were choſen by the people.

The Officers in the Provincial Eſtabliſhments, or King's Governments, were originally appointed by the King, or his Repreſentative the Governor.

When a vacancy happened, the Governor was empowered to fill it up; and his appointment ſtood until the King thought proper to ſupercede it. But ſee more on this head, under title Governor, *poſt*.

However, in Virginia, South Carolina, and ſome other Colonies, Acts of Aſſembly have from time to time been aſſented to, which appointed men to executive Offices; and those innovations in the Constitution passed *sub silentio* at the Boards in England, at times when little attention was paid to Colony matters.

By the 22 Geo. III. c. 75. it is enacted, "That "from thenceforth no office to be exercised in "any Colony or Plantation, then, or at any time "thereafter, belonging to the Crown of Great "Britain, shall be granted longer than for such "time as the grantee, or person appointed, shall "discharge the duty thereof in person, and be- "have well therein. And in case he shall be "wilfully absent, without a reasonable cause, to "be allowed by the Governor and Council, they "may remove him from his office; but if he "thinks himself aggrieved by such amotion, he "may appeal to his Majesty in Council, where "such amotion shall be finally judged of, and "determined: but the Governor and Council "may give such leave of absence, as they shall "see occasion; and in case of leave of absence, "or vacancy by death, or amotion, they are to "provide for the due discharge of the duties of "the office, until the King's pleasure shall be "known: but nothing in that act shall operate "to the prejudice of any subsisting grant of an "office, or to prevent an office being granted, "determinable at pleasure."

The Colonies have also Courts of Justice of their own; some of which sit by authority of letters patent, issued by the Governor on the first settlement of the Colony; and others under Act of Assembly, which establishes the style of the Court, its jurisdiction, and mode of proceeding.

The style of those courts, and the extent of their jurisdiction were different in different Colonies,

nies. In ſome it was called the General Court, or Supreme Court of Judicature, and had the ſame powers within the Colony, that the King's Bench, Common Pleas, and Exchequer, have in England. In other Colonies, they had a Court ſtyled the King's Bench and Common Pleas, which exerciſed civil and criminal juriſdiction: and there are a third ſort of Colonies in the Weſt Indies, in which Pleas of the Crown are cognizable by a Grand Seſſions (or King's Bench and Grand Seſſions), and civil matters by a diſtinct Court called the Common Pleas. In ſeveral of the Colonies on the Continent, before the Civil War, they had a Court in each county or diſtrict, that decided queſtions of property to a conſiderable amount; but there was an appeal to the ſuperior Court, which alſo decided matters in the firſt inſtance, that exceeded the juriſdiction of the County Courts. By means of thoſe County Courts, they had a great number of Judges in ſuch Colonies, who were, in general, unacquainted with the law; and little decorum was obſerved in the Courts where they preſided. But in the Colonies, where they had no County Courts, and the Judges of the ſuperior Court went in circuit throughout the Province, juſtice was more impartially adminiſtered, and greater decorum was obſerved, than in thoſe Colonies where the County Courts were eſtabliſhed: for four or five gentlemen might be found, who were ſkilled in the law, and capable of executing a judicial office when it was impoſſible to meet with an hundred in any Province, who were qualified to exerciſe the powers of judicature: nor could a Colony raiſe ſalaries for a number of able lawyers, to induce them to quit a lucrative practice at the bar,

bar, in order to go on the bench; whereas the raising competent salaries for four or five Judges, was no great burden on any country, when it was considered what benefits the Public derived from the services of men of learning and integrity. Besides, whenever there is in any country a number of courts independent of each other, the rule of decision is not uniform, and where there are many Judges in a Colony, scarce any question can come on, but some of them are interested in the decision as friends or relations to one of the parties. In an Island in the West Indies, where the King's Bench and Grand Sessions was composed of the Lieutenant Governor, Members of the Council, Judges of the Common Pleas, the Barons of the Exchequer, and the Justices of the Peace, I think I have seen instances of partiality. But the reader will meet with more observations of this sort, in the following parts of this work.

From the decrees of the Courts of Chancery in the Colonies, an appeal lies to the King in Council here in England.

And from the judgments of the Courts of Common Law, in the Colonies, a Writ of Error lies to the Governor and Council of the Colony; and from their decision, an appeal (in the nature of a Writ of Error) lies to the King in Council here in England.

" On an appeal to the King in Council from " the Plantations, the proceedings must be trans- " mitted, and the party appealing must proceed " within a year after the appeal is allowed in the " Plantations." 2 Lord Raymond, 1447.

" But a cause cannot be transmitted for dif- " ficulty, but must be determined one way or " other." Id. 1448.

"A Writ of Error lies to reverſe a judgment "in any dominions belonging to England." Vaughan's Rep. 290. 402. Show. Parl. c. 33.

For which the reaſons are, 1ſt, That without ſuch Writ, the law appointed, or permitted, to ſuch inferior dominion, might be inſenſibly changed within itſelf, without the aſſent of the dominion ſuperior.

2dly. Judgments might be then given to the diſadvantage or leſſening of the ſuperiority, which cannot be reaſonable; or to make the ſuperiority to be only of the King, not of the Crown of England. Vaughan's Rep. 402. Show. Parl. c. 33.

The General Aſſemblies in the Colonies, which are their Houſe of Commons, together with their Council of State, being their Upper Houſe, with the concurrence of the King, or his repreſentative the Governor, make laws ſuited to their own emergencies. 1 Black. Com. 108.

But it has been already obſerved, that the commiſſions to the Governors, and alſo the Colony Charters expreſsly provided, "that thoſe "laws were not to be repugnant, but as near "as might be agreeable to the laws and ſtatutes "of Great Britain."

It was alſo particularly declared by ſtatute 7 & 8. W. III. c. 22. "That all laws, bye-laws, "uſages, and cuſtoms, which ſhould be in prac-"tice in any of the Plantations, repugnant to "any law made or to be made in this king-"dom, relative to the ſaid Plantations, ſhould "be utterly void, and of none effect."

In all the Provincial Eſtabliſhments or King's Governments, except Virginia, the ſtyle of the legiſlature, before the Civil War, was, "the Go-"vernor, Council, and Aſſembly," (or "Ge-"neral

" neral Aſſembly") and in ſome of them, the Houſe of Repreſentatives was called " the Com-" mons Houſe of Aſſembly." But the ſtyle of the legiſlature in Virginia was, " the Governor, " Council, and Burgeſſes in General Aſſembly," and the Province itſelf was called, " The Co-" lony and Dominion of Virginia." However the reader will ſee the ſtyle of the different legiſlatures in the Colonies, in a ſubſequent part of this work. Before the Civil War in America, the Houſes of Repreſentatives would not conſent to any law, in which the Council was ſtyled the Upper Houſe of Aſſembly, and therefore in every Act of Aſſembly they were called " Council," although in their own Journals, they were ſtyled, " Upper Houſe of Aſſembly;" but after the reduction of Georgia by the King's forces in 1779, the Commons Houſe of Aſſembly there were ſtruck with the propriety of diſtinguiſhing when the Council acted as an executive body, or Council of State to aſſiſt the Governor; and when they formed a Houſe of Legiſlature. And in moſt of the Acts of Aſſembly that paſſed in Georgia, between the reduction of it in 1779, and the evacuation in 1782, the Council was ſtyled the Upper Houſe of Aſſembly.

On the paſſing the Act of the 5 Geo. III. c. 12. " For granting and applying certain Stamp Du-" ties, &c. in the Britiſh Colonies and Planta-" tions in America," (which Act was repealed by 6 Geo. III. c. 11.) ſeveral of the Colonies claimed the ſole and excluſive right of impoſing taxes upon themſelves: whereupon the ſtatute 6 Geo. III. c. 12. was made, which expreſsly declares, " That all his Majeſty's Colonies and " Plantations in America, have been, and are, " and of right ought to be, dependent upon the

" Imperial

" Imperial Crown and Parliament of Great Bri-
" tain; who have full power and authority to
" make laws and ſtatutes of ſufficient validity to
" bind the Colonies and people of America, ſub-
" jects of the Crown of Great Britain, in all
" caſes whatſoever." But by 18 Geo. III. c. 12.
ſ. 1. " The King and Parliament of Great Bri-
" tain declare, that from thenceforth they will
" not impoſe any duty, tax, &c. payable in any
" of the King's Colonies, Provinces, and Plant-
" ations in North America or the Weſt Indies,
" except for the regulation of commerce: the
" produce whereof is always to be applied to
" the uſe of the Colony in which it is levied,
" &c."

The authority of the Mother Country over the Colonies was alſo exemplified by 7 Geo. III. c. 59. for ſuſpending the legiſlation of New York —14 Geo. III. c. 19. for ſuſpending the trade of the harbour of Boſton—14 Geo. III. c. 39. for ſuppreſſing riots in the Maſſachuſett's Bay—14 Geo. III. c. 45. for regulating the government of the Maſſachuſett's Bay (by which Act its Charter was made void)—14 Geo. III. c. 54. for providing quarters for the King's troops in North America—15 Geo. III. c. 10. 18. to reſtrain the trade of the twelve Colonies, from New Hampſhire to South Carolina incluſive—16 Geo. III. c. 5. to prohibit all trade and intercourſe with the Thirteen Colonies, from New Hampſhire to Georgia incluſive, during the rebellion—— 17 Geo. III c. 7. to enable the Admiralty to grant commiſſions to privateers, to make prize of the ſhips and cargoes of the ſaid Thirteen Colonies, and of thoſe that traded with them—17 Geo. III. c. 9. 18 Geo. III. c. 1. 19 Geo. III. c. 1. 20 Geo. III. c. 5. 21 Geo. III. c. 2.

22 Geo.

22 Geo. III. c. 1. to empower the King to detain persons charged with, or suspected of high treason in America, or on the high seas, or for piracy—20 Geo. III. c. 46. s. 10. to indemnify the Commanders in Chief in America, and all persons acting under them, for all acts done in suppressing the rebellion there.

But some of these statutes were repealed, and the rest are become obsolete, since Great Britain has acknowledged the Independency of the Thirteen United States of America.

I have already observed, that Sir William Blackstone, in his Commentaries, says, "That "the British American Plantations are principally conquered or ceded countries; and "therefore the common law of England, as "such, has no allowance or authority there." However, the Crown has from time to time established the common law of England in all the British American Plantations, except Quebec or Canada. That province was ceded to Great Britain by the treaty of Paris, concluded the 10th of February 1763; and at the time of the cession, Canada contained above sixty-five thousand inhabitants, who were of the church of Rome, and had always been governed by the customs of Paris. It was therefore both just and prudent, to indulge the inhabitants with the exercise of their religion (subject to the King's supremacy), and to make the laws of the country the rule of decision there, in all matters of controversy relative to property and civil rights. But the constitution of Great Britain would not permit the criminal laws of a despotic government (which were enforced without the intervention of a jury) to continue in any of its plantations: and therefore the statute 14 Geo. III. c. 83. was made, which (after

(after eſtabliſhing the boundaries of Quebec) " provides for the government of that Province— " permits to the inhabitants the exerciſe of the " Romiſh religion (ſubject to the King's ſupre- " macy)—makes the laws of Canada the rule of " deciſion there, in all matters of controverſy " relative to property and civil rights; but eſta- " bliſhes the criminal law of England in that " province." They have no Houſe of Repre- ſentatives in Canada: however, the abovemen- tioned Act " empowers the Governor and le- " giſlative Council to make laws;" (which the Act calls Ordinances) but they cannot lay a tax on the Province: the power of doing that reſides ſolely in the Britiſh Parliament, except that the legiſlative Council may impower the inhabitants of any town or diſtrict in the Province, to levy and apply rates and taxes for the purpoſe of making roads, and erecting and repairing public buildings, or for any other purpoſes reſpecting the local convenience and œconomy of ſuch town or diſtrict.

By the 14 Geo. III. c. 88. " Certain duties " which were impoſed by the French King in " Canada, are diſcontinued, and other duties, in " lieu of them, are eſtabliſhed by the Britiſh " Parliament in that Province, to defray the " charges of the adminiſtration of juſtice, and " the ſupport of the civil Government there." I have already obſerved, that great part of Que- bec or Canada hath been ceded to the United States of America, as will appear by conſulting Faden's Map, lately publiſhed.

CHAP. II.

Of the Regulations to which the Commerce of the British American Colonies was subjected before the Civil War broke out there—With such Alterations as have taken place since that Time, down to the present Period.

I HAVE already observed, in the preceding Chapter, that the Colonies in America, which belong to different nations in Europe, were established for the promotion of trade, and are called Colonies of Commerce.

"The Colonies formed by the Europeans in "America, are (according to Montesquieu) "under a kind of dependence, of which there is "scarcely an instance in all the Colonies of the "ancients, whether we consider them as holding "of the State itself, or of some trading Com-"pany established in the State." Spirit of Laws, b. xxi. c. 17.

"The design of those Colonies, is to trade on "more advantageous conditions than could "otherwise be done with the neighbouring "people, with whom all advantages are reci-"procal. It has been established, that the Mo-"ther Country alone shall trade in the Colonies, "and that from very good reason, because the "design of the settlement, was the extension of "commerce, and not the foundation of a city, "or of a new empire." Ibid.

"Thus it is still a fundamental law of Europe, "that all commerce with a foreign Colony shall "be regarded as a mere monopoly, punishable "by the laws of the country. And in this case, "we are not to be directed by the laws and pre-"cedents

"cedents of the ancients, which are not appli-
"cable. It is likewise acknowledged, that a commerce established between the Mother Countries, does not include a permission to trade in the Colonies, for these always continue in a state of prohibition." Ibid.

"The disadvantage of a Colony, that loses the liberty of commerce, is visibly compensated by the protection of the Mother Country, who defends it by her arms, and supports it by her laws." Ibid.

"From hence follows a third law of Europe, that when a foreign commerce with a Colony is prohibited, it is not lawful to trade in its seas, except in such cases as are excepted by treaty." Ibid.

"Nations who are, with respect to the whole universe, what individuals are in a State, like these are governed by the law of nature, and by particular laws of their own making. One nation may resign to another the sea, as well as the land." Ibid.

Mr. Selden, in his *Mare Clausum*, has proved, "that the sea is capable of occupancy and dominion, naturally, as well as the land." Vaughan's Rep. 188.

By statute 4 Geo. III. c. 15. s. 33, 34. "Foreign vessels found at anchor, or hovering within two leagues of the shore of any British American dominion, and not departing, unless distressed, in forty-eight hours after notice, were liable to be forfeited, together with the goods, except French vessels fishing on the coast of Newfoundland, between the limits permitted by treaty." See also, s. 35. to prevent British vessels from trading with the French at Saint Pierre's and Miquelon.

"The

"The great distance of our Colonies, is not "an inconvenience that affects their safety, for "if the Mother Country, on whom they depend "for their defence, is far distant, no less distant "are those nations by whom they may be afraid "of being conquered." Spirit of Laws, b. xxi. c. 17.

But this observation does not hold true, since the Thirteen United States of America are acknowledged to be independent; for they are much nearer to the American Colonies, belonging to the different European powers, than the respective nations are, on whom those Colonies depend. "Besides this distance is the cause "that those who are established there, cannot "conform to the manner of living in a climate "so different from their own. They are obliged "therefore, to draw from the Mother Country "all the conveniencies of life. Our Colonies in "the Charribbee Islands, are under an admirable "regulation in this respect; the subject of their "commerce is, what we neither have, nor can "produce, and they want what is the subject of "ours." Spirit of Laws, b. xxi. c. 17.

The Dutch formerly carried on a considerable trade to the British American Colonies, until they were excluded by the Long Parliament, of which Sir William Blackstone gives the following account:

"The most beneficial statute for the trade and "commerce of these kingdoms is the Navigation Act, the rudiments of which were first "framed in 1650," (Scobell, 132.) "with a narrow partial view, being intended to mortify "our own sugar islands, which were disaffected "to the Parliament, and still held out for Charles "the Second, by stopping the gainful trade which

"they

" they then carried on with the Dutch," (Mod. Un. Hiſt. 41. 289.) " and at the ſame to clip the " wings of thoſe our opulent and aſpiring neigh- " bours. This prohibited all ſhips of foreign " nations from trading with any Engliſh Plant- " ations, without licence from the Council of " State. In 1651," (Scobell, 176.) " the pro- " hibition was extended alſo to the Mother Coun- " try; and no goods were ſuffered to be im- " ported into England, or any of its depend- " encies, in any other than Engliſh bottoms, or " in the ſhips of that European nation, of which " the merchandiſe imported was the genuine " growth or manufacture. At the Reſtoration, " the former proviſions were continued, by ſtatute " 12 Car. II. c. 18. with this very material im- " provement, that the maſter, and three-fourths " of the mariners, ſhall alſo be Engliſh ſubjects." 1 Black. Com. 418. 419.

But in time of war, it has been uſual to paſs an Act of Parliament, to permit Britiſh Merchant veſſels to be navigated by three-fourths foreign ſeamen. See 21 Geo. III. c. 11. which is the laſt act of that ſort.

The ſtatute 15 Car. II. c. 7. After reciting, " That his Majeſty's Plantations beyond the ſeas, " are inhabited and peopled by his ſubjects of " this his kingdom of England, for the main- " taining a greater correſpondence and kindneſs " between them, and keeping them in a firmer " dependence upon the Mother Country; and " rendering them yet more beneficial and advan- " tageous to it, in the further employment and " increaſe of Engliſh Shipping and Seamen; vent " of Engliſh woollen, and other manufactures and " commodities; rendering the navigation to and " from the ſame more ſafe and cheap; and

" making

" making this kingdom a ſtaple not only of the
" commodities of thoſe Plantations, but alſo of
" the commodities of other countries and places,
" for the ſupplying of them; and it being the
" uſage of other nations to keep their Plantation
" Trade to themſelves: It enacts, That no com-
" modity of the growth, production, or manu-
" facture of Europe, ſhall be imported into any
" Land, Iſland, Plantation, Colony, Territory,
" or Place to his Majeſty belonging, but what
" ſhall be ſhipped in England, Wales, or Ber-
" wick, and in Engliſh-built ſhipping, whereof
" the maſter and three-fourths of the mariners,
" at leaſt, to be Engliſh, under the forfeiture of
" ſhip and cargo."

By the 7 and 8 W. III. c. 22. ſ. 2. " No goods
" or merchandiſe ſhall be imported into, or ex-
" ported out of, any Colony, or Plantation, but in
" ſhips built in England, Ireland, or the Colo-
" nies," (except prize ſhips legally condemned,
20 Geo. II. c. 45. ſ. 9.) " and wholly owned by
" the people thereof, or any of them, under for-
" feiture of ſhip and goods." And ſee ſ. 17. for
regiſtering all ſhips trading there. But by the
13 Geo. III. c. 26. " A foreigner may purchaſe
" a ſhare in a Britiſh ſhip, with the conſent in
" writing of the owners of three-fourth parts in
" value, at leaſt, indorſed on the certificate of
" the regiſter before two witneſſes, otherwiſe the
" contract, &c. to be void."

By the 15 Geo. II. c. 31. ſ. 1. " No ſhip or
" veſſel required (by 7 and 8 W. III. c. 22. and
" 5 Ann. c. 8.) to be regiſtered, and carrying
" goods, &c. to or from any of his Majeſty's
" Plantations in America, or to or from one
" Plantation to another, ſhall be permitted to
" trade, or be deemed qualified for that purpoſe,
" within

"within the intent of the ſaid Acts, until the "maſter or perſon having charge of the ſaid ſhip "or veſſel, ſhall upon oath (or in caſe of "a Quaker, upon affirmation) before the Go- "vernor or Collector of the Cuſtoms, where the "ſame ſhall arrive, give a juſt and true account "of the name and burthen thereof, and of the "place from whence ſhe came, and of the other "particulars, according to the form of the oath "ſet forth in the Act, under the forfeitures in "the ſaid Act mentioned." But,

By 3 and 4 Ann. c. 8, 13 Geo. I. c. 5. 3 Geo. II. c. 12. 4 Geo. III. c. 15 and 19. 9 Geo. III. c. 28. "Horſes, victuals, and linen cloth from "Ireland; ſalt from any part of Europe; wines "of the growth of Madeira, and of any of the "Weſtern Iſlands; and goods neceſſary for the "fiſhery from Jerſey or Guernſey, may be im- "ported directly into the Britiſh Colonies in "America." And,

By the Act of Union, 5 Ann. c. 8, Article 4. "All the ſubjects of the united kingdom of Great "Britain, ſhall have full freedom and intercourſe "of trade and navigation to and from any part or "place within the ſaid united kingdom, and the "dominions and plantations thereunto belong- "ing." Alſo,

By the 20 Geo. III. c. 10. "Any goods which "may be imported from Britiſh America, &c. "to Great Britain, may be imported directly to "Ireland, and exported from thence, if the Iriſh "Parliament impoſes the ſame duties as are paid "in Great Britain."

Some American produce was permitted to be carried directly to a foreign market, without being firſt brought to Great Britain.

For,

For, "Any vessel built in Great Britain, and "navigated according to law, and belonging to "any of his Majesty's subjects, of which the major "part shall be residing in Great Britain, and the "residue in Great Britain, or in some of his "Majesty's Sugar Colonies in America, may load "sugars of the growth of the said Colonies, or "any of them, and carry the same from thence "to any part of Europe, under certain restric-"tions and regulations." See the 12 Geo. II. c. 30. extended to all ships belonging to Great Britain by 15 Geo. II. c. 33. s. 5.—The Act of the 12 Geo. II. c. 30. was continued down from time to time, and by 18 Geo. III. c. 45. s. 3. is continued to September 1785, &c.

And before the Civil War broke out in America, "Any vessel belonging to his Majesty's "subjects residing in Great Britain, and navi-"gated according to law, might load rice in "North Carolina, South Carolina, Georgia, East "and West Florida, and carry the same directly "to any part of Europe, southward of Cape Fi-"nisterre, without carrying the same to any other "Plantation, or to Great Britain, under certain "regulations." See the 3 Geo. II. c. 28. allowing this liberty to rice from Carolina—8 Geo. II. c. 19. extending it to Georgia—5 Geo III. c. 45. s. 19. extending it North Carolina—10 Geo. III. c. 31. 11 Geo. III. c. 39. extending it to East and West Florida. But North Carolina, South Carolina, and Georgia, are now acknowledged to be independent; and East and West Florida are ceded to Spain.

All the produce of the British American Plantations, was divided into enumerated and non-enumerated Articles. The enumerated Articles, were those particularly named in 12 Car. II. c. 18.

s. 18.

ſ. 18, 19. 15 Car. II. c. 7. ſ. 9. 22, 23 Car. II. c. 26. ſ. 10, 11, 12, 13. 7 & 8 W. III. c. 22. 3 & 4 Ann. c. 5. ſ. 12. 3 & 4 Ann. c. 10. 8 Geo. I. c. 15. ſ. 24. 8 Geo. I. c. 18. ſ. 22. which enumerated Articles are ſugar, cotton, wool, tobacco, indico, ginger, dying woods, rice, molaſſes, furs, and copper ore of the Plantations; tar, pitch, turpentine, maſts, yards, bowſprits, coffee, pimento, cocoa-nuts, whale fins, raw ſilk, hides and ſkins, pot and pearl aſhes of America; and all thoſe articles before the Union, muſt have been brought to England only—after the 5 Ann. c. 8. art. 4. to Great Britain only—and ſince the 20 Geo. III. c. 10. they muſt be brought to Great Britain or Ireland, except that ſugars may be carried directly to any foreign port, under the reſtrictions of 12 Geo. II. c. 30.—and that, before the Civil War, rice might have been carried to the ſouthward of Cape Finiſterre, under the Acts 3 Geo. II. c. 28. &c.

The non-enumerated articles, are thoſe which the ſeveral Acts regarding the Colonies do not ſpecify.

By 4 Geo. III. c. 15. ſ. 28. 5 Geo. III. c. 45. ſ. 22. 6 Geo. III. c. 52. ſ. 30. 7 Geo. III. c. 2. 9 Geo. III. c. 28. ſ. 3. The non-enumerates might be carried to any part of Europe to the ſouthward of Cape Finiſterre—to any of the Britiſh Colonies in America—to any port of Spain within the Bay of Biſcay—to Ireland—and to Jerſey or Guernſey (except rum to thoſe two laſt mentioned Iſlands) as well as to Great Britain.

Such lumber, as is ſpecified in 8 Geo. I. c. 12. ſ. 2. might be carried to any of the Britiſh Colonies in America—to any place in America, Africa, or Aſia—to Ireland—the Madeiras—the Azores—and to any part of Europe to the ſouthward of Cape Finiſterre—and iron might be

carried

carried to any British Colony in America—to any place in America, Africa, or Asia—and to Ireland, as well as to Great Britain, to which place only all the above articles must have been formerly imported. But since the Union of England and Scotland, and the making the 20 Geo. III. c.10. with respect to Ireland, the Scotch and Irish are intitled to the same free trade and navigation to and from British America, as the English have

Several free ports were also opened in two British Islands in the West Indies; for by 6 Geo. III. c. 49. s. 1. "Live cattle, and all manner of "goods and commodities, the growth or pro-"duce of any Colony or Plantation in America, "not under the dominion of his Majesty, his "heirs and successors, except tobacco, might "be imported into Prince Rupert's Bay, and "Roseau in the Island of Dominica, from any "foreign Colony or Plantation in America, in "any foreign sloop, schooner, or other vessel "whatsoever, not having more than one deck." (expired as to Dominica)—And by sect. 2. "Live "cattle, and all manner of goods and commo-"dities, the growth or produce of any Colony or "Plantation in America, not under the dominion "of his Majesty, his heirs and successors, ex-"cept sugars, coffee, pimento, ginger, melasses, "and tobacco, may, in like manner, be im-"ported into Kingston, Savanna la Mar, Mon-"tego Bay, and Santa Lucca, in the Island of "Jamaica, from any foreign Colony or Planta-"tion in America, in any foreign sloop, schooner, "or other vessel whatsoever, not having more "than one deck."

This Act was continued and amended by the 13 Geo. III. c. 73. But by 14 Geo. III. c. 41. and

21 Geo.

21 Geo. III. c. 29. it is continued as to Jamaica only, and will be in force until November 1787, &c.

Since the former part of this chapter was compiled, two Acts have been passed by the British Parliament, in consequence of the late peace.—The first is statute 23 Geo. III. c. 26. intituled, "An Act to repeal so much of two Acts made in "the 16th and 17th years of the reign of his present Majesty, as prohibits trade and intercourse "with the United States of America. By this "Statute, so much of the 16 Geo. III. c. 5. (as "prohibits all trade and intercourse with the "Thirteen Colonies, in the Act named, during "the continuance of the rebellion within the said "Colonies respectively, &c.) And also, so much "of the 17 Geo. III. c. 7. (as enables the Com-"missioners for executing the office of Lord High "Admiral of Great Britain, to grant commis-"sions to the commanders of private ships of war "and vessels employed in trade, or retained in his "Majesty's service, to take, and make prize of "all such ships and vessels, and their cargoes, as "are therein mentioned, for a limited time) so "far as such Acts extend to prohibit trade and "intercourse with the territories now composing "the United States of America, or to authorise "any hostilities against the persons or properties "of the subjects and citizens of the said United "States, after the respective periods set forth in "his Majesty's Proclamation, for the cessation of "hostilities between Great Britain and the United "States of America, bearing date the 14th day "of February 1783, are repealed."

The second statute is 23d Geo. III. c. 39. intituled, "An act for preventing certain instruments "from being required from ships belonging to "the United States of America; and to give to "his

" his Majeſty, for a limited time, certain powers " for the better carrying on trade and commerce " between the ſubjects of his Majeſty's domi- " nions, and the inhabitants of the ſaid United " States."

By this act, " No manifeſt, certificate, or " other document, is required for any ſhip or " veſſel belonging to the United States of Ame- " rica, arriving from thence, at, or clearing out " from, any port in this kingdom, for any place " within the ſaid United States, excepting ſuch " bonds as are required, duly to export, and not " to reland any goods entitled to a drawback or " bounty, or which are prohibited to be uſed " or worn in this kingdom.—Which bond may " be diſcharged upon a certificate under the " hands and ſeals of any officers appointed by " the United States for that purpoſe; and where " no ſuch officer is appointed, then the bond " may be diſcharged upon a certificate under the " hand and ſeal of any Magiſtrate of the ſaid " United States, certifying that there is no ſuch " officer at ſuch place; and that oath hath been " made before ſuch Magiſtrate, by the maſter, or " other perſon having the charge of ſuch ſhip, " that the goods for which ſuch certificate is re- " quired, were duly landed by him within the " ſaid United States.

" And his Majeſty in Council may, by orders " publiſhed from time to time, give ſuch di- " rections, and make ſuch regulations, with re- " ſpect to duties, drawbacks, or otherwiſe, for " carrying the trade between the territories of " Great Britain and thoſe of the United States, " as to his Majeſty in Council ſhall appear moſt " expedient and ſalutary. But the act, and the " powers and authorities thereby given to his

" Majeſty,

"Majeſty, and all orders publiſhed in conſe-
"quence thereof, are to be in force until the
"20th of December 1783, and no longer."

CHAP. III.

Of the Thirteen United States of America, whoſe Independence hath been lately acknowledged by Great Britain.

IN the year 1775, the Civil War broke out in the Maſſachuſett's Bay, and ſoon extended it-ſelf throughout all the Thirteen Britiſh Colonies, from New Hampſhire to Georgia incluſive. Numbers of the inhabitants of thoſe Colonies, ſenſible of the happineſs they enjoyed under the Government of Great Britain, were averſe to the meaſures carried on in America: but many of them acquieſced through fear. However, there were ſome who (remembering their allegiance to their Sovereign, and their gratitude to Great Britain) adhered to their loyalty at every riſk; and are now reſpected by men of every denomination. I could adduce inſtances of conduct in loyaliſts, that would do honour to human nature; but there is one which I cannot paſs over, becauſe it ſhews with what firmneſs men will act, when they are conſcious that they have taken the right ſide of a queſtion.—A fort was reduced by the Americans on the River Savannah; and ſuch of the loyal militia as were in garriſon there, had the alternative offered them, of enliſting with the Americans, or being put to death. Amongſt the loyaliſts was a young man who deſired a few minutes to conſider of the propoſal; and after a ſhort pauſe, he reſolutely anſwered, "That he "preferred

" preferred death to disgrace;" on which he was immediately cut down with a broad sword.

The Thirteen United Colonies declared themselves to be Free and Independent States on the 4th of July 1776. I leave it to those who write the History of the Civil War in America, to specify the arts that were used in the Continental Congress, to bring about the declaration of Independency.

On the 9th of July 1778, Articles of Confederation and perpetual Union were agreed upon in the Continental Congress held at Philadelphia; but those Articles of Confederation were not finally ratified until the 1st of March 1781, when the State of Maryland, by their Members in Congress, on that day acceded thereto, and completed the same.

The principal parts of the Articles of Confederation are,

" That the style of the Confederacy shall be " The United States of America;" but each State " retains its sovereignty, freedom, and independence, and every power, jurisdiction and right, " which is not expressly delegated to the United " States in Congress.——The States enter into a " firm league of friendship, for their common " defence, the security of their liberties, and their " mutual and general welfare, against all attacks " on account of religion, sovereignty, trade, or " any other pretence.——The free inhabitants " of each State (paupers, vagabonds, and fugitives excepted) shall be entitled to all privileges and immunities of free citizens in the " several States, and shall have free ingress and " regress, and all the privileges of trade and " commerce, subject to the same duties and restrictions as the inhabitants; but such restric-

" tions

" tions are not to extend to the removal of pro-
" perty imported into any State, to any other
" State, of which the owner is an inhabitant;
" and no impoſition, duties, or reſtriction, are
" to be laid by any State on the property of the
" United States, or either of them.——Perſons
" charged with treaſon, felony, or other high
" miſdemeanour, flying from juſtice, ſhall, upon
" demand, be delivered up: and full faith and
" credit ſhall be given, by each State, to the
" records, acts, and judicial proceedings, of the
" Courts and Magiſtrates of the other States.—
" Delegates are to be annually appointed by
" each State, to meet in Congreſs on the firſt
" Monday in November; but each State may
" recal its Delegates within the year, and ſend
" others for the remainder of the year. No State
" is to be repreſented in Congreſs by leſs than
" two, nor more than ſeven Members; and no
" perſon is to be a Delegate for more than three
" years in ſix, nor, whilſt a Delegate, can he hold
" an office under the United States, for which
" he receives any ſalary, fees, or emoluments.
" Each State is to maintain its own Delegates,
" whilſt they act as ſuch: and in determining
" queſtions in Congreſs, each State ſhall have
" one vote. Freedom of ſpeech and debate in
" Congreſs, ſhall not be queſtioned out of it;
" and the Members ſhall be protected from ar-
" reſt and impriſonment in going to, coming
" from, and attendance on Congreſs, except
" for treaſon, felony, or breach of the peace.—
" No State, without the conſent of the others in
" Congreſs, is to ſend or receive an embaſſy, or
" enter into any conference, &c. with any King,
" Prince, or State; nor ſhall any perſon in office
" under the United States, or any of them, ac-

" cept

" cept of any present, emolument, office or title, " from any King, Prince, or foreign State: nor " shall the United States, in Congress assembled, " grant any title of Nobility. No two or more " States, shall enter into any treaty, &c. without " the consent of the Continental Congress. And " no State shall lay any imposts, or duties inter- " fering with treaties entered into by the Con- " tinental Congress, with any King, &c. in pur- " suance of any treaties already proposed by " Congress to the Courts of France and Spain.— " No vessels of war, or body of forces, are to be " kept up in peace by any State, except such as " are deemed necessary by the Continental Con- " gress; but every State is to keep up a well dis- " ciplined militia, sufficiently accoutered, with " a proper quantity of field pieces, tents, arms, " ammunition, and camp-equipage: But no State " is to engage in a war without consent of the " Continental Congress, unless it is actually in- " vaded, or receives advice that some Indian " Nation intends so to do, and the danger will " not admit of the Continental Congress being " assembled and consulted. And no State is to " grant commissions or letters of marque to any " vessel, except after war is declared by the Con- " tinental Congress; and then only against the " State at war, and under the regulations esta- " blished by the Continental Congress; except " against pirates, and for so long as the danger " continues, or until the Continental Congress " shall determine otherwise.—When land forces " are raised for the common defence, all officers " under the rank of Colonel shall be appointed " by the State that raises them; and all vacancies " are to be filled up by the State that first made " the appointment.—All expences incurred for

" the

" the common defence, and allowed by the Con-
" tinental Congreſs, ſhall be defrayed out of a
" common treaſury ſupplied by the ſeveral States,
" in proportion to the value of land within each,
" as the Continental Congreſs ſhall from time
" to time direct: but the taxes ſhall be laid and
" levied by the Legiſlatures of the ſeveral States,
" within the time agreed upon by the Continen-
" tal Congreſs, who have alſo the ſole power of
" determining on peace or war (except in caſes
" of invaſion, &c. as before mentioned); ſending
" and receiving ambaſſadors; entering into trea-
" ties and alliances (but not to reſtrain the Le-
" giſlature of each State from impoſing ſuch
" duties on foreigners, as their own people are
" ſubject to, nor from prohibiting the exporta-
" tion or importation of any goods); of eſtabliſh-
" ing rules for deciding on captures by land or
" water, and in what manner thoſe taken by the
" forces in the ſervice of the United States ſhall
" be appropriated; of granting letters of marque
" and repriſal in times of peace; appointing
" Courts for the trial of piracies and felonies on
" the high ſeas; and eſtabliſhing Courts for ap-
" peal in all caſes of captures; but no Member
" of the Continental Congreſs is to be a Judge
" of any of the ſaid Courts.—The Continental
" Congreſs is alſo the laſt reſort on appeal, in all
" diſputes between two or more States, concern-
" ing boundary, juriſdiction, or any other cauſe:
" and on the petition of either party, they finally
" determine all controverſies concerning the pri-
" vate right of ſoil, claimed under different
" grants of two or more States, whoſe juriſ-
" dictions, as they may reſpect ſuch lands, and
" the States which paſſed ſuch grants, are adjuſted;
" the ſaid grants, or either of them, being at
" the

" the same time claimed to have originated an-
" tecedent to such settlement of jurisdiction;
" which authorities of the Continental Congress,
" in both cases, are to be exercised in the man-
" ner particularly directed in the 2d section of
" the 9th Article of Confederation: but no State
" shall be deprived of territory for the benefit of
" the United States.—The Continental Congress
" hath also the sole power of regulating the
" alloy and value of coin, struck by their own
" authority, or that of the respective States; fix-
" ing the standard of weights and measures; ma-
" naging all affairs with the Indians, not Mem-
" bers of any State (but not to infringe the le-
" gislative right of any State within its own li-
" mits); establishing and regulating post-offices
" throughout all the States, and exacting such
" postage as may defray the expence of the of-
" fice; appointing all naval officers, and all but
" regimental officers, in the land forces of the
" United States; and commissioning all officers
" whatsoever in such service; and making rules
" for the Government, and directing the opera-
" tions of all the Continental land and naval
" forces.—The Continental Congress is also to
" appoint a Committee to sit in the recess of
" Congress, named, "a Committee of the States,"
" and to consist of one Delegate from each State:
" to appoint such other Committees, and civil
" officers, as may be necessary for managing the
" general affairs of the United States under their
" direction: to appoint one of their number to
" preside; but none is to be President more than
" one year in three: to ascertain the sums of
" money to be raised for the service of the United
" States, and to apply the same: to borrow
" money, or emit bills of credit: to build and

" equip

" equip a navy: to agree upon the number of " land forces, and to make requisitions from each " State for its quota, in proportion to the number " of its white inhabitants, which requisition " is to be binding; and the Legislature of each " State is to appoint the regimental officers, and " raise, clothe, arm, and equip the men (at the " expence of the United States) who are to " march at the time, and to the place appointed " by the Continental Congress.—But not less than " Nine of the United States in Congress, can engage " in a war; or grant letters of marque and " reprisal in time of peace; or enter into any " treaties or alliances; or coin money; or regulate " the value thereof; or ascertain the necessary " expence for the defence of the United " States; or emit bills, or borrow money on the " credit of the United States; or appropriate " money; or agree upon the number of vessels " of war to be built or purchased; or the number " of land or sea forces to be raised; or appoint " a Commander in Chief of the army or " navy. And no question, except for adjournment " from day to day, shall be determined, " unless by the votes of a majority of the United " States in Congress; who have a power to adjourn " to any place within the United States, " and for any time within the year, not exceeding " six months at a time. And they are to " publish the Journals monthly, except such parts " relating to treaties, alliances, or military operations, " as in their judgment require secrecy: " and the Yeas and Nays on any question shall " be entered on the Journal, if desired by a " Delegate, who shall also be furnished with a " transcript of the Journal on request (except " those which require secrecy, as above mentioned)

" tioned) to be laid before the Legislature of his " State.—The Committee of the States, or any " Nine of them, are authorised to execute (in the " recess of Congress) such of the powers of Con- " gress, as the United States, in Congress as- " sembled, by the consent of Nine States, shall " from time to time think expedient to vest " them with; but no power can be delegated to " the Committee, for the exercise of which, by " the Articles of Confederation, the voice of Nine " States, in the Congress of the United States, " is requisite.—No other Colony can be admit- " ted into the Confederation, unless such admis- " sion be agreed to by Nine States.—All bills of " credit emitted, monies borrowed, and debts " contracted, by or under the authority of Con- " gress, before the assembling of the United " States, in pursuance of the Confederation, are " considered as a charge against the United States, " and for payment thereof the United States, and " the public faith, are pledged.—Every State is " to abide by the determination of the Continen- " tal Congress, on all questions which, by the " Confederation, are submitted to them; and " the Articles of the Confederation are to be in- " violably observed by every State, and the union " is to be perpetual; nor is any alteration to be " made in the Articles, unless in the Continental " Congress, and the same is afterwards confirmed " by the Legislature of every State.

" Every Article of the Confederation and per- " petual Union, and all matters therein con- " tained, were ratified by the Delegates, in the " name and behalf of their Constituents; and the " Delegates signed the Confederation, and so- " lemnly plighted the faith of their respective " Constituents, that they should abide by the de-

" termination

" termination of the Continental Congreſs, in all " queſtions ſubmitted to them by the Confede- " ration; and that the Articles thereof ſhould be " inviolably obſerved by the States, they reſpec- " tively repreſented; and that the Union ſhould " be perpetual."

The UNITED STATES of AMERICA have adopted different Conſtitutions or forms of Government; and there are not any two States in which the forms of Government agree in every particular. Theſe Conſtitutions have alſo been agreed to at different times; one of them ſo early as January 1776, and another of them not till 1780.

The Conſtitution or form of Government in NEW HAMPSHIRE, was eſtabliſhed in the Provincial Congreſs at Exeter, on the 5th of January 1776, (in conſequence of a recommendation from the Continental Congreſs) to continue during the conteſt with Great Britain.

" The Provincial Congreſs aſſumed the name, " power, and authority of a Houſe of Repreſenta- " tives for the Colony of New Hampſhire, and " then proceeded to chuſe twelve reputable " Freeholders and Inhabitants of the Colony out " of the five Counties, to be a diſtinct and ſepa- " rate Branch of the Legiſlature, by the name " of the Council for the Colony of New Hamp- " ſhire; which Council was to continue till the " third Wedneſday in December following, and " any ſeven of them were to be a quorum to do " buſineſs. But if the diſpute with Great Britain " continued longer than that year, and the Con- " tinental Congreſs gave no directions to the " contrary, the Council was to be choſen by the " people of each reſpective County, as the Coun- " cil and Houſe of Repreſentatives ſhould order: " and precepts in the name of the Council and Aſ-

" ſembly,

" sembly, signed by the President of the Council, " and Speaker of the House of Representatives, " are to issue annually, at or before the 1st of " November, for the choice of a Council and " House of Representatives, to be returned the " third Wednesday in December, in such manner " as the Council and Assembly shall prescribe. " And (by a resolution of the Council and As- " sembly of the 19th of September 1776) as any " new towns and settlements in the State shall " increase in inhabitants, precepts are to issue for " sending Delegates to the Council and Assembly, " proportionally with other parts of the State.— " The Council appoint their President; and in " his absence the senior Councillor presides.— " The Secretary is appointed by both branches, " and may be a Councillor or otherwise as they " chuse.—No act or resolve is to be valid, and " put in execution, unless agreed to and passed " by both branches of the Legislature.—All " public Officers for the Colony, and each " County (except the Clerks of the executive " Courts, who are to be appointed by the re- " spective Courts), are appointed, and their con- " tinuance in office determined by the two " Houses, except Clerks and County Treasurers, " and Recorders of Deeds.—And a Treasurer " and Recorder of Deeds for each County, are " annually chosen by the people of each County " respectively; and the votes for such Officers " are to be returned to the respective Courts of " General Sessions of the Peace in the County, " there to be ascertained as the Council and As- " sembly direct.

" All bills, resolves, or votes for raising, levy- " ing and collecting of money, are to originate " in the House of Representatives.—At any Ses-

" sions

" ſions of the Council and Aſſembly, neither
" Branch ſhall adjourn for any longer time than
" from Saturday till the next Monday, without
" conſent of the other."

MASSACHUSETT'S BAY.

The Conſtitution or frame of Government of the State of Maſſachuſett's Bay, was agreed upon by the Delegates of the people of that State in Convention, at Cambridge, begun the 1ſt of September 1779, and continued by adjournment to the 2d of March 1780.

In the ſummary of this and ſome other Conſtitutions that follow, I have, for the ſake of perſpicuity, arranged the ſeveral particulars more methodically than they are in the Conſtitution at large.

" The Convention forms the territory former-
" ly called the Province of Maſſachuſett's Bay,
" into a free, ſovereign, and independent Body
" Politic, or State, by the name of the Com-
" monwealth of Maſſachuſett's.

" No ſubject is to be moleſted for worſhipping
" God in the manner and ſeaſon moſt agreeable
" to his conſcience, or for his religious ſenti-
" ments, if he doth not diſturb the public peace,
" or obſtruct others in their religious worſhip:
" and the Legiſlature is to require the ſeveral
" towns, &c. to make ſuitable proviſion, at their
" own expence, for the public worſhip of God,
" and the ſupport of public Proteſtant teachers,
" where ſuch proviſion is not made voluntarily;
" and to enjoin all ſubjects to attend public
" teachers at ſtated ſeaſons, if there be any on
" whom they conſcientiouſly can attend; but the
" towns, &c. have the excluſive right of electing
" public

" public teachers, and contracting with them " for their fupport: and all monies paid by the " fubject, to the fupport of public worfhip and " public teachers, are, if he requires it, to be " uniformly applied to the fupport of thofe of " his own fect; but if he attends none, then the " the monies are to be paid towards the fupport " of the teacher of the parifh or precinct where " raifed; and every denomination of Chriftians " demeaning themfelves peaceably, and as good " fubjects, are to be equally under the protection " of the law; and no fubordination of any one " Sect to another, is ever to be eftablifhed by " law.

" The Governor of the Commonwealth of " Maffachufett's, is the fupreme executive Ma- " giftrate, and ftyled, " His Excellency."—He " is chofen annually by the Freeholders and " other Inhabitants; muft have refided in the " State feven years; have a freehold there worth " *L.* 1000, and declare himfelf to be of the " Chriftian religion: He can affemble the Coun- " cillors at difcretion; and he, and not lefs than " Five Members, can make a Council for order- " ing the affairs of the Commonwealth, accord- " ing to law.—He is Governor of the Common- " wealth, Commander in Chief by fea and land, " and hath all powers incident to the offices of " Captain General and Admiral, agreeable to " the rules of the Conftitution.—He can, with " the advice of Council, pardon all criminals, " after conviction, except thofe impeached by " the Houfe: and, with the advice and confent " of Council, he appoints all judicial Officers, " Attorney and Solicitor General, Sheriffs, Coro- " ners, and Regifters of Probate; and is to have an " honourable ftated falary eftablifhed by ftanding

" law.

" law.—All commiſſions are in the name of the
" Commonwealth, under the Great Seal, ſigned
" by the Governor, and atteſted by the Se-
" cretary.

" The Lieutenant Governor is annually elected
" in the ſame manner as the Governor: he is
" ſtyled, " his Honour;" and muſt be qualified
" as to religion, property, and reſidence, as the
" Governor is; and in the Governor's abſence
" he is Preſident of the Council, but has no
" vote; and is always a Member of the Coun-
" cil, except when the Governor's chair is va-
" cant. If the Governor is dead, or abſent from
" the Commonwealth, the Lieutenant Governor
" (during ſuch vacancy) exerciſes all ſuch powers
" as the Conſtitution veſts in the Governor when
" preſent.

" Nine Councillors are annually choſen from
" among the perſons returned for Councillors
" and Senators, by joint ballot of the Senators
" and Repreſentatives aſſembled in one room;
" and thoſe who accept the office of Councillors,
" vacate their ſeats in the Senate.—The Council-
" lors rank next after the Lieutenant Governor;
" the Governor aſſembles them at his diſcretion,
" and Five at leaſt, with the Governor, make a
" Board. Whenever the Governor and Lieute-
" nant Governor are dead, or abſent, the Council,
" or a majority during ſuch vacancy, exerciſe
" thoſe powers which the Conſtitution veſts in the
" Governor when preſent.

" The Senate is the firſt branch of the Le-
" giſlature, and annually elected by the Free-
" holders and Inhabitants; and each Senator
" muſt have a freehold worth *L.* 300, or a per-
" ſonal eſtate worth *L.* 600: they are Judges of
" the elections, returns, and qualifications of their
" Members,

" Members, determine their own rules of pro-
" ceeding, chuſe their own Preſident and Of-
" ficers; but can adjourn themſelves no longer
" than two days at a time.—They are a Court to
" determine all impeachments made by the Houſe
" of Repreſentatives againſt any Officer for mal-
" adminiſtration: however, their judgment ex-
" tends no farther than removal from, and diſ-
" qualification to hold any place of truſt, honour,
" or profit; but the Delinquent is liable to in-
" dictment at law.—Not leſs than Sixteen of the
" Senate can make a quorum to do buſineſs.

" The Houſe of Repreſentatives is choſen by
" the Freeholders and Inhabitants, and each
" Member muſt have reſided one year in the
" town he repreſents, and own there a freehold
" worth *L.* 100, or any rateable eſtate of the
" value of *L.* 200; and on his ceaſing to be qua-
" lified he loſes his ſeat.

" The Repreſentatives are annually choſen in
" May; they are the grand Inqueſt of the Com-
" monwealth, and all their impeachments are
" tried by the Senate. All money-bills originate
" with the Repreſentatives; but the Senate may
" propoſe or concur in amendments of them, as
" of other bills: they can adjourn themſelves no
" longer than two days at a time; and ſixty Mem-
" bers make a Houſe. They are Judges of their
" own returns, elections and qualifications, chuſe
" their own Speaker, appoint their own Officers,
" and ſettle the rule of proceeding in their
" own Houſe. They can impriſon every perſon
" (not a Member) for diſreſpect to the Houſe;
" contemptuous behaviour in its preſence; or
" threatening the body or eſtate of any Member
" in the town where the General Court ſits; or
" aſſaulting a Member; or aſſaulting or arreſt-
" ing

" ing a perſon ordered to attend the Houſe; or " reſcuing one arreſted by its order. The Go- " vernor and Council, and the Senate, have " the ſame power of puniſhing contempts; " but neither of the three Bodies can impriſon " for more than thirty days. And both Houſes " may determine caſes of right and privilege, by " their own Committees or otherwiſe, as each " Houſe thinks beſt.

" The Legiſlature is formed by the Senate and " Houſe of Repreſentatives, and each has a ne- " gative on the other. They are ſtyled, " The " General Court of Maſſachuſett's;" and all laws " run, " Be it enacted by the Senate and Houſe " of Repreſentatives, in General Court aſſembled, " and by the authority of the ſame." Both Houſes " meet on the laſt Wedneſday in every May: the " Governor, with the advice of Council, may, " during the Seſſion of the General Court, ad- " journ or prorogue them to any time they deſire: " in their receſs, he may prorogue them for not " more than ninety days in any one receſs, and " may call them together before the end of the " adjournment or prorogation, if the welfare of " the Commonwealth requires it; and he muſt " diſſolve them on the day preceding the laſt " Wedneſday in every May. If both Houſes " diſagree about the time of adjournment or pro- " rogation, the Governor can, with the advice " of Council, adjourn or prorogue them, not ex- " ceeding ninety days, as the public good may " require: and in caſe of an infectious diſtemper, " or other danger to the health or lives of the " Members of the General Court, he may direct " the Seſſion to be held in ſome other place than " that where they were to meet.—No bill or re- " ſolve of the Senate or Houſe of Repreſentatives

" ſhall become a law, until the Governor reviſes
" it, and in caſe of his approbation, he is to ſign
" it; but he may within five days, after any bill
" or reſolve is preſented to him, return it with
" his objections thereto in writing, to the Houſe
" in which it originated. And if, after recon-
" ſideration, two-thirds of the Members preſent
" in each Houſe, approve of the bill or reſolve,
" it ſhall have the force of a law; but in all ſuch
" caſes, the votes of both Houſes ſhall be deter-
" mined by Yeas and Nays, and the names of the
" perſons voting for, or againſt the bill or re-
" ſolve, ſhall be entered upon the public records
" of the Commonwealth. The General Court
" can conſtitute Courts of Record or others, to
" be held in the name of the Commonwealth,
" with power to try all criminal and civil mat-
" ters; and all Writs are to iſſue in the name of
" The Commonwealth of Maſſachuſett's," under
" the Seal of the Court, and the *teſte* of the firſt
" Juſtice thereof, who is not a party; and are to
" be iſſued out, and ſigned by the Clerk of ſuch
" Court. The General Court names all Officers
" whoſe appointment is not otherwiſe provided
" for; and monies raiſed by them, are iſſued by
" Warrant of the Governor, with the advice and
" conſent of Council, for the public ſervice, as
" the Acts direct. All judicial Officers (whoſe
" appointment is not otherwiſe provided for) are
" nominated by the Governor, with the advice
" and conſent of the Council, during good be-
" haviour, but may be removed by the ſame au-
" thority, upon addreſs of both Houſes of Le-
" giſlature. The Judges of the Supreme Judicial
" Court, have honourable ſalaries, eſtabliſhed by
" ſtanding law; and each branch of the Legiſla-
" ture, as well as the Governor and Council, can
" require

" require their opinions upon important queſtions " of law, and ſolemn occaſions. All cauſes of " marriage, divorce, and alimony, and all ap- " peals from the Judges of Probate, are to be " determined by the Governor and Council, un- " til the legiſlature ſhall make other proviſion. " But the legiſlative department, is never to ex- " erciſe the executive and judicial powers; the " executive is never to exerciſe the legiſlative and " judicial powers; and the judicial is never to " execute the legiſlative and executive powers, " and all Officers muſt take the Oath of Alle- " giance, and Oath of Office ſet forth in the " Conſtitution. All laws formerly adopted, and " uſually practiſed in the Courts of Law (except " ſuch as are repugnant to the Conſtitution) are " to remain, until altered by the Legiſlature; but " the Trial by Jury is to remain ſacred in all " Caſes, unleſs in ſuch laws as the Legiſlature " may make for the government of the army and " navy, concerning matters ariſing on the high " ſeas, and cauſes relating to mariners wages.

" The Maſſachuſett's form of Government, is " ordered to be enrolled on parchment, depoſited " in the Secretary's Office, and is a part of their " laws; and printed copies of the form of Go- " vernment, are to be prefixed to all future edi- " tions of their Book of Laws.

" In order to adhere to the principles of the " Conſtitution, to correct the violations of it, " and to form ſuch alterations, as from expe- " rience ſhall be found neceſſary, the General " Court, in 1795, is to iſſue precepts for conveen- " ing the qualified voters, to collect their ſen- " timents on the neceſſity or expediency of re- " viſing the Conſtitution, in order to amend- " ments; and if two thirds of the qualified voters

" of

"of the State, who assemble, vote for a revision and amendment, then the Towns are to elect Delegates to meet in Convention for that purpose; and the Delegates are to be chosen in the same manner and proportion, as the House of Representatives is by the Constitution."

The State of RHODE-ISLAND *and* PROVIDENCE PLANTATIONS.

King Charles the Second, in the 15th year of this reign (which was 1663) granted a Charter of Incorporation to the inhabitants of those Plantations, by the name of "The Governor and Company of the English Colony of Rhode Island, and Providence Plantations in New England in America;" to be holden of him, his heirs, and successors, as of his manor of East Greenwich in Kent, in free and common soccage. In that Charter, the King grants the Governor and Company the legislative, executive, and judicial powers, reserving to himself, as an acknowledgment of his sovereignty, a render of the fifth part of the gold and silver ore that should be found within the territory. In pursuance of the Charter, one Governor, one Deputy Governor, ten assistants were annually elected, and six freemen for Newport; four for each of the towns of Providence, Portsmouth, and Warwick; and two for each other place, town, or city, were elected every six months by the Freemen, and were called the General Assembly, which had full power and authority given them by the Charter, to make such laws, statutes, &c. as were not contrary or repugnant unto, but as near as might be agreeable to the laws

laws of the realm of England, considering the nature and constitution of the place and people there, to establish courts, and constitute officers; reserving an appeal to the King in England in all matters of public controversies. Under the title, "Rhode Island," in the collection of the Constitutions of the States of America, is inserted the Charter of King Charles the Second; and it is said, "That since the commencement of hostilities "by Great Britain, the State of Rhode-Island "and Providence Plantations has not assumed a "form of Government different from that con-"tained in the Charter. For in that, the King "ceded to the Governor and Company all "powers, legislative, executive, and judicial, re-"serving to himself, as an acknowledgment of "his sovereignty, a render of the fifth part of the "gold and silver ore that should be found within "the territory. The Governor, Chief Magi-"strates, and Legislators, are chosen by the "Freemen as usual; and all judicial and exe-"cutive officers are annually elected by the Go-"vernor and Company, or Upper and Lower "House of Assembly. All process, original and "judicial, formerly issued in the King's name, "but now issues in the name of the Governor and "Company. The oaths of allegiance and office, "are made conformable to the principles of the "Revolution. The Governor, in his legislative "capacity, cannot give a negative to any Act of "the two Houses; but, in common with the other "Magistrates, has one voice only.

"The State is divided into five Counties, in "each of which there is a Court of Common "Pleas, and General Sessions of the Peace, held "twice every year, for the trial of all causes not "capital, that arise within their limits; from

"which

" which an appeal lies to the superior Court of
" Judicature, Court of Assize, and General Goal
" Delivery, whose jurisdiction extends over the
" whole State, and who also sit twice a year in
" each County. The Constitution admits not of
" religious establishments, any farther than de-
" pends upon the voluntary choice of individuals.
" All men professing one Supreme Being, are
" equally protected by the laws; and no parti-
" cular Sect can claim pre-eminence."

The State of CONNECTICUT.

King Charles the Second, in the 14th year of his reign (which was 1662), granted a Charter of Incorporation to the inhabitants of Connecticut, of the same tenor with that of Rhode-Island. An account of the Constitution of Connecticut is inserted amongst the other Constitutions of the American States, and seems to be the same, in most respects, with that which is contained in their Charter, except that the name of the Governor and Company is substituted in the room of that of the King. The Connecticut Charter is not prefixed to the account of its Constitution, but the Charter may be seen in the second volume of Almon's Parliamentary Register.

The account of the Constitution of Connecticut, says, " That it is divided into six Counties,
" and each County is divided into a number of
" Towns. Each Town has a right to send two Re-
" presentatives to the General Court or Assembly.
" The General Court consists of two branches,
" called the Upper and Lower House. The
" Upper House is composed of the Governor,
" Deputy Governor, and twelve Assistants or
" Counsellors; and the Lower House, of the Re-
" presentatives of the several Towns. This Court
" has

"has the ſole power to make and repeal laws, "grant levies, diſpoſe of lands belonging to the "State, to particular towns and perſons; to "erect and ſtyle judicatories and officers, as they "ſhall ſee neceſſary, for the good government of "the People; and alſo to call to account any "Court, Magiſtrate, or other Officer, for any "miſdemeanor or mal-adminiſtration; and for "juſt cauſe, may fine, diſplace, or remove them, "or deal otherwiſe, as the nature of the caſe "ſhall require; and they act in any other manner "that concerns the good of the State, except "the election of Governor, Deputy Governor, "Aſſiſtants, Treaſurer, and Secretary, which is "done by the Freemen at the yearly Court of "Election, unleſs there be any vacancy, by rea-"ſon of death or otherwiſe, after the Election, "which may be filled up by the General Court. "That Court has power alſo, for reaſons ſatis-"factory to them, to grant ſuſpenſion, releaſe, "and goal delivery, upon reprieve, in capital "and criminal caſes. The General Court has "two ſtated Seſſions annually on the ſecond "Thurſdays of May and October.

"The Governor, or, in his abſence, the De-"puty Governor, may call the Aſſembly, on ſpe-"cial emergencies, to meet at any other time. "The Governor, Deputy Governor, Aſſiſtants, "and Secretary, are annually elected on the ſe-"cond Thurſday in May. The Repreſentatives "are newly choſen for each ſtated Seſſion. The "Judges and Juſtices are annually appointed by "the General Court; the ſame perſons are com-"monly re-appointed from time to time, during "their capacity to ſerve, unleſs guilty of miſbe-"haviour. The Sheriffs are appointed by the "Governor and Council without limitation of "time;

" time; but may be superseded by the authority
" that appointed them. The Governor for the
" time being, is Captain General of the Militia;
" the Deputy Governor is Lieutenant General,
" the other General and Field Officers are ap-
" pointed by the General Court, and commis-
" sioned by the Governor. The Captains and
" Subalterns are chosen by the votes of the Com-
" pany and Householders within the limits of
" the Company; the persons so chosen must be
" approved of by the General Court, and com-
" missioned by the Governor before they can exe-
" cute their offices. All the military Officers
" hold their offices during the pleasure of the
" Assembly, nor can they resign their commis-
" sions without leave of the Captain General,
" under penalty of doing duty in the ranks as
" private soldiers. The mode of electing the
" Governor, Deputy Governor, Assistants, Trea-
" surer, and Secretary is, that the Freemen in the
" several Towns meet on the Monday next after
" the first Tuesday in April annually (being the
" day appointed by law for that purpose, and for
" chusing representatives), and give in their votes
" for the persons they chuse for such offices re-
" spectively, with their names written on a piece
" of paper, which votes are received, and sealed
" up by a Constable in the Freemens Meeting.
" The votes for each of the said officers are put
" in a different paper; and on the outside of the
" paper is written the name of the town, and of
" the office for which the names are given in:
" these papers are sent by the Representatives to
" the General Court, to be held on the second
" Tuesday in May next ensuing the Election, at
" which time, after the House of Representatives
" have chosen a Speaker and Clerk, a Committee
" of

" of Members of both Houſes is choſen to ſort " and count the votes, and to declare the names " of the perſons choſen to the ſaid offices. Any " Freeman qualified to vote for Repreſentatives, " &c. may be elected to any office in the Go- " vernment. In chooſing Aſſiſtants, twenty per- " ſons are nominated by the Votes of the Free- " men, given in at their Meeting for chooſing " Repreſentatives in September annually: theſe " Votes are ſealed up, and ſent to the General " Court in the October following, when the Votes " are counted by a Committee of both Houſes, " and the twenty perſons, who have the greateſt " number of Votes, ſtand in nomination, out of " which number Twelve, are choſen as Aſſiſtants " by the Freemen, in the April following, in the " manner above deſcribed. The qualifications " requiſite to entitle a perſon to vote at the elec- " tion of the Officers of Government, are, ma- " turity in years, quiet and peaceable behaviour, " a civil converſation, and forty ſhillings free- " hold, or forty pounds perſonal eſtate: if the " ſelect men of the town certify a perſon quali- " fied in thoſe reſpects, he is admitted a Free- " man, on his taking an oath of fidelity to the " State.

" The names of all that are thus admitted, are " inrolled in the Town Clerk's Office, and con- " tinue Freemen during life, unleſs disfranchiſed " by a Sentence of the ſuperior Court, on convic- " tion of a miſdemeanor. The Governor, or, in " his abſence, the Deputy Governor in the Up- " per Houſe, and the Speaker of the Lower " Houſe of Aſſembly, have a caſting voice, when " the Members of the reſpective Houſes, includ- " ing the Governor and Speaker, are equally di- " vided in opinion on any queſtion.

" There

"There is in this State a superior Court, consisting of one Chief Judge, and four other Judges, who have authority in all criminal cases, extending to life, limb, and banishment; and they also determine all civil actions, brought by appeal from the County Courts, or on Writs of Error. This Court has also authority in all matters of divorce. There are two stated Sessions of the superior Court in each County annually.

"There are also County Courts held in the several Counties, consisting of one Judge, and four Justices of the Quorum, who have jurisdiction in all criminal cases, arising within their respective Counties, where the punishment does not extend to life, limb, or banishment. The County Courts have also original jurisdiction in all civil actions, wherein the demand exceeds forty shillings. The superior and County Courts try matters of fact by a Jury, according to the course of the common law.

"Justices of the Peace have authority to determine civil actions, where the demand does not exceed forty shillings. They also have authority in some cases of a criminal nature, punishable by fine not exceeding forty shillings; or whipping, not exceeding ten stripes; or setting in the stocks.

"This State is also divided into a number of probate districts, less than Counties; in each of which is appointed a Judge for the probate of wills, granting administration on intestates estates, appointing guardians for minors, ordering distribution of intestates estates, &c. An appeal lies from any decree of this Court to the superior Court. The superior County

"and

"and probate Courts appoint their reſpective "Clerks.

"The General Court has, till very lately, been "the only Court of Chancery in this State. But "by a late law, the County Courts determine "matters of equity, from five pounds to two "hundred pounds value; the ſuperior Court "from two hundred to eight hundred pounds "value, and the General Aſſembly determines all "caſes, exceeding the laſt mentioned ſum.

"All Attornies at Law, are admitted and "ſworn by the County Courts; there is no At-"torney General, but there uſed to be one King's "Attorney in each County, who is now ſtyled "Attorney to the Governor and Company."

As the account of the Conſtitution of Connecticut is ſhort, I have inſerted it at length, with the alteration of ſome inaccuracies; but the language is ſtill incorrect in ſeveral places. There is no date to the account of the Conſtitutions of Connecticut and Rhode Iſland.

NEW YORK.

The Conſtitution of the State of New York was eſtabliſhed by the Convention (authoriſed and empowered for that purpoſe), April 20, 1777.

As that Conſtitution differs, in many reſpects, from the Conſtitution of every other American State, I ſhall give it more at length than ſome of the Conſtitutions that follow: and, for the ſake of perſpicuity, I have arranged it differently to what it ſtands in the Conſtitution at large.

"The ſupreme executive power of the State, "is veſted in a Governor, choſen once in three "years, and as often as the Government becomes

" vacant. He muſt be a Freeholder of the State, " and elected by thoſe poſſeſſed of freeholds in " the four great diſtricts, worth one hundred " pounds more than the debts charged on them. " The Governor, by virtue of his Office, is Ge- " neral and Commander in Chief of the Militia, " and Admiral of the Navy. He may convene " the Legiſlature on extraordinary occaſions, and " prorogue them from time to time, not exceed- " ing ſixty days in one year. He may, at his " diſcretion, reprieve and pardon all crimes, ex- " cept treaſon or murder; and there he may " ſuſpend the execution until the Legiſlature " meets, who ſhall either pardon the criminal, " grant him a farther reprieve, or direct his exe- " cution. He is to inform the Legiſlature, at " every Seſſions, of the condition of the State, ſo " far as reſpects his department—he is to recom- " mend ſuch matters to them as concern its " welfare—to correſpond with the Continental " Congreſs, and other States—to tranſact all bu- " ſineſs with the Officers of Government, civil, " and military—to take care that the laws are " faithfully executed—and to expedite ſuch " meaſures as may be reſolved on by the Legiſ- " lature.

" The Lieutenant Governor is choſen in the " ſame manner, and for the ſame term as the Go- " vernor. He is Preſident of the Senate, but " has only a caſting voice when they are equally " divided. In caſe of the Governor's being im- " peached, removed, dead, abſent, or having " reſigned, he executes the office, until another " Governor is choſen, or the abſent or impeached " one, is returned or acquitted. But if in a war, " the Governor is out of the State, at the head " of the militia, and by the conſent of the Le-

" giſlature,

" giſlature, he ſtill continues in the command of
" the forces by ſea and land.

" When the Lieutenant Governor adminiſters " Government, or is unable to preſide at the Se- " nate, they ſhall elect one of their own Mem- " bers to be their Preſident *pro hac vice*; and in " caſe of the death or other diſability (above- " mentioned) of the Governor and Lieutenant " Governor, the Preſident of the Senate admi- " niſters Government until the next election by " the people, unleſs the temporary diſabilities of " the Governor and Lieutenant Governor are in " the mean time removed.

" The ſupreme legiſlative power is veſted in " two diſtinct bodies, called " The Aſſembly of " the State of New York," and " The Senate " of the State of New York," who together form " the Legiſlature, and are to meet once at leaſt " in every year, for the diſpatch of buſineſs.

" The Aſſembly ſhall conſiſt of at leaſt ſe- " venty Members, and never exceed three hun- " hundred; and to prevent an increaſe beyond " the laſt number, the Legiſlature from time to " time is by law to apportion the Repreſentatives " amongſt the Counties, in proportion to the " number of Electors, ſo that the Repreſentation " of the People may remain proportionate. The " Aſſembly is annually choſen in the ſeveral Coun- " ties in the proportion mentioned in the Conſti- " tution, by the male inhabitants of full age, " reſiding within one of the Counties for ſix " months next before the Election: and each " Elector muſt have a freehold worth twenty " pounds within the County, or a tenement of " forty ſhillings a year, and have paid taxes; and " if required by the returning Officer, muſt take " the Oath of Allegiance to the State. The Aſ-

" ſembly

" ſembly chooſe their own Speaker, are Judges of " their own Members, and proceed to buſineſs, " as Aſſemblies of right formerly did; and a " majority makes a Houſe to proceed to buſineſs.

" The Senate at firſt conſiſted of twenty-four " Freeholders choſen out of the four great di- " ſtricts (into which the Province is divided for " the purpoſe of electing the Governor, Lieu- " tenant Governor, and Senate) by ſuch Free- " holders as elect the Governor and Lieutenant " Governor. The firſt Senate was choſen for " four years, and immediately after the Election " was divided by lot into four claſſes, ſix in " each claſs, and numbered 1, 2, 3, and 4, " that the ſeats of the Members of the firſt claſs, " might be vacated at the end of the firſt year, " the ſecond claſs, the ſecond year, and ſo on " continually, ſo that the fourth part of the Se- " nate, as nearly as poſſible, may be annually " choſen; but the number of Senators is never to " exceed one hundred; to prevent which, the " Legiſlature, from time to time, is by law to " apportion the Senators amongſt the diſtricts, in " proportion to the number of Electors, ſo that " the Repreſentation of the People may for ever " remain proportionate. But, although the ſu- " preme legiſlative power is veſted in the Aſ- " ſembly and Senate; yet to prevent laws being " hoſtilely paſſed inconſiſtent with the ſpirit of the " Conſtitution, the Governor, Chancellor, and " Judges of the Supreme Court, or any two of " them, with the Governor, are a Council to " reviſe all bills that have paſſed the Senate and " Aſſembly, before they become laws; and if " within ten days, after a Bill is preſented for " reviſal, it ſhall appear improper to a majority " of the Council of Reviſal, they are to return

" it,

"it, with their objections in writing, to that "House in which it originated; and if, after re- "consideration by both Houses separately, two "thirds of the Members present in each House "approve of the Bill, it is a law, notwithstanding "the objections of a majority of the Council of "Revisal.

"Neither House has a power to adjourn itself "longer than two days, without mutual consent; "and whenever they disagree, a conference is to "be held, in the presence of both Houses, by "Committees chosen by ballot. The doors of "both Houses are to be open to all persons, ex- "cept when the welfare of the State requires their "debates to be kept secret; and their Journals "are to be kept like those of the Assembly in the "King's time, and published from day to day, "unless where secrecy is necessary. The style of "all laws is, "Be it enacted by the people of the "State of New York, represented in Senate and "Assembly;" and all Writs, and other proceed- "ings, run in the name of the People of the "State of New York, and are tested in the name "of the Chancellor, or Chief Judge of the Court, "from whence they issue.

"The Treasurer of the State is appointed by "Act of the Legislature, which originates with "the Assembly, but he cannot be elected out of "either House; and all Officers, whose mode of "election is not directed by the Constitution, are "appointed by a Council, consisting of the Go- "vernor (or other person that administers Go- "vernment for the time) who is President thereof; "and one Senator from each district, nominated "by the Assembly. When the Council of Ap- "pointment is equally divided, the President has "a casting voice; but no vote at other times. A

" majority of the Council of Appointment makes " a quorum, and with their consent, the Pre-" sident appoints all Officers, who are not other-" wise elected by the Constitution; and all com-" missioned Officers, civil and military, are com-" missionated by the Governor; but no Senator " is eligible to the Council of Appointment for " two years successively.

" The Chancellor, Judges of the Supreme " Court, and first Judge of every County Court, " are appointed during good behaviour, or till " the age of sixty. The Chancellor, and Judges " of the Supreme Court, can hold no other of-" fice, except that of Delegate to the General " Congress, upon special occasions; and the first " Judge of each County Court, can hold no other " office, except that of Senator or Delegate to " the General Congress; but when elected to dif-" ferent offices (except as above), they have their " option in which to serve.

" Sheriffs and Coroners are appointed anually, " but cannot serve more than four years suc-" cessively; nor can the Sheriff hold any other " Office.

" The Register, and Clerks in Chancery, are " appointed by the Chancellor; the Clerks of the " Supreme Court, by the Judges thereof; the " Clerk of the Court of Probates, by the Judge " thereof; and the Register and Marshal of the " Court of Admiralty, by the Judge thereof; " and they are to continue during the pleasure of " those who appoint them. Attornies, Solicitors, " and Counsellors at Law, are appointed by the " Court in which they practise—are licensed by " the First Judge, and regulated by the rules and " orders of such Court.

" Where

" Where the continuance of any Officer is not
" aſcertained by the Conſtitution, he continues
" during the pleaſure of the Council of Appoint-
" ment, but the Puiſne Judges of the County
" Court, and the Juſtices of the Peace, have
" new Commiſſions, at leaſt, once in three
" years.

" Town Clerks, Superviſors, Aſſeſſors, Con-
" ſtables, Collectors, and all other Officers for-
" merly eligible by the people, ſtill continue to
" be elected by them, as the Act of the Legiſla-
" ture directs; and Loan Officers, County Trea-
" ſurers, and Superviſors Clerks, are appointed
" as the law directs. Delegates to the Conti-
" nental Congreſs, are annually appointed by the
" Senate and Aſſembly: each Houſe openly no-
" minates as many perſons as are equal to the
" whole number of Delegates to be appointed;
" after the nomination, both Houſes meet, and
" ſuch as are named in both liſts, are Delegates;
" and out of thoſe names that are not in both
" liſts, one half is choſen by joint ballot of both
" Houſes ſo met together.

" For the trial of impeachments and correction
" of errors, there is a Court, conſiſting of the Pre-
" ſident of the Senate, and a majority of the Se-
" nators, the Chancellor, and Judges of the Su-
" preme Court. But where the Chancellor, or
" either of the Judges is impeached, he is
" ſuſpended from his office until he is acquitted;
" and on an appeal from a decree in Chancery,
" or on a Writ of Error from the Supreme Court,
" the Chancellor, in the firſt caſe, and the Judges
" in the ſecond, ſhall aſſign the reaſons for the
" decree or judgment, as the caſe may be; but
" cannot vote for the affirmance or reverſal.

" The

" The Assembly may impeach all Officers for " mal or corrupt conduct; but two thirds of the " members present must agree in the impeach- " ment and judgment thereon; and previous to " the trial, they must be sworn, " truly and im- " partially to try and determine the charge in " question, according to evidence." The judg- " ment on impeachment, shall extend no farther " than to removal from office, and disqualifica- " tion to hold any place of honour, trust, or pro- " fit; but the person convicted on impeachment " may, nevertheless, be indicted, and punished " according to law; and in every trial, on im- " peachment or indictment, the defendant is al- " lowed Counsel, as in other cases: and no mem- " ber is to be disfranchised, or deprived of his " rights, but by the law of the land, or the judg- " ment of his Peers.

" The Statute Laws of England and Great " Britain, and the Acts of Assembly under the " King's Government, which together formed the " law of New York, on 19th of April 1775, are " the law of the State, but subject to alteration " by the Legislature. The temporary Acts are " to expire at the times limited, and all such " parts of the common and statute law, and Acts " of Assembly, as establish any denomination of " Christians, or their Ministers, or which con- " cern the allegiance to, or the sovereignty of " the King of Great Britain, repugnant to the " Constitution, are abrogated; but the Resolu- " tions of the Provincial Congresses, and the " Convention of the Colony of New York, not " repugnant to the Constitution, are part of the " law of the State, subject to the alteration of the " Legislature. All grants by the King of Great " Britain, or under his authority, after the 14th

" of

" of October 1775, are declared void; but the " Conftitution does not affect any grant of lands " or charter prior to that day; and all Officers " who by charter were appointed by the King's " Governor, are now appointed by the Council of " Appointment.

" The free exercife of every religion is allow- " ed; but no Minifter or Prieft of any denomi- " nation can hold any civil or military office.

" The militia is at all times to be armed and " difciplined, as well in peace as war; and ma- " gazines of warlike ftores are to be eftablifhed " in every County. Quakers are excufed from " bearing arms; but muft pay the State, in lieu " thereof, fuch fums as the Legiflature may " direct.

" The trial by Jury is to remain inviolate for " ever; and no act of attainder is to be paffed " by the Legiflature for crimes, except thofe " committed before the termination of the war, " and fuch Acts are not to work a corruption of " blood.——The Legiflature can inftitute no " Courts, but what proceed according to the " courfe of the Common Law.

" The Legiflature may naturalize all perfons " who fettle in the State, become fubjects of it, " take an oath of allegiance to it, and abjure " all foreign allegiance and authority in matters " ecclefiaftical and civil."

NEW JERSEY.

The Conftitution of New Jerfey was eftablifhed in the Provincial Congrefs at Burlington, in that Province, on 2d July 1776, by the advice of the Continental Congrefs, and was to be void if a reconciliation between Great Britain and the Colonies

Colonies took place, otherwiſe to remain inviolable.

" The Conſtitution veſts the Government in a " Governor, Legiſlative Council, and General " Aſſembly.

" The Governor is elected annually by a ma- " jority of votes of the Council and Aſſembly " jointly, at their firſt meeting after their elec- " tion.—He has the ſupreme executive Power, " is conſtant Preſident of the Council, and has " a caſting vote in their proceedings.—He is " Captain-General and Commander in Chief, " Chancellor, and Ordinary or Surrogate Gene- " ral.

" The Vice-Preſident is choſen by the Coun- " cil, and, in the abſence of the Governor, the " Vice-Preſident acts as Governor.

" On the ſecond Tueſday in October (with " the power of adjournment from day to day) " the inhabitants of each County worth *L.* 50 a- " piece, proclamation money, in clear eſtate, " choſe one Member of the Legiſlative Council, " and three Members of Aſſembly, each of whom " muſt have reſided in the County a year next " before his election; the Councillor muſt have " at leaſt *L.* 1000, proclamation money, and " each Member of Aſſembly *L.* 500, like money, " within the County; but the majority of Re- " preſentatives in Council and General Aſſembly " may add to, or diminiſh, the number or pro- " portion of Members of Aſſembly for any Coun- " ty; ſo that the Repreſentatives in Aſſembly " are not leſs than thirty-nine.—The Council " are, in all reſpects, a Free and Independent " Branch of the Legiſlature, and have the like " powers as the Aſſembly, except that they can- " not prepare or alter a money bill. The Go-

" vernor,

" vernor, and three or more Councillors, make
" a privy Council: and the Governor, and ſeven
" of the Council at leaſt, make a quorum, to
" determine appeals in the laſt reſort, in all caſes,
" as during the King's Government; and they
" can pardon treaſon, felony, or other offences.

" The Aſſembly chuſe their own Speaker, and
" other Officers; are Judges of the qualifications
" of their Members; ſit upon their own adjourn-
" ments; empower their Speaker to convene
" them when any extraordinary occurrence ren-
" ders it neceſſary; and prepare bills to be paſſed
" into laws. The Governor or Vice-Preſident
" muſt convene the Council whenever the Aſ-
" ſembly ſits; and the Speaker of the Aſſembly
" is, immediately after an adjournment, to give
" the Governor or Vice-Preſident notice of the
" time and place to which the Aſſembly is ad-
" journed.

" The laws run, " Be it enacted by the Coun-
" cil and General Aſſembly of this Colony, and
" it is hereby enacted by the authority of the
" ſame."

" The Council and Aſſembly make the Great
" Seal, which is called " The Great Seal of the
" Colony of New Jerſey;" and is kept by the
" perſon that adminiſters Government, to be uſed
" as occaſion requires.

" The Council and Aſſembly appoint the Judges
" of the Supreme Court for ſeven years, the
" Judges of the Inferior Court of Common Pleas
" in each County, Juſtices of the Peace, Clerks
" of the Supreme Court, Clerks of the Inferior
" Court of Common Pleas and Quarter Seſſions,
" Attorney General, and Provincial Secretary
" for five years; and the Perſon that adminiſters
" Government commiſſions them: but all thoſe

" Officers

" Officers may be re-appointed, and are liable to " be diſmiſſed, when adjudged by the Council " to be guilty of miſbehaviour, on impeachment " of the Aſſembly.

" The Sheriffs and Conſtables are elected an- " nually by the People; and the Sheriffs are com- " miſſioned by the Governor, or in his abſence " by the Vice-Preſident; and all commiſſions " and writs run thus, " The Colony of New " Jerſey to A. B. greeting." General and Field " Officers of Militia are appointed by the Coun- " cil and Aſſembly; the Captains and Subalterns " are choſen by the Companies.

" All criminals are allowed witneſſes and coun- " ſel; and indictments conclude, " Againſt the " peace of this Colony, the Government and " dignity of the ſame." The eſtate of a *felo de* " *ſe*, or any thing occaſioning death, are not for- " feited.

" No religion is eſtabliſhed; and a perſon pro- " feſſing himſelf of any Proteſtant Sect, and de- " meaning himſelf peaceably, may hold any of- " fice, ſit in either Houſe of Legiſlature, and " enjoy every other privilege; but no Officer, " except a Juſtice of the Peace, can ſit in the " Aſſembly.

" The Acts of Aſſembly, and ſo much of the " common and ſtatute law of England as were " uſed in the King's time, remain, till altered " by the Legiſlature, except ſuch parts as are " repugnant to the Conſtitution; and the trial " by Jury is to remain for ever.

" Every Member of the Legiſlature, before he " takes his ſeat, is ſworn not to aſſent to any law " repealing annual elections, and the trial by " Jury; nor to alter thoſe parts of the Conſtitu-

" tion

" tion which forbid the eſtabliſhment of any one
" religion in preference to another, &c."

PENNSYLVANIA.

The Conſtitution of the Commonwealth of Pennſylvania was eſtabliſhed, agreeable to the direction of the Continental Congreſs, by the General Convention, held at Philadelphia from the 15th of July to the 28th of September 1776.

" The Commonwealth or State of Pennſylvania
" is governed by an Aſſembly of the Repreſent-
" atives of the Freemen (who are veſted with the
" Supreme Legiſlative power), and a Preſident
" and Council (who are veſted with the Supreme
" Executive power).

" The Preſident and Vice-Preſident of the
" Council are choſen annually, by joint ballot
" of the Council and General Aſſembly. The
" Council is choſen by the Freemen of the State,
" who are twenty-one years old, have reſided in
" the State a year next before the election, and
" paid taxes. And the ſons of ſuch Freemen,
" if twenty-one, vote, although they have not
" paid taxes.—Philadelphia, and each County,
" chuſes one Councillor a-piece; and ſuch a ro-
" tation was at firſt eſtabliſhed, that a number will
" always remain in Council who are acquainted
" with buſineſs.—No Councillor can ſerve longer
" than three years ſucceſſively, and he cannot be
" re-elected till the expiration of four years from
" his laſt ſervice: each Councillor is a Juſtice of
" the Peace for the whole Commonwealth.—
" The Preſident and five Councillors make a
" quorum, and appoint and commiſſionate Judges,
" naval Officers, Judge of the Admiralty, At-
" torney General, and ſuch other civil and mili-

" tary Officers as the General Aſſembly, or the
" people, do not chuſe by the Conſtitution, or
" laws ſubſequent thereto.—They correſpond
" with other States, tranſact buſineſs with the
" Officers of Government, and prepare matters
" to lay before the Aſſembly.—They determine
" on impeachments, taking the aſſiſtance of the
" Judges of the Supreme Court for advice only.
" —They can remit all fines, and pardon all
" crimes, except thoſe proſecuted by impeach-
" ment (which can be remitted or mitigated by
" the Legiſlature only), and for treaſon and mur-
" der; the Preſident and Council can reprieve,
" but not pardon, till the end of the Seſſions of
" Aſſembly next after conviction.

" The Preſident and Council are to take care,
" that the laws are faithfully executed, the mea-
" ſures agreed on by the Aſſembly expedited;
" and they are to draw on the Treaſury for the
" monies appropriated by the Aſſembly.—They
" lay embargoes, prohibit the exportation of any
" commodity (in the receſs of the Aſſembly only),
" not exceeding thirty days: they grant ſuch li-
" cences as are directed by law; and, in caſes of
" neceſſity, may call the General Aſſembly to-
" gether before the day they are adjourned to:
" they have a Secretary, keep fair books of their
" proceedings; and every Councillor may enter
" his diſſent, and the reaſons for it.—The Preſi-
" dent is Commander in Chief of the Forces of
" the State; but cannot command in perſon,
" except with the advice of the Council, and ſo
" long as they approve of it; and in the abſence
" of the Preſident, the Vice-Preſident adminiſters
" that office.

" The General Aſſembly of Repreſentatives of
" the Freemen of Pennſylvania," are annually
" choſen

" chosen for the Cities and Counties by the Free-
" men by ballot, and must have resided in the
" place they represent for two years next before
" their election. An Assembly-man can serve
" only four years in seven, and can hold no other
" office except in the militia.—The General
" Assembly chuse their own Speaker, and other
" Officers, and the Treasurer of the State: they
" sit on their own adjournments; prepare bills,
" and enact them into laws; judge of the elec-
" tions and qualifications of their Members; can
" expel a Member, but not a second time for the
" same cause; administer oaths or affirmations,
" on examination of witnesses; redress griev-
" ances; impeach State criminals; grant Char-
" ters of Incorporation; constitute towns, bo-
" roughs, cities, and counties; and have all
" powers necessary for the Legislature of a free
" State; but cannot alter any part of the Con-
" stitution.

" Two-thirds of the whole Members elected,
" make a House; and before they proceed to
" business, each must take an oath of allegiance
" to the State, and an oath not to injure or
" abridge the rights of the people; and must sign
" a declaration " Of belief in one God, the Crea-
" tor and Governor of the world, the Rewarder
" of the good, and the Punisher of the wicked,"
" and " an acknowledgment that the Scriptures
" of the Old and New Testament are given by
" Divine Inspiration;" which declaration is the
" only religious test required of any civil Officer
" or Magistrate.

" The doors of the Assembly are to be open,
" except when the welfare of the State requires
" them to be shut; and the Yeas and Nays on
" any question (when it is not by ballot) are to
" be

" be taken down, if two Members require it,
" and the proceedings must be printed weekly:
" and that improper laws may not be enacted, all
" bills of a public nature are to be printed before
" they are read the last time, and are not to be
" passed into laws till the following Session, ex-
" cept on occasions of sudden necessity.—The style
" of the laws is, " Be it enacted, and it is here-
" by enacted by the Representatives of the Free-
" men of the Commonwealth of Pennsylvania,
" in General Assembly met, and by the authority
" of the same:" and when a law passes, it is sealed
" with " the Seal of the Laws of Pennsylvania,"
" which is kept by the Assembly, and not used
" for any other purpose: the wages of the Re-
" presentatives, and other State charges, are paid
" out of the Treasury.—Any Officer whatsoever
" may be impeached by the General Assembly,
" before the President and Council, who hear and
" determine the impeachment.

" The Judges of the Supreme Court of Judi-
" cature have fixed salaries, and are commission-
" ated for seven years; but can hold no other
" office, and may be re-appointed.—And that
" Court, as well as the several Courts of Common
" Pleas, have some of the powers of a Court of
" Chancery.—The Freemen in each County elect
" Justices of the Peace for seven years, and She-
" riffs and Coroners for one year; and all elec-
" tions whatsoever are by ballot; and all com-
" missions in the name and by the authority of
" the Freemen of the Commonwealth of Pennsyl-
" vania, under the State Seal (which is kept by
" the Council), signed by the President, and at-
" tested by the Secretary.

" The trial by Jury remains; all prosecutions
" are in the name and by the authority of the
" Freemen

" Freemen of the Commonwealth of Pennſyl-
" vania; indictments conclude, " Againſt the
" peace and dignity of the ſame;" and the ſtyle
" of all proceſs is, " The Commonwealth of
" Pennſylvania."

" Any foreigner, on taking the oath of al-
" legiance, may purchaſe and transfer land; after
" one year's reſidence, is a free denizen; and
" after two year's reſidence, may be elected a Re-
" preſentative.

" Delegates to the Continental Congreſs are
" choſen by ballot by the General Aſſembly an-
" nually, at their firſt meeting, can ſerve only
" two years ſucceſſively, may be ſuperſeded at
" any time, and holding a Continental office,
" cannot be elected.

" There is no Eccleſiaſtical Eſtabliſhment;
" every mode of worſhip is allowed; and no
" man acknowledging the being of a God, is
" deprived or abridged of any civil right as a
" citizen.

" On the ſecond Tueſday of October, in every
" ſeventh year, the Freemen chuſe two perſons
" in each City and County, named the " Council
" of Cenſors," who may call a Convention, exa-
" mine into the conduct of the Legiſlative and
" Executive Branches, inquire into the laying
" and collecting of the taxes, ſend for perſons,
" papers, and records, paſs public cenſures, order
" impeachments, and recommend the repealing
" of laws that are contrary to the Conſtitution.
" —They continue only one year after election;
" but may call a Convention to meet in two
" years after their ſitting, if there is a neceſſity of
" amending the Conſtitution.—But the propoſed
" amendments muſt be promulgated ſix months
" before the Convention is elected, that the
" people

" people may confider of them, and inftruct
" their Delegates."

DELAWARE.

The Government of the Counties of Newcaftle, Kent, and Suffex, upon Delaware, are in all public and other writings, now called, " The " Delaware State ;" and the Conftitution or Syftem of Government was agreed to by the Reprefentatives, in full Convention, on the 20th of September 1776.

The Prefident, or Chief Magiftrate, is chofen for three years (or until the fitting of the then next General Affembly) by joint ballot of the Legiflative Council and Houfe of Affembly; and the box is examined by the Speakers of both Houfes, in the prefence of the other Members; and if the numbers are equal, the Speaker of the Council has an additional cafting voice; but the Governor cannot be reelected until he has been three years out of that office; he has an adequate moderate falary whilft he continues; in cafe of his death, inability, or abfence from the State, the Speaker of the Legiflative Council is Vice-Prefident, and if he is dead, difabled, or abfent from the State, the Speaker of the Houfe of Affembly has the powers of a Prefident, until the General Affembly makes a new nomination.

The Governor draws for the money appropriated by the General Affembly, and is accountable to them for it.—With the advice of the Privy (or Executive) Council, he lays embargoes, or prohibits the exportation of any commodity (when the General Affembly is not fitting) for thirty days or lefs.—He can pardon or reprieve (where the law does not forbid it), except the profecution is carried on by the Houfe of Affembly, and then the pardon or reprieve muft be by a refolve of that Houfe.—And the Governor may exercife all other Executive Powers of Government, where he is not reftrained by the Conftitution, or by law.

Four Privy Councillors (not in the Continental pay or fervice) are chofen by ballot, two by the Legiflative Council, and two by the Houfe of Affembly; and the accepting the office of a Privy Councillor vacates a feat in the Legiflature.

A Privy Councillor continues only two years, and cannot be re-elected as fuch for the three next years, and they are ballotted out in rotation by the Legiflative Council and Houfe of Affembly.—The Prefident convenes the Privy Council when and where he thinks moft convenient; three Members make a quorum, their proceedings are entered on record, and figned by them, to be laid before the General Affembly when called for; and each Member may enter his diffent.—With the advice and confent of the Privy Council, the Prefident embodies the militia, and acts as Captain-General and Commander in Chief of the military force of the State.

The Legiflature is called "The General Affembly of Delaware," and confifts of two Branches, *viz.* "The (Legiflative) Council," and "The Houfe of Affembly." The Legiflative Council is chofen by the Freemen for three years, and go out in rotation: it confifts of Nine Members (three for each County), who muft be upwards of twenty-five years old, and have a freehold in the County where chofen.

The Houfe of Affembly is chofen by the Freemen annually, on the 1ft of October, and confifts of twenty-one Members, ſeven for each County, each of whom muſt have a freehold where choſen —Each Houſe chuſes its own Speaker, and other Officers; judges of the qualifications and elections of its Members; ſettles its own rule of proceedings; directs writs of election for ſupplying intermediate vacancies; can expel any Member for miſbehaviour; but not a ſecond time in the ſame Seſſions, for the ſame offence; and both Houſes have all other powers neceſſary for the Legiſlature of a Free and Independent State.—All bills and ordinances may originate, be altered, amended, or rejected, by either Houſe, except money-bills, which muſt originate in the Houſe of Aſſembly; but may be altered, amended, or rejected, by the Legiſlative Council.—Both Houſes ſit at the ſame time and place; and each Houſe adjourns itſelf, of which each Speaker immediately gives the other notice. The Preſident cannot prorogue, adjourn, or diſſolve the General Aſſembly; but with the advice of the Privy Council, or on application of the majority of either Houſe, he can call them together before the time to which they ſtand adjourned. The Houſe of Aſſembly can impeach the Preſident (when out of office), and all other Officers, before the Legiſlative Council, for mal-adminiſtration, &c. If the party impeached is found guilty, he may be diſabled to hold any office, removed from it, or ſubjected to ſuch pains and penalties as the law directs; and all Officers are to be removed, on conviction of miſbehaviour by impeachment, or at common law; or if the General Aſſembly addreſſes for ſuch removal.

The Sheriffs and Coroners are choſen annually by the Freemen; but the Preſident and General Aſſembly, by joint ballot appoint the three

Juſtices

Juftices of the Supreme Court, the Judge of the Admiralty, and the four Juftices of the Common Pleas and Orphan's Court, in each County, who continue during good behaviour, but can hold no other office; and the Common Pleas, and Orphan's Court, have the power of holding inferior Courts of Chancery, as in the King's time, until the Legiflature directs otherwife.

The General Affembly appoints all the Officers in the army and navy; the Chief Juftice of the Supreme Court appoints its Clerks; the Juftices of the Common Pleas for each County appoint the Recorders of Deeds; and in cafe of a vacancy of any office, which is filled up by the Prefident and General Affembly, the Prefident and Privy Council may appoint till a new election.—The Prefident commiffions all Officers under the Great Seal of the State, which is made by the Legiflative Council and Affembly, kept by the Prefident, affixed to all Laws and Commiffions, and ufed as occafion may require; the Commiffions run in the name of "The Delaware State," and are tefted by the Prefident.

Every Member of the Legiflature, and Officer, before he acts, takes an Oath or Affirmation of Allegiance to the State, and fubfcribes a Declaration of Faith "In God the Father, and in Jefus "Chrift his only Son, and the Holy Ghoft, one "God bleffed for evermore; and acknowledges "the Holy Scriptures of the Old and New Tefta-"ment to be given by Divine Infpiration."—And Officers alfo take an oath of office.—But no religious Eftablifhment is allowed; nor is any Clergyman or Preacher of the Gofpel permitted to hold any civil office, or to be a Member of the Legiflature.—And the enflaving of Negroes, &c. is difallowed.

The

The Common Law of England, the Acts of Assembly in force on the 15th of May 1776, and such parts of the Statute Law of England used in the King's time, as are not repugnant to the Constitution, continue in force until altered by the Legislature.—Writs run in the name of "The "Delaware State," are tested in the name of the Chief Justice, and under the Seal of the Court from whence they issue: and indictments conclude, "Against the Peace and Dignity of the "State." In place of an appeal to the King in Council, "The Court of Appeals" is instituted, consisting of Nine Members, *viz.* the President for the time being, and Three to be appointed by the Legislative Council, and Three by the House of Assembly, who continue during good behaviour; and the vacancies are supplied by new elections.

But no Member of the Legislature can hold any office, except that of a Justice of the Peace, which he is for the whole State; and the Justices of the Common Pleas are Conservators of the Peace in their respective Counties.

Delegates to the Continental Congress are annually chosen by joint ballot of both Houses of Legislature, who may supersede them within the year.

Some parts of the Constitution are never to be violated on any pretence; and the others not to be altered without the consent of five parts in seven of the Assembly, and seven Members of the Legislative Council.

MARYLAND.

The Conſtitution or form of Government of Maryland, was agreed to and paſſed in a Convention of the Delegates, held at Annapolis the 14th of Auguſt 1776.

The Governor is choſen annually on the ſecond Monday of November, by joint ballot of the Senate and Houſe of Delegates; each of whom muſt firſt take an oath, "To elect, without favour, &c. "the Perſon he believes to be beſt qualified for "the office."—The Governor muſt be above twenty-five years of age, have reſided in the State above five years next before the election, own a freehold eſtate worth *L.* 1000, current money, and have a real and perſonal property there, worth in the whole *L.* 5000.—He cannot continue more than three years ſucceſſively, nor be re-elected till the expiration of four years after he has been out of that office.—He muſt take an Oath of Allegiance to the State; ſubſcribe a Declaration of Belief in the Chriſtian Religion; take a ſecond Oath, "That he will not receive "any part of the profits of an office held by "another, or ariſing on any agency, &c.;" and a third Oath, "That he will not vote for any Of-"ficer, through favour, &c. but for him that is "beſt qualified, &c.; and that he neither has "promiſed, nor will promiſe, his vote or intereſt "in favour of any perſon."—And if he is convicted by two witneſſes, of receiving any of the profits of an office held by another, whilſt he is himſelf in office, his appointment is void, and he ſuffers the puniſhment of perjury, or is baniſhed the State for ever, or diſqualified for ever from holding

holding any office or place of trust or profit, as the Court may adjudge.

Upon the Governor's death, resignation, or removal out of the State, the first named of the Council qualifies himself, and acts as Governor; but must immediately call the General assembly together (giving not less than 14 days notice of their meeting), when a Governor is to be appointed for the residue of the year.

The Senators and Delegates (first taking such an oath as before chusing a Governor), do, on the 2d Tuesday of November yearly, by joint ballot, elect five to be the Council to the Governor, each of whom must be above twenty-five years old, have resided in the State above three years next before his election, and own a freehold therein worth above *L.*1000 currency.—The Council must take the same Oaths, and subscribe the same Declaration as the Governor; their Clerk (who is appointed by them) must take the Oath of Fidelity to the State, and also an Oath to keep secret such matters as the Board shall direct.—Their proceedings are entered on record, to be laid before either House of Legislature that calls for them; and the Governor, or any Member of the Board, may require the advice of the Council in writing, signed by them.—The Governor, with the advice and consent of Council, can embody the militia, and alone has the direction of it, and of the regular land and sea forces of the State, according to law; but he cannot command in person, unless the Council advise it, and then no longer than they approve of it.—Where the concurrence of the Council is not required, he may alone exercise all the other executive Powers of Government, according to law; he may reprieve or pardon, where the law does not forbid; during the

recess

recefs of the General Affembly, he may embargo fhipping, and prevent the exportation of any commodity, not exceeding thirty days in a year; but he muft call the General Affembly before the embargo expires, and he may compel quarantine, if there are ftrong grounds to fufpect a veffel has the plague on board, or, that the place fhe came from, was infected with it. But the Governor is not, under any pretence, to exercife any power or prerogative, by virtue of any law, ftatute, or cuftom of England or Great Britain.

Three Councillors make a board; the Governor (and in his abfence, the firft named in the Council) prefides there, and votes where the Council is divided; and in cafe of a vacancy in the Council, the Members, by ballot, elect another for the refidue of the year.

The Governor, with the advice and confent of the Council, appoints the Chancellor, Judges, Attorney General, and Regifters of the Land Office, during good behaviour; and naval Officers, thofe in the land and fea fervice, and militia, Surveyors, and all other civil Officers of Government (except Affeffors, Conftables, Overfeers of the Roads, &c.) for one year; but removeable for mifbehaviour on conviction in a court of law. The Sheriffs are elected by the Freemen every third year, and the regifters of wills are recommended by both Houfes of Legiflature, and commiffioned by the Governor. The Judges and Juftices appoint their refpective Clerks; but where an office (not in the appointment of the Governor) becomes vacant, the Governor, with the advice of Council, appoints and commiffions, until another is elected, chofen, or recommended, as the cafe may be. The Council make the Great Seal of the State, which is

kept

kept by the Chancellor, and affixed to all laws, commissions, grants, and other public testimonials, as formerly; and all public commissions and grants, run in the name of "The "State of Maryland, &c." are signed by the Governor, and attested by the Chancellor, except military commissions, which are not attested by the Chancellor, nor have the Seal of the State.

The Legislature consists of two branches, a Senate and an House of Delegates, which are styled, "The General Assembly of Maryland." The Senate is chosen in the following manner: On the first of September, in every fifth year, the Freemen above twenty-one years of age, that have resided in the County, where they vote, for one year next before the Election, and own a freehold of fifty acres therein, or have a property in the State, worth above thirty pounds currency, chuse two persons in each county (and one for Annapolis, and one for Baltimore) called Electors of the Senate, any twenty-four of whom may, out of their own body or the people at large, by ballot, elect fifteen Senators that are above twenty-five years of age, have resided in the State three years next before the Election, and have real and personal property there, worth one thousand pounds currency; but the Electors of the Senate, before they proceed, take an oath of fidelity to the State, and also an oath, "to elect "without favour, &c. such persons for Senators, "as in their judgment, &c. they believe best "qualified for the office." But in case of a vacancy, the Senate elects another Senator for the residue of the five years; and they also chuse their President by ballot; and the President and a majority of the Senate make a House.

The

The Senate judges of the Elections and qualifications of their Members, and any, except money bills (to which they can only assent or dissent) may originate there; and to (other than money) bills from the House of Delegates, they may assent, dissent, or propose amendments. And that the Senate may exercise their judgment in passing laws, and not be compelled to reject a money bill, the House of Delegates are not to blend with a money bill, any thing that does not immediately relate thereto: and to prevent altercation about such bills, the Constitution declares, That no bill imposing duties or customs for the mere regulation of commerce, or inflicting fines for the reformation of morals, or to inforce the execution of the laws, by which an incidental revenue may arise; but only bills assessing, levying, or applying taxes or supplies for the support of government, or the current expences of the State, or appropriating money in the Treasury, are to be deemed money bills.

The House of Delegates is chosen on the first Monday in October annually, by the Freemen, qualified as aforesaid to vote for Electors of the Senate. There are four Delegates for each County, two for the city of Annapolis, and two for the town of Baltimore; but as well the Delegates, as the Electors of the Senate for Annapolis, are chosen by the Burgesses. The Delegates must have resided in the County where chosen, one year next preceding the Election, be above twenty-one years old, and have real and personal property in the State worth five hundred pounds currency.

The House of Delegates chose their Speaker by ballot, and he and a majority of Members, make a House, who judge of the elections and qualifications

cations of the Delegates; and in case of a vacancy, the Speaker issues his Warrant for the Election of another Member, of which, at least, ten days clear notice must be given. The House of Delegates originate all money bills—propose bills to the Senate—receive bills offered by them, and assent, dissent, or propose amendments thereto—inquire, by oath, into all complaints, grievances, and offences, as the grand inquest of the State—commit for any crime to the public goal, till discharged by due course of law—expel a member for a great misdemeanor, but not a second time for the same offence—examine and pass all accounts of the State, relating to the collection or expenditure of the revenue, or appoint auditors to adjust them—call for persons, papers, and records—and direct the prosecution of all office bonds, made payable to the State.

They also imprison for a contempt in their view—obstruction to their proceedings—breach of privilege by arresting (on civil process) or assaulting a Member in the Session, or coming to or returning from it—assaulting or obstructing their Officers on duty, or a witness or other person, attending on, coming to, or going from the House—or rescuing a person committed by them: and the Senate exercises the same powers in similar cases.

The House of Delegates appoint a Treasurer for the Western, and another for the Eastern Shore, and also the Commissioners of the Loan Office during pleasure, but if a vacancy happens in the recess of the General Assembly, the Governor, with the advice of Council, appoints and commissions a proper person to fill up such vacancy, till the General Assembly meets, which they do annually on the first Monday of November,

vember, and oftener, if neceſſary; and each Houſe appoints its own Officers, and ſettles its own rules of proceeding. And the ſtyle of the laws, is, "Be it enacted by the General Aſſembly "of Maryland," when a bill paſſes, the General Aſſembly, the Speaker of the Houſe of Delegates preſents it to the Governor in the Senate, who ſigns it, and affixes the Great Seal thereto in the preſence of both Houſes.

There is a Court of Appeals, compoſed of ſeveral perſons, whoſe judgment is final in all appeals from the Court of Chancery, General Court, and Court of Admiralty; the Chancellor is appointed by the Governor (with the advice and conſent of the Council) during good behaviour, and is removable only for miſbehaviour, on conviction in a Court of Law, or addreſs of the General Aſſembly. The ſuperior Court of common law, which was formerly called the Provincial Court, is now called "the General Court," and has three Judges, who are appointed by the ſame authority, that appoints the Chancellor, continue during good behaviour, and are removeable only for miſbehaviour, by conviction at law, or addreſs of the General Aſſembly. All writs run in the name of "The State of Maryland;" and indictments conclude, "againſt the peace, govern-"ment, and dignity of the State."

The trial by Jury remains, and the common law of England; and ſuch Engliſh and Britiſh Statutes as were formerly uſed in the Courts of Law and Equity; and all Acts of Aſſembly, down to the firſt of June 1774 (except ſuch as are altered by the Convention, &c.) remain in force, until amended or repealed by the legiſlature. There is no religious eſtabliſhment, nor is any teſt required on admiſſion into office, except the Oath of Fidelity to the State—the Oath

of

of Office—and a declaration of Belief in the Chriſtian Religion. A gift, ſale, or deviſe to a Teacher of the Goſpel, or to any religious Sect, or in truſt for their ſupport, and to go in ſucceſſion, without leave of the Legiſlature, is void, except a ſale, gift, &c. not exceeding two acres, for a Church, &c. or burying Ground; but the Churches, Chapels, Glebes, and other property belonging to the Church of England, at the time the Conſtitution was aſſented to, are to remain to the Church of England for ever.

No part of the Conſtitution is to be altered or aboliſhed, unleſs the bill, for that purpoſe, paſſes the General Aſſembly, is publiſhed three months before the next Election, and is confirmed by the General Aſſembly in the firſt Seſſion after the new Election of Delegates.

VIRGINIA.

The Conſtitution or form of Government of Virginia was agreed to in a General Convention, held at Williamſburgh, from the 6th of May to the 5th of July 1776.

The legiſlative, executive, and judiciary departments, are to be ſeparate and diſtinct, ſo that neither is to exerciſe the powers properly belonging to the others; nor is any perſon to exerciſe the powers of more than one of them at the ſame time, except that the Juſtices of the County Courts are eligible to either Houſe of Aſſembly.

The Governor or Chief Magiſtrate is choſen annually by joint ballot of both Houſes of Aſſembly—he can continue no longer than three years ſucceſſively, and is not eligible until four years after he has been out of office. He has an adequate, but moderate ſalary, and with the advice of the Council of State, exerciſes the executive powers

powers of Government, according to the laws of the Commonwealth; but is not, under any pretence, to exercise any power or prerogative, by virtue of any law, custom, or statute of England. But he may, with the advice of the Council of State, reprieve, or pardon, where the prosecution is not carried on by the Delegates, or the law otherwise directs; in which cases, no reprieve or pardon can be granted, but by resolve of the House of Delegates.

A Privy Council or Council of State, consisting of eight Members, is chosen by joint ballot of both Houses of Assembly, either from their own Members, or the people at large, to assist in the administration of Government. The Council, out of their own members, annually chose a President, who in the death or absence of the Governor from the Government, acts as Lieutenant Governor. Four Councillors make a board—their advice and proceedings are entered on record—signed by the Members present (to which either may enter his dissent), and are laid before the General Assembly, when called for. A sum appropriated by the Legislature is divided amongst the Councillors annually, in proportion to their attendance; and whilst Councillors, they cannot sit in either House of Assembly. Every third year, two Councillors are balloted out by both Houses of Assembly, and they are ineligible for the next three years; and all vacancies in the Council are supplied by new Election, by ballot of both Houses of Assembly. The Council appoints their own Clerk, who has a settled salary, and swears to keep secret such matters as the board directs. The Governor, with the advice of the Council, embodies the militia, and has the sole direction of them; and with the like advice (and the recommendation of the reſpective County Courts) he appoints or ſuſpends militia officers—orders a court martial, on complaint of miſbehaviour or inability, and ſupplies vacancies, when happening in actual ſervice—appoints Juſtices of the Peace—and approves of and commiſſions Sheriffs and Coroners, when nominated by the reſpective County Courts—and the Juſtices appoint the Conſtables.

The Judges of the Supreme Court of Appeals of the General Court, of the Chancery, and of the Admiralty, and the Secretary and Attorney General, are appointed by joint ballot of both Houſes, during good behaviour, and the Treaſurer for one year; but they are commiſſioned by the Governor, and all commiſſions and grants run in the name of, "The Commonwealth of Virginia," are under the Seal of the Commonwealth, and teſted by the Governor. The Governor (when he is out of office) the Judges of the General Court, and all other officers, are impeachable by the Houſe of Delegates for mal-adminiſtration, corruption, or otherwiſe endangering the ſafety of the State. The Attorney General (or other perſon appointed by the Houſe of Delegates) proſecutes the impeachment in the General Court, according to the laws of the land, unleſs the Judges of the General Court are the ſubjects of it, in which caſe, it is proſecuted in the Court of Appeals; and if the delinquent is found guilty, he is diſabled to hold any office under Government, is removed from it *pro tempore*, or ſubjected to ſuch pains or penalties as the law directs.

The two diſtinct branches, called "The Senate," and "The Houſe of Delegates," form a complete

complete Legiſlature, and are named "The General Aſſembly of Virginia."

The Senate conſiſts of twenty-four Members, thirteen conſtitute a Houſe to proceed to buſineſs. For their Election, the different Counties are divided into twenty-four diſtricts, and each County, in a diſtrict (at the time of electing Delegates) votes for one Senator, who is a reſident and freeholder within the diſtrict, or duly qualified according to law, and is upwards of twenty-five years of age. Within five days after the Election, the Sheriffs of each County meet; and, from the poll taken in their reſpective Counties, return, as a Senator, him who has the greateſt number of votes in the whole diſtrict. To keep up this Aſſembly, by rotation, the diſtricts are equally divided into four claſſes, and numbered by lot. At the end of one year, after the General Election, the ſix Members elected by the firſt diviſion are diſplaced, and the vacancies occaſioned thereby are ſupplied from ſuch claſs or diviſion, by new Election, in the manner beforementioned. This rotation is applied to each diviſion, according to its number, and continued in due order annually.

The Houſe of Delegates conſiſts of two Repreſentatives choſen for each County, and for the diſtrict of Weſt Auguſta annually; if actual reſidents or freeholders in the ſame, or thoſe duly qualified according to law: and one Delegate or Repreſentative is choſen annually for the city of Williamſburgh, one for the borough of Norfolk, and one for each of the other cities and boroughs, to whom the Legiſlature may in future allow a particular repreſentation. But when a city or borough decreaſes ſo, that the number of Voters, for ſeven years ſucceſſively, is reduced lower than the

the number of Voters in ſome one County in Virginia, ſuch decayed city or borough thenceforth ceaſes to ſend a Delegate or Repreſentative to the General Aſſembly.

The right of ſuffrage in the Election of Members for both Houſes, remains as it was at the time the Conſtitution was agreed to. Each Houſe chooſes its own Speaker—appoints its own Officers—ſettles its own rules of proceeding—and directs Writs of Election for ſupplying intermediate vacancies. All laws originate in the Houſe of Delegates, may be approved of, or rejected by the Senate, or may be amended by them, with conſent of the Houſe of Delegates, except money bills, which in no inſtance can be altered by the Senate, but muſt be wholly approved of, or rejected by them. Either Houſe of the General Aſſembly may adjourn itſelf. The Governor cannot prorogue or adjourn them during their Seſſion, nor diſſolve them at any time; but by advice of the Council of State; or on an application of a majority of the Houſe of Delegates, he may, if neceſſary, call them before the time to which they ſtand prorogued or adjourned.

All eſcheats, penalties, and forfeitures, which formerly went to the King, now go to the Commonwealth, except ſuch as the Legiſlature may aboliſh, or otherwiſe provide for.

Writs run "In the name of the Common-"wealth of Virginia;" and are teſted by the Clerks of the ſeveral Courts, out of which they iſſue. Indictments conclude, "Againſt the peace "and dignity of the Commonwealth."

The territories contained within the Charters, erecting the Colonies of Maryland, Pennſylvania, North and South Carolina, are for ever confirmed to thoſe Colonies reſpectively, with all rights what-

whatſoever which Virginia might have thentofore claimed, except the free navigation and uſe of the Rivers Potomaque and Pokomoque, with the property of the Virginia ſhores and ſtrands, bordering on either of the ſaid rivers, and all improvements made or to be made thereon. The weſtern and northern extent of Virginia, in all other reſpects, ſtands, as fixed by the Charter of King James I. in the year 1609, and by the treaty of peace between Great Britain and France in 1763, unleſs the Virginia Legiſlature ſhould eſtabliſh one or more Governments, weſtward of the Allegheney Mountains; and no purchaſes of lands are to be made of the Indian natives, but on behalf of the public, by authority of the General Aſſembly.

The Delegates to the Continental Congreſs are choſen annually, by joint ballot of both Houſes of Aſſembly; and may, in the mean time, be ſuperſeded in the ſame manner.

NORTH CAROLINA.

The Conſtitution or form of Government of North Carolina was agreed to, and reſolved upon, by the Provincial Congreſs aſſembled at Halifax, December 18, 1776.

The Governor, and ſeven Councillors of State (to adviſe him in the execution of his office) are annually elected by the Senate and Houſe of Commons jointly, by ballot, at their firſt meeting after each annual Election. The Governor is Captain General and Commander in Chief of the Militia; and, in caſe of his death, inability, or abſence from the State, the Speaker of the Senate exerciſes the powers of Government; and in caſe of his death, &c. the Speaker of the Houſe of Commons,

mons, until the return of the abſentee, or a new nomination by the Houſe of Commons. Four Councillors make a quorum, their advice and proceedings are entered on a journal, and ſigned by the Members preſent, who may either of them enter his diſſent to any part of it; and the journal is to be laid before the General Aſſembly when called for, in which no Councillor can ſit. The Governor draws for, and applies ſuch monies as are voted by the General Aſſembly for the contingencies of Government, and is accountable to them for the ſame. With the advice of the Council of State, he lays embargoes—prohibits the exportation of any commodity in the receſs of the General Aſſembly, not exceeding thirty days at a time—grants pardons and reprieves (except where the proſecution is carried on by the General Aſſembly, or the law directs otherwiſe; and, in that caſe, he may, in the receſs of the General Aſſembly, reprieve until they ſit again), and exerciſes all the other executive powers of Government, as limited by the Conſtitution and laws of the State.

The legiſlative authority is veſted in two diſtinct branches, "a Senate," and "Houſe of "Commons," both dependent on the people.

The Senate is compoſed of Repreſentatives annually choſen by ballot, one for each County in the State, by the Freemen, aged twenty-one, who have reſided within the State a year next before the Election, and own fifty acres of land apiece at the time of the Election, and had it for ſix months next before.

And Freemen who have paid public taxes, and are, in other reſpects, qualified as abovementioned (except as to land, which is not neceſſary) annually choſe by ballot two Members

of

of the Houſe of Commons for each County (in which the Voters reſide), and one Member for each of the Towns of Edentown, Newbern, Wilmington, Saliſbury, Hillſborough, and Halifax. But each Member of the Senate, and of the Houſe of Commons, muſt have uſually reſided one year next before the Election, in the County in which he is choſen; and the Senator muſt own, at leaſt, three hundred acres of land in fee; and the Commoner, at leaſt, one hundred acres in fee or for life, and muſt have had it for ſix months next before the Election.

"The Senate," and "The Houſe of Com-"mons," aſſembled for the purpoſe of legiſlation, is denominated, "The General Aſſembly."

Each Houſe chooſes its Speaker and other Officers—judges of the qualifications and elections of its Members—ſits upon its own adjournments from day to day—and prepares bills to be paſſed into laws. The two Houſes direct Writs of Election for ſupplying intermediate vacancies; and alſo, jointly, by ballot, adjourn themſelves to any future day and place. All bills are read three times in each Houſe, and ſigned by the Speakers of both Houſes, before they paſs into laws. And neither Houſe can proceed to buſineſs, unleſs the majority of the Members is preſent. Every Member of the Legiſlature, before he ſits, muſt take an oath to the State; and every one appointed to an office, before he enters on the execution of it, muſt take an oath to the State, and an oath of office.

The Senate and Houſe of Commons, by joint ballot, appoint Judges of the Supreme Courts of Law and Equity – Judges of the Admiralty and Attorney General (during good behaviour)—Generals and Field Officers of the Militia—and

all

all Officers of the regular army of the State—Treaſurers for the State (annually)—and a Secretary for three years.

No receiver of public money, till accounted for and paid, can ſit in the Legiſlature, or hold an office—and no Treaſurer—regular Officer in the Army or Navy—Contractor or Agent for ſupplying them—Judge of the Supreme Court of Law or Equity—Judge of the Admiralty—Secretary of the State—Clergyman or Preacher of the Goſpel—or perſon that denies the Being of God, the truth of the Proteſtant Religion—the divine authority of the Old or New Teſtament, or that holds religious principles incompatible with the freedom and ſafety of the State, can ſit in the Legiſlature or Council. And a perſon coming within the above deſcription of an Infidel, or of holding religious principles dangerous to the State, is alſo incapable of any office in the civil department.

Juſtices of the Peace are recommended by the Legiſlature, and hold during good behaviour; and they, and all other officers are commiſſioned by the Governor. The Commiſſions run "in "the name," and under "the Great Seal of the "State of South Carolina," and are teſted and ſigned by the Governor. No perſon can hold more than one lucrative office at a time; but the appointments of Militia Officers, and Juſtices of the Peace, are not conſidered as lucrative.

The Governor, and any other Officer, may be proſecuted, on impeachment of the General Aſſembly, or preſentment of the Grand Jury, of any Supreme Court.

All Writs run, "In the name of the State of "North Carolina," and are teſted and ſigned by the Clerks of the reſpective Courts: and indictments

ments conclude, " Againſt the peace and dignity " of the State."

The Legiſlature is to regulate entails, ſo as to prevent perpetuities. The declaration of rights, and the trial by Jury are to remain inviolable. There is no religious eſtabliſhment, but every mode of worſhip is tolerated. Foreigners ſettling in the State, and taking an oath of allegiance to it, may hold real eſtate, and after a year's reſidence, are deemed free citizens.

Delegates to the Continental Congreſs are annually choſen by ballot of the General Aſſembly, and may be ſuperſeded, in the mean time, in the ſame manner, and cannot be elected for more than three years ſucceſſively.

The limits of the province are aſcertained; but the legiſlature is not prevented from eſtabliſhing one or more governments to the weſtward.

The titles of perſons holding under the laws formerly in force, or under grants made by King George the Second, or his predeceſſors; or the Lords Proprietors are not affected by the Conſtitution.

SOUTH CAROLINA.

On the 26th day of March 1776, a Conſtitution or form of Government was agreed to by the Provincial Congreſs of South Carolina, and " eſtabliſhed until an accommodation between " Great Britain and America could be ob" tained."

But on the 19th Day of March 1778, an Act was paſſed by the Preſident and Commander in Chief, the Legiſlative Council, and General Aſſembly, intituled, " An Act for eſtabliſhing the " Conſtitution of the State of South Carolina," which

which recites, that the Constitution in 1776 was only temporary—that the United Colonies of America were constituted independent States, by the declaration of the Continental Congress of 4th July 1776; and that it therefore became necessary to frame a Constitution suitable to that event. It then proceeds to enact, that the articles in that Act, agreed upon in General Assembly, are to be the Constitution and form of Government of the State, unless altered by the legislative authority.

By that Act, the style of the Country is thereafter to be, "The State of South Carolina;" and the legislative authority is vested in a General Assembly, consisting of two distinct bodies, "A Senate," and "A House of Representatives," who at their first meeting after each Election, jointly, by ballot, chose (from among themselves, or the people at large) a Governor and Commander in Chief, a Lieutenant Governor (both of them for two years)—a Privy Council of eight Members for two years (half of whom are elected yearly), all of whom must be of the Protestant Religion. Each of them must have a freehold of the clear value of 10,000 *l.* currency; the Governor and Lieutenant Governor must have resided in the State for ten years; and each of the Councillors for five years, next preceding his Election, and on their Election, they must respectively take an oath of qualification in the House of Representatives. There must be a majority of both Houses present to elect a Governor or Lieutenant Governor. The executive authority is vested in the Governor and Commander in Chief (who serves two years, and cannot be re-elected till the end of four); but he cannot adjourn, prorogue, or dissolve the General Assembly

ſembly; however (with the conſent of the Privy Council) he may, if neceſſary, convene them before the time, to which they ſtand adjourned. He cannot commence war, conclude peace, or enter into final treaty, without the conſent of the Senate and Houſe of Repreſentatives; but, with the conſent of the Privy Council, he may, in the receſs of the General Aſſembly, lay embargoes, or prohibit the exportation of any commodity, not exceeding thirty days.

If the Governor is impeached, or his place vacated by removal, death, &c. the Lieutenant Governor ſucceeds him for the remainder of the time; and the Privy Council chooſes another Lieutenant Governor out of their body. And if the Lieutenant Governor is impeached, or his place vacated by removal, death, &c. the Privy Council choſe one of themſelves to ſucceed him for the remainder of the time, or till a new nomination by the General Aſſembly.

The Privy Council conſiſts of the Lieutenant Governor and the eight Councillors, five of whom make a quorum, to adviſe the Governor and Commander in Chief, when required; but he is not bound to conſult them, unleſs the law directs it. If, during the receſs of the General Aſſembly, a Councillor dies, or departs the State, the Privy Council choſe one in his room, until the Legiſlature nominates another. The Clerk of the Privy Council keeps a regular journal of their proceedings, to be laid before the Legiſlature when required by either Houſe; and any Councillor, that deſires it, may enter his opinion, with the reaſons at large. The Governor may, under his hand and ſeal, empower a Councillor to act in his room, where he and the Lieutenant Governor are ſick or abſent from the ſeat of Government,

vernment, and whilst such Councillor acts for the Governor, he does not vacate his seat in the Legislature or Privy Council; but no Military Officer, Judge or Father, Son or Brother of the Governor, can be a Privy Councillor.

On the last Monday in November, in every second year, the Senators, and the Members of the House of Representatives, are chosen for the Parishes and Districts (to meet on the first Monday in January following), by free white Men, who acknowledge the being of a God, believe in a future state of Rewards and Punishments, have attained twenty-one years of age, and have resided in the State one year before the election.—And each Voter must have a freehold of fifty acres of land, or a town lot, and owned it for six months before the election; or must have been taxed for six months before the election, in a sum equal to that raised on fifty acres of land. Any Elector, if required, must take an Oath or Affirmation of his qualification.

Every Senator, and every Member of the House of Representatives, must be a Protestant; the Senator must be thirty years old, and have resided in the State at least five; and if he resides in the parish or district where chosen, he must have a freehold worth *L.* 2000 currency, clear of debt; and if he does not reside there, he must have a freehold in the parish or district where elected, worth *L.* 7000 currency, clear of debt.

A Member in the House of Representatives, must have resided in the State three years previous to his election, and if he does not reside in the parish or district where chosen, he must have a freehold there worth *L.* 3500 currency, clear of debt.

Thirteen

Thirteen Senators make a quorum; but the Prefident, or any three Members, may adjourn from day to day. Not lefs than fixty-nine Members make a Houfe of Reprefentatives to do bufinefs; but the Speaker, or any feven Members, may adjourn from day to day.

The Senate and Houfe of Reprefentatives meet at the Seat of Government, unlefs war or ficknefs renders it unfafe; in either of which cafes, the Governor, with the confent of the Privy Council, may, by proclamation, appoint a more convenient place.

All money-bills for the fupport of Government, originate in the Houfe of Reprefentatives; the Senate cannot alter or amend them, but may reject them; and no money can be drawn out of the Public Treafury but by the legiflative authority of the State. All other bills and ordinances may take their rife in the Senate or Houfe of Reprefentatives, and may be altered, amended, or rejected, by either of them. Acts and ordinances, when paffed the General Affembly, have the Great Seal affixed to them by a joint Committee of both Houfes, who wait on the Governor to receive and return the Seal.—They are then figned in the Senate Houfe, by the Prefident of the Senate, and the Speaker of the Houfe of Reprefentatives; and from that time have the force of a law, and are lodged in the Secretary's Office.

The Senate and Houfe of Reprefentatives refpectively, enjoy all other privileges which the Commons Houfe of Affembly at any time claimed, or exercifed.—Neither Houfe hath power to adjourn itfelf longer than three days at a time, with the confent of the other.—The Governor can neither adjourn, prorogue, or diffolve them; but with

with the conſent of the Council, he may, if neceſſary, convene them before the time to which they ſtand adjourned.—If a bill hath been rejected by either Houſe, it cannot be brought in again the ſame Seſſion, without leave of the Houſe, and ſix days previous notice.—Each Houſe chuſes its own Officers by ballot; and during a receſs, the Preſident of the Senate, and the Speaker of the Houſe of Repreſentatives, on giving not leſs than three weeks, nor more than thirty-five days notice of election, iſſue writs for filling up, in their reſpective Houſes, vacancies occaſioned by death.

A Member of either Houſe accepting any appointment, but that of a Militia Officer or Juſtice of the Peace (except where he acts for the Governor, in his abſence or ſickneſs) vacates his ſeat; but may be re-elected, if he is not Secretary of State, a Commiſſioner of the Treaſury, an Officer of the Cuſtoms, a Regiſter of Meſne Conveyances, a Clerk of a Court of Juſtice, a Sheriff, a Powder-Receiver, a Clerk of the Privy Council, or either Houſe of Legiſlature, Surveyor-General, or Commiſſary of Military Stores, neither of whom can ſit in either Houſe of Legiſlature.

The Senate and Houſe of Repreſentatives jointly, nominate the Juſtices of the Peace during pleaſure, and all other Judicial Officers (except thoſe of the Court of Chancery, of which the Lieutenant-Governor, and a majority of the Privy Council are Judges), during good behaviour (but removable on addreſs of the Senate and Houſe of Repreſentatives); the Sheriffs for two years, two Commiſſioners of the Treaſury, the Secretary of the State, the Regiſters of Meſne Conveyances, the Attorney-General, Surveyor-General, Powder-Receiver, Collectors and Comptrollers

rollers of the Cuftoms for two years, and all Officers in the Army or Navy above the rank of Captain.

But all thefe Officers are commiffioned by the Governor, who, with the confent of the Council, appoints all other neceffary Officers during pleafure, and fills up the vacancies in thofe which are in the appointment of the Legiflature, until they elect others.

Every civil and military Officer, before he acts, muft take an Oath, " Acknowledging South Ca-" rolina to be a Free, Independent, and Sove-" reign State *, abjuring the King of Great Bri-" tain, fwearing to defend the State againft him, " his heirs, fucceffors, abettors, &c. (to the ut-" moft of his power), and to ferve the State with " fidelity and honour."

The Houfe of Reprefentatives can impeach all Officers of the State, for mal and corrupt conduct, who are not amenable to any other Jurifdiction; but two-thirds of the Members prefent muft confent to it; the Senators, and fuch Judges of the State as are not Members of the Houfe of Reprefentatives, try the impeachment, and take an Oath, " Truly and impartially to try and de-" termine the charge in queftion, according to " evidence." Two-thirds of the Members prefent muft agree in every judgment, except that of acquittal, and the party accufed is allowed counfel.

All Perfons and religious Societies are tolerated, who acknowledge one God, a future ftate of rewards and punifhments, and that God is publicly

* I fhudder when I read this Oath, which many in South Carolina muft abhor; but as the King has not a more loyal Servant than I am, I hope I fhall not be blamed for fetting out the fubftance of the Oath in this Publication.

to

to be worſhipped.—But none except Chriſtian Proteſtants (of all denominations) are eſtabliſhed, and they enjoy equal religious and civil privileges.—The reſpective Societies of the Church of England continue incorporated; and they and all other religious Societies hold the property they poſſeſſed at the time the Act was made.—And whenever fifteen male Proteſtants, not under twenty-one years of age, agree to unite in a Society, for the purpoſes of religious worſhip, they ſhall (on complying with the terms thereafter mentioned) be conſtituted a Church, and regarded in law as of the Eſtabliſhed Religion of the State; and on a petition to the Legiſlature ſhall be incorporated, and enjoy equal privileges. But every ſuch Chriſtian Society muſt give itſelf a name, by which it ſhall be called and known in law; and all that aſſociate with them for the purpoſes of worſhip, ſhall be eſteemed as belonging to the Society ſo called. But previous to the Eſtabliſhment and Incorporation, every ſuch Society muſt ſubſcribe in a Book the following five Articles, or elſe it cannot entitle itſelf to be incorporated and eſteemed as a Church of the Eſtabliſhed Religion of the State.

1ſt, That there is one eternal God, and a future ſtate of rewards and puniſhments.

2d, That God is publicly to be worſhipped.

3d, That the Chriſtian Religion is the true religion.

4th, That the Holy Scriptures of the Old and New Teſtament are of Divine Inſpiration, and are the Rule of Faith and Practice.

5th, That it is lawful, and the duty of every Man, being thereunto called by thoſe that govern, to bear witneſs to truth.

But

But it is provided, that every one, when called to make an appeal to God, as a witneſs to truth, ſhall be permitted to do it in that way which is moſt agreeable to the dictates of his own conſcience.

The majority of every religious Society, or the perſons appointed by them, have a right of electing their own Clergy; but no Miniſter can officiate until he has ſubſcribed the above Five Articles, and alſo made and ſubſcribed the Declaration ſet forth in the Conſtitution.—And no Miniſter of the Goſpel, or public Preacher of any religious perſuaſion, is eligible as Governor, Lieutenant-Governor, a Member of the Senate, Houſe of Repreſentatives, or Privy Council, nor till two years after he has ceaſed to exerciſe his paſtoral function.

The Delegates to the Continental Congreſs are annually choſen by joint ballot of the Senate and Houſe of Repreſentatives, and no Member of the Legiſlature vacates his ſeat on being choſen a Delegate.

No part of the Conſtitution can be altered, without ninety days previous notice, and the conſent of a majority of the Members of the Senate and Houſe of Repreſentatives.

GEORGIA.

Few Countries have undergone ſo many changes as Georgia has, in the courſe of fifty years. His late Majeſty King George the Second, by Letters Patent of the 9th of June, in the fifth year of his reign (which was 1732), granted ſeven-eighths of all the lands, from the Northern Stream of the River Savannah along the Sea-coaſt, to the moſt Southern Stream of the River Alatamaha, and Weſtward,

Weſtward, in direct lines, to the South Seas, and all the Iſlands to the Eaſt within twenty leagues of the coaſt, to the Truſtees for eſtabliſhing the Colony of Georgia in America, and their ſucceſſors; and erected thoſe territories into one independent and ſeparate Province, by the name of Georgia, with a power of Legiſlation, &c. in the Truſtees for twenty-one years, when ſuch form of government was to be eſtabliſhed, as the King or his ſucceſſors ſhould appoint, and ſhould be agreeable to law.

Mr. Oglethorpe (now the Senior General in his Majeſty's ſervice), was the firſt Truſtee's Governor of Georgia. He arrived with the Settlers from England at Beaufort in South Carolina on the 20th of January 1732-3, Old Style, and in Georgia in February following.

On their landing they met only one white man, who was an Indian trader; for although the country now called Georgia was included in the Charters of the Lords Proprietors of Carolina, and grants had from time to time been made of lands on the South ſide of the River Savannah, yet the Indians had either cut off or driven away thoſe who attempted to ſettle them: but there were ſeveral Indians ſettled at a place called Yamacraw, within a quarter of a mile of the ſpot where the town of Savannah now ſtands. Thoſe Indians received General Oglethorpe and the Settlers with great courteſy, and permitted them to ſettle in the country; for the General ſhewed great addreſs in conciliating the affections of the Indians, and no diſturbances happened between them and the white people, until after General Oglethorpe left the country.——When I went to Georgia in the year 1769 ſome of the firſt Settlers were alive, from

from whom I learned ſeveral facts relative to the firſt ſettlement of that country.

The Truſtees, during their Government of Georgia, enacted three laws for that country: one of them was a law to prevent the importation of negroes and rum; and another of them was a law for the purpoſe of regulating the trade with the Indians, and laying a tax on the Indian traders, for defraying the charge of the ſalaries allowed by the Truſtees to their Officers in Georgia: and the Colony, which was thus taxed by a law enacted by the Truſtees Council at a Tavern in London, afterwards denied the right of Parliament to tax the Colonies, and joined in the Civil War.

On the 20th of June 1752, the Truſtees ſurrendered their Charter to his late Majeſty King George the Second; but he being then in Hanover, the Lords Juſtices continued the form of Government by a Preſident and Aſſiſtants (under his Majeſty), until the King ſhould make other proviſion for the government thereof: and on the 6th of Auguſt 1754, John Reynolds, Eſq; a Captain in the Navy, was appointed the firſt King's Governor of Georgia, who arrived there the October following, and took upon himſelf the government of the Province on the 30th of that month.

Georgia made but little progreſs in population and agriculture during the government of Mr. Reynolds, and his immediate ſucceſſor Mr. Ellis; but under the long adminiſtration of Sir James Wright, the laſt Governor, it made ſuch a rapid progreſs in population, agriculture, and commerce, as no other country ever equalled in ſo ſhort a time.—By his Majeſty's Proclamation of the 7th of October 1763, the lands between the rivers Alatamaha and St. Mary were annexed to Georgia, which made it a better rice Colony than South Carolina, as it then contained more good River Swamp.

The disturbances broke out in the other Colonies some time before they reached Georgia, there being a greater proportion of Loyalists in that Province than in any other of the Thirteen Colonies: and it was not till the 18th of January 1776, that the Governor and Council were made prisoners, and the King's Government was totally subverted there.—Georgia continued in possession of the Americans until the 29th of December 1778, when his Majesty's forces under Lieutenant Colonel Campbell landed there, and on the same day took possession of Savannah the capital, and its neighbourhood. On the 4th of March 1779, the King's Civil Government was re-established in Georgia, by proclamation; and matters bore a promising appearance until the 12th of September following, when the Count D'Estaign landed there, and on the 16th summoned the Town of Savannah to surrender to the arms of France. On the 9th of October following the besiegers, consisting of about 4500 French, and 2500 Americans, were repulsed with considerable loss.—On the the 19th of October, the enemy quitted the lines before Savannah, and on the 21st the French embarked, and the Americans marched off to South Carolina.

During the siege of Savannah, the enemy plundered the country of most of the moveable property; and the Town of Savannah was greatly injured by a heavy fire of cannon and mortars, for several days: but notwithstanding the reduced state of the country, and the frequent incursions of the enemy by sea and land, the inhabitants

began

began to plant their lands; and the King's loyal subjects flattered themselves that a few years would restore the Province to the flourishing state it was in before the civil war, until the melancholy news of Lord Cornwallis's capitulation at York Town reached Savannah, on the 9th of November 1781, and reduced the inhabitants almost to a state of despair.—To add to their affliction, an express arrived at Savannah from Charlestown, on the 5th of December following, with an account of the enemy's marching in force against Savannah; and the names of several were mentioned whom the Americans intended to put to death when they entered the town.—Fortunately for the Loyalists, the enemy was not so numerous as they at first expected; but soon afterwards the communication between Savannah and the country was for the most part cut off.—On the 14th of June 1782, orders were received at Savannah from the Commanding Officer at Charlestown, for the evacuation of Georgia; but the news did not transpire till the following day. Nothing could exceed the distress to which the Loyalists were then reduced; they had no other alternative but that of leaving the country with the loss of their property (for little besides negroes could be carried off), or of staying behind with the prospect of the harshest treatment from an enraged enemy.—The embarkation took up some weeks; the heat of the weather was extreme; few evenings passed without a violent gust of thunder and rain.—The Loyalists were encamped on a small sandy Island, called Tybee, where there was no good water; and the flies and mosquitos abounded beyond description.—To add to their affliction, many were apprehensive of being left behind, for want of shipping to carry them away: in this situation

tion several died daily, from the heat of the season, and the drinking unwholesome water.—The Editor returned to Georgia on the 14th of July 1779, and was not out of that Province until he left it on the evacuation, which took place the 24th of July 1782, when the last division of transports sailed. He was a witness of several melancholy scenes that happened there in the course of those three years; and if he is not out of pocket by this work, he means, with God's leave, to publish a Narrative of the troubles that happened in Georgia, as well before the Crown Officers left that Province, on the subversion of the King's Government in 1776, as from his return to Georgia in 1779, until the evacuation thereof in 1782, having kept a diary of what passed; the whole of which he has now by him, except one volume, containing a period of some months, which was burned in his quarters during the siege of Savannah.

In the following account of the Constitution of Georgia, I have taken notice of several material circumstances, in which it differs from that which prevailed when it was under the Government of the King of Great Britain.

On the 20th of April 1776, the Provincial Congress in Georgia made several orders and regulations (which were to continue for six months, or until the further order of the Continental Congress), by which they appointed a President or Commander in Chief, a Council, Judges, and other Officers, and fixed the salaries they were to receive. They also directed, that the Common and Statute Law, and Acts of Assembly thentofore in force in Georgia (which did not interfere with their proceedings, or those of the Continen-

tal

tal Congreſs) ſhould continue, until otherwiſe ordered.

And the Conſtitution of the State of Georgia was unanimouſly agreed to in Convention (in conſequence of the recommendation of the Continental Congreſs, and their declaration of Independency), on the 5th of February 1777.

Whilſt Georgia continued under the King's Government, the Governor was appointed by his Majeſty during pleaſure, as in all the other Provincial Eſtabliſhments or King's Governments: but now the State Governor is choſen annually (by ballot) by the Repreſentatives of the People, on the 1ſt day of their meeting; he muſt have reſided three years in the State, and is eligible only one year in three. The King's Governor was Captain-General and Governor in Chief in and over the Province of Georgia, and Chancellor, Vice-Admiral, and Ordinary of the ſame; and was ſtyled "His Excellency." The State Governor is Captain-General and Commander in Chief over all the Militia, and other Military and Naval Forces belonging to the State, and is ſtyled "His Honour." The King's Governor was the firſt branch of the Legiſlature, had a power of rejecting all bills offered to him for his aſſent, iſſued writs for the electing Repreſentatives to ſit in the Commons Houſe of Aſſembly, and convened, adjourned, prorogued, and diſſolved both Houſes of Legiſlature, except that from Saturday to Monday they might adjourn themſelves.—The State Governor has not the leaſt ſhare in the Legiſlative Power; he cannot adjourn, prorogue, or diſſolve the Houſe of Aſſembly; but with the advice of the Executive Council, he has power to call them together upon any emergency, before the time to which they ſtand adjourned.—

The

The King's Governor was Chancellor of the Province.—The State Governor has no judicial power of any ſort.—The King's Governor was Vice-Admiral of the Province, and, as occaſion required, exerciſed the powers and authorities veſted in him by his commiſſion of Vice-Admiral.—It does not appear by the Conſtitution that the State Governor has any ſuch title; he commands the Naval Forces of the State, and, as I apprehend, grants commiſſions to privateers, &c. The King's Governor was Ordinary of the Province, and as ſuch, he collated to all Benefices, and granted Probate of Wills, and Letters of Adminiſtration, of Inteſtates Eſtates.—The State Governor has no ſuch authorities; for every religious Sect chuſes its own Miniſters; and there is now a Regiſter of Probates in each County, for proving Wills, and granting Letters of Adminiſtration.—The King's Governor had the appointment to all offices that became vacant, until his Majeſty's pleaſure was known, and his appointments to many of them were never ſuperſeded by the Crown.—The State Governor has only the appointment of the Militia Officers, during good behaviour; but all commiſſions, civil and military, are iſſued by him, under his hand, and the Great Seal of the Province; and he can fill up all intermediate vacancies till the enſuing Election.—The King's Governor was, in ſome inſtances, reſtrained by his inſtructions, and in others by Act of Aſſembly, from doing certain Executive Acts of Government, without the advice of the Council; but there were caſes in which ſuch advice was not neceſſary.—It does not appear by the Conſtitution, that the State Governor can do one Executive Act of Government without the advice of the Executive Council.—The

King's

King's Governor could pardon all crimes except treafon and murder; and there he could only reprieve: he could remit no fine above ten pounds; but he could fufpend the payment of it until the King's pleafure was known.—The State Governor can neither pardon a crime nor remit a fine; but he may reprieve a criminal, or fufpend the payment of a fine, until the Affembly meets, with whom the power of pardon and remiffion lies.—The King's Governor could refide in that part of the Province which he thought moft convenient for tranfacting the public bufinefs, and might direct the Legiflature to meet there.—The State Governor muft refide at fuch place as the Houfe of Affembly for the time being fhall appoint; but he is impowered, with the advice of the Executive Council, to exercife the executive powers of Government, according to the laws of the State, and the Conftitution thereof. And he and every other Officer of the State is liable to be called to account by the Houfe of Affembly.

The oaths taken by the King's Governor are fet forth in the following part of this Work.—The State Governor takes the following oath, "I A. B. elected Governor of the State of "Georgia, by the Reprefentatives thereof, do "folemnly promife and fwear, That I will, during "the term of my appointment, to the beft of "my fkill and judgment, execute the faid office "faithfully and confcientioufly, according to law, "without favour, affection, or partiality: That "I will, to the utmoft of my power, fupport, "maintain, and defend the State of Georgia, "and the Conftitution of the fame; and ufe my "utmoft endeavours to protect the people there-"of in the fecure enjoyment of all their rights, "franchifes, and privileges; and that the laws

"and

" and ordinances of the State be duly observed; " and that law and justice, in mercy, be executed " in all judgments. And I do farther solemnly " promise and swear, That I will peaceably and " quietly resign the Government to which I have " been elected, at the period to which my conti- " nuance in the said office is limited by the Con- " stitution. And lastly, I do also solemnly swear, " That I have not accepted of the Government " whereunto I am elected, contrary to the Ar- " ticles of this Constitution.—So help me God."

This Oath is to be administered to the Governor by the Speaker of the Assembly: and the Constitution directs the same Oath to be administered by the Speaker to the President of the Council.—Now it seems strange how the President of the Council can swear, " That he is elected Go- " vernor of the State of Georgia," or that he will " execute the said office," &c.—The Governor's Oath is part of the Constitution, and is set out in it.—The Speaker of the Assembly is, by the Constitution, directed to administer the same Oath (that is the Governor's Oath) to the President of the Council.—The Speaker of the House of Assembly (as well as every other Member of that House) swears, " That he will execute the trust " reposed in him, to the support of the Consti- " tution, &c." And the last Article of the Constitution says, " That no alteration shall be made " in this Constitution, without Petitions from a " majority of the Counties, and the Votes in each " County within the State: and then the As- " sembly is to order a Convention to be called " for that purpose, specifying the alterations to " be made, according to the Petitions preferred " to the Assembly by the majority of the Coun-

" ties

" ties as aforesaid." I cannot conceive how these contradictions are to be reconciled.

The King's Council consisted of Twelve Members in Ordinary, and Two extraordinary Members, who were appointed by the Crown (during pleasure), either by Mandamus to the Governor, commanding him to admit them as such, or else their names were inserted in the King's instructions to the Governor: but when, by means of death, or absence, the number of Councillors in the Province was less than seven, in that case the Governor could fill up the vacancies, so as to increase the number of resident Members to seven, until the King's pleasure was known. If the Governor was dead, or absent from the Province, the Lieutenant-Governor took the command,—was styled "His Honour," and had half the salary and half the fees whilst he administered government; but when the Governor was on the spot, the Lieutenant-Governor had no salary or perquisite. If the Governor and Lieutenant-Governor were both of them dead, or absent from the Province, then the senior Member of the Council in Ordinary administered Government, and had the same allowance as the Lieutenant-Governor, whilst his command continued. But neither of the two extraordinary Members of the Council (who were the Surveyor-General of the Customs, and the Superintendant-General of Indian Affairs), altho' senior in the Council, could administer government in the absence of the Governor and Lieutenant-Governor; for in that case the command devolved on the Senior Member of the Council in Ordinary.

The State (Executive) Council are chosen by the Representatives of the People, out of their own body, by ballot, on the first day of their

meeting

meeting after their Election, and the number of Councillors muſt fluctuate, for the Repreſentatives chuſe two Councillors for each County, that elects ten Repreſentatives; but if a County has not ſuch a number of Members as intitles them to elect ten Repreſentatives, then the Houſe of Repreſentatives chuſes no Councillors for that County; and therefore, as the Counties increaſe in population, the number of Councillors encreaſes in proportion.

The King's Council was one of the three branches of the Legiſlature, and then ſtyled itſelf the Upper Houſe of Aſſembly; it was alſo the Privy Council to the Governor, to aſſiſt him with their advice in the adminiſtration of government. Five made an Upper Houſe or a Council; but if there were not ſo many on the ſpot, then three Members were ſufficient for either of thoſe purpoſes. As a Council, they met whenever the Governor thought proper to ſummon them, and on ſuch occaſions the Governor preſided, and propoſed matters to them for their advice thereon. As an Upper Houſe, they met at the ſame time that the Commons Houſe of Aſſembly did, and the Lieutenant Governor (if he was one of the Council, and on the ſpot) preſided; but if the Lieutenant Governor was not in the Houſe, the Senior Member of the Council preſent, ſat as Preſident of the Upper Houſe.

The State Council is merely an executive body, to adviſe the Governor in the adminiſtration of government, and they have no further concern with Legiſlation, than that all laws muſt be ſent to them after the ſecond reading, and they are to peruſe them and give their advice thereon, and to return them, with their remarks, to the Aſſembly in five days; but the ſole power of Legiſlation

giſlation reſides in the Repreſentatives of the people, called the Houſe of Aſſembly; it is therefore ſurpluſage in the Conſtitution to annex the epithet "Executive" to Council, as there is no legiſlative Council in the State. One State Councillor for each County attends in monthly rotation, where the Governor reſides, except when the Aſſembly ſits, and then all muſt attend, unleſs ſick, &c. The firſt day of meeting, after they are choſen, the Executive Council proceeds to the choice of a Preſident; but the Governor may preſide in the Executive Council, at all times, except when they are taking into conſideration, and peruſing the laws and ordinances offered to them by the Houſe of Aſſembly; and in the abſence or ſickneſs of the Governor, the Preſident of the Council exerciſes all the powers of the Governor.

When the King's Council ſat as a legiſlative body, they were convened by the Governor, and obſerved the ſame form of proceeding that is uſed in the Houſe of Lords in Great Britain (except that no Member had a right to make a proxy, nor could they adjourn themſelves longer than from Saturday to Monday); and every Member might make his proteſtation, or enter his diſſent to any vote of the Houſe, agreeable to the method obſerved in the Houſe of Lords. But when the King's Council ſat as an executive body to adviſe the Governor, no Member could enter his proteſtation, for the opinion of the majority of the board was entered as the ſenſe of the whole Council. Each Member, on his firſt admiſſion to the Council Board, took the State Oaths; and alſo an oath not to reveal the ſecret debates of the Council, &c. the form of which Oath is ſet forth in the following part of this work. And the

the Clerk, Messenger, and Doorkeeper were appointed by the Governor.

The State Council settle their own rules of proceeding—vote by Counties, and not individually; and any Member may enter his protest against any measures in Council that he has not consented to, provided he does it within three days. And when any affair that requires secrecy is laid before the Governor and the Executive Council, the Governor must administer the oath of secrecy to the Council, their Secretary, and the other Officers necessary to carry the business into execution.

Under the King's Government, Georgia was divided into parishes, which were extensive; and some of these parishes sent one Representative a piece, other parishes sent two Representatives a piece, and there were parishes that sent three Representatives a piece to the Commons House of Assembly. Christ Church was the only parish that sent more than three Representatives to the Commons House of Assembly, and that was owing to its being the first settled part of the country, in consequence of which, it was divided into five districts, each of which returned one Member; and Savannah, the capital of the Province, and the seat of Government (which was situate in Christ Church Parish) returned four Members to the Commons House of Assembly. Had not the Civil War broke out, the western part of the Province, called the Ceded Lands, would have been divided into parishes, and the number of Representatives consequently increased. After the reduction of Georgia by his Majesty's forces, a bill, for that purpose, passed both Houses of Assembly; but before it could be carried into execution, the news of Lord Cornwallis's misfortune at York Town reached Savannah, and the evacuation of Georgia took place in a few months after. The Writs of Election were iſſued by order of the Governor in Council, under the Great Seal of the Province, and teſted by the Governor, returnable in forty days. When a vacancy happened in the Commons Houſe of Aſſembly, after the general Election, the Houſe applied to the Governor by addreſs, and a Writ of Election iſſued to ſupply the vacancy. There was a Provoſt Marſhal for the whole Province (in the nature of the Sheriff of a County in England) appointed by the Crown. The Principal reſided in Great Britain, and rented out the office to a deputy, who was ſtyled Acting Provoſt Marſhal, and was the returning Officer for every pariſh and diſtrict, but he was by law impowered to appoint Deputies in the different pariſhes, *pro hac vice*, to hold the Elections for him. The qualification of an Elector was fifty acres of land in the pariſh or diſtrict where he voted; and of a Repreſentative 500 acres of land in any part of the Province. The Repreſentatives, when convened, were called the Commons Houſe of Aſſembly, and choſe their own Speaker, who was preſented to the Governor for his approbation. The Commons Houſe of Aſſembly continued, until the Governor thought proper to diſſolve them, and they could not adjourn themſelves longer than *de die in diem*, except from Saturday to Monday; but in other reſpects, they claimed moſt of the privileges of the Houſe of Commons in Great Britain, and, at times, attempted to exert ſome powers that they were not intitled to. Their proceedings were conformed to thoſe of the Commons in Great Britain, and they choſe their own Meſſenger and Door-keeper, but the Governor appointed the Clerk. Being a ſubordinate Legiſlature, they

ſhould

ſhould not have attempted to make laws repugnant to thoſe of Great Britain; but they would ſoon have altered the Conſtitution the Crown gave them, had it not been for the negative of the Upper Houſe, and the right the Governor had to refuſe his aſſent to ſuch laws as he did not approve of. They claimed and enjoyed the excluſive right of originating money bills, and would not ſuffer the Upper Houſe to alter or amend them: however, if there was any impropriety in a money bill, the Upper Houſe ſent down an amendment in a private way; but the meſſage purported that the Upper Houſe agreed to the bill, without amendments. The Commons Houſe did not expreſsly deny the Upper Houſe the right of originating or amending any other than money bills; but ſeveral years before the ſubverſion of the King's Government, they ſeldom, if at all, paſſed a bill that originated in the Council, nor would they allow it the title of Upper Houſe. But the Commons Houſe, that was elected after the re-eſtabliſhment of the King's Government, paſſed ſeveral bills that originated with the Council, and ſuffered the Style of Upper Houſe to ſtand in thoſe bills. Before the Civil War, the Commons Houſe neither received nor claimed wages; but affected great popularity, although, at times, they did ſome things with a high hand; and it required great addreſs in a Governor to keep them in tolerable temper after the Stamp Act paſſed.

The State of Georgia is now divided by the Conſtitution into Counties, ſeveral of which are named after ſome leading men in both Houſes of Parliament. The number of Repreſentatives in each County, depends on the number of Electors; for a County that has ten may chuſe one Repreſentative,

ſentative, and ſo in proportion, according to the number of Electors, until they amount to 100, who may chuſe ten Repreſentatives; which is the greateſt number that any County can elect. The returning Officers, are two Juſtices of the Peace for each County; and the Repreſentatives are elected by ballot by the male white inhabitants not under twenty-one years old, each of whom muſt have paid taxes for a capital of ten pounds (or be of a mechanic trade), and have reſided in the State ſix months; and each Elector, if required, muſt ſwear or affirm (as the caſe may be) that he owes allegiance to the State, and will ſupport the Conſtitution thereof. But in the Counties of Glyn and Cambden, which are ſubject to alarms, and have few reſidents, the qualifications are different, until the number of inhabitants increaſes. The town of Savannah is allowed four Members, and the town of Sunbury two Members, to repreſent their trade. An Elector has only one vote, and muſt give it in the County where he reſides: if he neglects to ballot, he forfeits a ſum not exceeding five pounds, unleſs he has a reaſonable excuſe. But no perſon, having a title of nobility, can vote, be elected, or hold any poſt of honour, profit, or truſt, until he gives up ſuch diſtinction, in the manner the Legiſlature directs; and then he enjoys the benefits of a free citizen. Every Repreſentative (except thoſe for Glyn and Cambden Counties) muſt have reſided twelve months in the State, and three months in the County where he is elected; he muſt be a Proteſtant, twenty-one years old, and own 250 acres of land, or ſome property worth 250 *l.* He muſt ſwear, "to "bear true allegiance to the State—truly to per-"form the truſt repoſed in him—to execute the "ſame

" ſame to the beſt of his knowledge for the be-
" nefit of the State, and the ſupport of the Con-
" ſtitution—and that he has obtained his Election
" without fraud or bribe." And after five Repreſentatives are met, they adminiſter the oath to each other. The Repreſentatives are elected annually on the firſt Tueſday in December, and meet the firſt Tueſday in January, where the laſt Houſe directed. And when they have, at their firſt meeting after each Election, choſen a Governor, and two executive Councillors (for each County that elects ten Members) out of their own body, the Repreſentatives that remain are called "The Houſe of Aſſembly," and conſtitute the Legiſlature of the State. The Conſtitution, indeed, ſays, that all laws ſhall be ſent to the executive Council, after the ſecond reading, for their peruſal and advice; that they ſhall be returned in five days, with their remarks thereon; and that the Committee of the Council ſent with the propoſed amendments to any law, ſhall deliver their reaſons for ſuch propoſed amendments, ſitting and covered, all the Houſe of Aſſembly, except the Speaker, being uncovered; but I apprehend that the Houſe of Aſſembly may reject their amendments, and paſs the law notwithſtanding; however, the Conſtitution is not ſufficiently explicit on the occaſion. The Conſtitution gives the Houſe of Aſſembly power to make ſuch laws and regulations as may be conducive to the good order and well being of the State, provided they are not repugnant to the true intent and meaning of the Conſtitution: they have alſo power to repeal all laws injurious to the people; but all bills muſt be read three times on different days, except in caſes of neceſſity and danger. The Houſe of Aſſembly chuſes its own Speaker

and

and Officers, ſettles its own rules of proceeding, directs Writs of Election for ſupplying intermediate vacancies, and adjourns itſelf to any time within the year. No civil or military Officer (except Juſtices of the Peace, and thoſe who have Commiſſions in the Militia) can ſit in the Houſe of Aſſembly. After the ſubverſion of the King's Government, the Houſe of Aſſembly voted themſelves wages, and one year it took the whole taxes of the Province to pay them, as I have heard.

The appointment of the Civil Officers is not veſted in the executive power, as was the caſe during the King's Government; but they are annually elected by the County in which they act, except the Juſtices of the Peace, Attornies at Law, and the Regiſters for proving Wills, and granting Letters of Adminiſtration, who are appointed by the Houſe of Aſſembly; and no perſon can hold more than one office of profit at the ſame time.

After Georgia became a King's Government, Mr. Reynolds, the firſt King's Governor, in purſuance of an inſtruction from the Crown, iſſued Letters Patent under the Great Seal of Georgia, dated the 12th of December, in the 28th year of George the Second, conſtituting a Court of Record by the name of "The General Court," to be holden four times a year, with the ſame juriſdiction in Georgia, that the King's Bench, Common Pleas, and Exchequer, exerciſe in England. On the 14th of November 1755, Governor Reynolds alſo iſſued Letters Patent for eſtabliſhing a Court of Seſſion of Oyer and Terminer, and General Gaol delivery, to be holden twice a year. The civil buſineſs was tranſacted at the General Court, and the criminal buſineſs at the Court of Oyer and Terminer, for which purpoſe Grand

Juries

Juries were returned twice a year. But as the Judges of the General Court, and the Judges of the Court of Session of Oyer and Terminer, were the same individuals, the latter Court was thought to be superfluous, and a Gaol Delivery only twice a year, was considered as not sufficient in a warm, unwholesome climate, where men suffered much from the length of confinement in a close gaol; and therefore, on the re-establishment of the King's Government, the Chief Justice drew up an Act to transfer the business of the Sessions to the General Court, and to cause four Grand Juries to be returned every year, instead of two. This Act passed into a law, the Court of Session no longer transacted any business, and there was a Gaol Delivery in the General Court four times a year. Georgia being a young Colony, the General Court was stationary at Savannah; but as the western boundary of the Province was 160 miles from Savannah, after the last cession made by the Indians to the Crown; a bill was therefore brought in to divide the Province into Circuits, and to enable the Judges of the General Court to hold Circuit Courts twice a year, for those places that were distant from Savannah: however, the evacuation of Georgia took place before the bill passed into a law. The presiding Judge, was styled "Chief Justice of Georgia," was a Barrister at Law, and had a salary of 500 *l.* sterling a year, raised by annual grant of Parliament. His attendance at Westminster Hall must necessarily have given him some degree of legal knowledge, and the salary and established fees enabled him to appear in the character of a gentleman, and to give due attention to his office, without prosecuting any other profession for a maintenance. The Chief Justice was appointed by warrant,

under

under his Majeſty's Sign Manual and Signet, which commanded the Governor to make out Letters Patent under the Great Seal of Georgia; and under that commiſſion the Chief Juſtice acted. The appointment of the Aſſiſtant Judges, who were three in number, and had no ſalaries (unleſs on the death or abſence of the Chief Juſtice), was left to the Governor. Before the Civil war broke out, the adminiſtration of juſtice was ſaid to give ſatisfaction to the Public. For I have already obſerved, that where there is a Superior Court in a Colony, which has juriſdiction over the whole country, and the Judges go in circuit to thoſe places which are diſtant from the ſeat of government, four men may be found who are capable of exerciſing a judicial office; nor will it be a great burden on any Colony, to provide ſalaries for them, ſo as to enable them to give their attention to the duties of their office, without applying themſelves to any other profeſſion for a maintenance.

However, after the Colonies declared themſelves to be independent, and Georgia became a State, the Conſtitution eſtabliſhed a Superior Court in each County, which tries all matters civil and criminal ariſing there, unleſs the parties reſide in different Counties, and then the action is tried in that County where the defendant reſides; but in queſtions concerning real eſtates, the action is tried in the County where the real eſtate lies. Each Court has a Chief Juſtice, and three or more of the Juſtices that reſide in the County: there are at preſent eight Counties, and as the number of Counties increaſes, ſo will the number of Judges. The Jury are judges of law as well as of fact, and are not allowed to bring in a ſpecial verdict; but if they doubt of the law, muſt apply

apply to the Judges on the bench, each of whom gives his opinion in rotation. It is probable, the Judges know as little of law as the Jurors, being annually elected, and having such small salaries, that no man of abilities would accept of an office which must take up great part of his time. The Common Jury are sworn, "to bring in a verdict, "according to law, and the opinion they enter-"tain of the evidence, provided it is not repug-"nant to the rules and regulations contained in "the Constitution." Now it seems rather strange, that a Jury should be sworn to bring in a verdict, according to law, when it is natural to suppose they do not understand it. Besides, how can a verdict, according to law, be repugnant to the Constitution, unless the law and the Constitution clash with each other? There seems to be no Writ of Error from the Superior Court to the Governor and Council, as was the case under the the King's Government; but if, in civil cases, either party is dissatisfied with the verdict of the Common Jury, he may enter an appeal, and demand a new trial by a Special Jury, nominated as the Constitution directs; and from their verdict there is no appeal. This seems to be the first instance of an appeal from one Jury to another; and as the Special Jury is sworn "to "bring in a verdict according to law, and the "opinion they entertain of the evidence, pro-"vided it be not repugnant to justice, equity, "and conscience, and the rules and regulations "contained in the Constitution of which they "shall judge," it is supposed the Special Jury are intended to supply the place of a Court of Equity, there being no other tribunal of that sort established by the Constitution. Extraordinary as the oath of a Common Juryman is, that of a

Special

Special Juror is yet more so; for a Special Juror is not only sworn to bring in a verdict according to law, although it is probable he knows nothing about it; but the oath supposes that the law may be repugnant to justice, equity, conscience, and the constitution, and of this, it is said, the Jury shall judge. Now the Special Jury is the last resort in all cases; and as they are impowered to judge where the law is repugnant to the Constitution (and can decide against law whenever they please, by saying it is contrary to the Constitution), they have it therefore in their power to change the law as often as they think proper. In Georgia, a Judge is now a very useless being; for as the special Jury is the dernier resort, from whose decision there lies no appeal, it is supposed the Court cannot set aside a verdict, and grant a new trial; and as the Jury are commanded by the Constitution to judge of the law as well as the fact, and are sworn to bring in a verdict according to law, &c. I apprehend that no question of law can be brought before the Court by demurrer, neither can the Court decide the law arising on a Special Verdict, as the Jury is forbid to bring one in. One single right the Constitution has reserved to the Bench, which is that of telling the Jury what the law is, when they doubt about it, although it is natural to suppose that the Judges know no more of the law than the Juror themselves do.

During the King's Government, there was a Court of Vice Admiralty to judge of captures at sea, and other maritime causes, which had a Judge appointed by the Crown, who proceeded according to the course of the civil law, and the established method of determination used in Great Britain, and other maritime nations. But now the

the Constitution directs, that all captures by sea and land shall be tried in the County to which they are carried, in a special Court, called by the Chief Justice, or in his absence by the senior Justice, upon application of the. captors or claimants; and the cause is to be determined in ten days. The proceedings are to be the same as in the superior Courts, unless, after the second trial, an appeal is made to the Continental Congress; and all maritime causes are to be tried in like manner. I cannot readily conceive how questions of capture can be tried according to the mode of proceeding used in the superior Court, where the common law process is adopted, and the Jury is sworn to give their verdict according to law: for it has been holden by some of the greatest lawyers in Europe, that any other method of trial, than that now used by Courts of Admiralty, would be manifestly unjust, absurd, and impracticable; and those Courts proceed according to the course of the civil law, and found their decisions on the law of nations, and particular treaties.

The Courts of Conscience, established by Act of Assembly during the King's Government, continue as before, except that their jurisdiction, which was formerly limited to 8 *l.* is now extended to 10 *l.*

Before the Civil War, the Attornies at Law (who also act as Counsel) were admitted by the General Court, but now they are admitted by the House of Assembly.

I apprehend the laws continue much as they were in the King's time, except as to the instances above-mentioned, and also with respect to real estates, which cannot be entailed; and where the owner dies intestate, his estate is divided, ac-

cording

cording to the Statute of Diſtributions of 22 & 23 Car. II. c. 10.

Every religion is tolerated, that is not repugnant to the peace and ſafety of the State; but no Clergyman of any denomination is allowed to ſit in the Legiſlature.

Delegates to the Continental Congreſs are annually appointed by the Houſe of Aſſembly, by ballot, are deemed a part of that Houſe, and have a right to ſit, debate, and vote there.

The Conſtitution ſays, that the legiſlative, executive, and judiciary departments ſhall be ſeparate and diſtinct, ſo that one ſhall not exerciſe the powers properly belonging to the other. How well this rule has been obſerved in drawing up the Conſtitution, the reader will judge for himſelf.

Having now got through the Conſtitutions of the Thirteen United States of America, I ſhall make a few obſervations on them: and firſt, with reſpect to Georgia (a Province in which I reſided ſeveral years), I muſt obſerve, that no country ever enjoyed a greater ſhare of liberty than Georgia did from the time it became a King's Government, down to the breaking out of the Civil War. It is true, there was a ſtrong tendency to democracy, for the Commons Houſe of Aſſembly graſped at powers that did not belong to them, and they ſometimes oppoſed meaſures which tended to the good of the community, merely becauſe they did not originate with themſelves. The Council, as a legiſlative body, loſt its weight and influence in the country, becauſe the Members were appointed only during pleaſure, and therefore, the Commons Houſe of Aſſembly, from jealouſy, ſuppoſed they acted under influence; but had the Upper Houſe of Aſſembly been

been a diftinct body from the Council, and had the Members been appointed for life, and the hereditary title of Baronet been conferred on them, and fome other leading men in the country, I am inclined to think that Province never would have joined in the Civil War. For fuch a mixture of ariftocracy, and thefe hereditary honours (which muft have ftood or fallen with the King's Government) would have engaged a number of leading men in the intereft of the Crown, fufficient to counterbalance the influence that the popular demagogues had in the country. And it is probable, that if the fame experiment had been made in all the Provincial Eftablifhments, they would ftill have continued to be Britifh Governments. There was alfo another fatal practice, which greatly weakened the King's caufe in all the American Colonies, I mean the beftowing almoft every lucrative office in America, that could be exercifed by Deputy, on fome perfon refiding in Great Britain, who employed a Deputy, with a flender allowance, to execute the office for him: this Deputy had neither weight in the Province, nor any intereft in the Government under which he lived; for in cafe of a change he could not be worfe, but having gained fome official knowledge, he might hope to be a principal, if a revolution took place. Befides the Colony Governors, who were deprived of every appointment of confequence, had nothing in their power therewith to ftop the mouths of thofe demagogues that endeavoured to throw the Country into confufion, and they thereby became infignificant. Some of us who wifhed well to the King's Government, lamented this unhappy practice; but the fame prevailed down to the breaking out of the Civil War. However, notwith-

ftanding

ſtanding theſe inconveniencies, Georgia continued under the King's Government to be one of the moſt free and happy countries in the world—juſtice was regularly and impartially adminiſtered—oppreſſion was unknown—the taxes levied on the ſubject were trifling—and every man that had induſtry, became opulent—the people there were more particularly indebted to the Crown, than thoſe in any other Colony—immenſe ſums were expended by Government in ſettling and protecting that country—troops of rangers were kept up by the Crown for ſeveral years—the Civil Government was annually provided for by vote of the Houſe of Commons in Great Britain, and moſt of the inhabitants owed every acre of land they had to the King's free gift: in ſhort, there was ſcarce a man in the Province that did not lie under particular obligations to the Crown. As a proof of the amazing progreſs that Georgia made, I ſhould obſerve, that when Governor Reynolds went to that province in 1754, the exports did not amount to 30,000l. a year; but at the breaking out of the Civil War, they could not be much leſs than 200,000 *l.* ſterling. The caſe is now quite altered, for moſt of the gentlemen of diſtinction and property in Georgia were Loyaliſts, and on the evacuation they left the country, and carried off their Negroes; and others of the Loyaliſts were cruelly murdered for their attachment to their Sovereign. I am perſuaded that not a tenth part of the white inhabitants, that were in Georgia at the breaking out of the Civil War, remain there at this time; and the proportion of Negroes is much leſs. Should the Repreſentatives continue to vote themſelves wages, as they did before Colonel Campbell reduced the Country, the whole taxes of the Province will not be ſufficient

ficient for that purpose; and what is to become of their Governor, and the numerous train of civil Officers? Georgia is also subjected to another disagreeable circumstance beyond any other of the Thirteen States, which is this: The Southern Colonies are overrun with a swarm of men from the western parts of Virginia and North Carolina, distinguished by the name of Crackers. Many of these people are descended from convicts that were transported from Great Britain to Virginia at different times, and inherit so much profligacy from their ancestors, that they are the most abandoned set of men on earth, few of them having the least sense of religion. When these people are routed in the other provinces, they fly to Georgia, where the winters are mild, and the man who has a rifle, ammunition, and a blanket, can subsist in that vagrant way, which the Indians pursue; for the quantity of deer, wild turkies, and other game there, affords subsistence; and the country being mostly covered with woods, they have it always in their power to construct temporary huts, and procure fuel. The Eastern Coast of Georgia, in which they plant rice, is at this time thinly settled on account of the emigration of the Loyalists, and the greatest proportion of inhabitants are Negro slaves: whereas in the western parts, the inhabitants are numerous, and daily increase by the accession of the Crackers from the other Provinces; and it is highly probable that these people will in time overrun the rice part of the country, as the Tartars in Asia have done by the fruitful cultivated provinces in the southern parts of that country. What induces me the rather to think so, is, that during the King's Government these Crackers were very troublesome in the settlements, by driving off gangs

gangs of horſes and cattle to Virginia, and committing other enormities: they alſo occaſioned frequent diſputes with the Indians, whom they robbed, and ſometimes murdered: the Indians in return, according to their cuſtom, murdered the firſt white man they met, by way of retaliation. To a ſimilar ſituation with thoſe Crackers, would the diſciples of Hume reduce the people of this country, could they ſucceed in aboliſhing Chriſtianity, and perſuading the world to believe that moral and natural defects are on the ſame footing. Georgia being bounded by the moſt northern ſtream of the River Savannah, it expands greatly in that quarter, forms part of the weſtern boundary of South Carolina, and joins North Carolina. Since the late proviſional treaty, no other nation but the Indians can conteſt with them the right to that large and fertile country, which lies between Georgia and the River Miſſiſſippi. During the Civil War, the Americans loſt much of that apprehenſion which they formerly entertained of the Indians, for the Crackers, who are deſtitute of every ſenſe of religion, which might withhold them from acts of perfidy and cruelty, have been diſcovered to outdo the Indians in bearing hunger and fatigue; and as they lead a ſavage kind of life, they are equally ſkilled in the arts of buſh fighting, and diſcovering the enemy by their tracks: Theſe men will naturally ſettle faſt in the weſtern parts of North Carolina and Georgia; and as the Indians dwindle away before them, they certainly threaten ruin to the civilized parts of the rice Colonies, who have not now a common parent to call to their aſſiſtance. How much ſoever I may deteſt the conduct of ſome men in America in bringing on the Civil War, and the conſequent

ruin

ruin of their country; yet Christianity forbids me to wish ill to an individual: how much more then does it forbid the wishing ill to thousands: and had I abilities to suggest hints that would conduce to the good of my greatest enemies, I should rejoice in having an opportunity of doing it.

I now beg leave to make some observations on the United States in general.—By this time the reader must have observed, that the Constitutions of all these States are Democratical; and however specious that form of government may appear in theory, yet, as a great Author has observed, in a popular State virtue is a necessary spring; and I do by no means agree, that the Americans are more virtuous than the rest of mankind. I shall quote from Montesquieu a passage, in which he has described the situation of England during the Civil War.

"A very droll spectacle it was, in the last "century, to behold the impotent efforts the "English made for the establishment of Demo-"cracy. As those who had a share in the direc-"tion of public affairs were void of all virtue, as "their ambition was inflamed by the success of "the most daring of their Members, as the spirit "of faction was suppressed only by that of a suc-"ceeding faction, the Government was con-"tinually changing. The people, amazed at so "many revolutions, sought every where for a "Democracy, without being able to find it. At "length, after a series of tumultuary motions "and violent shocks, they were obliged to have "recourse to the very government they had so "odiously proscribed." Whether this description will ever suit America, time only can discover; it is said that, even now, the majority of the people there is averse to independency; and

when

when it was offered to the Congreſs, their apprehenſions ſeemed to increaſe. Had thoſe men read Monteſquieu and De Lolme on the Conſtitution of England, they would not (to uſe the words of the firſt Author), have built a Chalcedon, when they had a Byzantium before their eyes.

Many efforts were made by Great Britain to recover America from the deluſion they were under: the 18 Geo. III. c. 13. "Enabled his Ma-"jeſty to appoint Commiſſioners, with ſufficient "powers to treat, conſult, and agree upon the "means of quieting the diſorders ſubſiſting in "certain of the Colonies, Plantations, and Pro-"vinces of North America." In purſuance of this Act, the King did from time to time appoint Commiſſioners to treat with the Americans; and as the Congreſs could not ſafely reject the offers made by the Britiſh Commiſſioners in a peremptory manner, evaſive anſwers were returned, and the people were deceived with the falſe repreſentation of an interview with the Britiſh Commiſſioner: but there was a party in the Congreſs, which influenced the deliberations of that Body againſt a Reconciliation; and when General Burgoyne's Defeat, and the Conciliatory Motion made in the Houſe of Commons, had elevated the Congreſs, they with arrogance rejected the ſecond Propoſals made by Great Britain. As nothing ſhort of Independency would ſatisfy the leading Men in Congreſs, the Act of 22 Geo. III. c. 46 was made, "To enable his Majeſty to conclude a peace or "truce with certain Colonies in North America, "therein mentioned," but which impliedly gave the King a power to declare them Independent; and ſuch was the conſtruction which the Houſe of Commons put on that Act, in their Debate on the late Peace.

In pursuance of that Act, Mr. Oswald was sent to Paris to treat with the American Commissioners, and on the 30th of November 1782, Provisional Articles were signed at Paris by the British and American Commissioners, to take effect when Terms of Peace were agreed upon between Great Britain and France, and his Britannic Majesty should be ready to conclude such Treaty accordingly. By the Provisional Articles, his Britannic Majesty acknowledges the Thirteen United States of America (in the Articles particularly named) to be Free, Sovereign and Independent States; and for himself, his heirs and successors, relinquishes all claims to the government, propriety, and territorial rights of the same.

The affection I have for my native country, induces me to recommend one measure to Government, which, however chimerical it may appear, will, I flatter myself, give no offence to any one. I would, in the first place, premise, that I do not take upon me to question the attachment of the present set of men in the West Indies to their Sovereign and Parent State; but those Islands change their inhabitants in a few years; a new race may be inclined to give the Mother Country as much trouble as the Colonies on the Continent have done; and it is by no means clear, that the North Americans will refuse them their assistance. —If those Islands should become independent, Great Britain would have no footing in the West Indies, unless the following plan was adopted:— The cession of Gibraltar would insure to Great Britain such of the Spanish Islands in the West Indies as she might chuse to ask for. Let some Island of a moderate size be pitched upon, that is naturally defensible, and has a good harbour, capable

pable of receiving and heaving down line of battle ſhips.—Let an Act of Parliament be made, which unalienably annexes this Iſland to Great Britain. —After reſerving lands ſufficient for Fortifications, a Dock-yard, Churches, and other public Places, let the lands on the harbour be laid out in town lots, and the reſt of the Iſland in farm lots or plantations, not exceeding a ſmall number of acres; and let it be provided by the Act, that no perſon ſhall hold more than one town lot, and one farm lot; and if more ſhould come to him by deſcent, or otherwiſe, he ſhall be obliged to ſell the overplus number within a given time, or elſe they ſhall be forfeited to the Crown.

This Iſland being intended merely as an emporium, provide that no ſugar-canes, cotton, or indigo, ſhall be raiſed on it, but that the inhabitants ſhall be confined to the raiſing ſtock and proviſions.—Make this Iſland a free port; give the people the trial by jury, and eſtabliſh every other part of the Conſtitution of England, except that of a right to chuſe Repreſentatives.—And let every grant of a town or farm lot have a clauſe inſerted in it, to run with the land, expreſsly ſtipulating, that there never ſhall be a power of legiſlation in the Iſland, but that the Parliament of Great Britain ſhall always exerciſe the powers of legiſlation and taxation over it.—A man who purchaſed lands in the Iſland, and voluntarily ſettled there under ſuch a reſtriction, could never complain of the want of a Colony Legiſlature; and as the Parliament would pay every attention to the proſperity of the Iſland, and the encouragement of trade, ſuch a Colony would be as free as any the Engliſh ever had, and much more happy. The Iſland might be rendered as ſtrong as art, combined with nature, could make it, and ſhould always

always have a ſtrong garriſon.—If the Governor was an able civilian, and the Judges good common lawyers, the inhabitants would ſuffer no oppreſſion; but if the gentleman who commanded the forces was the Governor of the Iſland, it might undo every thing.—Such an Iſland would probably have an immenſe trade, and be of great importance to the commerce and manufactures of this country. In a Colony ſettled on ſuch a plan, where the inhabitants enjoyed the benefits of the Common Law of England, and had regular Courts of Juſtice eſtabliſhed, every thing would probably remain quiet, unleſs a General Aſſembly was convened, and then a ſcene of confuſion might enſue; for, as an ingenious writer in the year 1770 obſerved, "When you put every Colony on the "ſame footing with the Mother Country, it be-"comes an independent Government. The Bri-"tiſh Empire is no longer to be governed by the "ſame general tenor of laws. It ceaſes to be "one, it is at beſt but a confederacy of petty "States. Inſtead of the Empire's being ſtrength-"ened with Provinces, it is weakened by raiſing "rivals, where there only ought to be ſubjects." I muſt own, I never could conceive any juſt medium between the ſupremacy of Parliament over the Colonies in all caſes, on the one hand, and the Independency of the Colonies, on the other. Having juſt taken up a book which exactly expreſſes my thoughts, I ſhall quote a paſſage from it—"The Britiſh Parliament muſt be the ſu-"preme power in all the Britiſh dominions; and "if ſo, all the Britiſh dominions ought to pay "obedience, in all caſes, to all the laws in which "they are mentioned, that may be enacted by "the Britiſh Parliament; and to refuſe obedience

"in

"in any ſuch caſe, is to declare themſelves an "independent people."

No good man would wiſh to revive the queſtion concerning the right of the Britiſh Parliament to tax the Colonies; and the 18 Geo. III. c. 12. hath declared, "That the King and Parliament "of Great Britain will not impoſe any duty, tax, "&c. payable in the Colonies, except for the "regulation of commerce." The ſupreme and abſolute authority of the Britiſh Empire is veſted in the King and Parliament, and to their direction in all caſes I do moſt dutifully ſubmit; but although the 18 Geo. III. may be concluſive as to thoſe Britiſh Colonies which are already ſettled, yet that Act cannot extend to thoſe which may hereafter be acquired, nor reſtrain the King and Parliament from ſettling them on what terms they may think proper. And as I apprehend there are at preſent no thoughts of extenſive Coloniza-tion, we ought to ſettle a few Iſlands in different parts of the world, in the nature of free ports, and on the plan above mentioned, in order to ſecure our commerce. Every man of diſcernment muſt be convinced, that the Eaſt India Company will not long be able to hold the extenſive countries they now command: and the ſooner ſomething is done in the Indian ocean, on the plan I have propoſed, the better it may be for this country. I flatter myſelf that no man entertains a greater regard for true liberty, and the happy Conſtitution of this Iſland, than I do; but altho' it might be intended to benefit mankind, by eſtabliſhing the counterpart of our excellent Conſtitution in the large Provinces on the Continent of America, yet there can be no reaſon for convening a Colony Legiſlature in ſuch ſmall Iſlands as may hereafter be ſettled, for the ſole purpoſe

of

of commerce; and if they enjoy the Common Law of England, and are under the immediate and ſole direction of the ſupreme Legiſlature of the Empire, they will have no reaſon to complain.

As far as lies with an obſcure individual, I wiſh, on all occaſions, to conſult the intereſts of Chriſtianity, the good of my country, and the welfare of mankind: the purity of my intentions will therefore afford me conſolation, let the fate of my projects be what they may.—It is the great pride of my life that I was born in this Iſland, which is the only ſpot on earth that enjoys a free and happy Conſtitution: may it continue in its preſent purity to the lateſt poſterity! But it has often hurted my feelings to reflect, that after Great Britain had ſettled a number of Colonies at an immenſe expence, protected them againſt the French and Indians, given them a free form of Government, and inſtead of cramping their commerce by taxes, encouraging it by drawbacks and bounties, ſo that they became the moſt happy people on earth—That thoſe Coloniſts, from an exceſs of liberty and affluence, ſhould wantonly follow the lead of factious men, and join the ancient enemies of their country, to the intended deſtruction of their Parent State, and their own ruin, is more than human nature can bear with patience.—When ſeveral turbulent men united to involve the Province where I reſided in the civil war, I did, in my charges to Grand Juries, and on other occaſions, point out to them the ill conſequences that would attend the ſubverſion of the King's Government; the event has juſtified my predictions; and having diſcharged my duty to my King and country, I mean, if God ſpares me life and health, to publiſh a Narrative of my conduct,

conduct, which will not depend on bare assertion, but authentic vouchers.

CHAP. IV.

Of the Governor of a Provincial Establishment, or King's Government, and of the powers and authorities with which he is vested by his Commissions and Instructions.

PROVINCIAL Establishments being the only species of American Governments that now remain to Great Britain, I shall confine myself to them, except where I have occasion to speak incidentally, of some few particulars regarding the Proprietary and Charter Governments, at the time they were under the Crown of Great Britain.

I have already observed, in a former part of this work, that in a Provincial Establishment, or King's Government, the Governor is named by the King, and is his Representative or Deputy. He is styled "Captain-General and Governor in "Chief in and over the Province, and Chan-"cellor, Vice-Admiral, and Ordinary of the "same:" and has the title of "Excellency" given him, in consequence of his being the King's immediate Representative.

I shall lay before the Reader a modern form of a Governor's Commission, which contains the recital of the Act made in the 6th year of his present Majesty, for altering the oath of abjuration, &c.; and also the recital of the 22 Geo. II. c. 33. for amending, explaining, and reducing into one Act of Parliament, the laws relating to the government of his Majesty's ships, vessels, and forces

forces by sea.—The dates in this commission are arbitrary, and the name of any particular Province is omitted.—I flatter myself there cannot be the least disrespect to Government in publishing this form of a Governor's commission, as some have already appeared in print.

After the commission of Governor, will appear that of Vice-Admiral, and then some account of the powers and authorities with which a Governor is vested by his commission and instructions.

G. R.

GEORGE the Third, by the Grace of God, of Great Britain, France, and Ireland King, Defender of the Faith, and so forth: To our trusty and well beloved A. B. Esq;

GREETING:

WHEREAS we did, by our Letters Patent under our Great Seal of Great Britain, bearing date at Westminster the first day of January, in the eighteenth year of our reign, constitute and appoint C. D. Esq; Captain-General and Governor in Chief in and over our Province of F——, and the territories depending thereon in America, for and during our will and pleasure; as by the said recited Letters Patent (relation being thereunto had) may more fully and at large appear: Now know you, that we have revoked and determined, and by these presents do revoke and determine the said recited Letters Patent, and every clause, article, and thing therein contained.

And further know you that we, reposing especial trust and confidence in the prudence, courage and loyalty of you the said A. B. of our especial grace, certain knowledge, and mere motion, have

thought

thought fit to conftitute and appoint you the faid A. B. to be our Captain-General and Governor in Chief in and over our Province of F——, and the territories depending thereon in America: And we do hereby require and command you to do and execute all things in due manner that fhall belong unto your faid command, and the truft we have repofed in you, according to the feveral powers and directions granted or appointed you by this prefent commiffion, and inftructions herewith given you, or by fuch further powers, inftructions, and authorities, as fhall at any time hereafter be granted or appointed you under our Signet and Sign Manual, or by our order in our Privy Council, and according to fuch reafonable laws and ftatutes as now are in force, or hereafter fhall be made and agreed upon by you, with the advice and confent of our Council, and the Affembly of our faid Province under your government, in fuch manner and form as is herein after expreffed.

And our will and pleafure is, that you the faid A. B. after the publication of thefe our Letters Patent, do, in the firft place, take the oaths appointed to be taken by an Act paffed in the firft year of the reign of King George the Firft *, intituled, "An Act for the further fecurity of his Ma-" jefty's perfon and government, and the fucceffion of the Crown in the heirs of the late Princefs Sophia, being Proteftants, and for extinguifhing the hopes of the pretended Prince of Wales, and his open and fecret abettors." And by an Act paffed in the fixth year of our reign †, intituled, "An Act for altering the oath of abjuration, and the affurance; and for amending fo

* 1 Geo. I. ft. 2. c. 13. † 6 Geo. III. c. 53.

"much

" much of an Act of the ſeventh year of her late " Majeſty Queen Ann, intituled, An Act for the " improvement of the Union of the two King- " doms, as after the time therein limited requires " the delivery of certain liſts, and copies therein " mentioned, to perſons indicted of high treaſon, " or miſpriſion of treaſon." As alſo, that you make and ſubſcribe the declaration mentioned in an Act of Parliament made in the twenty-fifth year of the reign of King Charles * the Second, intituled, " An Act for preventing dangers which " may happen from Popiſh recuſants." And likewiſe, that you take the oath uſually taken by the Governors in the Plantations, for the due execution of the office and truſt of our Captain-General and Governor in Chief in and over our ſaid Province of F——, and the territories depending thereon, for the due and impartial adminiſtration of juſtice: and further, that you take the oath required to be taken by Governors of Plantations, to do their utmoſt, that the ſeveral laws relating to trade and the Plantations be duly obſerved: which ſaid oaths and declaration our Council of our ſaid Province, or any three of the Members thereof, have hereby full power and authority, and are required to tender and adminiſter unto you, and in your abſence to our Lieutenant-Governor, if there be any upon the place; all which being duly performed, you ſhall yourſelf adminiſter unto each of the Members of our ſaid Council; as alſo to our Lieutenant-Governor, if there be any upon the place, the oaths mentioned in the ſaid Acts, intituled, " An Act for " the further ſecurity of his Majeſty's perſon and " government, and the ſucceſſion of the Crown

* 25 Cha. II. c. 2.

" in

"in the heirs of the late Princeſs Sophia, being "Proteſtants, and for extinguiſhing the hopes of "the pretended Prince of Wales, and his open "and ſecret abettors." And an Act for altering the oath of abjuration, and the aſſurance; and for amending ſo much of an Act of the ſeventh year of her late Majeſty Queen Ann, intituled, "An Act for the improvement of the Union of "the two Kingdoms, as after the time therein "limited requires the delivery of certain liſts, "and copies therein mentioned, to perſons in- "dicted of high treaſon, or miſpriſion of treaſon;" as alſo to cauſe them to make and ſubſcribe the afore mentioned declaration, and to adminiſter to them the uſual oath for the due execution of their places and truſts.

And we do hereby give and grant unto you full power and authority to ſuſpend any of the Members of our ſaid Council from ſitting, voting, or aſſiſting therein, if you ſhall find juſt cauſe for ſo doing; and if there ſhall be any Lieutenant-Governor, him likewiſe to ſuſpend from the execution of his command, and to appoint another in his ſtead until our pleaſure be known: and if it ſhall at any time happen, that, by the death, departure out of our ſaid Province, or ſuſpenſion of any of our ſaid Councillors, or otherwiſe, there ſhall be a vacancy in our ſaid Council (any three whereof we do hereby appoint to be a quorum), our will and pleaſure is, that you ſignify the ſame unto us by the firſt opportunity, that we may, under our Signet and Sign Manual, conſtitute and appoint others in their ſtead. But that our affairs may not ſuffer at that diſtance, for want of a due number of Councillors, if ever it ſhould happen that there be leſs than ſeven of them reſiding in our ſaid Province, we do hereby give and

and grant unto you the ſaid A. B. full power and authority to chuſe as many perſons out of the principal Freeholders, inhabitants thereof, as will make up the full number of our ſaid Council to be ſeven, and no more; which perſons, ſo choſen and appointed by you, ſhall be, to all intents and purpoſes, Councillors in our ſaid Province, until either they ſhall be confirmed by us, or that, by the nomination of others by us, under our Sign Manual and Signet, our ſaid Council ſhall have ſeven or more perſons in it.

And we do hereby give and grant unto you full power and authority, with the advice and conſent of our ſaid Council, from time to time as need ſhall require, to ſummon and call General Aſſemblies of the ſaid Freeholders and Planters within your government, according to the uſage of our Province of F——. And our will and pleaſure is, that the perſons thereupon duly elected by the major part of the Freeholders of the reſpective Counties and places, and ſo returned, ſhall, before their ſitting, take the oaths mentioned in the ſaid Acts, intituled, "An Act for "the further ſecurity of his Majeſty's perſon and "Government, and the ſucceſſion of the Crown, "in the heirs of the late Princeſs Sophia, being "Proteſtants, and for extinguiſhing the hopes of "the pretended Prince of Wales, and his open "and ſecret abettors:"—and "An Act for al-"tering the oath of abjuration, and the aſſu-"rance; and for amending ſo much of an Act "of the ſeventh year of her late Majeſty Queen "Ann, intituled, An Act for the improvement "of the Union of the two Kingdoms, as after "the time therein limited, requires the delivery "of certain liſts, and copies therein mentioned, "to perſons indicted of high treaſon, or miſ-

"priſion

"prision of treason:"—as also, make and subscribe the afore-mentioned declaration (which oaths and declaration you shall commissionate fit persons, under our Seal of F———, to tender and administer unto them): and until the same shall be so taken and subscribed, no person shall be capable of sitting, though elected.

And we do hereby declare, that the persons so elected and qualified shall be called and deemed The General Assembly of that our Province, and the territories depending thereon.

And you the said A. B. by and with the consent of our said Council and Assembly, or the major part of them respectively, shall have full power and authority to make, constitute, and ordain laws, statutes, and ordinances, for the public peace, welfare, and good government of our said Province, and of the people and inhabitants thereof, and such others as shall resort thereto, and for the benefit of us, our heirs and successors: which said laws, statutes, and ordinances, are not to be repugnant, but as near as may be agreeable to the laws and statutes of this our kingdom of Great Britain.

Provided that all such laws, statutes and ordinances, of what nature or duration soever, be, within three months or sooner after the making thereof, transmitted unto us under our Seal of F———, for our approbation or disallowance of the same; as also duplicates thereof by the next conveyance.

And in case any or all of the said laws, statutes, and ordinances, being not before confirmed by us, shall at any time be disallowed, and not approved, and so signified by us, our heirs or successors, under our or their Sign Manual and Signet, or by order of our or their Privy Council, unto you

you the ſaid A. B. or to the Commander in Chief of our ſaid Province for the time being; then ſuch and ſo many of the ſaid laws, ſtatutes and ordinances, as ſhall be ſo diſallowed, and not approved, ſhall from thenceforth ceaſe, determine, and become utterly void and of none effect; any thing to the contrary thereof notwithſtanding.

And, to the end that nothing may be paſſed or done by our ſaid Council or Aſſembly, to the prejudice of us, our heirs or ſucceſſors, we will and ordain, that you the ſaid A. B. ſhall have and enjoy a negative voice in the making and paſſing of all laws, ſtatutes and ordinances, as aforeſaid: and you ſhall and may likewiſe, from time to time, as you ſhall judge it neceſſary, adjourn, prorogue, and diſſolve all General Aſſemblies as aforeſaid.

And our further will and pleaſure is, that you ſhall and may uſe and keep the Public Seal of our ſaid Province of F——, for ſealing all things whatſoever that paſs the Great Seal of our ſaid Province under your government.

And we do further give and grant unto you the ſaid A. B. full power and authority from time to time, and at any time hereafter, by yourſelf, or by any other to be authoriſed by you in that behalf, to adminiſter and give the oaths mentioned in the ſaid Acts, intituled, "An Act for the further ſecurity of his Majeſty's perſon and Government, and the ſucceſſion of the Crown in the heirs of the late Princeſs Sophia, being Proteſtants, and for extinguiſhing the hopes of the pretended Prince of Wales, and his open and ſecret abettors:" and, "An Act for altering the oath of abjuration, and the aſſurance; and for amending ſo much of an Act of the ſeventh year of her late Majeſty Queen Ann, "intituled,

" intituled, An Act for the improvement of the " Union of the two Kingdoms, as, after the time " therein limited, requires the delivery of certain " lists, and copies therein mentioned, to persons " indicted of high treason or misprision of trea- " son," to all and every such person and persons as you shall think fit, who shall at any time or times pass into our said Province, or shall be resident or abiding there.

And we do further by these presents give and grant unto you the said A. B. full power and authority, with the advice and consent of our said Council, to erect, constitute, and establish such and so many Courts of Judicature and public Justice, within our said Province under your government, as you and they shall think fit and necessary for the hearing and determining of all causes, as well criminal as civil, according to law and equity, and for awarding execution thereupon; with all reasonable and necessary powers, authorities, fees, and privileges belonging thereunto: as also, to appoint and commissionate fit persons in the several parts of your government, to administer the oaths mentioned in the aforesaid Act, intituled, " An Act for the further security " of his Majesty's person and government, and " the succession of the Crown, in the heirs of the " late Princess Sophia, being Protestants, and for " extinguishing the hopes of the pretended Prince " of Wales, and his open and secret abettors;" and " An Act for altering the oath of abjuration, " and the assurance; and for amending so much " of an Act of the seventh year of her late Ma- " jesty Queen Ann, intituled, An Act for the " improvement of the Union of the two King- " doms, as, after the time therein limited, re- " quires the delivery of certain lists and copies

" therein

"therein mentioned, to persons indicted of high "treason, or misprision of treason;" as also to tender and administer the aforesaid declaration, unto such persons belonging to the said Courts, as shall be obliged to take the same.

And we do hereby authorise and impower you to constitute and appoint Judges, and in cases requisite, Commissioners of Oyer and Terminer, Justices of the Peace, and other necessary Officers and ministers in our said Province, for the better administration of justice, and putting the laws in execution; and to administer, or cause to be administered unto them, such oath or oaths as are usually given for the due execution and performance of offices and places, and for the clearing of truth in judicial causes.

And we do hereby give and grant unto you full power and authority, where you shall see cause, or shall judge any offender or offenders in criminal matters, or for any fines or forfeitures due unto us, fit objects of our mercy, to pardon all such offenders, and to remit all such offences, fines, and forfeitures, treason and wilful murder only excepted; in which cases, you shall likewise have power, upon extraordinary occasions, to grant reprieves to the offenders, until, and to the intent that, our royal pleasure may be known therein.

And we do, by these presents, authorise and impower you to collate any person or persons to any churches, chapels, or other ecclesiastical benefices within our said province and territories aforesaid, as often as any of them shall happen to be void.

And we do hereby give and grant unto you the said A. B. by yourself or by your captains and commanders, by you to be authorised, full power and authority to levy, arm, muſter, command, and employ all perſons whatſoever, reſiding within our ſaid Province of F——, and other the territories under your government; and, as occaſion ſhall ſerve, to march them from one place to another, or to embark them, for the reſiſting and withſtanding of all enemies, pirates, and rebels, both at ſea and land; and to tranſport ſuch forces to any of our plantations in America, if neceſſity ſhall require, for the defence of the ſame againſt the invaſions or attempts of any of our enemies; and ſuch enemies, pirates, and rebels, if there ſhall be occaſion to purſue and proſecute in or out of the limits of our ſaid Province and Plantations, or any of them; and if it ſhall ſo pleaſe God them to vanquiſh, apprehend, and take, and being taken, either according to law to put to death, or keep and preſerve alive, at your diſcretion; and to execute martial law in time of invaſion, war, or other times, when by law it may be executed; and to do and execute all and every other thing and things, which, to our Captain General and Governor in Chief, doth or ought of right to belong.

And we do hereby give and grant unto you full power and authority, by and with the advice and conſent of our ſaid Council, to erect, raiſe, and build, in our ſaid Province of F——, and the territories depending thereon, ſuch and ſo many forts and platforms, caſtles, cities, boroughs, towns, and fortifications, as you, by the advice aforeſaid, ſhall judge neceſſary; and the ſame, or any of them, to fortify and furniſh with ordnance, ammunition, and all ſorts of arms fit and neceſſary for the ſecurity and defence of our ſaid Province; and, by the advice aforeſaid, the ſame again,

again, or any of them, to demolish or dismantle, as may be most convenient.

And forasmuch as divers mutinies and disorders may happen by persons shipped and employed at sea, during the time of war; and to the end that such as shall be shipped and employed at sea during time of war, may be better governed and ordered, we do hereby give and grant unto you the said A. B. full power and authority to constitute and appoint Captains, Lieutenants, Masters of Ships, and other Commanders and Officers, and to grant to such Captains, Lieutenants, Masters of Ships, and other Commanders and Officers Commissions, to execute the law martial during the time of war, according to the directions of an Act passed in the twenty-second year of the reign of our late Royal Grandfather *, intituled, "An Act for amending, explaining, "and reducing into one Act of Parliament the "laws relating to the government of his Majesty's "ships, vessels, and forces by sea;" and to use such proceedings, authorities, punishments, corrections, and executions upon any offender or offenders, who shall be mutinous, seditious, disorderly, or any way unruly either at sea, or during the time of their abode and residence in any of the ports, harbours, or bays of our said province and territories, as the case shall be found to require, according to the martial law, and the said directions, during the time of war as aforesaid.

Provided that nothing herein contained shall be construed to the enabling you, or any by your authority, to hold plea, or have any jurisdiction

* 22 Geo. II. c. 33.

of

of any offences, caufe, matter, or thing committed or done upon the high fea, or within any of the havens, rivers, or creeks of our faid Province and territories under your government, by any Captain, Commander, Lieutenant, Mafter, Officer, Seaman, Soldier, or other perfon whatfoever, who fhall be in our actual fervice and pay, in or on board any of our fhips of war, or other veffels acting by immediate commiffion or warrant from our Commiffioners, for executing the office of our High Admiral of Great Britain; or from our High Admiral of Great Britain for the time being, under the Seal of our Admiralty; but that fuch Captain, Commander, Lieutenant, Mafter, Officer, Seaman, Soldier, or other perfon fo offending, fhall be left to be proceeded againft, and tried, as their offences fhall require, either by commiffion under our Great Seal of Great Britain, as the Statute of the twenty-eighth of Henry the Eighth directs, or by Commiffion from our faid Commiffioners for executing the office of our High Admiral of Great Britain, or from our High Admiral of Great Britain for the time being, according to the aforementioned Act, intituled, "An Act for amending, explaining, and reducing into one Act of Parliament "the laws relating to the government of his Majesty's fhips, veffels, and forces by fea, and not "otherwife."

Provided neverthelefs, that all diforders and mifdemeanors, committed on fhore by any Captain, Commander, Lieutenant, Mafter, Officer, Seaman, Soldier, or other perfon whatfoever belonging to any of our fhips of war, or other veffels, acting by immediate commiffion or warrant from our faid Commiffioners for executing the office of our High Admiral of Great Britain, or from

from our High Admiral of Great Britain for the time being, under the Seal of our Admiralty, may be tried and punished, according to the laws of the place, where any such disorder, offence, and misdemeanor shall be committed on shore, notwithstanding such offenders be in our actual service, and borne in our pay on board any such our ships of war, or other vessels, acting by immediate commission or warrant from our said Commissioners for executing the office of our High Admiral of Great Britain, or from our High Admiral of Great Britain for the time being as aforesaid; so as he shall not receive any protection for the avoiding of justice for such offences committed on shore, from any pretence of his being employed in our service at sea.

And our further will and pleasure is, that all public monies raised, or which shall be raised by any Act to be hereafter made within our said Province, and other the territories depending thereon, be issued out by warrant from you, by and with the advice and consent of our Council, and disposed of by you for the support of the government, and not otherwise.

And we do hereby likewise give and grant unto you full power and authority, by and with the advice and consent of our said Council, to settle and agree with the inhabitants of our province and territories aforesaid, for such lands, tenements, and hereditaments, as now are, or hereafter shall be in our power to dispose of, and them to grant to any person or persons upon such terms, and under such moderate quit-rents, services, and acknowledgments, to be thereupon reserved unto us, as you, by and with the advice aforesaid, shall think fit: which said grants are to pass, and be sealed by our Seal of our said Province of

F——;

F——; and being entered upon record by ſuch officer or officers, as are or ſhall be appointed thereunto, ſhall be good and effectual in law againſt us, our heirs, and ſucceſſors.

And we do hereby give you the ſaid A. B. full power and authority to order and appoint fairs, marts, and markets, as alſo ſuch and ſo many ports, harbours, bays, havens, and other places for the convenience and ſecurity of ſhipping, and for the better loading and unloading of goods and merchandiſes in ſuch and ſo many places, as by you, with the advice and conſent of our ſaid Council, ſhall be thought fit and neceſſary.

And we do hereby require and command all Officers and Miniſters, civil and military, and all other inhabitants of our ſaid Province and Territories depending thereon, to be obedient, aiding, and aſſiſting unto you, the ſaid A. B. in the execution of this our Commiſſion, and of the powers and authorities herein contained; and in caſe of your death or abſence out of our ſaid province and territories depending thereon, to be obedient, aiding, and aſſiſting unto ſuch perſon as ſhall be appointed by us to be our Lieutenant Governor, or Commander in Chief of our ſaid Province for the time being; to whom we do therefore by theſe preſents give and grant all and ſingular the powers and authorities herein granted, to be by him executed and enjoyed during our pleaſure, or until your arrival within our ſaid province and territories.

And if, upon your death or abſence out of our ſaid province and territories depending thereon, there be no perſon upon the place commiſſionated or appointed by us to be our Lieutenant Governor, or Commander in Chief of our ſaid Province, our will and pleaſure is, that the eldeſt Councillor, whoſe name is firſt placed in our ſaid

inſtructions

inſtructions to you, and who ſhall, at the time of your death or abſence, be reſiding within our ſaid Province of F———, ſhall take upon him the adminiſtration of the government, and execute our ſaid commiſſion and inſtructions, and the ſeveral powers and authorities therein contained, in the ſame manner, and to all intents and purpoſes, as other our Governor and Commander in Chief of our ſaid Province, ſhould or ought to do in caſe of your abſence until your return, or in all caſes, until our further pleaſure be known therein.

And we do hereby declare, ordain, and appoint that you the ſaid A. B. ſhall and may hold, execute, and enjoy the office and place of our Captain General and Governor in Chief in and over our Province of F———, and the territories depending thereon, together with all and ſingular the powers and authorities hereby granted unto you, for and during our will and pleaſure.

In witneſs whereof, we have cauſed theſe our Letters to be made Patent.

Witneſs ourſelf at Weſtminſter, the firſt day of January, in the twenty-third year of our reign.

By Writ of Privy Seal,
YORKE and YORKE.

The
Great Seal
of
GREAT BRITAIN.

In Charter Governments, ſuch as Connecticut and Rhode Iſland, where the Governor was annually choſen by the people, in the ſame manner

as

as a Mayor is in a Corporation in England, it would have been improper to have trusted such elected Governor (who was frequently a man of little knowledge or consequence) with the command of the Militia in the Province over which he presided. In such cases therefore, before the Civil War, it was usual to insert in the Commission of the Governor of the Provincial Establishment, or King's Government, next to such Charter Government, a clause, appointing the King's Governor Captain General and Commander in Chief of the Militia and Forces by sea and Land; and of all forts, &c. in such Charter Government; which clause was in the following words:

"And whereas there are divers Colonies adjoining to our Province of F——, for the defence and security whereof, it is requisite that due care be taken in time of war; we have therefore thought it necessary for our service, and for the better protection and security of our subjects inhabiting those parts, to constitute and appoint, and we do by these presents constitute and appoint you the said A. B. to be our Captain General and Commander in Chief of the Militia, and of all the forces by sea and land within our Colony of G——, and of all our forts and places of strength within the same; and for the better ordering, governing, and ruling our said Militia, and all our forces, forts, and places of strength within our said Colony of G——, we do hereby give and grant unto you the said A. B. and in your absence to our Commander in Chief of our Province of F——, all and every the like powers as in these presents are before granted and recited, for the ruling, governing, and ordering our Militia, and all our forces, forts, "and

" and places of ſtrength within our Province of
" F———, to be exerciſed by you the ſaid A. B.
" and in your abſence from our territories and
" dominion of F———, by our Commander in
" Chief of our Province of F———, within our
" ſaid Colony of G———, for and during our
" pleaſure."

COMMISSION of VICE ADMIRAL.

GEORGE the Third, by the Grace of God of Great Britain, France, and Ireland King, Defender of the Faith, to our beloved A. B. Eſq. our Captain General and Governor in Chief in and over our Province of F———, in America.

GREETING:

WE confiding very much in your fidelity, care, and circumſpection in this behalf, do, by theſe preſents, which are to continue during our pleaſure only, conſtitute and depute you the ſaid A. B. Eſq our Captain General and Governor in Chief aforeſaid, our Vice Admiral, Commiſſary, and Deputy in the Office of Vice Admiralty in our Province of F——— aforeſaid, and the territories depending thereon in America, and in the maritime parts of the ſame and thereto adjoining whatſoever; with power of taking and receiving all and every the fees, profits, advantages, emoluments, commodities, and appurtenances whatſoever due, and belonging to the ſaid office of Vice Admiral, Commiſſary, and Deputy in our Province of F———, and the territories depending thereon, and maritime parts of the ſame and adjoining to them whatſoever, according to the ordinances and ſtatutes of our High Court of Admiralty in England.

And

And we do hereby remit and grant unto you the aforefaid A. B. our power and authority in and throughout our province of F—— aforementioned, and the territories depending thereon, and maritime parts whatfoever of the fame and thereto adjacent, and alfo throughout all and every the fea-fhores, public ftreams, ports, frefh water rivers, creeks, and arms, as well of the fea as of the rivers and coafts whatfoever of our faid Province of F——, and the territories depending thereon, and maritime parts whatfoever of the fame and thereto adjacent, as well within liberties and franchifes, as without; to take cognizance of, and proceed in, all civil and maritime caufes, and in complaints, contracts, offences, or fufpected offences, crimes, pleas, debts, exchanges, accounts, charter-parties, agreements, fuits, trefpaffes, injuries, extortions, and demands, and bufinefs civil and maritime whatfoever, commenced or to be commenced between merchants, or between owners and proprietors of fhips and other veffels, and merchants or others whomfoever, with fuch owners and proprietors of fhips and all other veffels whatfoever, employed or ufed within the maritime jurifdiction of our Vice Admiralty of our faid Province of F——, and the territories depending thereon, or between any other perfons whomfoever, had, made, begun, or contracted for any matter, thing, caufe, or bufinefs whatfoever, done or to be done within our maritime jurifdiction aforefaid, together with all and fingular their incidents, emergencies, dependencies, annexed or connexed caufes whatfoever or howfoever, and fuch caufes, complaints, contracts, and other the premifes above faid, or any of them, which may happen to arife, be contracted, had or done, to hear and determine according

cording to the rights, ſtatutes, laws, ordinances. and cuſtoms anciently obſerved.

And moreover, in all and ſingular complaints, contracts, agreements, cauſes, and buſineſſes civil and maritime, to be performed beyond the ſea, or contracted there, howſoever ariſing or happening: and alſo in all and ſingular other cauſes and matters, which in any manner whatſoever touch or any way concern, or anciently have and do, or ought to belong unto the maritime juriſdiction of our aforeſaid Vice-Admiralty in our ſaid Province of F——, and the territories depending thereon, and maritime parts thereof, and to the ſame adjoining whatſoever; and generally, in all and ſingular all other cauſes, ſuits, crimes, offences, exceſſes, injuries, complaints, miſdemeanors, or ſuſpected miſdemeanors, treſpaſſes, regrating, foreſtalling, and maritime buſineſſes whatſoever, throughout the places aforeſaid, within the maritime juriſdiction of our Vice Admiralty of our Province of F—— aforeſaid, and the territories depending thereon by ſea or water, on the banks or ſhores of the ſame howſoever done, committed, perpetrated or happening.

And alſo to enquire by the oaths of honeſt and lawful men of our ſaid Province of F——, and the territories depending thereon, and maritime parts of the ſame and adjoining to them whatſoever, dwelling both within liberties and franchiſes and without, as well of all and ſingular ſuch matters and things, which of right, and by the ſtatutes, laws, ordinances, and the cuſtoms anciently obſerved were wont and ought to be enquired after, as of wreck of the ſea, and of all and ſingular the goods and chattels of whatſoever traitors, pirates, manſlayers, and felons howſoever offending within the maritime juriſdiction of our Vice-

Vice-Admiralty of our Province of F—— aforementioned, and the territories depending thereon, and of the goods, chattels, and debts of all and ſingular their maintainers, acceſſaries, councillors, abettors, or aſſiſtants whomſoever.

And alſo of the goods, debts, and chattels of whatſoever perſon or perſons, felons of themſelves, by what means, or howſoever coming to their death within our aforeſaid maritime juriſdiction, whereſoever any ſuch goods, debts, and chattels, or any part thereof, by ſea, water, or land in our ſaid Province of F——, and the territories depending thereon, and maritime parts of the ſame and thereto adjacent whatſoever, as well within liberties and franchiſes as without, have been or ſhall be found forfeited, or to be forfeited, or in being.

And moreover, as well of the goods, debts, and chattels, of whatſoever other traitors, felons, and manſlayers whereſoever offending, and of the goods, debts, and chattels of their maintainers, acceſſaries, counſellors, abettors, or aſſiſtants, as of the goods, debts, or chattels of all fugitives, perſons convicted, attainted, condemned, outlawed, or howſoever put or to be put in exigent for treaſon, felony, manſlaughter, or murder, or any other offence or crime whatſoever; and alſo concerning goods waived, flotſon, jetſon, lagon, ſhares and treaſure found or to be found; deodands, and of the goods of all others whatſoever taken or to be taken, as derelict, or by chance found, or howſoever due or to be due; and of all other caſualties, as well in, upon, or by the ſea and ſhores, creeks or coaſts of the ſea, or maritime parts, as in, upon, or by all freſh waters, ports, public ſtreams, rivers, or creeks, or places overflown whatſoever, within the ebbing and

and flowing of the ſea or highwater, or upon the ſhores and banks of any of the ſame within our maritime juriſdiction aforeſaid, howſoever, whenſoever, or by what means ſoever ariſing, happening or proceeding, or whereſoever ſuch goods, debts, and chattels, or other the premiſes, or any parcel thereof may or ſhall happen to be met with, or found within our maritime juriſdiction aforeſaid.

And alſo concerning anchorage, laſtage, and ballaſt of ſhips, and of fiſhes royal, namely ſturgeons, whales, porpoiſes, dolphins, kiggs, and grampuſſes, and generally of all other fiſhes whatſoever, which are of a great or very large bulk or fatneſs, anciently by right or cuſtom, or any way appertaining or belonging to us.

And to aſk, require, levy, take, collect, receive, and obtain for the uſe of us, and to the office of our High Admiral of Great Britain aforeſaid for the time being, to keep and preſerve the ſaid wreck of the ſea, and the goods, debts, and chattels of all and ſingular other the premiſes; together with all and all manner of fines, mulcts, iſſues, forfeitures, amerciaments, ranſoms, and recognizances whatſoever forfeited or to be forfeited, and pecuniary puniſhments for treſpaſſes, crimes, injuries, extortions, contempts, and other miſdemeanors whatſoever, howſoever impoſed or inflicted, or to be impoſed or inflicted for any matter, cauſe, or thing whatſoever in our ſaid Province of F——, and the territories depending thereon, and maritime parts of the ſame and thereto adjoining, in any Court of our Admiralty there held or to be held, preſented or to be preſented, aſſeſſed, brought, forfeited, or adjudged; and alſo all amerciaments, iſſues, fines, perquiſites, mulcts, and pecuniary puniſhments

what-

whatſoever, and forfeitures of all manner of recognizances, before you or your Lieutenant, Deputy or Deputies in our ſaid Province of F——, and the territories depending thereon, and maritime parts of the ſame and thereto adjacent whatſoever, happening or impoſed, or to be impoſed or inflicted, or by any means aſſeſſed, preſented, forfeited, or adjudged, or howſoever by reaſon of the premiſes, due or to be due in that behalf to us, or to our heirs and ſucceſſors.

And further to take all manner of recognizances, cautions, obligations, and ſtipulations, as well to our uſe, as at the inſtance of any parties, for agreements or debts, or other cauſes whatſoever, and to put the ſame into execution, and to cauſe and command them to be executed; and alſo to arreſt, and cauſe and command to be arreſted, according to the civil and maritime laws, and ancient cuſtoms of our ſaid court, all ſhips, perſons, things, goods, wares, and merchandiſes, for the premiſes and every of them, and for other cauſes whatſoever concerning the ſame, whereſoever they ſhall be met with, or found throughout our ſaid Province of F——, and the territories depending thereon, and maritime parts thereof and thereto adjoining, as well within liberties and franchiſes as without; and likewiſe for all other agreements, cauſes, or debts, howſoever contracted or ariſing, ſo that the Goods or perſons may be found within our juriſdiction aforeſaid.

And to hear, examine, diſcuſs, and finally determine the ſame, with their emergencies, dependencies, incidents, annexed and connexed cauſes and buſineſſes whatſoever; together with all other cauſes, civil and maritime, and complaints, contracts, and all and every the reſpective premiſes

premiſes whatſoever above expreſſed, according to the laws and cuſtoms aforeſaid, and by all other lawful ways, means, and methods, according to the beſt of your ſkill and knowledge.

And to compel all manner of perſons in that behalf, as the caſe ſhall require, to appear and to anſwer, with power of uſing any temporal correction, and of inflicting any other penalty or mulct, according to the laws and cuſtoms aforeſaid.

And to do and adminiſter juſtice, according to the right order and courſe of law, ſummarily and plainly, looking only into the truth of the facts.

And to fine, correct, puniſh, chaſtiſe, reform, and to impriſon, and cauſe and command to be impriſoned in any gaols, being within our Province of F—— aforeſaid, and the territories depending thereon, the parties guilty, and the contemners of the law and juriſdiction of our Admiralty aforeſaid, and violators, uſurpers, delinquents and contumacious abſenters, maſters of ſhips, mariners, rowers, fiſhermen, ſhipwrights, and other workmen and artificers whatſoever exerciſing any kind of maritime affairs, according to the rights, ſtatutes, laws, and ordinances, and cuſtoms anciently obſerved; and to deliver and abſolutely diſcharge, and cauſe and command to be diſcharged, whatſoever perſons impriſoned in ſuch caſes, who are to be delivered.

And to preſerve, or cauſe to be preſerved, the public ſtreams, ports, rivers, freſh waters and creeks whatſoever, within our maritime juriſdiction aforeſaid, in what place ſoever they be in our Province of F—— aforeſaid, and the territories depending thereon, and maritime parts of the ſame and thereto adjacent whatſoever, as well for the preſervation of our navy royal, and of the

fleets

fleets and veſſels of our kingdom and dominions aforeſaid, as of whatſoever fiſhes increaſing in the rivers and places aforeſaid.

And alſo to keep, and cauſe to be executed and kept, in our ſaid Province of F——, and the territories depending thereon, and maritime parts thereof and thereto adjacent whatſoever, the rights, ſtatutes, laws, ordinances and cuſtoms anciently obſerved.

And to do, exerciſe, expedite, and execute all and ſingular other things in the premiſes, and every of them, as they by right, and according to the laws and ſtatutes, ordinances, and cuſtoms aforeſaid ſhould be done.

And moreover to reform nets too cloſe, and other unlawful engines or inſtruments whatſoever for the catching of fiſhes whereſoever, by ſea, or public ſtreams, ports, rivers, freſh waters, or creeks whatſoever, throughout our Province of F—— aforeſaid, and the territories depending thereon, and maritime parts of the ſame and thereto adjacent, uſed or exerciſed, within our maritime juriſdiction aforeſaid whereſoever.

And to puniſh and correct the exerciſers and occupiers thereof, according to the ſtatutes, laws, ordinances, and cuſtoms aforeſaid.

And to pronounce, promulge, and interpoſe all manner of ſentences and decrees, and to put the ſame in execution; with cognizance and juriſdiction of whatſoever other cauſes, civil and maritime, which relate to the ſea, or which any manner of ways reſpect or concern the ſea, or paſſage over the ſame, or naval or maritime voyages, or our ſaid maritime juriſdiction, or the places or limits of our ſaid Admiralty and cognizance aforementioned, and all other things done, or to be done.

With

With power alſo to proceed in the ſame, according to the ſtatutes, laws, ordinances, and cuſtoms aforeſaid, anciently uſed, as well of mere office mixed or promoted, as at the inſtance of any party, as the caſe ſhall require and ſeem convenient: and likewiſe with cognizance and deciſion of wreck of the ſea, and of the death, drowning, and view of dead bodies of all perſons howſoever killed or drowned, or murdered, or which ſhall happen to be killed, drowned or murdered, or by any other means come to their death, in the ſea, or public ſtreams, ports, freſh waters, or creeks whatſoever, within the flowing of the ſea and high-water mark, throughout our aforeſaid Province of F——, and the territories depending thereon, and maritime parts of the ſame, and thereto adjacent, or elſewhere within our maritime juriſdiction aforeſaid.

Together with the cognizance of Mayhem in the aforeſaid places, within our maritime juriſdiction aforeſaid, and flowing of the ſea and water there happening; with power alſo of puniſhing all delinquents in that kind, according to the exigencies of the law and cuſtoms aforeſaid.

And to do, exerciſe, expedite, and execute all and ſingular other things, which in and about the premiſſes only ſhall be neceſſary or thought meet, according to the rights, ſtatutes, laws, ordinances, and cuſtoms aforeſaid.

With power of deputing and ſurrogating in your place for the premiſſes, one or more deputy or deputies, as often as you ſhall think fit; and alſo with power from time to time of naming, appointing, ordaining, aſſigning, making, and conſtituting whatſoever other neceſſary, fit, and convenient Officers and Miniſters under you, for the ſaid office, and execution thereof in our ſaid Province

vince of F——, and the territories depending thereon, and maritime parts of the ſame, and thereto adjacent whatſoever.

Saving always the right of our High Court of Admiralty of England, and alſo of the Judge and Regiſter of the ſaid Court, from whom or either of them, it is not our intention in any thing to derogate by theſe preſents; and ſaving to every one who ſhall be wronged or grieved by any definitive ſentence or interlocutory decree, which ſhall be given in the Vice-Admiralty Court of our Province of F—— aforeſaid, and the territories depending thereon, the right of appealing to our aforeſaid High Court of Admiralty of England.

Provided neverthelefs, and under this expreſs condition, that if you the aforeſaid A. B. our Captain-General and Governor in Chief, ſhall not yearly, to wit, at the end of every year, between the feaſt of Saint Michael the Archangel and All Saints, duly certify, and cauſe to be effectually certified (if you ſhall be thereunto required) to us, and our Lieutenant Official, Principals, and Commiſſary-General and Special, and Judge and Preſident of the High Court of our Admiralty of England aforeſaid, all that which from time to time, by virtue of theſe preſents, you ſhall do and execute, collect or receive in the premiſſes, or any of them, together with your full and faithful account thereupon, to be made in an authentic form, and ſealed with the Seal of our Office, remaining in your cuſtody, that from thence, and after default therein, theſe our Letters Patent of the Office of Vice-Amiralty aforeſaid, as above granted, ſhall be null and void, and of no force or effect.

Further

Further we do, in our name, command all and singular our Governors, Justices, Mayors, Sheriffs, Captains, Marshals, Bailiffs, Keepers of all our Gaols and Prisons, Constables, and all other our Officers and faithful Liege Subjects whatsoever, and every of them, as well within liberties and franchises as without, that in and about the execution of the premisses, and every of them, they be aiding, favouring, assisting, submissive, and yield obedience, in all things as is fitting to you, the aforesaid A. B. our Captain-General and Governor in Chief of our Province of F—— aforesaid, and to your Deputy whomsoever, and to all other Officers by you appointed, and to be appointed, of our said Vice-Admiralty of F—, aforesaid, and the territories depending thereon, and maritime parts of the same, and thereto adjoining, under pain of the law, and the peril which will fall thereon.

Given at London in the High Court of our Admiralty of England aforesaid, under the Great Seal thereof, the first day of January, in the year of our Lord 1783, and of our reign the * twenty-third.

(Signed) GODF. LEE TARRANT, Registrar.

The Commission of Captain-General and Governor in Chief, &c. is, in the first place, to be inrolled in the High Court of Chancery;—it is then to be recorded in the Treasury Chambers at Whitehall;—and lastly, in the Secretary's Office of that Province over which the Governor is appointed to preside.—The Commission of Vice-Admiral is to be registered in the High Court of

* This date is arbitrary, there being no Commission of a Vice-Amiral of that year.

Admiralty

Admiralty in England; and in the Secretary's Office of the Province in which the Governor is appointed Vice-Admiral.

A Governor, on his arrival in the Province over which he is appointed to command, muſt (agreeable to the directions of his commiſſion and inſtructions) in the firſt place, cauſe his commiſſion of Captain-General and Governor in Chief, &c. and alſo of Vice-Admiral, to be read and publiſhed at the firſt meeting of the Council, and alſo in ſuch other manner as hath been uſually obſerved on like occaſions;—in the next place, he muſt take the oaths to Government, and adminiſter the ſame to each of the Council, and then he muſt make and ſubſcribe, and cauſe the Members of the Council to make and ſubſcribe, the declaration againſt tranſubſtantiation;—he muſt then take the oath uſually taken by the Governors in the Plantations, for the due execution of the office and truſt of Captain-General and Governor in Chief in and over the Province to which he is appointed, and for the due and impartial adminiſtration of juſtice there, and he muſt alſo cauſe the oath of office to be adminiſtered to the Members of the Council;—in the laſt place, he muſt take the oath (required to be taken by Governors of the Plantations) to do his utmoſt that the ſeveral laws relating to trade and the Plantations be duly obſerved;—which oaths and declaration the Council of the Province, or any three of the Members thereof, are empowered to adminiſter.—It is alſo uſual for a Governor, when he enters on his office, to iſſue a proclamation for continuing all perſons in their employments, until further order.

OATH

OATH *of* ALLEGIANCE *by the* 1 Geo. I. *st.* 2. *c.* 13.

I A. B. do sincerely promise and swear, that I will be faithful, and bear true allegiance to his Majesty King George: So help me God.

OATH *of* SUPREMACY, *by the* 1 Geo. I. *st.* 2. *c.* 13.

I A. B. do swear, That I do from my heart abhor, detest and abjure, as impious and heretical, that damnable doctrine and position, that Princes excommunicated or deprived by the Pope, or any authority of the See of Rome, may be deposed or murdered by their subjects, or any other whatsoever. And I do declare, That no foreign Prince, Person, Prelate, State, or Potentate, hath, or ought to have any jurisdiction, power, superiority, pre-eminence, or authority, ecclesiastical or spiritual, within this realm: So help me God.

OATH *of* ABJURATION, *by the* 6 Geo. III. *c.* 53.

I A. B. do truly and sincerely acknowledge, profess, testify and declare in my conscience, before God and the world, That our sovereign Lord King George is lawful and rightful King of this realm, and all other his Majesty's dominions and countries thereunto belonging. And I do solemnly and sincerely declare, That I do believe in my conscience, that not any of the descendants of the person who pretended to be Prince of Wales, during the life of the late King James the Second, and since his decease pretended to be, and took upon himself the style and title of King of England, by the name of James the Third, or of Scotland by the name of James the Eighth, or the style and title of King of Great Britain, hath any right

right or title whatſoever to the Crown of this realm, or any other the dominions thereunto belonging: and I do renounce, refuſe and abjure any allegiance or obedience to any of them. And I do ſwear, That I will bear faith and true allegiance to his Majeſty King George, and him will defend, to the utmoſt of my power, againſt all traiterous conſpiracies and attempts whatſoever, which ſhall be made againſt his Perſon, Crown or dignity. And I will do my utmoſt endeavour to diſcloſe and make known to his Majeſty, and his ſucceſſors, all treaſons and traiterous conſpiracies, which I ſhall know to be againſt him or any of them. And I do faithfully promiſe, to the utmoſt of my power, to ſupport, maintain and defend, the ſucceſſion of the Crown againſt the deſcendants of the ſaid James, and againſt all other perſons whatſoever; which ſucceſſion, by an Act, intituled, An Act for the further limitation of the Crown, and better ſecuring the rights and liberties of the ſubject, is and ſtands limited to the Princeſs Sophia, Electreſs and Dutcheſs Dowager of Hanover, and the heirs of her body, being Proteſtants. And all theſe things I do plainly and ſincerely acknowledge and ſwear, according to theſe expreſs words by me ſpoken, and according to the plain common ſenſe and underſtanding of the ſame words, without any equivocation, mental evaſion, or ſecret reſervation whatſoever. And I do make this recognition, acknowledgment, abjuration, renunciation, and promiſe heartily, willingly, and truly, upon the true faith of a Chriſtian: So help me God.

DECLARATION *against* TRANSUBSTANTIATION, *by the* 25 C. II. *c.* 2. *s.* 9.

I A. B. do declare, That I do believe that there is not any transubstantiation in the Sacrament of the Lord's Supper, or in the elements of bread and wine, at or after the consecration thereof by any person whatsoever.

OATH *of a* GOVERNOR, *for the due Execution of his Office.*

You do swear, That you will faith and true allegiance bear unto his most Sacred Majesty King George the Third, and to his heirs and successors, and that you will well and truly execute the office and trust of Captain-General and Governor in Chief in and over the Province of F——, according to the best of your skill and knowledge, and according to the power to you granted by virtue of his Majesty's Letters Patent, bearing date at Westminster the 1st day of January, in the 23d year of his said Majesty's reign: So help you God.

By 12 Car. II. c. 18. intituled, An Act for the encouraging and increasing of shipping and navigation, s. 2. it is enacted, That all Governors of Plantations shall, before their entrance into their government, take a solemn oath, to do their utmost that all the matters and things in that Act contained, shall be punctually and *bona fide* observed, according to the true intent and meaning thereof; and if any Governor shall be willingly negligent in doing his duty accordingly, he shall be removed from his government.

By 15 Car. II. c. 7. intituled, An Act for the encouragement of trade, s. 8. it is enacted, That all Governors or Commanders of Plantations, &c. shall,

ſhall, before their entrance upon the execution of ſuch truſt or charge, take a ſolemn oath, before ſuch perſon or perſons as ſhall be authoriſed by his Majeſty to adminiſter the ſame, to do their utmoſt within their reſpective governments or commands, to cauſe that Act to be truly obſerved, in relation to the trade of ſuch Plantations, &c. under penalty of being removed out of their governments and commands;—and if any of them ſhall be found to have willingly offended, contrary to what by that Act is required of them, they ſhall be turned out of their governments, and be uncapable of the government of any other Plantations, &c. and forfeit *L.* 1000; half to the King, and half to him that will ſue for the ſame in any of the Plantations, or in any Court of Record in England.

By 7 & 8 Wil. III. c. 22. intituled, An Act for preventing frauds, and regulating abuſes in the Plantation trade, ſ. 4. it is enacted, That all Governors and Commanders in Chief of Engliſh Colonies or Plantations, before their entrance into their government, ſhall take a ſolemn oath, to do their utmoſt that all the clauſes, matters, and things contained in that Act, and the Acts therein recited, relating to the ſaid Colonies and Plantations, be punctually and *bona fide* obſerved, according to the true intent and meaning thereof, (which oath ſhall be taken before ſuch perſon or perſons as his Majeſty ſhall appoint); and upon complaint and proof, made by the oath of two or more credible witneſſes, that any Governors or Commanders in Chief have neglected to take the ſaid oath at the times aforeſaid, or have been willingly negligent in doing their duty accordingly, the Governor ſo neglecting or offending, ſhall be removed from his government, and forfeit *L.* 1000.

And by 8 & 9 Wil. III. c. 20. ſ. 69, all Governors and Commanders in Chief of any Engliſh Colonies or Plantations ſhall, at their entrance upon their reſpective governments, or within the ſpace of ſix months after the ſame, take a ſolemn oath to do their utmoſt, that all the clauſes, matters, and things contained in the Acts of Parliament therein recited, or any of them theretofore paſſed, and then in force, relating to the ſaid Colonies and Plantations, ſhould be punctually and *bona fide* obſerved, according to the true intent and meaning thereof (which oath ſhall be taken before ſuch perſon or perſons as ſhall be appointed by his Majeſty, his heirs or ſucceſſors, who are thereby authoriſed to adminiſter the ſame), ſo far as appertains to the Governors or Commanders in Chief reſpectively.

See alſo 4 Geo. III. c. 15. intituled, An Act for granting certain duties in the Britiſh Colonies and Plantations in America, &c. ſ. 39; which ſection (after reciting the 4th ſection of the 7 & 8 Wil. III. c. 22. relative to Governors of Plantations, which 4th ſection is herein before recited) enacts, That all Governors or Commanders in Chief of any Britiſh Colony or Plantation ſhall, before their entrance into their government, take a ſolemn oath, to do their utmoſt that all the clauſes, matters, and things contained in any Act of Parliament theretofore made, and then in force, relating to the ſaid Colonies and Plantations; and that all and every the clauſes contained in that Act ſhould be punctually and *bona fide* obſerved, according to the true intent and meaning thereof; ſo far as appertains unto the ſaid Governors or Commanders in Chief reſpectively, under the like penalties, forfeitures, and diſabilities, either for neglecting to take the ſaid oath, or for wittingly

tingly neglecting to do their duty accordingly, as are mentioned and expressed in the said Act of the 7 & 8 Wil. III.; and that the oath thereby required to be taken, shall be administered by such person or persons as had been, or should be, appointed to administer the oath required to be taken by the 7 & 8 Wil. III.

The OATH *to be taken by every Governor and Commander in Chief of any Colony or Plantation, to do his utmost that all Acts of Parliament, relating to the Colonies and Plantations be punctually observed.*

You do swear, That you will, to the best of your skill and power, so long as you shall continue in the government and command of his Majesty's Province of F——, well and truly execute and perform all matters and things which, by the statute made in the 12th year of the reign of King Charles the Second, intituled, An Act for the encouraging and increasing of shipping and navigation; and the other statute made in the 15th year of his said Majesty's reign, intituled, An Act for the encouragement of trade; and also the Act made in the 7th & 8th years of the reign of his late Majesty King William, intituled, An Act for preventing frauds, and regulating abuses in the Plantation trade; and also all other Acts which have been made, and are in force, for the better regulating and securing the Plantation trade, you are required, as Captain-General and Governor in Chief of the said Province, to be sworn to the performance of: So help you God.

Every Governor of a Colony, together with his commission, receives a large body of instructions, a copy of which I have by me, but the whole are too voluminous to be inſerted here: nor does the Editor chuſe to publiſh them all, unleſs (in caſe of another Edition of this Work) he obtains leave from Government to inſert them therein at length.

Every Governor of a Province, by his commiſſion of Captain-General and Governor in Chief, and by his commiſſion of Vice-Admiral, and the inſtructions which accompany them, is veſted with the following powers:

1. He is Captain-General of the forces by ſea and land within his Province; and where a Provincial Eſtabliſhment or King's Government joined a Charter-Colony, it was uſual to make the Governor of the Provincial Eſtabliſhment Captain-General of the forces by ſea and land within ſuch Charter-Colony, as I have already obſerved. The Governor has alſo the appointment of all Militia Officers.

2. As Governor in Chief, he is one of the conſtituent parts of the General Aſſembly of his Province, and has the ſole power of convening, adjourning, proroguing, and diſſolving the General Aſſembly; he may alſo give or refuſe his aſſent to any bill which has paſſed the Council and Aſſembly. The Governor has alſo the diſpoſal of ſuch employments as his Majeſty does not diſpoſe of himſelf; and with reſpect to ſuch offices as are uſually filled by the immediate appointment of his Majeſty, if vacancies happen by death or removal, the Governor appoints to ſuch offices until they are filled up from home; and the perſons appointed by the Governor receive all the profits and emoluments of ſuch offices, until they are ſuperſeded by the King's appointment of others.

3. The

3. The Governor has the cuſtody of the Great Seal, and is Chancellor within his Province, with the ſame powers of judicature that the Lord High Chancellor has in England.

4. The Governor is Ordinary within his Province; and by virtue of the King's Commiſſion, he collates to all vacant Benefices: he hath alſo the power of granting Probate of Wills, and Adminiſtration of Inteſtates Effects, by virtue of his inſtructions.

5. The Governor preſides in the Court of Errors, of which he and the Council are Judges, to hear and determine all appeals, in the nature of Writs of Error, from the Superior Courts of Common Law in the Province.

6. The Governor is uſually named firſt in the ſtanding commiſſion, iſſued under the 11 & 12 Wil. III. c. 7. for the more effectual ſuppreſſion of piracy.

7. The Governor is alſo Vice-Admiral within his Province; but he does not ſit in the Court of Vice-Admiralty, there being a Judge of that Court, who is uſually appointed from England. —In time of war, commiſſions to privateers are iſſued by the Judge of the Court of Vice-Admiralty, in conſequence of a warrant from the Governors.

1. As to the office of Captain-General—the Governor, as Captain-General of the forces by ſea and land, had formerly the command, not only of the militia, but alſo of all the regular forces within his Province; and every Weſt India Governor has at preſent the command of the militia, and alſo of the regulars within the Iſland, unleſs a General Officer is on the ſpot; but it was found neceſſary to take away, in a great meaſure, from the Governors on the Continent, the command

command of ſuch regular forces as might happen to be within their reſpective Provinces, and to appoint a Commander in Chief of all the regular forces in the Britiſh Colonies on the Continent of America, independent of every Provincial Governor; in order (as it is ſuppoſed) that ſuch Commander in Chief of the forces might, in caſe of an Indian war, or a foreign invaſion, be able to collect his Majeſty's troops together, to defend that part of the Continent which was attacked by the enemy. Had the command of the King's forces been continued in the Provincial Governors, each of whom was Commander in Chief in his own Province, there would have been no ſuperior to direct the removal of the regulars to that part of the Continent which was attacked by, or in danger from an enemy; or the Governors of thoſe Provinces under whoſe juriſdiction the regular forces happened to be, might, from an affectation of importance, from diſputes between them, or from an ill-founded apprehenſion of danger to their own Provinces, prevent the troops from marching to thoſe places where his Majeſty's ſervice required their preſence. However, all Provincial Governors have yet the command of the militia within their reſpective Provinces, and the appointment of all Militia Officers.

And with reſpect to the regulars before the Civil War, where the Commander in Chief of the forces, or Brigadier-General of the diſtrict, had given no ſpecific orders, the Civil Governor might have interfered in ſuch inſtances as are ſet forth in his Majeſty's orders, which follow, viz.

His

His Majesty's Orders, *ascertaining the Power and Authority of the Civil Governors over his Majesty's forces stationed in the respective Provinces in North America.*

His Majesty's intentions are, that according to his commissions granted for that purpose, the orders of his Commander in Chief, and under him of the Brigadiers General, commanding in the Northern and Southern Departments, in all military affairs, shall be supreme, and must be obeyed by the troops as such, in all the Civil Governments in America.

That, in cases where no specific orders have been given by the Commander in Chief, or by the Brigadier-General commanding in the district, the Civil Governor in Council, and where no Council shall subsist, the Civil Governor may, for the benefit of his government, give orders for the marching of troops, the disposition of them, for making and marching detachments, escorts, and such purely military services within his government, to the Commanding Officer of the troops, who is to give proper orders for carrying the same into execution; provided they are not contradictory to, or incompatible with, any orders he may have received from the Commander in Chief, or the Brigadier General of the district.

And the Commanding Officer is, from time to time, duly to report, with all convenient expedition, to the Commander in Chief, or to the Brigadier General, such orders as he shall have received from the Civil Governor.

That the Civil Governor shall give the word, in all places where he shall be within his Province, except where the Commander in Chief, or Brigadier-General, shall be in the same place.

That

That the return of the ſtate and condition of of the troops, magazines, and fortifications, ſhall be made to the Governors, as well as to the Commander in Chief and Brigadier-General.

That the Civil Government is not to interfere with the detail of the military regimental duty and diſcipline; the reports concerning which are to be made to the commanding Officer, who is to make his general report to the Civil Governor.

When the Commander in Chief or Brigadier-General ſhall be preſent, all military orders are to be iſſued by them only.

On the eſtabliſhment of the Staff of the Army in North America, it became neceſſary to ſettle the rank and precedency of the Officers of the Army, and of the Governors and Commanders in Chief of Provinces: which eſtabliſhment, before the Civil War, was as follows:

RANK *and* PRECEDENCY *of the Commander in Chief of his Majeſty's forces, Governors, Lieutenant Governors, and Commanders in Chief of his Majeſty's Provinces, Colonels, and other Field Officers of his Majeſty's troops in North America, as eſtabliſhed by the King, under his royal Sign Manual. Given at St. James's, December 17th* 1760.

GEORGE. R.

1. The Commander in Chief of our forces, by Commiſſion under our Great Seal of Great Britain.

2. Captains General and Governors in Chief of our Provinces and Colonies, when in their reſpective governments, as appointed by Commiſſion under our Great Seal of Great Britain.

3. General Officers upon the Staff.

4. Captains-General and Governors in Chief of our Provinces and Colonies, when out of their reſpective governments.

5. Lieu-

5. Lieutenant-Governors and Prefidents of Council, when Commanders in Chief of our Provinces and Colonies, in their refpective governments.

6. Colonels.

7. Lieutenant-Governors and Prefidents of Council, when Commanders in Chief of our Provinces and Colonies, out of their refpective governments.

8. Lieutenant-Governors of our Provinces and Colonies, not being Commanders in Chief, in their refpective governments.

9. Lieutenant-Governors of our Provinces and Colonies, not being Commanders in Chief, out of their refpective governments.

10. Governors of Charter Colonies, when in their refpective Colonies.

11. All Field Officers under the rank of Colonels.

12. Lieutenant-Governors of Proprietary Governments, out of their refpective governments.

13. Governors of Charter Colonies, out of their refpective Colonies.

All Captains-General and Governors in Chief of our Provinces and Colonies, to take rank according to the dates of their Commiffions.

All Lieutenant-Governors of our Provinces, the fame.

All Lieutenant-Governors of Proprietary Governments, the fame.

Governors of Charter-Colonies according to the date of their Charters.

It may not be improper to infert in this place the rules of precedence between men and women in America.

RULES *of* PRECEDENCY *compared and adjusted from the several Acts and Statutes made and provided in England, for the Settlement of the Precedency of* MEN *and* WOMEN *in* AMERICA. *By Joseph Edmonson Mowbray, Herald.*

Governor of the Province,	His Wife.
Lieutenant Governor,	His Wife.
President of the Council,	His Wife.
Members of his Majesty's Council,	Their Wives.
Speaker of the Commons House of Assembly,	His Wife.
Chief Justice,	His Wife.
Treasurer,	His Wife.
Associate Judges,	Their Wives.
Baronets,	Their Wives.
His Majesty's Attorney General,	His Wife.
Judge of the Admiralty,	His Wife.
Secretary of the Province,	His Wife.
Members of the Commons House of Assembly,	Their Wives.
Mayor,	His Wife.
Aldermen,	Their Wives.
Members of the Corporation,	Their Wives.

The Members of the Assembly, Crown Officers, &c. of any particular Province, have no other rank out of their Province, than what belongs to them in their private capacity as men.

The Widow of a late Governor has not any precedency as such.

A Governor of one Province, or his Wife, coming into another Province, have not, in that Province where they visit, any precedency above their rank in private life.

2dly, As Governor in Chief, the Governor of every Provincial Establishment, hath the sole power of convening, adjourning, proroguing, and dissolving

diſſolving the General Aſſembly, and neither Houſe of Aſſembly could adjourn itſelf longer than from Saturday to Monday. But ſee more on this head in Chap. 7.

3dly, The Governor has the cuſtody of the Great Seal: and in moſt of the Colonies he (or in caſe of his death or abſence from the government, the Commander in Chief for the time being) is ſole Chancellor; but in the Iſlands of Barbadoes, Antigua, and Montſerrat, in the Weſt Indies, the Council ſit as Judges in the Court of Chancery with the Governor; however the Chancery Proceſs is iſſued by the Governor, and teſted in his name. In South Carolina, alſo before the Civil War, the Council ſat as Judges with the Governor in the Court of Chancery.

The proceedings in Chancery in the Colonies, are ſimilar to thoſe of the High Court of Chancery in England; and the books of practice uſed in England, govern the practice of the Chancery in the Colonies, except in a few trifling inſtances, which are varied, according to the local circumſtances of the Colonies.

In the government of the Leeward Charibbee Iſlands, they have upwards of fifty rules and orders of practice in the High Court of Chancery, throughout thoſe Iſlands, moſt of which have been extracted from the books of practice in England, and are therefore not worth tranſcribing, except the 4th, which has been productive of ſo much miſchief, that I cannot avoid taking notice of it.

4. "That all ſervices of Subpœna's ſhall be on "the party himſelf, or left at his dwelling houſe "with one of his family, or at his place of re- "ſidence; or, if the party be off the Iſland, at his "laſt place of reſidence, if he, or ſhe hath no Attornies,

" Attornies, Agents, or Guardians; and if he " or ſhe hath any Attornies, Agents, or Guar- " dians, ſervice of Subpœna ſhall be good on " ſuch Attorney, Agent, or Guardian."

This rule has been conſtrued much to the injury of creditors, as will appear from the practice that has prevailed in thoſe Iſlands, which I ſhall exemplify, by ſtating a caſe that frequently happens.

A perſon formerly reſided for a ſhort time in one of the Leeward Charribbee Iſlands, but left it many years ago, and is ſettled in England. He has a juſt demand againſt an inhabitant of one of the Leeward Iſlands, and ſends out a power of Attorney, in order to enable ſome perſon there to proceed at common law for the recovery of ſuch debt: the Attorney accordingly does proceed; and the debtor has no defence to make; but, for the purpoſe of gaining time, he files a Bill in Chancery againſt the Plaintiff at Law, cauſes a copy of the Subpœna to be left at his laſt place of abode, and then procures the perſon, who ſerved it, to make affidavit, that he left a copy of ſuch Subpœna at the laſt place of abode of the creditor; although perhaps ſuch creditor left the Iſland a dozen years before, and the debt has been recently contracted. The Plaintiff at Law being in England, cannot put in an anſwer by the time preſcribed by the rules of the Court; and whether proceſs of contempt iſſues, or a *dedimus* is prayed to take his anſwer; in either caſe, an injunction goes, and the Plaintiff at Law is kept out of his juſt debt for a long time.

Some merchants and tradeſmen in England will remember this practice, to their ſorrow.

The Chancery Proceſs in the Colonies, is copied from the Proceſs of the High Court of Chan-

cery

cery in England, except that the Subpœna is made returnable immediately; and, in case of a contempt, the Plaintiff (when a commission of rebellion is returned *non est inventus*) proceeds to sequestration, without an order for a Serjeant at Arms.

In drawing a bill in Chancery in the Colonies, at the top of the Bill, on the left hand, you mention the name of the Island or Province, thus:

Antigua in Chancery, }

or

Nova Scotia in Chancery. }

At the top of the Bill, on the right hand, you direct the Bill thus:

> To his Excellency George Thomas, Esq; Captain General and Governor in Chief in and over all his Majesty's Leeward Charibbee Islands in America, and Chancellor, Vice Admiral, and Ordinary of the same.

Or, if it is in a Province on the Continent, thus:

> To his Excellency A. B. Esq; Captain General and Governor in Chief in and over his Majesty's Province of Nova Scotia, and Chancellor, Vice Admiral, and Ordinary of the same.

You then begin the Bill, thus:

"Humbly complaining, sheweth unto your "Excellency, your Orator, &c."

And

And ſo proceed as in other caſes, uſing the words, " Your Excellency," inſtead of " Your " Lordſhip."

Before the Civil War, the ſtyle of a Governor of Virginia, was different from that of any other Governor, and was as follows:

" His Excellency John Earl of Dunmore, his " Majeſty's Lieutenant and Governor General of " the Colony and Dominion of Virginia, and " Vice Admiral of the ſame."

An appeal lies from the deciſion of a Court of Chancery in the Colonies, to his Majeſty in Council, provided the value of the property in diſpute exceeds five hundred pounds ſterling; but for further directions on this head, ſee title, Appeal.

If a Defendant in Chancery is litigious, he may occaſion great delay to the Plaintiff; for an appeal lies from an interlocutory order made by a Court of Chancery in the Colonies, to his Majeſty in Council; and ſo *toties quoties*; by which means, the Plaintiff may be kept out of his juſt demand many years.

When the Governor happens to be a Lawyer, the buſineſs is properly conducted. A Civilian was Governor of Barbadoes, and a common Lawyer of Georgia, for many years; during their adminiſtration, the government of thoſe Colonies was carried on with much reputation, and greatly to their credit. But when the Governor is not a Lawyer, he is generally under the influence of ſome Counſel or Attorney, who makes his decrees for him, and frequently directs every other act of government. If this tutor happens to be a man of integrity and abilities, the buſineſs goes on well; but if he is a raſh ignorant man, the Governor is led into many imprudent meaſures, and perhaps is recalled in diſgrace. I ſhall mention

tion ſome inſtances of inattention in Governors, which may ſerve as a caution to others.

When I was in the Weſt Indies, I ſaw a grant of lands in one of the Ceded Iſlands, in which the King was made to ſay, that he granted thoſe lands, "with the advice and *conſent* of the Go-"vernor," as if a Governor's conſent was neceſſary, to enable the King to grant away his own lands. I believe moſt of the grants in thoſe Iſlands run in that form.

A Governor in the Weſt Indies aſſented to an Act of Aſſembly for bringing down freſh water to the town of B———, &c. which Act was to be executed by the Council and Aſſembly; and amongſt other powers which they gave themſelves, was the following very extraordinary one, "That "where any doubt or difficulties ſhould ariſe, "touching the meaning or conſtruction of that "Act, or any defects ſhould appear in the powers "thereby inveſted in the Commiſſioners, the ſame "ſhould and might be explained, corrected, "amended, ſupplied, and enlarged, by any order "or declaration to be made, by the Council and "Aſſembly of that Iſland."

The Commiſſioners were the Council and Aſſembly; and this clauſe of the Act gave them a power of legiſlation independent of the Crown, and erected them into a Court of Judicature, by which means, the legiſlative and judiciary powers were united in the ſame body of men, and the Council and Aſſembly were rendered perfectly deſpotic with reſpect to the ſubject matter of that Act. I told the Governor that this Act would be diſallowed by the King; and ſo it turned out. In the laſt reign, a man was convicted of a capital crime in a Province on the Continent, and, agreeable to the uſual practice, a Rule of Court was made

made for his execution on a day certain: the Governor (who was a military man) ordered the Provoſt Marſhal to hang up the convict before the day appointed for his execution, which was accordingly done. The Governor was ſaid to be a well meaning man; but, perhaps, he might think, that as he had a power to reprieve, he had therefore a right to order the execution, whereas he was committing felony. 1 Hawkins P. C. 70.

Some military Governors, inſtead of taking the trouble to looſe the Gordian knot of the law, have cut it through with the ſword.

In Barbadoes, Antigua, Montſerrat, and South Carolina, it ſhould ſeem that the Governors aſſented to Acts of Aſſembly, to enable the Council to ſit as Judges in the Court of Chancery, without adverting to the conſequences of it. By an Act of Aſſembly in the Iſland of Antigua, made in the year 1715, reciting that by long experience, great corruptions, delays, and other inconveniencies, had been found by Courts of Chancery being held in that Iſland by one perſon; for preventing the like evils, and that the inhabitants of Antigua might be under the ſame regulation, and enjoy the ſame advantage that Barbadoes had for many years paſt, to the great encouragement of trade, and general ſatisfaction of all his Majeſty's good ſubjects in that Iſland, it was enacted, That from thenceforth all Courts of Chancery holden for the Iſland of Antigua, ſhould conſiſt of the Captain General or Governor in Chief of the ſaid Leeward Iſlands for the time being, and five or more of the Council of that Iſland, except where any Councillor happened to be a party, and then three Councillors ſhould be ſufficient.

Notwithſtanding this ſpecious recital, I am inclined to think that the making the Council in

Antigua

Antigua Judges in the Court of Chancery with the Governor, has been productive of several inconveniencies.

In those Islands where the Governor is sole Judge in Equity, and holds a Court of Chancery whenever he is applied to for that purpose, should an Advocate have occasion to make a motion in Chancery, he waits on the Governor, without any previous notice; and if a cause is to be heard, a short notice is sufficient, that the Governor may be in the way, and disengaged from other business. The Court of Chancery is therefore always open for those Islands, in which the Governor is sole Chancellor; but, in Antigua and Montserrat, five Councillors must be summoned, and attend, before a common motion can be made in the Chancery of that Island. And as the Governor seldom goes to Montserrat, and the Council there cannot hold a Court of Chancery without him, the inhabitants of that Island will labour under great inconveniencies, until the Act of Assembly respecting the Court of Chancery is repealed, and the Governor again becomes sole Chancellor of that Island.

Again, in general, a Governor has fewer connections in the country, and is less liable to influence than any one of the Council, who, for the most part, are natives. A gentleman, who has interest to get a government, must be a man of some character and distinction; he is responsible for his conduct, and has at stake the loss of office: when he sits alone (be his disposition what it may) he will hardly venture to commit any flagrant acts of injustice. But when a dozen Councillors are placed on the bench with him, *defendit numerus*; and, if they are inclined to do mischief, they keep each other in countenance; and there are thirteen to divide the censure amongst

amongst them. It very seldom happens, that either of these Councillors has been bred to the law; and a Governor can have little assistance, and the country little benefit from a dozen gentlemen being placed on the Chancery Bench, who know nothing of law. Besides, in such small countries as Barbadoes, Antigua, and Montserrat, scarce any cause can come on, in which all that sit on the bench are totally uninterested. Where the Governor is sole Chancellor, if any doubt arises in the progress of a cause, he may take time to consider what decree to make; but where the Council sit as Judges with him, I apprehend they generally decide off hand; for any doubt would occasion a fresh meeting.

One of the most extraordinary decisions I ever met with, was in the Court of Chancery in a Colony, where the Council sat as Judges with the Governor, and at a time when many of the Council sat on the bench.

A bill was filed, and a *ne exeat* obtained. The Defendant gave notice of motion to discharge the *ne exeat*; which being irregular, the Court seemed inclined to discharge it. The Plaintiff's Counsel, encouraged at this disposition in the Court, altered his application, and moved to dismiss the bill; which the Court ordered accordingly. Now I will not take upon me to say, that the case disclosed by the Plaintiff in his bill was sufficient to found a decree in his favour; nay, to place the conduct of the Council in the most favourable point of view, I will even admit that the bill would have been dismissed at the hearing: yet I apprehend, this was the first instance of a bill's being dismissed on a motion, for want of merits, without even a previous notice for that purpose, or the least pretence, that the Plaintiff had neglected to prosecute his cause ac-

cording

cording to the rules of the Court. Had the gentlemen of the Council looked into any common book of practice, they might have ſeen that a bill could not be diſmiſſed before hearing, unleſs for want of proſecution; or where the Plaintiff proceeded to ſue both at law and in equity for the ſame thing, and refuſed to make his election (in which Court he would proceed) within the time preſcribed by the Court. I muſt do the Governor the juſtice to ſay, that the matter was carried before it came to his turn to give his voice, and therefore he did not vote at all; and it ſeemed to me, that what he ſaid, did not tend to an approbation of what was done.

4. The Governor is ordinary within his Province; and by virtue of the King's Commiſſion, he collates to all vacant benefices. He hath alſo the power of granting probate of wills and adminiſtration of inteſtates effects, by virtue of his inſtructions.

I have not the laws of South Carolina by me; but in that Province, one of their Governors formerly aſſented to an Act of Aſſembly, by which the parochial Clergy were put entirely in the power of the veſtries, who could force a miniſter to quit at any time, by refuſing to give him a certificate to enable him to receive his ſalary. The Veſtries carried this power to ſuch a length, that for ſome years before the Civil War, they would not permit a Miniſter to apply to the Governor for collation; but the Clergy continued to officiate merely during the pleaſure of the Veſtries. The Clergy in America do not receive tithes, but in moſt of the Colonies before the Civil War (except the New England Provinces, where the Independents had the upper hand), an Act of Aſſembly was made, to divide the Colony into pariſhes, and to eſtabliſh religious worſhip therein,

according

according to the rites and ceremonies of the Church of England, and alſo to raiſe a yearly ſalary for the ſupport of each parochial miniſter; but in moſt of theſe Acts of Aſſembly, there was a clauſe, which provided, that no Miniſter ſhould exerciſe any eccleſiaſtical juriſdiction.

In ſome Colonies, the Miniſter's ſtipend or ſalary was raiſed in money; in others, the Act of Aſſembly directed it to be raiſed in ſugar, and in Virginia it was raiſed in tobacco; but, as the quantum of the ſalary, and the mode of raiſing it, were different in almoſt every Colony, it would be endleſs to take notice of all the Acts of Aſſembly that were made for that purpoſe.

On the breaking out of the Civil War in America, moſt of the Clergy of the Church of England adhered to their loyalty, and acted a part ſuitable to the bleſſed religion which they preached. But the propriety of their conduct, and the ſacred order to which they belonged, did not protect them from the perſecution of their enemies. Many of them have taken ſhelter in Great Britain, and others in different Colonies. I met ſeveral of them at New York, and frequently attended divine worſhip at the City Hall, where they preached in rotation. I was much edified with their truly goſpel doctrine, for their diſcourſes were intended to mend the heart, and not to miſlead the head with fine ſpun theories; and they delivered themſelves with that zeal, which diſtinguiſhes thoſe who feel what they preach to others. Amongſt men of this primitive ſtamp, I ſhould mention Mr. Leaming, and the two Sayers from Connecticut, was it not that good men are dead to the applauſe of the world, and look for their reward in another country, where merit will not be miſtaken or overlooked.

The

The following form of a Collation will anſwer the purpoſe of a precedent in any Colony.

Antigua.

The Seal at Arms.

By the Honourable A. B. Eſq; Preſident of the Council of his Majeſty's Iſland of St. Chriſtopher, and Commander in Chief, Chancellor, Vice Admiral, and Ordinary for the time being in and over all his Majeſty's Leeward Charibbee Iſlands in America.

HIS Majeſty having been graciouſly pleaſed by Letters Patent under the Great Seal of Great Britain to authoriſe me to collate orthodox Miniſters to all and every the pariſhes in the ſaid Iſlands; and the pariſh of St. John, in the Iſland of Antigua, being vacant by the death of the late incumbent, and the Rev. C. D. Clerk, being recommended to me as a perſon well qualified to take on him the Cure of Souls in the ſaid Pariſh, I do hereby conſtitute and collate the ſaid C. D. to be Clerk Miniſter of the ſaid Pariſh of St. John, in the ſaid Iſland of Antigua, with full power to have, hold, receive, and enjoy all ſuch rights, dues, perquiſites, and advantages, as do, or of right may belong to him, either by law or cuſtom.

Given under my Hand and Seal at Arms in the Iſland of St. Chriſtopher, and counterſigned by my Secretary the 28th day of January 1767, and in the ſeventh year of his Majeſty's reign.

To the Churchwardens and Veſtry of the Pariſh of St. John, in the Iſland of Antigua.

By his Honour's Command, A. B.

E. F. Deputy Secretary.

In

In the government of the Leeward Charibbee Iſlands, there are a Captain General and Governor in Chief, and a Lieutenant General of all the Iſlands; and there are alſo Lieutenant Governors of the Iſlands of Antigua, Montſerrat, Nevis, and Saint Chriſtopher's reſpectively. In the death or abſence of all thoſe, the Senior Member of the Council of the Iſland of Saint Chriſtopher's, is Commander in Chief for the time being. There is at preſent a Lieutenant Governor of Tortola, and the other Virgin Iſlands; but I apprehend, that he is ſubordinate to the Members of the Council of the ſeveral Iſlands firſt abovementioned, and that each of them would, in ſucceſſion, take the command of the Leeward Charribbee Iſlands before him. There was alſo a Lieutenant General of the Southern Charibbee Iſlands whilſt they formed one government, but one of thoſe Iſlands hath been lately ceded to France, and the other three are ſeparate governments.

The power of a Governor of a Colony, to grant probate of Wills, is delegated to him by his inſtructions. In the Eccleſiaſtical Courts in England, there are two methods of proving a Will; one in common form, by the oath of the Executor; the other *per teſtes*. Floyer's Proctors Practice 120. Hetley 77.

In the Weſt India Iſlands, that I am acquainted with, every will is proved *per teſtes*, or at leaſt *per teſtem*, by one of the ſubſcribing witneſſes thereto, unleſs they are all out of the Iſland; and in that caſe, it is uſual for one of the executors, and ſome perſon who is acquainted with the handwriting of the Teſtator, to go before the Ordinary, and make oath, that they are acquainted with the Teſtator's hand-writing, and that they believe

believe the name ſubſcribed to the Will is of his hand-writing; and the executor farther ſwears, that the writing produced, is the Laſt Will and Teſtament of the Teſtator; but where either of the ſubſcribing witneſſes is on the ſpot, and attends to prove the Will, the executor takes no oath, nor does he return any inventory into the Secretary's Office: however, the Will and Probate are always carried to the office, to be regiſtered at full length. In thoſe Iſlands, where there is no particular Regiſter's Office for regiſtering Deeds and Wills, they are then lodged in the Secretary's Office for that purpoſe.

In caſe of a Will, to which there is no ſubſcribing witneſs, or of the notes of a Will, or of a Teſtamentary Schedule, they proceed as near to the practice of the Eccleſiaſtical Courts in England, as local circumſtances will admit.

In moſt of the Colonies on the Continent before the Civil War, a Will was proved in common form by the executor's going before the Ordinary (or before ſome perſon by him deputed for that purpoſe), and making oath, that the writing produced was the Laſt Will and Teſtament of the Teſtator; that he would produce to the appraiſers, that ſhould be appointed by the Ordinary, all the goods, &c. of the Teſtator, that ſhould come to his hands, poſſeſſion, or knowledge; and that he would well and truly adminiſter all and ſingular the goods, &c. of the Teſtator, and pay his debts and legacies, as far as his eſtate would extend, and the law charge him (the executor); and that he would make a true inventory of the rights and credits of the Teſtator, and exhibit the ſame, together with the appraiſement of his goods and chattels, certified under the hands of the appraiſers, into the Secretary's Office of the Province,

vince, within the time prescribed by law. The appraisers also took an oath, to make a just and true appraisement, and to return the same, under their hands, to the executor, within the time prescribed by law. This was the substance of those two oaths; but they were usually set out at large in the Act of Assembly, which pointed out the duties required of executors and administrators.

In the Ecclesiastical Courts in England, if a party is contumacious, they proceed to excommunication; and then, on a certificate from the Bishop to the King in Chancery, a writ *de Excommunicato Capiendo* issues; but the Ordinary's jurisdiction in such of the Colonies, as I am acquainted with, was defective in this, that the Ordinary had no power to compel obedience to his sentence. Some years ago, a Lieutenant Governor of South Carolina (who commanded in the absence of the Governor) did proceed to excommunicate a contumacious party; but I never heard what became of it. However, in some Colonies, they might have had Acts of Assembly, for strengthening the hands of the Ordinary.

In the West Indies, the Probate or Affidavit of the due execution of a Will, is always written either under, or on the back of the will: when it is written under the Will, it is in the following form:

ANTIGUA. Before his Excellency G. T. Esq; Captain General and Governor in Chief in and over all his Majesty's Leeward Charibbee Islands in America, and Chancellor, Vice Admiral, and Ordinary of the same.

PERSONALLY appeared W. B. of the said Island of Antigua, Surgeon, one of the subscribing

ſcribing witneſſes to the before written Will of E. M. late of the ſaid Iſland of Antigua, Widow, deceaſed, who being duly ſworn on the Holy Evangeliſts of Almighty God, maketh oath, and ſaith, That he was preſent, and did ſee the ſaid E. M. make her mark over againſt the Seal, at the foot of the ſaid before written Will; and that the ſaid E. M. did ſign, ſeal, publiſh, and declare the before writing as and for her Laſt Will and Teſtament, in the preſence of this Deponent, and of the other ſubſcribing witneſſes thereto, who ſubſcribed their names to the ſaid before written Will, in the preſence of the ſaid Teſtatrix, and in the preſence of each other: And this Deponent further ſaith, he verily believes, in his conſcience, that the ſaid E. M. was, at the time of her executing her ſaid Will, of ſound and diſpoſing mind, memory, and underſtanding: And this Deponent further ſaith, That the name or letters W. B. ſubſcribed as a witneſs to the ſaid Will, and that the names J. M. and M. O. alſo ſubſcribed as witneſſes to the ſaid Will, are of the reſpective proper hand-writing of this Deponent, and of J. M. of the ſaid Iſland of Antigua, Pilot, and M. O. of the ſaid Iſland of Antigua, Widow.

W. B.

Sworn before me, this
day of October,
in the year of our
Lord 1764.

When the Probate is written on the back of the Will, it muſt be varied accordingly, by uſing the words, "the within written Will." Inſtead of the words, "the before written Will."

In the Iſland of Jamaica, where the ſubſcribing witneſſes to a Will, live at a diſtance, it is uſual to ſue out a Dedimus, to impower Commiſſioners to take

take the affidavit of the subscribing witnesses (or one of them) of the due execution of the Will.

DEDIMUS.

Jamaica.

George the Second, by the grace of God of Great Britain, France, and Ireland, King, and of Jamaica, Lord, Defender of the Faith, &c. To our trusty and well-beloved Thomas Frowers and Nicholas Plisham, of the parish of Portland, Esqrs; Know ye, That we have constituted, authorized, and appointed, and by these presents do constitute ye, or either of ye, to administer an oath unto Alexander Wilson, Joseph Barnett, and Samuel Orr, or any other that are witnesses, and can make oath of the signing, sealing, publishing, and declaring, of the last Will and Testament of R— J—, late of the parish of Portland, planter, deceased; and thereof you, or either of you, are to make due return, under your, or either of your hands and seals, unto our Captain-General and Governor in Chief of our said Island, or to the Governor in Chief of the same for the time being, with this power annexed; so that such proceedings may be ordered therein as may be according to law—Witness his Excellency Edward Trelawny, Esq; Captain-General and Governor in Chief of our said Island at St. Jago de la Vega the twenty-eighth day of January, in the year of our Lord One thousand seven hundred and forty seven, and in the twenty-first year of our reign.

Edward Trelawny.

Passed the Secretary's Office—
Wastel Briscoe,
Secretary.

(L. S.)

The

The Return indorſed on the *Dedimus.*

The return of the within Dedimus appears by the ſchedule annexed.

NICHOLAS PLISHAM.

Affidavit of the due Execution of the Will, taken before one of the Commiſſioners.

Memorandum, this ſixteenth of September one thouſand ſeven hundred and forty-eight, perſonally appeared before me, Alexander Wilſon of the pariſh of Portland, planter, one of the ſubſcribing witneſſes to the annexed will of R— J—, who being duly ſworn by virtue of the Dedimus annexed, made oath, That he was preſent and did ſee R— J— the teſtator, being then of ſound mind and memory, ſign, ſeal, publiſh, and declare the ſaid annexed Will as and for his Laſt Will and Teſtament, and that at the ſame time Joſeph Barnett and Samuel Orr were preſent, and ſubſcribed their names as witneſſes to the ſame, in the preſence of the ſaid Teſtator: he likewiſe makes oath, That he knows nothing of any other Will or Wills ſince made by the ſaid Teſtator, in prejudice of ſaid annexed Will.—Sworn before me the day and year above written.

NICHOLAS PLISHAM. (L. S.) ALEX. WILSON.

The Dedimus, Will, and the Affidavit of the Execution of the Will, muſt be annexed together, and then returned into the Secretary's Office.

In the Province of Pennſylvania (which was a Proprietary Government before the Civil War) wills were proved before the Regiſter General: and

and a Probate out of his Office in Philadelphia was in the following form:

SEAL.

By the tenor of theſe preſents, I William Plumſted, Regiſter-General for the Probate of Wills, and granting Letters of Adminiſtration in and for the Province of Pennſylvania, do make known unto all people, That on the day of the date hereof, at Philadelphia in the Province aforeſaid, before me was proved, approved, and inſinuated, the Laſt Will and Teſtament of D— P— deceaſed (a true copy whereof is to theſe preſents annexed), having whilſt he lived, and at the time of his death, divers goods, chattels, rights and credits within the ſaid Province, by means whereof the approbation and inſinuation of the ſaid Laſt Will and Teſtament, and the committing the adminiſtration of all and ſingular the goods, chattels, rights and credits which were of the ſaid decedent, and alſo the auditing the accompts, calculations, and reckonings of the ſaid adminiſtration, and a final diſmiſſion from the ſame to me is manifeſtly known to belong, and adminiſtration of all and ſingular the goods, chattels, rights and credits of the ſaid decedent any wiſe concerning; and his Laſt Will and Teſtament was committed to M— P—, executrix in the ſaid Teſtament named, chiefly of well and truly adminiſtrating the goods, chattels, rights and credits of the ſaid decedent, and making a true and perfect inventory thereof, and exhibiting the ſame into the Regiſter-General's Office at Philadelphia, at or before the 2 . d day of January next; and rendering a true and juſt account, calculation, and reckoning of the ſaid adminiſtration, when thereunto lawfully required, being duly ſworn thereto.

In

In teſtimony whereof I have hereunto ſet my hand and Seal of Office, at Philadelphia, the 23d day of December, in the year of our Lord one thouſand ſeven hundred and ſixty-two.

W. Plumsted, Reg. Gl.

In the name of God, Amen. I D— P—, late of Antigua, but now of the Borough of Southwark, in the Province of Pennſylvania, blackſmith, being ſick and weak in body, &c. (here ſet out the Will at length.)

Philadelphia, 23d December 1762. Then perſonally appeared Francis Sewer and Philip Thomas, two of the witneſſes to the foregoing Will, and on oath did declare, they ſaw and heard D— P—, the Teſtor therein named, ſign, ſeal, publiſh and declare the ſame Will for and as his Laſt Will and Teſtament, and that at the doing thereof he was of ſound mind, memory, and underſtanding, to the beſt of their knowledge.

Coram, W. Plumsted, Reg. Gl.

In the Weſt-Indies, where a government conſiſts of many Iſlands, and the Governor is out of the Iſland (where a Will is to be proved) but within the government, the Preſident of the Iſland where the Will is to be proved, uſually takes the probate or affidavit of the execution of ſuch Will; but if the Teſtator leaves effects in different Iſlands in the government, then, to ſave the expence and trouble of proving the Will before the different Preſidents in thoſe Iſlands in which the effects lie, the ſhorteſt way is, to prove the Will before the Governor in Chief, as Ordinary of all the Iſlands; and then to have the Will regiſtered in thoſe Iſlands where there are any effects of the Teſtator, in the ſame manner as in England, when the

the deceased has *bona notabilia* in different dioceses, the Will must be proved in the Prerogative Court of the Archbishop of Canterbury.

The Governor, as Ordinary, has also the power of granting administration of Intestates effects: but if a government consists of many Islands, and the Governor is out of that Island in which the Intestate's effects lie, but within the government, the President of the Council of that Island where such Intestate's effects lie, usually grants letters of administration within that Island where such effects are, and from whence the Governor is then absent:—but if the Intestate leaves effects within different Islands, in that case, to prevent the trouble of applying for as many administrations as there are Islands in which the Intestate had effects, the best way is, to petition the Governor for administration of all the effects of the Intestate within the government, in the same manner as an application is made to the Prerogative Court in England, where the deceased had *bona notabilia* in different dioceses.

In the West India Islands, the method of obtaining letters of administration is, to petition the Governor for that purpose, who, without issuing any citation, grants the prayer of such Petition, and frequently, without giving any time to those who are better intitled to administration, to oppose the same:—when the petition is granted, the Administrator gives bond, with securities in the Secretary's Office, faithfully to administer the intestate's effects. according to law, and to render a just and true account of his administration upon oath, when he shall be thereto lawfully required. —A warrant of appraisment also issues, and the appraisers are to make an inventory and appraisment of the goods and chattels of the Intestate,

and

and to return the ſame with all convenient ſpeed into the Secretary's Office; and they are to ſwear thereto if lawfully required.

In the Colonies on the Continent, no letters of adminiſtration were granted before the Civil War, until a citation had been iſſued, and read in the church by the miniſter during the time of divine ſervice, on the Sunday before ſuch letters of adminiſtration were granted; and the adminiſtrator and appraiſers were ſworn to the effect ſet forth, under the head of executors, except that the part of the oath, which, in the caſe of an executor, ſtated, that he believed the writing produced to be the Laſt Will of the deceaſed, in the caſe of an adminiſtrator was altered, by inſerting inſtead thereof, the words following, *viz.* "That the deceaſed "made no will, as far as the deponent knew and "believed;"—in other reſpects, the adminiſtrator conducted himſelf in the ſame manner as an executor was before obſerved to do.

The haſty method of proceeding in the Weſt Indies, in the granting of letters of adminiſtration in the manner before ſet forth, hath been productive of many inconveniencies.—Some years ago, a perſon in the Iſland of Jamaica petitioned the Governor for letters of adminiſtration of the eſtate and effects of a man who had left the Iſland, and was ſtated in the petition to be dead;—the prayer of the Petition was granted, and letters of adminiſtration obtained;—and ſome time afterwards, the perſon ſuppoſed to be dead returned to the Iſland;—on which the then Governor ordered, that for the future no letters of adminiſtration ſhould be granted, until previous notice of the application for them was given, by an advertiſement in the news paper.

I ſhall

I ſhall here furniſh the Reader with the mode of application for Letters of Adminiſtration in ſome of the Weſt India Iſlands.

A PETITION *for Letters of Adminiſtration.*

St. CHRISTOPHER'S. To the Honourable J. V. Eſq; Preſident of his Majeſty's Council of his Iſland of St. Chriſtopher, and Commander in Chief, Chancellor, Vice-Admiral, and Ordinary for the time being, in and over all his Majeſty's Leeward Charibbee Iſlands in America;

The humble Petition of F. C. of the ſaid Iſland of St. Chriſtopher, Gentleman, and Mary his Wife (which ſaid Mary is the only ſurviving Child of N. K. late of the ſaid Iſland of St. Chriſtopher, Gentleman, deceaſed:)

Sheweth,

That the ſaid N. K. departed this life on or about the twentieth day of May laſt paſt, inteſtate, and unmarried, poſſeſſed of ſome perſonal eſtate within the government of his Majeſty's Leeward Charibbee Iſlands in America.

That as your Petitioner Mary is the only ſurviving child of the ſaid N. K. your Petitioners are adviſed, that they are well intitled to Letters of Adminiſtration of all and ſingular the goods and chattels, rights and credits, which were of the ſaid Inteſtate at the time of his deceaſe.

Your

Your Petitioners therefore humbly pray your Honour to grant unto them, and the ſurvivor of them, Letters of Adminiſtration, of all and ſingular the goods and chattels, rights and credits, which were of the ſaid N. K. at the time of his death, within the government of his Majeſty's Leeward Charibbee Iſlands in America, upon your Petitioner F. C. giving the uſual ſecurity into the Secretary's Office of this Iſland, on behalf of himſelf and your ſaid Petitioner Mary, faithfully to adminiſter the ſame, &c.

And your Petitioners ſhall ever pray, &c.

Dated this 17th day of Sept. 1766.

F. C.
M. C.

A PETITION *for Letters of Adminiſtration, with the Will annexed.*

ANTIGUA. To his Excellency G. T. Eſq; Captain-General and Governor in Chief in and over all his Majeſty's Leeward Charibbee Iſlands in America, and Chancellor, Vice-Admiral and Ordinary of the ſame;

The humble Petition of E. B. of the ſaid Iſland of Antigua, Gentleman, and Margaret his Wife:

Sheweth,

That W. C. late of the ſaid Iſland of Antigua, Gentleman, deceaſed, departed this life on the eight day of Auguſt, in the year of our Lord one thouſand ſeven hundred and ſixty-four, having firſt

first made his Last Will and Testament nuncupative, and thereby given his * real and personal estate to your Petitioner Margaret, who was a sister of the half blood to the said W. C.; which said Will nuncupative hath been duly proved before your Excellency.

That the said W. C. not having named any person or persons as executor or executors of his said Last Will and Testament, your Petitioners are advised, that it is necessary for them to take out Letters of Administration, with the said Will and Testament annexed.

Your Petitioners therefore humbly pray your your Excellency, that Letters of Administration of all and singular the goods and chattels, rights and credits, which were of the said W. C. at the time of his death, with his Last Will and Testament annexed, may be granted to your Petitioners, and the survivor of them, upon their giving the usual security into the Secretary's Office of this Island, faithfully to administer the same.

And your Petitioners will ever pray, &c.

Dated 26th of April 1765.

Granted
G. T.

E. B.
M. B.

I consent to the above
Petition. T. W.

* The stat. 29 Cha. II. c. 3. for prevention of frauds and perjuries, is not in force in Antigua; but neverthelefs it is conceived, that a devise of lands by a nuncupative Will was not good, even before the stat. of Cha. II. for the statutes of 32 Hen. 8. c. 1. and 34 Hen. 8. c. 5. which permitted the devising of lands by Will, direct it to be in writing.

Letters

Letters of Adminiſtration.

ANTIGUA. By his Excellency G. T. Eſq; Captain-General and Governor in Chief in and over all his Majeſty's Leeward Charibbee Iſlands in America, Chancellor, Vice-Admiral, and Ordinary of the ſame.

SEAL.

WHEREAS E. B. of the ſaid Iſland of Antigua, Gentleman, and Margaret his wife, by their Petition to me directed, have ſet forth, That W. C. late of the ſaid Iſland of Antigua, Gentleman, deceaſed, departed this life on the eighth day of Auguſt, in the year of our Lord one thouſand ſeven hundred and ſixty-four, having firſt made his Laſt Will and Teſtament nuncupative, and thereby given his real and perſonal eſtate to your Petitioner Margaret, who was a ſiſter of the half blood to the ſaid W. C.; which ſaid Will nuncupative hath been duly proved before me.

That the ſaid W. C. not having named any perſon or perſons as executor or executors of his ſaid Laſt Will and Teſtament, the Petitioners were adviſed, that it was neceſſary for them to take out Letters of Adminiſtration, with the ſaid Will and Teſtament annexed; the Petitioners therefore humbly prayed me, that Letters of Adminiſtration of all and ſingular the goods and chattels, rights and credits, which were of the ſaid W. C. at the time of his death, with his Laſt Will and Teſtament annexed, might be granted to the Petitioners, and the ſurvivor of them, upon their giving the uſual ſecurity into the Secretary's Office of this Iſland, faithfully to adminiſter the ſame.

ADMI.

ADMINISTRATION therefore, of all and singular the goods and chattels, rights and credits, which were of the said W. C. at the time of his death, with his Will annexed, is hereby granted unto the said E. B. and Margaret his wife, they having given bond, with security in the Secretary's Office of this Island, faithfully to administer the same according to law, and to render a just and true account of their administration upon oath, when they shall be thereto lawfully required.

Passed the Office. W. A. Dep. Sec.

Given under my hand and Seal this 30th day of April 1765. G. T.

Warrant of Appraisement.

ANTIGUA.

SEAL.

By his Excellency G. T. Esq; Captain-General and Governor in Chief in and over all his Majesty's Leeward Charibbee Islands in America, Chancellor, Vice-Admiral, and Ordinary of the same.

THESE are in his Majesty's name, to authorise and require you A. B, C. D, E. F, G. H, or any three of you, according to the best of your judgments and consciences, to inventory and appraise the goods and chattels of W. C. late of the said Island of Antigua, Gentleman, deceased, as the same shall be shewn unto you by E. B. and Margaret his wife, Administrator and Administratrix of all and singular the goods and chattels, rights and credits, which were of W. C. deceased, with his Will annexed, and return thereof, to make into the Secretary's Office of this Island, with all convenient speed; which return you are to make,

so

ſo that you may ſwear, if thereto lawfully requir-ed, that the ſame is a juſt and true Appraiſement; and for your ſo doing this ſhall be your warrant.

Paſſed the Office. W. A. Dep. Sec. Given under my Hand and Seal this 30th day of April 1765. G. T.

Another form of a PETITION *for Letters of Admini-ſtration.*

St. CHRISTOPHER'S. To the Honourable J V. Eſq; Preſident of the Council of his Majeſty's Iſland of St. Chriſtopher, and Commander in Chief, Chancellor, Vice-Admiral, and Ordinary for the time being, in and over all his Majeſty's Leeward Charibbee Iſlands in America;

The humble Petition of J. L. of the Iſland of St. Chriſtopher, Merchant:

Sheweth,

That W. D. Merchant, departed this life at the Iſland of St. Euſtatia, ſome time in the month of November laſt, poſſeſſed of divers goods and chattels, rights and credits, within his Majeſty's Leeward Charibbee Iſlands in America.

That the ſaid W. D. at the time of his death, left a widow in ſome part of Great Britain, and ſome time before his death made his Laſt Will and Teſtament in writing, at the Iſland of St. Croix, and appointed T. L, H. R, and G. H, all of the ſaid Iſland of St. Croix, Gentlemen, Executors of his ſaid Will.

That

That the said Executors, and every of them, have refused to act under the said Will, and have also refused to prove the same; so that your Petitioner hath not been able to get a copy of the said Will to annex to this his Petition.

That your Petitioner hath taken an assignment of a bond or obligation, entered into by the said W. D. in his life time, for a large sum of money, and by reason thereof is become the largest creditor of the said W. D. within your Honour's government: but as no person hath yet proved the said Will of the said W. D. nor taken out Letters of Administration of his personal estate, your Petitioner is altogether disabled from commencing any action or suit for the recovery of his said demand.

Your Petitioner therefore humbly prays your Honour to grant unto him Letters of Administration of all and singular the goods and chattels, rights and credits, which were of the said W. D. at the time of his death, within the government of his Majesty's Leeward Charibbee Islands in America, upon your Petitioner's giving the usual security faithfully to administer the same, &c.

And your Petitioner shall ever pray, &c.

Dated the 19th day of March 1767.

The inconveniencies arising from the hasty method of granting Letters of Administration in the West Indies, will appear by the two following Petitions, amongst many other instances:

PETI-

Petition *to revoke Letters of Adminiſtration granted to* W. S. *and to grant Letters of Adminiſtration to* J. B.

Antigua. To his Excellency G. T. Eſq; Captain-General and Governor in Chief in and over all his Majeſty's Leeward Charibbee Iſlands in America, and Chancellor, Vice-Admiral, and Ordinary of the ſame;

The humble Petition of J. B. of the Iſland of Antigua, Gentleman:

Sheweth,

That A. B. of the ſaid Iſland of Antigua, Gentleman, your Petitioner's late brother deceaſed, departed this life in the ſaid Iſland on the twenty-ninth day of Auguſt laſt paſt, inteſtate and unmarried, poſſeſſed of a conſiderable perſonal eſtate within your Excellency's government.

That your Petitioner was off from this Iſland at the time of the death of the ſaid A. B. and that on or about the thirtieth day of Auguſt laſt paſt, W. S. of the Iſland of Antigua, Merchant, preferred a Petition to your Excellency, therein ſetting forth, among other things, the death and inteſtacy of the ſaid A. B. and that the ſaid deceaſed was, at the time of his death, indebted to him the ſaid W. S. in the ſum of one hundred pounds or thereabouts; and that he had actually been at the expence of burying the ſaid deceaſed: the ſaid W. S. therefore humbly prayed your Excellency to grant unto him Letters of Adminiſtration of all and ſingular the goods and chattels, rights and credits, which were of the ſaid Inteſtate at the time of his death, upon the ſaid W. S. giving the

the usual security for the faithful administration thereof.

That the said Petition of the said W. S. was not opposed by any person whatsoever; and thereupon your Excellency was pleased to grant the same.

That your Petitioner and his Brother L. B. who is a minor, are the next of kin to the said deceased.

That your Petitioner is willing, and doth hereby offer to pay unto the said W. S. all such sum and sums of money as are justly due to him from the estate of the said deceased.

Your Petitioner therefore humbly prays your Excellency to revoke and declare null and void the Letters of Administration of the goods and chattels, rights and credits, of the said deceased, granted to the said W. S. to all intents and purposes in the law whatsoever; and to grant and commit Letters of Administration of the goods and chattels, rights and credits, of the said deceased, which are within your Excellency's government, anew to your Petitioner, upon his giving the usual security faithfully to administer the same; and that the said W. S. may be decreed to account on oath, before your Excellency, for all and singular the goods and chattels, rights and credits of the said deceased, which since his death have come to the hands, possession, or power of the said W. S. and that he may pay over unto your Petitioner such balance as shall appear to be in his hands.

And your Petitioner shall ever pray, &c.

Dated the day of February 1766.

Another

Another Form of a Petition *to revoke* Letters *of* Administration, &c.

Antigua. To his Excellency G. T. Esq. Captain General and Governor in Chief in and over all his Majesty's Leeward Charibbee Islands in America, and Chancellor, Vice Admiral, and Ordinary of the same:

The humble Petition of A. M. of the Island of Antigua, Gentleman;

Sheweth,

That C. J. late of the Island of Antigua, Sugar Refiner, deceased, departed this life on Tuesday the thirtieth day of October last, in the morning, at the house of G. B. of the Island of Antigua, Esq. situate in the town of St. John, in the said Island, having first made his last Will and Testament in Writing, bearing date the fifteenth day of August, in the year of our Lord 1761, and thereof appointed W. E. Gentleman (since deceased) executor.

That the said G. B. was considerably indebted to the said C. J. at the time of his death, for his salary, as a Sugar Refiner; nevertheless, the said G. B. concealed the death of the said C. J. for several hours, till he the said G. B. had prepared a Petition from himself to your Excellency for Letters of Administration of the goods and chattels, rights and credits, which were of the said C. J. at the time of his death, to be granted to him the said G. B. although the said C. J. was, at the time of his death, indebted to your Petitioner, and

and J. H. of the ſaid Iſland of Antigua, Eſq. in ſeveral conſiderable ſums of money.

That the ſaid G. B. by concealing the death of the ſaid C. J. in manner aforeſaid, procured Letters of Adminiſtration of the goods and chattels, rights and credits, which were of the ſaid C. J. at the time of his death, to be granted to him by your Excellency.

That as the ſaid C. J. duly made and executed ſuch laſt Will and Teſtament, as hereinbefore is mentioned; and as the ſaid W. E. the executor named in ſuch laſt Will and Teſtament is dead, and your Petitioner and the ſaid J. H. are the largeſt creditors of the ſaid C. J.

Your Petitioner therefore humbly prays your Excellency, that Letters of Adminiſtration of all and ſingular the goods and chattels, rights and credits, which were of the ſaid C. J. at the time of his death, with his ſaid laſt Will and Teſtament annexed, may be granted to your Petitioner, upon his giving the uſual ſecurity into the Secretary's Office of this Iſland, faithfully to adminiſter the ſame; and that the Letters of Adminiſtration, which have been granted unto the ſaid G. B. may be revoked.

And your Petitioner will ever pray, &c.

I the above named J. H. (being the largeſt creditor of the above named C. J.) do hereby humbly conſent to the prayer of the above written Petition, if your Excellency ſhall be pleaſed to approve of the ſame.

5. The Governor preſides in the Court of Errors, of which he and the Council are Judges, to

to hear and determine all Appeals, in the nature of Writs of Error, from the superior Courts of Common Law in the Province; and all Writs of Error are tested in his name, when he is on the spot: but in those governments, which consist of several Islands, it is provided by Act of Assembly, that, in the absence of the Captain General or Governor in Chief from the Island, the Lieutenant General, Lieutenant Governor; or if he is also out of the Island, the President, and Council of the Island are Judges of the Court of Errors, and then Writs of Error may be issued by and tested in the name of the President of such Island, and shall be made returnable before, and proceeded in by him and the Council of the said Island; but the number of Councillors necessary to constitute such Court of Errors, is different in some Islands to what it is in others.

These Appeals or Writs of Error, are allowed and regulated by his Majesty's instructions to his Governor: but in the West India Islands, Acts of Assembly have been passed to direct the mode of proceeding in Appeals or Writs of Error, in such particulars only, about which his Majesty's instructions are silent. In those Acts of Assembly, the Court held by the Governor and Council for correcting errors in proceedings in the superior Courts of common law in the Province, is called The Court of Errors; and the process for removing the proceedings, is called A Writ of Error; but the King's instructions call it An Appeal; by such instructions, liberty of Appeal is allowed from the judgment or sentence of the Courts of Common Law to his Excellency the Governor or Commander in Chief, and the Council; for which purpose, a Writ is to issue, returnable before the Governor and Council, who are to proceed to

hear

hear and determine ſuch Appeal, wherein ſuch of the Council, as ſhall be at that time Judges of the Court, from whence ſuch Appeal ſhall be ſo made, ſhall not be permitted to vote upon ſuch Appeal; but they may nevertheleſs be preſent at the hearing thereof, to give the reaſons of the judgment given by them in the cauſes, wherein ſuch Appeals ſhall be made. Liberty of Appeal is alſo allowed from the judgment or ſentence of the Governor or Commander in Chief and Council, and from the order or decree of the Court of Chancery to his Majeſty in his Privy Council; but ſuch liberty of Appeal is under the following reſtrictions:

1. No Appeal ſhall be allowed to the Governor in Council in any civil cauſe, unleſs the debt or damages, or the ſum or value appealed for, do exceed the ſum of 300*l.* ſterling; except the matter in queſtion relates to the taking or demanding any duty payable to the King, or to any fee of office, or annual rent, or other ſuch like matter or thing, where the rights in future may be bound; in all which caſes, an Appeal is admitted to the King in his Privy Council, though the immediate ſum or value appealed for be of leſs value.

2. That in all caſes of fines impoſed for miſdemeanors, no Appeals are permitted to the King in his Privy Council, except the fines, ſo impoſed, amount to or exceed the value 200*l.* ſterling.

3. That every ſuch Appeal to the Governor and Council be made within fourteen days after judgment or ſentence is pronounced in the Court below; and that the Appellant or Plaintiff in Error do give good ſecurity that he will effectually proſecute his Appeal or Writ of Error, and anſwer the condemnation money; and alſo pay ſuch coſts and

and damages as ſhall be awarded, in caſe the judgment or ſentence of the Court below ſhall be affirmed.

4. That no Appeal be allowed from the judgment or ſentence of the Governor and Council, or from the decree of the Court of Chancery to the King in his Privy Council; unleſs the debt, damages, or the ſum or value ſo appealed for, do exceed the ſum of 500 *l.* ſterling, except where the matter in queſtion relates to the taking or demanding any duty payable to the King, or to any fee of office, or an annual rent, &c. as above mentioned.

5. That ſuch Appeal to his Majeſty in his Privy Council be made within fourteen days after judgment or ſentence is pronounced by the Governor in Council, or after a decree is pronounced by the Governor in the Court of Chancery; and that the Appellant or Plaintiff in Error do give good ſecurity, that he will effectually proſecute his Appeal or Writ of Error, and anſwer the condemnation money; and alſo pay ſuch coſts and damages as ſhall be awarded by his Majeſty, in caſe the ſentence or judgment of the Governor and Council, or the decree of the Court of Chancery be affirmed.

In the Weſt India Iſlands, proviſion is uſually made by Act of Aſſembly, for directing the mode of aſcertaining the value of the matter in diſpute, and alſo in what time the Writ of Error ſhall be returnable, when a tranſcript of the record ſhall be made out, and when errors ſhall be aſſigned, and ſuch other incidental matters in the courſe of the proceeding, about which his Majeſty's inſtructions are ſilent; but on the Continent, theſe things are uſually provided for by Rule of Court, which being under the power of the Governor and

and Council, are amended from time to time: whereas in the West India Islands, sometimes ill judged Acts of Assembly are made for regulating the proceedings of the Courts of Justice, which take away from the Judges the power of amending the practice of the Courts; and it is not always an easy matter to prevail on the Assembly to amend one of their inconvenient laws.

On an Appeal from the judgment of the Governor and Council, or from the decree of the Court of Chancery to the King in Council, the proceedings must be copied fair, on large paper (for parchment is not used in the Colonies) by the Officer, who has the custody of the records; who, in some Colonies, is the Secretary of the Island or Province; in others, the Clerk of the Crown and Pleas; and, in others, the Prothonotary. When the proceedings are thus copied fair, the Officer, who has the custody of them, must make an affidavit that they are true copies, and have been compared with the original records. The proceedings and affidavit are then annexed together, the Governor or Commander in Chief puts the Great Seal to them, and they are then transmitted to Great Britain.

On an Appeal to the King in Council, from the Plantations, the proceedings must be transmitted, and the party appealing must proceed within a year after the Appeal allowed in the Plantations. 2 Lord Raymond 1447.—But a cause cannot be transmitted for difficulty, but must be determined one way or other. Id. 1448.

I shall here give the form of an Appeal, in the nature of a Writ of Error in a Colony, where the liberty of Appeal was entirely regulated by the King's instructions; and as this was the first instance of an Appeal in that Colony, there was no

Act

Act of Aſſembly, nor Rule of Court reſpecting Appeals; great care was therefore taken to conduct the proceedings in every reſpect, as near as poſſible to the King's inſtructions.

An APPEAL *(in the nature of a* WRIT *of* ERROR) *to the Governor and Council, from a Judgment given in the General Court.*

GEORGIA.

GEORGE the Third, by the Grace of God, of Great Britain, France, and Ireland King, Defender of the Faith, and ſo forth. To our truſty and well beloved A. B. Barriſter at Law, our Chief Juſtice of our Province of Georgia, greeting: Whereas by our fifty-ſecond inſtruction, to our Governor and Commander in Chief of our ſaid Province or Colony of Georgia, we have thought fit to authoriſe him, or the Commander in Chief of our ſaid Province for the time being, to permit and allow Appeals from any of the Courts of Common Law, in our ſaid Colony; and to iſſue a Writ for that purpoſe, returnable before him, and the Council of our ſaid Colony: provided, that in all ſuch Appeals, the value exceeds the ſum of three hundred pounds ſterling. And that ſecurity be firſt duly given by the Appellant, to anſwer ſuch charges as ſhall be awarded, in caſe the firſt ſentence be affirmed, as in the ſaid recited inſtruction is more fully contained. And whereas G. W. of our ſaid Province of Georgia, Eſquire, hath, by his Petition, alleged, that in the record and proceſs, and alſo in the giving of judgment of the Plaint, which was in our General Court of our ſaid Province of Georgia, before you the ſaid A. B. our Chief Juſtice of our ſaid Province of Georgia, and your Fellows,

Fellows, our Juftices of our faid General Court, by our Writ, between R. K. (on the demife of G. D.) and the aforefaid G. W. Efq; of a certain trefpafs and ejectment of farm, manifeft error hath intervened, to the great damage of him the faid G. W. as we from his complaint are informed. And whereas by the affidavit of the faid G. W. made before you, our faid Chief Juftice, it is alleged, that the premifes, mentioned in the declaration filed in the action aforefaid, with the improvements, are worth five hundred pounds lawful money of our faid Province. We therefore being willing, that the error, if any there be, fhould be corrected in due manner, and that full and fpeedy juftice fhould be done to the parties in this behalf, do command you, that, if judgment thereof be given, then (on the faid G. W's giving before you fuch fecurity, as by our faid in part recited inftruction is directed) the record and procefs of the Plaint aforefaid, with all things concerning them; to his Excellency our trufty and well beloved Sir J. W. Baronet, our Captain General and Governor in Chief in and over our faid Province of Georgia, and Chancellor, Vice Admiral, and Ordinary of the fame; and the Honourable Council of our faid Province, under your feal (to wit) on the day of next enfuing, diftinctly and openly you fend, and this writ; that the record and procefs aforefaid being infpected, our faid Governor, with the affent of our faid Council, may further caufe to be done therein for correcting that error, what of right, and according to the law and cuftom of England, in force in our faid Province of Georgia, ought to be done. Witnefs our faid Governor in Chief of our faid Province, in Council

Council, at Savannah, the day of February, in the fifteenth year of our reign.

By his Excellency's Command,
A. W. Clerk of the Council.

This Writ was ſigned by the Governor, and under the Great Seal of the Province.

I ſhall alſo give the reader the form of a Writ of Error in the Iſland of Nevis, which is perhaps the firſt inſtance in which a perſon, who was the chief or preſiding Judge in one Court, teſted and ſigned a writ, which commanded himſelf, as Chief Juſtice of another Court, to certify the proceedings in a cauſe determined before him. For Joſeph Herbert, who was Preſident of the Council in the Iſland of Nevis, was alſo Chief Juſtice of the Courts of King's Bench and Common Pleas there.

(SEAL *.)

GEORGE the Third, by the grace of God, of Great Britain, France, and Ireland King, Defender of the Faith, and ſo forth. To our truſty and well-beloved Joſeph Herbert, Eſq; Chief Juſtice of our Courts of King's Bench and Common Pleas, in our Iſland of Nevis, greeting: Whereas in and by a certain ſtatute or ordinance, made and paſſed by our Captain-General and Governor in Chief, in each, and over all our

* When the Governor is preſent, the Writ of Error, or Appeal, ought to be under the Great Seal of the Government; but when (as was the caſe here) the Governor is in another Iſland of the Government, then, as he has the Great Seal with him, the Writ of Error muſt, of neceſſity, be under the Seal at Arms of the Lieutenant-Governor or Preſident that iſſues it.

Leeward

Leeward Charibbee Islands in America; and also our Council, and the Assembly of our said Island of Nevis, at Charlestown in the same island, in the year of our Lord one thousand seven hundred and thirty-two, it was among other things enacted and ordained, That the Captain-General, or Governor in Chief of our Leeward Charibbee Islands, with four or more of the Council of our said Island of Nevis; and in the absence of the Captain-General or Governor in Chief, the Lieutenant-Governor or President of the Council, with the like number of the Council of the said Island of Nevis, should and might hear, try, and determine all errors to be brought of any judgments to be given in the said Courts of King's Bench and Common Pleas, or which were given by the Courts held by any former Act, for any sum, matter, Cause, or Thing; and that in the absence of the Captain-General, or Governor in Chief, the Lieutenant-Governor, or in his absence, the President of the Council might sign such Writ of Error, or other process thereupon, as in the said statute or ordinance is more fully contained. And because in the record and proceedings, as also in the rendition of the judgment of a plea of trespass on the case which was in our Court of Common Pleas, held in and for our said Island of Nevis, before the Honourable Joseph Herbert, Esq; and others his brethren, Justices of our Court of Common Pleas aforesaid, between J. S. Esq; Plaintiff, and T. B. Esq; Defendant, there is, as it is said, a manifest error, to the great damage of the said Thomas, as by his complaint we have received information. We therefore being willing, that the error aforesaid (if any shall be) should, according to the form of the statute or ordinance aforesaid, be corrected, and full and speedy jus-

tice

vice done to the parties aforesaid, in this behalf command you, That if judgment thereupon be given, then the records and proceedings aforesaid, with all things concerning the same, before the said Captain-General, or Governor in Chief, with four or more of our said Council, or in the absence of the said Captain-General, or Governor in Chief, before the said Lieutenant-General or President of the said Council, with the like number of the said Council, into our Court of Error aforesaid, at Charlestown aforesaid, on Tuesday, to wit, the second day of October next ensuing, you cause to be brought, that the said Captain-General, or Governor in Chief, with four or more of our said Council, and in the absence of the said Captain-General, or Governor in Chief, the said Lieutenant-Governor or President of the said Council, with the like number of our said Council; the records and proceedings aforesaid having seen and examined, may further cause to be done therein, what of right, and according to the form of the statute and ordinance aforesaid shall be to be done. Witness the Honourable Joseph Herbert, Esq; President of our said Council at Charlestown aforesaid, this third day of July, in the year of our Lord one thousand seven hundred and sixty-four, and in the fourth year of our reign.

JOSEPH HERBERT.

For the result of a Writ of Error in a prosecution for a Misdemeanor, see Title, Courts of Criminal Jurisdiction, hereafter.

6. The Governor is usually named first in the standing Commission issued under the * 11 & 12 Wil.

* On a reference to the Attorney and Solicitor-General of England, in the case of a man who was convicted in the Province

Wil. III. c. 7. for the more effectual suppression of Piracy; and if he chuses to sit, he is then President of the Court: if he does not sit, the senior Member of the Council then present presides.

Mr. Dudley, Governor of the Massachusett's Bay in New England, sat as President at the trial of Quelch and others at Boston, who were tried under the above-mentioned Act, 8 vol. State Trials, fol. 205.

This Act of the 11 & 12 Wil. III. is made perpetual by the 6 Geo. I. c. 19. s. 3. and is enforced by the 8 Geo. I. c. 24. which last mentioned act is made perpetual by 2 Geo. II. c. 28. s. 7. The proceedings under the statute of 11 & 12 Wil. III. are by the 4th section of that Act directed to be, according to the Civil Law, and the methods and Rules of the Admiralty. This Act became necessary, on account of such British settlements in different parts, as had no regular Courts of Justice established, and were not populous enough to furnish juries; such as the forts on the coast of Guinea, and elsewhere; but by the 4 Geo. I. c. 11. intitled, "An Act for the further "preventing Robbery, &c." and for declaring the law upon some points relating to pirates. In the 7th section, it is declared, That all persons who shall commit any offence or offences, for which they ought to be adjudged pirates, felons, or robbers by the said Act of 11 & 12 Wil. III. c. 7. may be tried and judged for every such offence, in such manner as is directed by the 28 Hen. VIII. c. 15. and shall be excluded from Clergy;

vince of South Carolina, in a Court held by virtue of a Commission issued under this Act, they reported as their opinion, That murder on the high seas was not triable under the 11 & 12 of Wil. III. c. 7. which speaks of piracies, felonies, and robberies, but does not mention murder.

and

and by the 9th ſection of 4 Geo. I. c. 11. that Act is extended to America; ſo that at preſent a pirate in the Britiſh Colonies in America may be tried either under the 11 & 12 Wil. III. c. 7. according to the courſe of the Civil Law, or under the 28 Hen. VIII. c. 15. according the courſe of the Common Law; but the 28 Hen. VIII. c. 15. was not extended to the Britiſh ſettlements in Aſia and Africa; becauſe in many of them there were no regular Courts of Juſtice eſtabliſhed, nor juries to be had.

I was preſent at two trials in America under the 11 & 12 Wil. III. c. 7. One of thoſe trials was in a Weſt India iſland, and the other on the Continent. In the firſt caſe, the priſoners eſcaped, becauſe they were tried according to the courſe of the Civil Law, and there was but one witneſs againſt them; and the Solicitor-General was not aware of the 4 Geo. I. c. 11. which impowered him to try them in the manner directed by the 28 Hen. VIII. c. 15.

7. The Governor is alſo Vice-Admiral within his province; and in time of war he iſſues his warrant to the Judge of the Court of Vice-Admiralty to grant commiſſions to privateers: but the Governor does not ſit in the Court of Vice-Admiralty himſelf, there being uſually a Judge of the Court of Vice-Admiralty appointed from England. See more on this head under the title, Court of Vice-Admiralty hereafter.

By 11 & 12 Wil. III. c. 12. all crimes and offences committed by any Governor, Lieutenant-Governor, Deputy-Governor, or Commander in Chief of any plantation or colony within his Majeſty's Dominions beyond the ſeas, contrary to the laws of this realm, or in force within their reſpective governments, ſhall be heard and determined in the King's Bench in England, or before such Commissioners, and in such county of this realm, as shall be assigned by his Majesty's commission, and by good and lawful men of the same county, and that such punishments shall be inflicted on such offenders as are usually inflicted for offences of the like nature committed here in England.

CHAP. V.

Of the Lieutenant-General and Lieutenant-Governor.

LIEUTENANT-GENERAL.

IN Governments consisting of several islands, there is a Lieutenant-General, who is next in succession to the Captain-General and Governor in Chief; and in case of his death or absence, the Lieutenant-General takes the command: he is usually also Lieutenant-Governor of one of the Islands in the Government; but Mr. Losack, the present Lieutenant-General of the Leeward Charibbee Islands, is not Lieutenant-Governor of either of them, as they were all filled before his appointment. A Governor, on his departure from the colony which he commands, delivers his commission and instructions to the Lieutenant-General, or other person next in command, who is then on the spot.

LIEUTENANT-GOVERNOR.

By virtue of his Majesty's commission and instructions to the Captain-General and Governor in Chief, the Lieutenant-Governor (in case of the death

death or abſence of the Governor out of the province) is inveſted with all the powers and authorities granted by ſuch commiſſion; to be executed and enjoyed by the Lieutenant-Governor during his Majeſty's pleaſure, or until the arrival of the Governor in Chief in the province.

Form of a Commiſſion of a Lieutenant-Governor.

George R.

(Signet.)

GEORGE the Third, by the Grace of God, King of Great Britain, France, and Ireland, Defender of the Faith, &c. To our truſty and well-beloved A. B. Eſq; greeting: We repoſing eſpecial truſt and confidence in your loyalty, courage, and prudence, do, by theſe preſents, conſtitute and appoint you to be our Lieutenant-Governor of our Province of C— in America; to have, hold, exerciſe, and enjoy the ſaid place and office during our pleaſure, with all rights, privileges, profits, perquiſites, and advantages to the ſame belonging or appertaining; and further, in caſe of the death or abſence of our Captain-General and Governor in Chief in and over our ſaid province of C—, now and for the time being: we do hereby authoriſe and empower you to execute and perform all and ſingular the powers and authorities contained in our commiſſion to our ſaid Captain-General and Governor in Chief, according to ſuch inſtructions as are already ſent, or hereafter ſhall from time to time be ſent unto him, or as you ſhall receive from us, and from our ſaid Captain-General and Governor in Chief of our ſaid province of C—, now and for the time being; and all and ſingular our officers, Miniſters,

ministers, and loving subjects of our said province, and all others whom it may concern, are hereby commanded to take due notice hereof, and to give a ready obedience accordingly. Given at our Court at St. James's, the first day of January, one thousand seven hundred and eighty-three, in the twenty-third year of our reign.

By his Majesty's Command,

D. E.

A. B. Esq; Lieut. Governor of C—.

A Lieutenant-Governor who takes the command of a Colony on the death or absence of the Governor in Chief, must take the same oaths, and subscribe the test in the same manner that a Governor in Chief does on his entrance on his Government, viz. He must take the oaths to Government, and make and subscribe the declaration against transubstantiation: he must then take the oath usually taken by the Governors in the Plantations, for the due execution of the office of Lieutenant-Governor and Commander in Chief for the time being of that Province, the command of which has devolved on him; and for the due and impartial administration of justice there; and, in the last place, he must take the oath (required to be taken by Governors of the Plantations) to do his utmost, that the several laws relating to Trade and the Plantations be duly observed; which oaths and declaration, the Council of the Province, or any three of the Members thereof, are empowered to administer.

CHAP.

CHAP. VI.

Of the COUNCIL.

THERE are in every Colony twelve Ordinary Members of the Council, who are appointed either by being named in the Governor's Inſtructions, or elſe by Mandamus.

In the Colonies on the Continent, before the Civil War, there were two extraordinary Members of the Council, viz. his Majeſty's Superintendant for Indian affairs, and the Surveyor-General of the Cuſtoms: but notwithſtanding the Governor in Chief, and Lieutenant-Governor, ſhould be both dead, or abſent from the Province, yet neither of thoſe two extraordinary Members of the Council could adminiſter government, though next in ſeniority, but the command devolved on the Ordinary Member of the Council next in ſeniority to ſuch Superintendant or Surveyor-General. When a Governor in Chief is appointed to a Colony, the names of all ſuch Members of the Council as are continued, and the names of all ſuch as are newly appointed, are inſerted in the Governor's Inſtructions; and under this authority they are ſworn in on the Governor's arrival in the Province; but as faſt as vacancies happen during the Governor's continuance in office, ſuch vacancies are filled up by the Crown by Mandamus: of which the following is a copy.

G. R.

TRUSTY and well-beloved, we greet you well. We being well ſatisfied with the loyalty, integrity, and ability of our truſty and well-beloved A. B. Eſq;

Esq; have thought fit hereby to signify to you, our will and pleasure, That forthwith, upon receipt of these presents, you swear and admit him the said A. B. to be our of Council in our Province of C— ; and for so doing, this shall be your warrant: and so we bid you farewel: Given at our Court at St. James's, the fifth day of March, 1771, in the eleventh year of our reign.

By his Majesty's Command,
HILLSBOROUGH.

A. B. Esq. to be of the Council of C—.

This is folded up like a letter; and on the margin of the outside is thus written,

"A. B. Esq. to be
"of the Council of
"C——."

And is directed thus:

"To our trusty and well-beloved D. E. Esq; "our Captain-General and Governor in Chief "in and over our Province of C— in America; "and in his absence to the President of our Coun-"cil, or Commander in Chief of our said Pro-"vince for the time being."

SIGNET. The Signet was on the outside, after the Mandamus was folded up.

Every Councillor must take the oaths of allegiance, supremacy, and abjuration, and subscribe the test; after which he must take the following oath of office:

You do swear, that you faith and true allegiance bear unto his Most Sacred Majesty King George the

the Third, and to his heirs and ſucceſſors, and ſhall be true and faithful to his Excellency J. R. Eſq; as he is commiſſionated Captain-General and Governor in Chief in and over this his Majeſty's Province; and that you will, in the place and office of his Majeſty's Councillor of this Province, well and faithfully ſerve his ſaid Majeſty, and promote the good of his Majeſty's affairs with your beſt advice and counſel;—you ſhall, with your beſt ability, defend this Province from all foreign invaſions and inteſtine inſurrections;—you ſhall not countenance or conceal any plot or ſeditious conſpiracy, or any treaſonable or ſeditious ſpeeches againſt his ſaid Majeſty, his heirs or ſucceſſors, or his ſaid Excellency, but you ſhall give ſpeedy notice hereof unto his ſaid Excellency, or to ſome Member of the Council:—the ſecret debates of the Council you ſhall not reveal directly nor indirectly: all which you ſhall, to the utmoſt of your ability, perform.

So help you GOD.

The Council in a Colony act in the following different capacities:

1. They are to give advice to the Governor or Commander in Chief for the time being, when thereunto required; and they ſtand in the ſame relation to the Governor in a Colony, that the Privy Council does to the King in Great Britain; in ſome caſes, the Governor can act without their advice and concurrence; and there are other caſes, in which the Governor is required by his inſtructions not to act, without the advice and concurrence of the Council, or the major part of them. There are alſo inſtances, in which a Commander in Chief, for the time being, cannot act, without the advice and concurrence of the majority of the Council;

Council; although a Governor in Chief could, in such cases, proceed without their advice. This depends on his Majesty's instructions, which every Governor and Commander in Chief should carefully attend to. When I was in the West Indies, a Governor took the advantage of this power vested in him, to suspend, a Member of the Council, for marrying his daughter without his consent. But this Act was disapproved of at home, and the suspended Member was restored by an order from home, as I afterwards heard.

2. The Council is one branch of the legislature, and in the Colonies on the Continent before the Civil War, when the Members of the Council sat in their legislative capacity, they were then called, The Upper House of Assembly in their minutes; but in the Acts of Assembly, they were called, The Council, in the same manner as in the West India Colonies. But for more under this head, see title General Assembly, hereafter.

3. The Council sit as Judges in the Court of Errors or Court of Appeal, as herein before is mentioned.

4. In some Colonies, the Council sit as Judges with the Governor in the Court of Chancery, as I have herein before observed.

5. The Council are named, in every Commission of the Peace, as Justices of the Peace throughout the whole Colony; whereas, in the Provinces on the Continent, which are divided into particular districts, all the Justices of the Peace (except the Council, the Judges of the Superior Courts, and a few more) were, before the Civil War, appointed for particular districts only.

Every

Every Member of the Council is appointed during his Majeſty's pleaſure only; and, with the conſent of the Council, may be ſuſpended by the Governor or Commander in Chief for miſbehaviour.

CHAP. VII.

Of the GENERAL ASSEMBLY.

THE General Aſſembly conſiſts of the Captain General and Governor in Chief (or in caſe of his death or abſence, of the Commander in Chief for the time being), the twelve Members of the Council, and the Houſe of Repreſentatives choſen by the people, which Repreſentatives are more or fewer, according to the extent of the Colony.

In the Provinces on the Continent, the number of Repreſentatives increaſed, as the boundaries were extended by ceſſions of land by the Indians. The Repreſentatives are ſtyled differently in different Colonies. In all the Weſt India Iſlands, they are called The Aſſembly; in Virginia, before the Civil War, they were ſtyled, The Houſe of Burgeſſes; in the Maſſachuſett's Bay, The Houſe of Repreſentatives; and in moſt of the other Colonies on the Continent, The Commons Houſe of Aſſembly.

The Governor, Council, and Aſſembly, in every Colony, is a ſubordinate Legiſlature, ſubject to the controul of the King and Parliament, who are ſupreme over all the Britiſh Empire. The Governor (or in caſe of his death or abſence, the Commander in Chief for the time being) as the King's Repreſentative, is the firſt branch of this ſubordinate Legiſlature, and hath the ſole

power

power of convening, adjourning, proroguing, and dissolving the General Assembly. Every Governor is forbid to suffer the Assembly to adjourn itself. In the Provinces on the Continent, where many of the Members lived at a distance from the town, it was usual for the Commons House of Assembly not to do business on a Saturday, but to go home on the Friday evening, and re-return to town on the Monday morning following. However, the Governor could not, consistent with his duty, permit the Commons House of Assembly to enter on their Journals an adjournment from Friday till Monday; but the Clerk of the Commons House of Assembly made an entry on the Journals every Saturday, in the manner following:

Saturday, December 16th, 1769.

" The House met according to adjournment, " and then adjourned 'till Monday morning, ten " of the clock."

And whenever the two Houses of Assembly were adjourned for the Christmas Holidays, or on any other occasion, it was always done by the Governor, in the manner following:

" Mr. Speaker, and Gentlemen of the Assembly, I do hereby adjourn the Commons " House of Assembly, until Monday the eighth " day of January next, then to meet for the dispatch of business; and it is accordingly adjourned to the 8th day of January next. Given " under my hand, at   this 20th day of " December 1769.

A. B.

" To the Honourable the Speaker " and Members of the Commons House of Assembly."

The

The late diſpoſition, the Colonies have ſhewn, makes it appear how neceſſary it was that the power of adjournment ſhould be lodged in the Governor only, and not entruſted with the Houſes of Aſſembly.

The Council, or (as it is called) Upper Houſe of Aſſembly, is an humble imitation of the Houſe of Lords.

The Aſſembly, or (as it is called in moſt of the Colonies on the Continent) Commons Houſe of Aſſembly, repreſents the people at large, and are choſen by them. The qualifications of the Electors, and the elected, are different in almoſt every Colony, and ſo is the continuance of the Houſe of Repreſentatives; for in ſome Colonies, they continued during the Governor's pleaſure; in other Colonies, they were elected annually; and ſeveral of the Governors formerly aſſented to Acts of Aſſembly, extending the democratical part of the Conſtitution of ſome Colonies beyond that of Great Britain, particularly in the Iſlands of St. Chriſtopher and Barbadoes, and in the Province of South Carolina, where, by Act of Aſſembly, the election of Repreſentatives was annual.

Some Governors in former reigns did alſo aſſent to Acts, giving the Houſes of Repreſentatives a power of appointing to executive offices, by enabling them to conſtitute the public Treaſurer, &c. in derogation of the undoubted prerogatives of the Crown, as the Reader may obſerve, by conſulting the Acts of Aſſembly of the different Colonies.

The proceedings of the Houſes of Aſſembly in the Colonies are conducted, and their Journals kept, in a manner much conformed to thoſe of the two Houſes of Parliament.

It will therefore be needleſs to enumerate particulars, as the Journals of the Houſes of Parliament

ment are the precedents by which the Legislatures in the Colonies conduct themselves. I shall only take notice of some things which are peculiar to the Colonies; and in the first place, it will be necessary to observe, that the enacting part of the Acts of Assembly differs in different Colonies, as will appear by the following extracts:

The enacting part of an Act of Assembly in the Island of Jamaica.

"WHEREAS some inconveniencies have already "happened, through the negligence and misbe- "haviour of some officers in the respective offices "of record of this Island: for the prevention of "such inconveniencies for the future, and the "rasing, embezzling, or destroying of any the "records or enrollments within this Island, we "your Majesty's most dutiful and loyal subjects, "the Council and Assembly of this your Ma- "jesty's Island, do beseech your Majesty that it "may be enacted; be it therefore enacted by the "Governor, Council, and Assembly of this your "Majesty's Island of Jamaica, and it is hereby "enacted and ordained by the authority of the "same, That if any person whatsoever shall make, "or cause to be made, any rasure, &c."

The Enacting Part of an Act of Assembly in the Island of Barbadoes.

"WHEREAS the several fortifications of this "Island are at this time very much gone to decay, "and it being absolutely necessary for the honour "of the government, as well as the safety of this "place, that the said fortifications should be well "and sufficiently repaired, and at all times for

"the

" the future kept and preserved in a good posture " of defence; be it enacted by his Excellency " Robert Lowther, Esq; Captain General and " Governor in Chief of this and other the Cha- " ribbee Islands, lying and being to windward of " Guadaloupe, the Honourable the Members of " his Majesty's Council, and the General As- " sembly of this Island, and by the authority of " the same, That every person in this Island, be- " ing seised or possessed of ten or more acres, " &c."

The Enacting Part of an Act of Assembly, in the Island of St. Christopher.

" WHEREAS the navigation of this Island la- " bours under great difficulties and disappoint- " ments by reason of the disorderly behaviour of " the sailors and seamen, occasioned chiefly by the " entertainment and credit they meet with in the " Punch-houses of this Island; and also by sailors " leaving the vessels they have been entered in, " before they have performed the voyage they " have been entered for, to which they are en- " couraged by their being shipped at higher " wages by the masters of other vessels.

" And whereas the laws already made, have " proved ineffectual for the prevention of the " mischiefs aforesaid, we your Majesty's most du- " tiful and loyal subjects, the Governor in Chief " in and over all your Majesty's Leeward Cha- " ribbee Islands in America, and the Council and " Assembly of your Majesty's Island of St. Chri- " stopher, humbly pray your most sacred Ma- " jesty, that it may be enacted:

" 2. And be it, and it is hereby enacted by the " King's most excellent Majesty, by and with the " advice

"advice and consent of the said Governor in "Chief, and the Council and Assembly of the "said Island of St. Christopher, That all sailors "and seamen, &c."

The enacting part of the Acts of Assembly in the other parts of the Leeward Charibbee Islands, is similar to that in the Island of St. Christopher above set forth. Formerly there was but one General Assembly for all the Leeward Charibbee Islands; but now there is a separate legislature for each of the Islands of Saint Christopher, Nevis, Montserrat and Antigua.

The Enacting Part of an Act of Assembly, of the Bermuda or Summer Islands.

"WHEREAS there hath been no current value as "yet set upon gold, which many times causeth "disputes and differences in passing the same; "and for prevention whereof for the future, we "therefore your Majesty's most dutiful and loyal "subjects, the Assembly of these your Majesty's "Bermuda or Summer Islands in America, do "most humbly beseech your Majesty, that it may "be enacted; and be it enacted by your Majesty's "Lieutenant Governor, Council, and Assembly, "and it is hereby enacted and ordained by the "authority of the same, That from and after "publication hereof, all pistoles of gold, &c."

The Enacting Part of an Act of Assembly in Virginia before the Civil War.

"WHEREAS it hath been found by experience, "that one Act of Assembly made in the seventh "year of the reign of our late sovereign Lord "King George the First, intituled, An Act for "the

" the supply of certain defects found in an Act, " prescribing the method for appointing Sheriffs, " is very useful and necessary; and it is since de- " termined and expired.

2. " Be it therefore enacted, by the Lieutenant " Governor, Council, and Burgesses, of this pre- " sent General Assembly; and it is hereby enacted " by the authority of the same, That the said Act, " made in the said seventh year of the reign of " our said late Lord the King, and every the " clauses, articles, and sentences therein con- " tained, shall and be, and are hereby revived " and made perpetual."

The Enacting part of an Act of Assembly of the Province of the Massachusett's Bay before the Civil War.

" WHEREAS the stated allowance by law for " grand Jurors, of two shillings *per diem*, during " their attendance at Court, is thought too little, " considering the great price of provisions and " other necessaries; be it enacted by his Excel- " lency the Governor, Council, and Representa- " tives, in General Court assembled, and by the " authority of the same, That the allowance of a " Grand Juror, during his attendance on the " Court, and also for his necessary travel to and " from the same for the future, be three shillings " *per diem*.

" And whereas a great part of the business of " the Superior Court, is often taken up in hear- " ing and granting petitions for the sale of land, " and no fee yet stated by law for the same; be " it further enacted by the authority aforesaid, " That the fee or allowance to the Judges of the " said Court, on such petitions, be two shillings a-piece to each Judge preſent at the hearing of ſuch petition, and no more."

The enacting Part of an Act of Aſſembly of the Province of New York, before the Civil War.

" WHEREAS the Act, intituled, An Act for
" licenſing Hawkers and Pedlars within this Pro-
" vince, is expired by its own limitation, and
" the ſame having by experience been found to
" be very beneficial; be it therefore enacted by
" the Governor, Council, and General Aſſembly,
" and by the authority of the ſame, That the
" ſaid Act, and every article, clauſe, and thing
" therein contained, be, and is hereby revived
" and continued to remain in force for and during
" the term of four years; excepting and reſerving
" from the penalties of the Act aforeſaid, Jere-
" miah Smith of Queen's County, who is hereby
" licenſed to trade as a petty Chapman within
" Queen's County only; any thing in the before
" recited Act to the contrary notwithſtanding."

The enacting part of an Act of Aſſembly in the Province of New Jerſey, is the ſame as that in New York, *mutatis mutandis.*

The enacting Part of an Act of Aſſembly in the Province of Georgia before the Civil War.

" WHEREAS the dangerous practice of hunt-
" ing by fire-light in the night-time, under the
" pretence of killing deer, is now become very
" common, by means whereof cattle are frequent-
" ly deſtroyed, to the manifeſt injury of the
" owners of the ſame; for remedy thereof, and
" in order to prevent as much as may be the like
" miſchiefs in future, we humbly pray his moſt

" Sacred

" Sacred Majeſty that it may be enacted, and
" be it enacted by his Excellency Sir James
" Wright, Baronet, Captain-General and Go-
" vernor in Chief in and over his Majeſty's Pro-
" vince of Georgia, by and with the advice and
" conſent of the Honourable Council, and the
" Commons Houſe of Aſſembly of the ſaid Pro-
" vince, in General Aſſembly met, and by the
" authority of the ſame, That from and after the
" firſt day of June next enſuing, &c."

I have already obſerved, that after the re-eſtabliſhment of the King's Civil Government in Georgia, the Council was ſtyled Upper Houſe, in moſt of the laws that paſſed.

Many of the Acts of Aſſembly in the Colonies are drawn in a looſe inaccurate manner, as will appear by the following ſpecimens:

In an Act of Aſſembly in the Iſland of Antigua is the following recital:

" WHEREAS *the want* of croſs Streets and
" Lanes, to paſs from Street to Street in the ſe-
" veral Towns of this Iſland, and proper allot-
" ments of Land for Market-places have been
" hitherto *much wanted*, &c."

In ſome Acts of Aſſembly of the Province of ——— are the following recitals:

" WHEREAS the Light-houſe on ———
" Iſland is in a *ruinous condition*, and if not ſpeedi-
" ly repaired muſt ſoon *decay*, &c."

Is not a Building in a *ruinous condition* already *decayed?*

" WHERE-

"WHEREAS Disputes and Differences fre-
"quently arise and happen between Merchants,
"&c. which cannot be determined by *Legal Pro-*
"*cess*, &c."

If such Disputes cannot be determined by *Legal Process*, How then are they to be determined?

It may appear trifling to the Reader to take notice of such absurdities; but it will be a foundation for the following useful hints to some of the Colony Legislatures, provided they will take notice of them.

In the Colonies, the Planters and Mechanics that get into the House of Representatives, frequently think themselves capable of adding a clause to, or altering the wording of a bill brought into the House of Assembly, without reflecting, that even statutes drawn by the ablest Judges in Westminster Hall, have occasioned doubts and law-suits.—I have known Bills passed in the Commons House of Assembly, and sent to the Upper House for concurrence, which have been so defective, both in language and sentiment, that they were incapable of any amendment otherwise than by drawing up a fresh form of a Bill, calculated to answer the same purposes with the Bill sent up. In the Upper House of Assembly, pains were accordingly taken to draw up a Bill, in the language of some Act in the Statute Book of Great Britain, in a case of a similar nature; and such draught has been sent down by way of an amendment with the Bill that passed the Commons House of Assembly. The Gentlemen below were not able to deny the absurdity of their own Bill, and have adopted the draught sent down in lieu of it; but they have disgraced it so much with ill-judged alterations, which they called amendments, that those who were concerned in drawing it have been ashamed to own it.

When an Act of Assembly has received the Governor's assent, it must be sent home to Great Britain within three months, for his Majesty's approbation or disallowance. If it receives his Majesty's approbation, the same is signified to the Governor by an order of the King in Council, which was formerly done in the following manner:

" At the Court at Kensington the 31st of December 1696.

PRESENT

The KING's Most Excellent Majesty in Council.

" Thomas, Lord Archbishop " of Canterbury
" Lord Keeper
" Lord Steward
" Lord Chamberlain
" Earl of Bridgewater
" Earl of Stamford
" Earl of Portland
" Earl of Monmouth
" Lord Viscount Dursley
" Lord Cornwallis
" Lord Coningsby
" Mr. Secretary Trumbull
" Mr. Chancellor of the " Exchequer
" Lord Chief Justice Holt.

" WHEREAS his Majesty has been pleased, " by his Royal Commission, bearing date the six " and twentieth day of October one thousand six " hundred and eighty-nine, in the first year of his " reign, to authorise the Governor, Councils, and " Assemblies of their Majesty's Leeward Charib- " bee Islands in America, jointly and severally, " to make, constitute and ordain laws, statutes, " and ordinances, for the public peace, welfare, " and good government of the said Islands; " which said laws, statutes, and ordinances, are " to be, as near as conveniently may be, agree- " able to the laws and statutes of this Kingdom, " and to be transmitted to his Majesty for his " Royal

" Royal approbation or disallowance of them; " and the Council of Trade having perused and " and considered certain laws, passed in the Ge- " neral Assembly of his Majesty's Island of Mont- " serrat, in the words following:

Here the several Acts of Assembly approved of by his Majesty, were recited.

" Which said laws having been presented to " his Majesty, at this Board, his Majesty was gra- " ciously pleased, with the advice of his Privy " Council, to declare his approbation of the same, " and, pursuant to his Royal pleasure thereupon, " the said laws are hereby confirmed, finally enact- " ed, and ratified accordingly.

W. Bridgman."

But now the method is, not to recite the Acts themselves in the order of Council, but only the titles of them; as will appear by the following form:

" P R E S E N T

" The King's Most Excellent Majesty,

" Lord President	" Viscount Falmouth,
" Duke of Queensberrry	" Viscount Ligonier
" Earl of Holdernesse	" Lord Berkeley of Stratton
" Earl of Cholmondeley	" Lord Grantham
" Earl of Bute	" Mr. Vice Chamberlain.

" Whereas, by Commission under the " Great Seal of Great Britain, the Governor, " Council, and Assembly of his Majesty's Pro- " vince of Georgia, are authorised and impowered " to make, constitute, and ordain laws, statutes, " and ordinances for the public peace, welfare, " and good government of the said Province, " which laws, statutes, and ordinances are to be,

" as

" as near as conveniently may be, agreeable to " the laws and ſtatutes of this kingdom, and to " be tranſmitted for his Majeſty's Royal appro- " bation or diſallowance: and whereas, in pur- " ſuance of the ſaid powers, an Act was paſſed in " the ſaid Province in May 1760, and tranſmit- " ted, intituled as follows, *viz.*

" An Act for ſtamping, imprinting, iſſuing, " and making current, the ſum of Seven " thouſand four hundred and ten pounds " Sterling, in Paper Bills of Credit, and for " applying and ſinking the ſame.

" Which Act, together with a repreſentation " from the Lords Commiſſioners for Trade and " Plantations thereupon, having been referred to " the conſideration of a Committee of the Lords " of his Majeſty's moſt Honourable Privy Coun- " cil for Plantation affairs, the ſaid Lords of the " Committee did this day report, as their opinion " to his Majeſty, that the ſaid Act was proper to " be approved. His Majeſty taking the ſame " into conſideration, was pleaſed, with the advice " of his Privy Council, to declare his approba- " tion of the ſaid Act; and, purſuant to his Ma- " jeſty's Royal pleaſure thereupon expreſſed, the " ſaid Act is hereby confirmed, finally enacted, " and ratified accordingly; whereof the Gover- " nor or Commander in Chief of his Majeſty's " Province of Georgia for the time being, " and all others whom it may concern, are to " take notice and govern themſelves accord- " ingly. W. SHARPE."

If a Governor has the leaſt doubt whether an Act of Aſſembly, to which he is requeſted to give his

his assent, is constitutional, or else infringes on his Majesty's prerogative, in that case, if he does not reject it, he ought at least to refuse his assent, until both Houses of Assembly agree to add a clause to such Act, suspending the execution thereof, until his Majesty's pleasure is known; which suspending clause may be in the words following:

" AND be it further enacted, That neither this " Act, nor any thing herein before contained, " shall be of any force, power, or efficacy; but " the same is wholly suspended, until his Sacred " Majesty's approbation and allowance thereof " shall be signified to the Governor or Com- " mander in Chief for the time being; any thing " herein before contained to the contrary there- " of in any wise notwithstanding."

Or it may be thus:

" PROVIDED lastly, and it is hereby de- " clared, That neither this Act, nor any part " thereof, shall take effect, until his most Sacred " Majesty shall notify his confirmation and allow- " ance thereof to his Governor or Commander " in Chief of this Province for the time being; " any thing herein before contained to the con- " trary in any wise notwithstanding."

CHAP.

CHAP. VIII.

Of Inferior COURTS *of Civil Jurisdiction.*

IN all the Colonies there are Inferior Courts of Civil Jurisdiction, which hold plea in personal actions to a certain amount; which limitation in some Colonies is greater, in others less. In Jamaica, besides the Supreme Court, which has jurisdiction over all the Island, and holds plea to any amount, there are also Courts which have jurisdiction within certain districts, and hold plea where the debt or damages amount to twenty pounds only; and in which Courts matters of fact are tried by a Jury, in the same manner as in the Supreme Court. But in some of the Islands to Windward, the Chief Justice of the Superior Court sits alone, to try actions to a certain amount without a Jury:—in other Islands, personal actions to a certain amount are brought on before all the Judges of the Court, and are decided without a Jury, after all the Jury actions are finished. In the Colonies on the Continent, there are Inferior Courts held before the Justices of the Peace for particular districts, in which all matters of debt or damage under a certain sum are tried by a Jury; and the extent of those Inferior Courts are in some places bounded by the parish, in other places by different divisions. If the debt or damages are under forty shillings, Two Justices, and Three Jurymen, are sufficient to decide on them; if above forty shillings, and under eight pounds, then there must be Two Justices and Twelve Jurymen. In some Colonies those Courts are called Courts of Conscience, and in others County Courts;

Courts; the form of their process, and the mode of their proceedings, are usually set out at large in the Acts of Assembly, by which they are established. Where the debt or damages are under forty shillings, there is usually no power of appeal allowed; bu in cases where the debt or damages exceed forty shillings, a Writ of Error is allowed, or liberty of appeal given to the Superior Court of Common Law. These Inferior Courts decide a great number of actions; but the Justices of Peace who preside therein are frequently plain men, and their proceedings are very irregular, little order or decorum being observed among them.

CHAP. IX.

Of the Superior COURTS *of Civil Jurisdiction.*

I SHALL first begin with the West India Islands, by observing, that, in the Island of Jamaica, the Superior Court of Common Law is called The Supreme Court, and is a King's Bench, Common Pleas, and Exchequer; and this being a large Island, it has of late years been divided into districts; and the Judges of the Supreme Court go in circuit round the Island.

In Barbadoes, the Island is divided into five precincts, for each of which there is a Court of Common Pleas, with a distinct set of Judges. The greatest length of this Island is about twenty miles and three quarters, and its greatest breadth about thirteen miles and three quarters:—it seems therefore very absurd to have so many distinct Superior Courts in such a small Island.—Had there been one Superior Court established for the whole

whole Island, in the center of it; in that case five Gentlemen, who had some experience in the law, might have been found to fill the Office of Judges: but it is not to be conceived, that such a small Island can afford to pay proper salaries to twenty-five Judges; by which means, none but a man who has little knowledge, and much vanity, will accept of the Office of a Judge, which is attended with little or no profit.

Antigua was formerly divided into two precincts; but at present there is only one Court of Common Pleas for the whole Island.

In the rest of the Leeward Charibbee Islands, the Superior Court of Common Law is a King's Bench and Common Pleas.

In all the Southern Colonies on the Continent, before the Civil War, the Superior Court was, a King's Bench, Common Pleas, and Exchequer.

I shall now make some observations on the proceedings of the Superior Courts of Civil Jurisdiction in the Colonies, which will apply to all the West India Islands, and also, as I apprehend, to all the Provinces on the Continent before the Civil War.—In the first place, all original Process, and even Writs of Dedimus Potestatem to Commissioners, to take renunciations of Dower, are issued by the Court of Common Law itself, and tested in the name of the Chief Justice:—and the Chancery issues no Writ in the form of a Præcipe, or Si te fecerit securum, or any other process whereon to found the proceedings of the Courts of Common Law, except Writs of Audita Querela, which must necessarily be issued by the Chancellor; and instances of the issuing of such Writs of Audita Querela, I have known in different Colonies. But I remember no case wherein the Chancellor issued any other Writ, to enable the

the Court of Common Law to hold plea; and by reason thereof, that which in Westminster Hall is Mesne Process, *viz.* the Summons in Dower, the Capias in Trespass, &c. are the original Process in the Colonies.

2. No real actions have ever been used in the Colonies, except actions of Dower; for all titles to land have been tried either by Ejectment, Trespass, or Replevin.

3. The mode of commencing actions in the Colonies is various:—In the West India Islands, they commence the action by filing the Declaration in the Office, and a copy of such Declaration, with a Summons, is served by one of the Marshall's Bailiffs on the Defendant: but if the Defendant is absent from the Island, and hath appointed an Attorney, then, if the Letter of Attorney is registered in the Secretary or Register's Office, the Declaration and Summons are to be served on such Attorney; or, if he is not to be met with, they are to be left at his dwelling-house or place of abode:—if no such Letter of Attorney is registered in the Office, then, if the Defendant has a Plantation in the Island, the Declaration and Summons must be served on the Manager or Overseer of such Plantation; and if neither of is to be met with, the Declaration and Summons must be left at the House upon such Plantation: but if the Defendant has no Plantation on the Island, the service must be, by nailing up a copy of the Declaration and Summons at the door of the Court-house. This mode of service is not perfectly the same in every stage of it, but is substantially the same in every Island.

On the Continent before the Civil War, their proceedings were more conformable to the prac-

tice

tice in Weſtminſter Hall: they had four Courts in the year: the action was commenced by ſuing out a Writ, which was made returnable on a day certain; and after the return of the Writ, the Plaintiff filed his Declaration.

In all the Weſt India Iſlands, the Superior Courts of Common Law have been eſtabliſhed by Acts of the General Aſſembly; for which *ſee* the Laws of each of theſe Iſlands. In moſt of the Colonies on the Continent, theſe Superior Courts of Common Law were eſtabliſhed by Letters Patent under the Great Seal of the Province, by the King's inſtructions to his Governor, on the firſt inſtitution of the King's government in the Province.

Under this head I have given no forms, becauſe the method of proceeding in Civil Actions in all the Colonies is conducted, as near as local circumſtances will admit, agreeable to the practice in the Court of Common Pleas in Weſtminſter Hall.

Letters Patent *for eſtabliſhing a General Court in the Province of Georgia.*

Georgia.

GEORGE the Second, by the grace of God of Great Britain, France, and Ireland, King, Defender of the Faith, and ſo forth. To all to whom theſe our preſent Letters ſhall come greeting; Know ye that we, tendering the ſtate and condition of our Province of Georgia, and being willing and deſirous that juſtice be duly and regularly adminiſtered therein, have thought fit to erect and conſtitute, and by theſe preſents do erect and conſtitute a Court of Record, by the name and ſtyle of the General Court, to be holden yearly

yearly at Savannah, within our ſaid Province, on the ſecond Tueſday in January, the ſecond Tueſday in April, the ſecond Tueſday in July, and the ſecond Tueſday in October, before our truſty and well-beloved Noble Jones and Jonathan Bryan, Eſqrs; or one of them, whom we hereby appoint our Juſtices thereof, during our pleaſure, and others our Juſtices appointed for the time being. And we do hereby give and grant unto the ſaid Noble Jones and Jonathan Bryan, and each of them, and all others our Juſtices of the ſaid General Court, for the time being, full power, juriſdiction and authority, to enquire, by the oaths of good and lawful men of the Province aforeſaid, and by other ways and means by which the truth of the matter may be better known and enquired into, of all treaſons, felonies, and other crimes and criminal offences whatſoever, done or committed within our ſaid Province by any perſons whatſoever, and the ſame to hear and determine, according to the laws and cuſtoms of our ſaid Province; ſaving to us, and our ſucceſſors, all fines, forfeitures, and amerciaments, and all other things to us on account thereof belonging and appertaining. And further, we give and grant to the ſaid Noble Jones and Jonathan Bryan, and each others our Juſtices of our ſaid General Court for the time being, full power, juriſdiction, and authority, to hold pleas in all and all manner of cauſes, ſuits, and actions whatſoever, as well criminal as civil, real, perſonal, and mixed, ariſing, happening, or being within our ſaid Province, where the ſum or thing demanded ſhall exceed the value of forty ſhillings ſterling; except only where the title to any freehold ſhall come in queſtion; and to proceed in ſuch pleas, ſuits, and actions, by ſuch ways, means, and proceſs, as may with

with the greateſt ſafety, diſpatch, and juſtice, bring the ſame to a final determination, and alſo to hear and determine all ſuch pleas, ſuits, and actions, and judgment thereupon to give, and execution thereof to award and iſſue, and this as fully and amply as can or may be done by our Courts of King's Bench, Common Pleas, and Exchequer in England, doing therein what of right and juſtice ought to be done.—In teſtimony whereof we have cauſed theſe our Letters to be made Patent, and the Seal of our ſaid Province to be affixed thereto. Witneſs our truſty and well-beloved John Reynolds, Eſq; our Captain-General and Governor in Chief in and over our ſaid Province of Georgia, the twelfth day of December, in the twenty-eighth year of our reign.

J. REYNOLDS.

By his Excellency's
command,
JAMES HABERSHAM,
Secretary.

The
Great Seal
of
GEORGIA.

CHAP.

CHAP. X.

Of the Superior COURTS *of Criminal Jurisdiction.*

IN England the criminal business is divided between the Assizes and Quarter Sessions.—But in the Colonies, the whole of the criminal business centers in one Court.—In Jamaica, St. Christopher's, and Nevis, the Superior Court has the same jurisdiction there as the King's Bench and Common Pleas have in England; and that was the case in some of the Colonies on the Continent before the Civil War.—But in the Islands of Barbadoes, Antigua, Montserrat, and in some other Colonies, the Criminal Court is distinct from the Common Pleas, and consists of a number of Judges, *viz.* of the Members of the Council, the Judges of the Common Pleas, the Justices of the Peace, and the Judge of the Court of Vice-Admiralty, &c.—This Court is inconvenient; for the Judges are, in general, unacquainted with the law, and often commit mistakes. Their number is so great, that should they do wrong, there is no getting at them. And as most of the principal men in the Colony sit in this Court, hardly any thing can come on but some of them are connected with it.

Such of the pleadings in criminal causes (as well as those in civil cases) which are drawn by Counsel, are conducted in a manner similar to that used in the Superior Courts in Westminster Hall:—but in all the Islands except Jamaica, the entry of the judgment, and the other Acts of the Court, are not entered at large, agreeable to the practice in England; but are short minutes made

by

by the Officer of the Court, who is frequently unacquainted with the law forms.

The following cafe happened whilft I refided in the Weft Indies:

The Town of ——— in the Ifland of ——, was laid out in parallel lines, interfecting each other at right angles.—One G— built a houfe in the middle of a ftreet there, called North Street, and an indictment for a nuifance was found againft him. When the indictment came on to trial, the Profecutor's Counfel afked ———, the Attorney General, on which fide he was concerned? to which he anfwered, That he was concerned for the Defendant.—It was then objected, That the Court ought not to fuffer the King's Attorney General to appear againft him; and the practice of the Courts in Weftminfter Hall was mentioned.—The Prefident of the Court faid, That the cuftom of that Country was different: and the Attorney General was fuffered to appear for the Defendant, who was found guilty of the nuifance.—The Attorney General, as Counfel for the Defendant, then moved, That judgment might be arrefted; but this motion was overruled: and then, on the motion of the Profecutor's Counfel, and agreeable to the doctrine in the 1 Hawkins P. C. 200. the Defendant was commanded by the Court to remove the nuifance at his own cofts; and judgment was refpited until the then next Seffions. The Defendant did not remove the nuifance; but brought a Writ of Error, which was made returnable before the day for holding the then next Seffions, and was therefore no Superfedeas. On this ground, the Profecutor's Counfel moved for the judgment of the Court, on the authority of the cafes of Baker and

and Bulstrode, 1 Ventris 255. Ayers and Lenthall, 3 Keble 308. Prydyerd and Thomas, 1 Ventris 96, and of 1 Siderfin 466. But notwithstanding these cases, the Court declined to give any judgment; and there the matter rested.

I shall trouble the Reader with no forms under this head; for the method of proceeding in criminal cases in the Colonies, is similar to that of the Superior Courts in England.—But process of outlawry hath never been issued in any Colony, either in civil or criminal cases, that I can learn. In those Colonies in which I resided, no such thing ever happened.

CHAP. XI.

Of the JUDGES *of the* SUPERIOR COURTS *in the* COLONIES.

EVERY Judge in the Colonies holds his Commission during his Majesty's pleasure, and the residence of such Judge in the Colony. The Chief Justices are in general appointed by warrant under his Majesty's Sign Manual and Signet, by the authority of which warrant, Letters Patent are made out in the Colony, tested by the Governor or commander in Chief for the time being, and under the Great Seal of the Colony. For these instruments, see the following forms: Wherever a salary is annexed to the office of Chief Justice, and the income is sufficient to induce a man of abilities to accept of it, a proper person is appointed from England to fill such office; but the Assistant Judges are, in general, appointed by the Governor, and are almost always unacquainted with the law. In such of the Colonies where the inhabitants

habitants are able to bear the expence of raiſing ſalaries for their Judges, it is not to be expected that Great Britain ſhould ſuſtain that expence; but the leading men in ſome Colonies may perhaps oppoſe every attempt to provide proper ſalaries for the Chief Judges by Act of Aſſembly, as they may expect to fill thoſe offices themſelves; whereas, if ſalaries were annexed to them, proper Judges would be ſent from England. In a northern climate, where men are phlegmatic, it would be difficult to prevail on an ignorant country eſquire to ſit in judgment on the lives and properties of his fellow-ſubjects, even if a ſalary was allowed him; but in ſouthern climates, where men in general have much vivacity, and a great love of power, we may obſerve, that without any knowledge of the law, they court theſe employments. It would be invidious to deſcend to particulars; but I cannot avoid obſerving, that ſeveral years ago, when I reſided in the Weſt Indies, and was converſant with four Iſlands, there was not in either of theſe Iſlands one Judge that had been regularly bred to the law. In ſome of the Weſt India Iſlands, it is neceſſary that there ſhould be three Judges on the Bench, in order to proceed to buſineſs, which is an inlet to much abuſe; for ſome of the Judges have frequently abſented themſelves, under different pretences, that there might be no Court. An inſtance of this kind happened ſome years ago in one of the Iſlands in the Weſt Indies that I was acquainted with. A Chief Judge had a Bond and Warrant of Attorney to confeſs judgment, ſtanding out againſt him; and by the law of the Iſland, ſuch a judgment could not be entered up, except at the ſitting of the Court: matters were ſo managed, that a number of Judges, ſufficient to hold

hold a Court, did not meet for a confiderable time, and the creditor was kept out of his money.

Formerly fome perfons in —— had taken an undue advantage of being privileged from arreft, on which the Legiflature of that Ifland, in the year 1740, paffed an Act, declaring, That from thenceforth no Judge, &c. or any other Minifter of the Law, fhould thereafter have privilege to enter any common appearance for the difcharge of any bail bond in any cafe whatfoever. Many years after this Act paffed, when I was in the Weft Indies, an Affiftant Judge was arrefted for debt:—at the next Court it was moved on his behalf, that he fhould be difcharged, on entering a common appearance. In vain did the Plaintiff's Counfel urge the Act of Affembly againft fuch application;—the gentleman on the Bench faid, That they only were Judges of their own privileges; and the Affiftant Judge's bond was difcharged on his entering a common appearance. I fhall only further obferve on this head, that, as the Judges there were in general unacquainted with the law, they frequently afked the opinion of fome leading Lawyer in matters that came before them; which gave fuch lawyer an amazing afcendency in the Ifland, as many who refided there muft remember.

WARRANT *under his Majefty's Sign Manual and Signet, for the Appointment of a Chief Juftice in one of the Colonies.*

GEORGE R.

TRUSTY and well-beloved, we greet you well. Whereas we have taken into our Royal confideration the loyalty, integrity, and ability of

our

our trusty and well-beloved A. B. Esq; we have thought fit hereby to authorise and require you forthwith to cause Letters Patent to be passed under the seal of our Province of C—, constituting and appointing him the said A. B. our Chief Justice of, and in our said Province, in the room of L. M. Esq; deceased. To have, hold, execute, and enjoy the said office unto him the said A. B. for and during our pleasure, and his residence within our said Province, together with all and singular the rights, profits, privileges, and emoluments unto the said place belonging, in the most full and ample manner, with full power and authority to hold the Supreme Courts of Judicature at such places and times as the same may and ought to be held within our said province: and for so doing, this shall be your warrant; and so we bid you farewel. Given at our Court at St. James's the twenty-third day of March 1769, in the ninth year of our reign.

By his Majesty's Command,

H——.

A. B. Esq; Chief Justice of C—.

This warrant was under the King's Signet, and directed to the Governor of C—, and in his absence, to the Commander in Chief there, exactly as in the Mandamus for a Member of the Council.

LETTERS PATENT *under the Great Seal of a Colony, for the Appointment of a Chief Justice, in pursuance of the before-mentioned Warrant.*

GEORGE the Third, by the Grace of God, of Great Britain, France, and Ireland, King, Defender of the Faith, &c. To all whom these presents

preſents ſhall come, greeting: Know ye, That we having taken into our Royal conſideration the loyalty, integrity, and ability, of our truſty and well-beloved A. B. Eſq; have conſtituted and appointed him the ſaid A. B. our Chief Juſtice of and in our Province of C— in America, in the room of L. M. Eſq; deceaſed, to have, hold, execute, and enjoy the ſaid office unto him the ſaid A. B. for and during our pleaſure; and his reſidence within our ſaid Province, together with all and ſingular the rights, profits, privileges, and emoluments unto the ſaid place belonging, in the moſt full and ample manner, with full power and authority to hold the Supreme Courts of Judicature at ſuch places and Times as the ſame may and ought to be held, within our ſaid Province. In Witneſs whereof we have cauſed theſe our Letters to be made Patent. Witneſs his Excellency D. E. Eſq; our Captain-General and Governor in Chief in and over our ſaid Province of C—, at F——, the firſt day of September, in the ninth year of our reign.

D, E.

By his Majeſty's Warrant, under his Royal Sign Manuel and Signet, dated at his Court at St. James's, the 23d day of March, 1769, in the ninth year of his reign.

Great Seal of C—.

CHAP.

CHAP. XII.

Of the COUNSEL *and* ATTORNIES *in the* COLONIES.

IN Jamaica and Barbadoes, the departments of Counſel and Attorney are diſtinct, and they have ſeveral gentlemen of ability in the Law, who attend at the bars in thoſe Iſlands. In St. Chriſtopher's, the branches of Counſel and Attorney were ſeparate, and only four Attornies were allowed, until the year 1764, when an Act of Aſſembly paſſed to enable any perſon admitted to the bar to practiſe as an Attorney and Solicitor, on taking the oath appointed to be taken by Attornies and Solicitors; and at this day, the departments of Counſel and Attorney are united in all the Colonies, except Jamaica and Barbadoes. The union of theſe two branches has been productive of much inconvenience; for the practical part has ſo much employed the attention of the Colony Advocates, that few of them have leiſure to attain to any conſiderable degree of knowledge. The law practitioners in the Colonies are of three ſorts; firſt, Gentlemen who have been called to the bar at the Inns of Court in London, and who are of courſe admitted to practiſe, on their producing certificates of their being called to the bar: ſecondly, thoſe who have ſerved Clerkſhips in Great Britain, Ireland, or the Colonies: and thirdly, thoſe who through intereſt are admitted to the bar, without ſerving a regular Clerkſhip, and who (according to the phraſe of the country) are ſaid to turn lawyers.

Of all the Barriſters who practiſed in the Colonies, and afterwards returned to England, few have

have attempted to practise at the bars here; for the following reasons: The Judges in the Colonies being, in general, unacquainted with the Law, order and decorum are not properly attended to, and little improvement can be got under such masters.

Most of the questions that arise in the Colonies are founded in litigation, and not in intricacy; and, as the gentleman of the bar in general go out there at an early period in life, before they are arrived at any considerable share of knowledge, they have it not in their power to gain much experience in the Colonies, and most of the Judges not being bred to the profession of the law, the Advocate, who has the greatest fluency, may sometimes be considered as the ablest lawyer.

CHAP. XIII.

Of the COURT *of* VICE-ADMIRALTY.

THE Court of Vice-Admiralty in the Colonies exercises three sorts of jurisdiction.

In the first place, it is the proper Court for deciding all Maritime Causes.

2dly, It is the Court for the trial of Prizes taken in time of war, or hostilities between Great Britain and any other State, to determine whether the Captures be or be not lawful prize. And,

3dly, The Court of Vice-Admiralty in the Colonies has a concurrent jurisdiction with the Courts of Record there, in the case of forfeitures and penalties incurred by the breach of any Act of Parliament relating to the trade and revenues of the British Colonies in America; for the informer or prosecutor hath the election of proceeding either in any Court of Record in the Colonies where

where ſuch offence is committed, or in the Court of Vice-Admiralty there, for the recovery of thoſe penalties and forfeitures.

In the firſt place, as to the juriſdiction exerciſed in the Court of Vice-Admiralty in the Colonies, in deciding all Maritime Cauſes, or Cauſes ariſing on the High Seas. I have only to obſerve, that it proceeds in the ſame manner that the High Court of Admiralty in England does.

The only book that I have met with, which treats of the practice of the High Court of Admiralty in England, is Clerke's Praxis Admiralitatis; and this is the book uſed by the practitioners in the Colonies. As there are few Admiralty forms to be met with in print, I ſhall give the Reader ſome precedents for his information.

INSTRUCTIONS *for the Execution of a Warrant from the Court of Admiralty to arreſt a Ship, agreeable to the Practice uſed in the High Court of Admiralty in England.*

THE Warrant muſt be executed by a perſon who can write and read, whoſe name muſt be firſt inſerted in the blank left in the beginning of the Warrant for that purpoſe, by his going on board the ſhip, and producing the Warrant to the Maſter, Commanding Officer, or ſome of the Crew on board, and declaring before them, that he doth, by virtue of the ſaid Warrant, arreſt the ſaid ſhip, her tackle, apparel, and furniture, at the ſuit of J. B. W. E. and Company, late mariners of the ſaid ſhip, in an action of £.—— Sterling, and that he doth cite all perſons in general, having or pretending to have any right, title, or intereſt in the premiſes, to appear at the time

time and place, and to the effect mentioned in the ſaid Warrant: then let him fix a copy on the mainmaſt, and leave it there; and after ſupplying the blanks in the certificate indorſed on the back of the Warrant, let him ſubſcribe his name thereto, and make oath thereof before a Maſter in Chancery, or the Mayor of the Town, and then let him return the Warrant to the Proctor in Doctors Commons.

Should you be apprehenſive the Maſter intends to run away with the ſhip, you may take the ſails on ſhore, or put a man on board to ſecure her under the arreſt.

A Certificate *of the Service of a* Warrant *from the Admiralty to arreſt a Ship.*

On the day of the month of in the year of our Lord this Warrant was duly executed, by arreſting the within mentioned ſhip the (whereof N. N. is Maſter) her tackle, apparel, and furniture, lying at and by citing all perſons in general, having or pretending to have any right, title, or intereſt therein, to appear at the time and place, and to the effect within mentioned.

P. S.

On the day of in the year of our Lord the aforeſaid P. S. was ſworn to the truth of the above Certificate, before me.

Libel

LIBEL *for Wages.*

St. CHRISTOPHER'S. In the Court of Vice-Admiralty, on the ſecond day of April, in the year of our Lord 1767, before the Honourable R. H. Eſq; Judge Surrogate of the Court of Vice-Admiralty, held for the Iſland of St. Chriſtopher.

Thomas Edwards, late mariner of a certain merchant ſhip, called the Kitty, whereof J. N. is Maſter, againſt the ſaid ſhip, her apparel, and furniture, and alſo againſt the ſaid J. N. in a certain cauſe of Subtraction of the Wages both Civil and Maritime.

Upon which day, H. P. as lawful Proctor of the ſaid Thomas Edwards, by all better and more effectual ways and means, and alſo to all intents and purpoſes in law whatſoever, doth ſay, allege, and in law propound articulately, as follows: (that is to ſay,)

Firſt, That in the month of June, in the year of our Lord 1766, the ſaid Ship the Kitty, whereof the ſaid J. N. then was, and is now maſter, being at the port of Briſtol, in the kingdom of Great Britain, and deſigned on a voyage to the Coaſt of Guinea, and from thence to the Weſt Indies, and ſo back again to the ſaid port of Briſtol, the ſaid J. N. did, by himſelf or agent, upon the high and open ſeas, within the ebbing and flowing thereof, and juriſdiction of the Court of Admiralty of the Iſland of St. Chriſtopher, ſhip and hire the ſaid Thomas Edwards to ſerve as Second Mate on board the ſaid ſhip on the ſaid voyage, at and after the rate of 3l. Sterling, money

ney of Great Britain, by the month; and the ſaid Thomas Edwards did, on or about the 18th day of June aforeſaid, go on board, and enter into ſervice of the ſaid ſhip; and the ſaid ſhip proceeded on the ſaid voyage, and took in a cargo of ſlaves on the ſaid coaſt of Guinea, and then came to the ſaid iſland of St. Chriſtopher, where ſhe delivered her ſaid loading; and the ſaid Thomas Edwards ſerved as Second Mate aforeſaid on board the ſaid ſhip, from the ſaid 18th day of June aforeſaid to the 3d day of March aforeſaid, being eight months and five days, which amounts to the ſum of 24 l. 7 s. 6 d. whereof received, in Sterling money, the ſum of 7 l. which being deducted from the ſum of 24 l. 7 s. 6 d. there remains due to the ſaid Thomas Edwards the ſum of 17 l. 7 s. 6 d. and the ſaid Thomas Edwards well and truly performed his office and duty of Second Mate on board the ſaid ſhip during all the ſaid time, and was obedient to the lawful commands of the Maſter thereof, and well and truly deſerved the ſaid monthly wages, and ſo much or greater monthly wages than was uſually given to perſons ſerving in ſuch capacity in other ſhips on the like voyage; and this was and is true; and ſo much the ſaid J. N. hath confeſſed and acknowledged to be true; and the party proponent doth allege and propound of any other time and place and ſalary, wages, ſum and ſums of money, and of every thing elſe, as ſhall appear from the proofs to be made in this cauſe.

Second, That all and ſingular the premiſes were and are true, public, and notorious, and thereof there was and is a public voice, fame, and report, and of which legal proof being made, the party proponent prays right and juſtice to be effectually adminiſtered

miniſtered to him and his party in the premiſes, &c.

There are very few Admiralty forms to be met with in print; and thoſe uſed in the Colonies are too looſe and inaccurate to deſerve notice.

From the Court of Vice-Admiralty in the Colonies an Appeal lies to the High Court of Admiralty of England. An Appeal may alſo be brought from the Court of Vice-Admiralty before the King in Council. 3 Black. Com. 69.

2dly, As to the juriſdiction which the Court of Vice-Admiralty in the Colonies exerciſes, for the the trial of prizes taken in time of war, or hoſtilities between Great Britain and any other State, to determine whether the Captures be or be not lawful prize.

When two powers are at war, they have a right to make prizes of the ſhips, goods, and effects of each other upon the high ſeas. Whatever is the property of the enemy may be acquired by capture at ſea; but the property of a friend cannot be taken, provided he obſerves his neutrality. Anſwer to the Expoſition of Motives in 1 Magens on Inſurances, 487.

By the Maritime Law of Nations, univerſally and immemorially received, there is an eſtabliſhed method of determination, whether the capture be, or be not, lawful prize.—Idem.

Before the ſhip or goods can be diſpoſed of by the Captor, there muſt be a regular judicial proceeding, wherein both parties may be heard, and condemnation thereupon as prize, in a Court of Admiralty, judging by the Law of Nations and Treaties.—Idem.

The proper and regular Court for theſe condemnations, is the Court of that State to whom the captor belongs.—Idem.

A claim

A claim of ship or goods must be supported by the oath of some body, at least as to belief.—Idem, fol. 488

If the sentence of the Court of Admiralty is thought to be erroneous, there is in every maritime country a superior Court of Review, consisting of the most considerable persons, to which the parties who think themselves aggrieved may appeal; and this Superior Court judges by the same rule which governs the Court of Admiralty, viz. The Law of Nations, and the treaties subsisting with that neutral power whose subject is a party before them.—Idem, 489.

If no Appeal is offered, it is an acknowledgment of the justice of the sentence by the parties themselves, and conclusive.—Idem.

In Great Britain and her Colonies, the property of prizes being given in war to the captors, the King cannot arbitrarily release the capture, but leaves all cases to the decision of the proper Courts, judging by the Law of Nations and Treaties, where there are any: and it never was imagined, that the property of a foreign subject, taken as prize on the high seas, could be affected by laws peculiar to England.—Idem, 505.

Every State has an equal right to erect Admiralty Courts for the trial of prizes taken by virtue of their respective commissions; but neither has a right to try the prizes taken by the other, or to reverse the sentences given by the other's tribunal. The only regular method of rectifying their errors, is by Appeal to the Superior Court. —Idem.

This is the clear Law of Nations; and by this method prizes have always been determined, in every other maritime country in Europe, as well as England.—Idem.

In

In caſe of prize veſſels taken in time of war, in any part of the world, and condemned in any Courts of Admiralty or Vice-Admiralty as lawful prize, the Appeal lies to certain Commiſſioners of Appeals, conſiſting chiefly of the Privy Council, and not to Judges Delegates: and this, by virtue of divers treaties with foreign nations, by which particular Courts are eſtabliſhed in all the maritime countries of Europe for the deciſion of this queſtion, whether lawful prizes or not: for this being a queſtion between ſubjects of different States, it belongs entirely to the Law of Nations, and not to the municipal laws of either country to determine it. The Original Court to which this queſtion is permitted in England, is the Court of Admiralty; and the Court of Appeal is, in effect, the King's Privy Council; the Members of which are, in conſequence of treaties, commiſſioned under the Great Seal for this purpoſe. In 1748, for the more ſpeedy determination of Appeals, the Judges of the Courts of Weſtminſter-hall, though not Privy Councillors, were added to the commiſſion then in being: but doubts being conceived concerning the validity of that commiſſion, on account of ſuch addition, the ſame was confirmed by Statute 22 Geo. II. c. 3. with a proviſo, that no ſentence given under it ſhould be valid, unleſs a majority of the Commiſſioners preſent were actually Privy Councillors. But this did not, I apprehend, extend to any future commiſſions.—3 Black. Com. 69, 70.

The moſt uſeful books to a lawyer in the Colonies, in queſtions on captures at ſea in time of War, are Grotius of War and Peace, Bynkerſhoeck's Queſtiones Juriſpublici, Vattel's Law of Nations, &c. and the Anſwer of the King of Great Britain to the Expoſition of the Motives of of the King of Pruſſia; which ſee at large in the 1ſt vol. of Magens on Inſurances, from 486 to 509. Vatell (b. 2. c. 7. ſ. 48) calls this an excellent piece on the Law of Nations.

When the King declares war againſt a foreign State, a Commiſſion under the Great Seal of Great Britain, iſſues to the Lords Commiſſioners for executing the office of Lord High Admiral of Great Britain and Ireland, &c. in the following form:

GEORGE R.

GEORGE the Second, by the Grace of God, of Great Britain, France, and Ireland, King, Defender of the Faith, &c. To our High Admiral of Great Britain and Ireland, &c. for the time being, and to our right truſty and well-beloved Councillor George Lord Anſon; our truſty and well-beloved William Ponſonby, Eſq; commonly called Lord Viſcount Duncannon; Thomas Villiers, Eſq; Sir William Rowley, Knight of the Bath; Edward Boſcawen, Eſq; our right truſty and well-beloved Couſin John Lord Viſcount Bateman, of our kingdom of Ireland; and our truſty and well-beloved Richard Edgecumbe, Eſq; our Commiſſioners for executing the Office of our High Admiral of Great Britain and Ireland, &c. and to our Commiſſioners for executing that Office for the time being, greeting; Whereas we, by our Declaration of the 17th day of May, in the year of our Lord 1756, for the reaſons therein contained, have declared war againſt France; theſe are therefore to authoriſe, and we do hereby authorize and enjoin you our High Admiral of Great Britain and Ireland, &c. for the time being, and you our ſaid Commiſſioners for executing the Office of our High Admiral

miral of Great Britain and Ireland, &c. and the Commiſſioners for executing the ſaid Office for the time being, or any three or more of you, to will and require our High Court of Admiralty in England, and the Lieutenant and Judge of the ſaid Court, and his Surrogate, as alſo the ſeveral Courts of Admiralty within our dominions; and they are hereby authoriſed and required to take cognizance of, and judicially to proceed upon, all and all manner of captures, ſeizures, prizes, and reprizals of all ſhips and goods already ſeized and taken, and which hereafter ſhall be ſeized and taken, and to hear and determine the ſame; and according to the courſe of Admiralty and Laws of Nations, to adjudge and condemn all ſuch ſhips, veſſels, and goods, as ſhall belong to France, or the Vaſſals and ſubjects of the French king, or to any other inhabiting within any of his countries, territories, and dominions, and all ſuch other ſhips, veſſels, and goods, as are or ſhall be liable to confiſcation, purſuant to the reſpective treaties between us and other Princes, States, and Potentates. In witneſs whereof, we have cauſed our Great Seal of Great Britain to be affixed to theſe preſents. Given at our Court at Kenſington, the 4th day of June, in the year of our Lord 1756, and in the 29th year of our reign

GREAT
SEAL OF
GREAT
BRITAIN.

On the receipt of this Commiſſion, the Lords of the Admiralty iſſue their Warrant to every Court of Vice-Admiralty in the Colonies; of which the following is a form;

By

(Admiralty Seal.)

By the Commiſſioners for executing the Office of Lord High Admiral of Great Britain and Ireland, &c.

WHEREAS his Majeſty has declared war againſt France, we do, in purſuance of his Majeſty's Commiſſion under the Great Seal of Great Britain, dated the 4th day of this inſt. June (a copy whereof is hereunto annexed) hereby will and require the Vice Admiralty Court of the Leeward Iſlands, and the Vice Admiral or his Deputy, or Judge of the ſaid Court, or his Deputy now and for the time being, to take cognizance of, and judicially to proceed upon all and all manner of captures, ſeiſures, prizes, and repriſals of all ſhips and goods already ſeiſed and taken, and which hereafter may be ſeiſed and taken, and to hear and determine the ſame; and according to the courſe of Admiralty and laws of nations, to adjudge and condemn all ſuch ſhips, veſſels, and goods, as ſhall belong to France, or the vaſſals and ſubjects of the French King, or any other inhabiting within any of his countries, territories, or dominions, and all ſuch other ſhips, veſſels, and goods as are or ſhall be liable to confiſcation, purſuant to the reſpective treaties between his Majeſty and other Princes, States, and Potentates, which ſhall be brought before them for trial and condemnation; and for ſo doing this ſhall be their ſufficient warrant. Given under our hands and ſeal of the office of Admiralty, this 5th day of June 1756, and in the 29th year of his Majeſty's reign.

ANSON.
BATEMAN.
R. EDGECUMBE.

To

To the Vice Admiralty Courts of the Leeward Islands, and the Vice Admiral or his Deputy, or Judge of the said Court, or his Deputy now and for the time being.

By Command of their Lordships,

J. CLEAVLAND.

I have not met with any Admiralty proceedings in Prize Causes in print; but here follow some precedents, which I collected when I was in the West Indies; they may be inaccurate in some respects, but, for want of others, I shall lay them before the Reader.

I would gladly have got some forms from the practisers in Doctors Commons, and I accordingly used endeavours for that purpose; but I did not succeed.

A Copy of the Proceedings in the Court of Vice Admiralty in Antigua, in the Case of a French Vessel and her Cargo, that were taken by an English Privateer.

ANTIGUA. At a Court of Vice Admiralty held for this Island, on Wednesday the 8th day of September 1756,

PRESENT:

The Hon. ROBERT CHRISTIAN, Esq. Judge Surrogate.

The Private Schooner of War, Mary, Edward Richards, Commander, against Schooner, Poisson Volant.

Proclamation being made, and the Court called and sat, and the execution of a monition duly issued in this cause being proved by the Marshal

Marſhal of this Court, John Hart, Eſq; Advocate for the Libellant, prayed that the Libel might be read, which was accordingly read in the following words:

ANTIGUA.
In the Court of Vice Admiralty. } Monday the 30th day of Auguſt 1756.

The Schooner Le Poiſſon Volant, whereof one Gaſper was Maſter.

Edward Richards, Commander of the Private Schooner of War, Mary,
againſt
The ſaid Schooner Poiſſon Volant, her Tackle, Apparel, and Furniture, and the Goods therein taken and ſeiſed.

THOMAS WARNER. On which day, Thomas Warner, as lawful Proctor of the ſaid Edward Richards, Commander of the ſaid private Schooner of War the Mary, by all lawful ways and means, and to all effects of law whatſoever, alleged, pleaded, and articulately propounded, as follows: (to wit,)

1. That on or about the 18th day of May 1756, war and hoſtility was declared by his Majeſty King George the Second againſt the French King, his ſubjects and vaſſals, and this was and is true, public, and notorious; and the party proponent doth

doth allege and propound of any other time, and all and every thing jointly and ſeverally.

2. That the ſaid Schooner Poiſſon Volant, whereof the ſaid Gaſper was Maſter, on or about the 13th of this inſtant Auguſt, being a French Schooner belonging to the French King, his vaſſals or ſubjects, was, by the ſaid private Schooner of War called the Mary, whereof the ſaid Edward Richards is Commander, taken and ſeiſed as lawful prize, and afterwards carried into the port of St. John in Antigua; and the party proponent doth allege and propound as before.

3. That the ſaid Schooner Le Poiſſon Volant and goods, were and are the ſchooner and goods belonging to the French King, his vaſſals or ſubjects, or others inhabiting within his countries, territories, or dominions, and ought to be confiſcated, condemned, and adjudged to be good and lawful prize, as being the ſchooner and goods of the enemies of the Crown of Great Britain; and the party proponent doth allege and propound as before.

4. That all and ſingular the premiſes were and are true, public, and notorious; and thereof there was and is a public voice, fame, and report, of which legal proof being made, the party proponent prays you Robert Chriſtian, Eſq; Judge Surrogate of the ſaid Court of Vice Admiralty, That right and juſtice be duly adminiſtered to him and his party in the premiſes; and that the ſaid ſchooner, her tackle, apparel, and furniture, and the goods taken therein, be pronounced to belong at the time of the capture of the ſame to the French King, his vaſſals, ſubjects, or others inhabiting within his countries, territories or dominions, and as ſuch liable and ſubject to confiſcation, and to be adjudged and condemned as

and

and for good and lawful prize by you, and your definitive sentence to be given in this behalf.

Which being read, proclamation was made to see if any person would come in to claim the said schooner, her tackle, apparel, and furniture, and her cargo; but no person appearing to claim the same, the following depositions taken *in preparatorio* were read:

ANTIGUA.
In the Court of Vice Admiralty.

INTERROGATORIES administered to witnesses *in preparatorio*, touching and concerning the seisure and taking of a certain Schooner, named Princess of Orange, alias Flying Fish, whereof Casparus Wyneburgh was Master, by the private Schooner of War Mary, whereof Edward Richards is Commander.

1. Where was you born, and where do you now live, and how long have you lived there, and where have you lived for seven years last past? are you subject to the Crown of Great Britain, or of what Prince or State are you a subject?

2. When, where, and by whom was the schooner and lading, goods and merchandises, concerning which you are now examined, taken and seised, and into what place or port were the same carried? whether was there any resistance made, or any guns fired against the said schooner, or persons who seised and took the same, and what and how many, and by whom?

3. Whether was you present at the time of the taking or seizing the schooner and her lading, goods and merchandises concerning which you are now examined, or how and when was you first made acquainted thereof? whether was the said

ſaid ſchooner and goods taken by a man of war, or a private man of war, and to whom did ſuch man of war, or private man of war belong? had they any commiſſion to act as ſuch, and from and by whom, and by what particular veſſel, or by whom was or were the ſaid ſchooner ſeized and taken? to what kingdom, country, or nation did the ſaid ſchooner ſo ſeized and taken belong, and under the colours of what kingdom, country, or nation did ſhe ſail at the time ſhe was ſo ſeized and taken? was the ſaid ſchooner, which was taken, a man of war, privateer, or merchant-man?

4. Upon what pretence was the ſaid ſchooner ſeized and taken? to what port or place was ſhe afterwards carried? whether was ſhe condemned, and upon what account, and for what reaſon was ſhe condemned, and by whom, and by what authority was ſhe ſo condemned?

5. Who by name was the maſter of the veſſel concerning which you are now examined, at the time ſhe was taken and ſeized? how long have you known the ſaid maſter? who firſt appointed him to be maſter of the ſaid ſchooner, and when did he take poſſeſſion thereof, and who by name delivered the ſame to him? where is the ſaid maſter's fixed place of habitation with his wife and family, and how long has he lived there? what countryman is he by birth, and to what Prince or State ſubject?

6. What number of mariners belonged to the ſaid ſchooner at the time ſhe was taken and ſeized? what countrymen are they, and where did they all come on board? whether had you, or any of the officers or company, or mariners belonging to the ſaid ſchooner or veſſel, any part, ſhare, or intereſt in the ſaid ſchooner concerning which you are

are now examined, and what in particular, and the value thereof, at the time the ſaid ſchooner was ſo taken, or the ſaid goods ſeiſed?

7. Whether did you belong to the ſchooner or veſſel concerning which you are now examined, at the time ſhe was taken and ſeized? how long had you known her? when and where did you firſt ſee her? of what burthen was ſhe? how many guns did ſhe carry? and how many or what number of men did belong to, or were on board the ſaid ſchooner at the time ſhe was taken, or at the beginning of the engagement before ſhe was taken? and of what country building was ſhe? what was her name, and how long had ſhe been ſo called? whether do you know of any other name ſhe was called by? and what were ſuch names, as you know or have heard?

8. To what ports and places was the ſaid ſchooner or veſſel concerning which you are now examined bound, the voyage wherein ſhe was taken and ſeized? to and from what ports or places did ſhe ſail the ſaid voyage before ſhe was taken and ſeized? where did the voyage begin, and where was the voyage to have ended? what ſort of lading did ſhe carry at the time of her firſt ſetting out on the ſaid voyage, and what particular ſort of lading and goods had ſhe on board at the time ſhe was taken and ſeized, proceeding upon a lawful trade? had ſhe at that time any, and what prohibited goods on board her?

9. Who were the owners of the ſaid ſchooner and veſſel, and goods concerning which you are now examined, at the time ſhe was taken and ſeized? how do you know they were the owners of the ſaid ſchooner and goods at that time? of what nation are they by birth, and where do they

live

live with their wives and families? and to what Prince or State are they subjects?

10. Was there any bill of sale made to the owners of the said schooner? in what month or year, and where and before what witnesses was the same made, and when did you last see it, and what is become thereof?

11. In what port or place was the lading, which was on board the schooner at the time she was taken and seized, first put on board the said schooner? in what month and year was the lading so put on board? what were the several qualities and quantities, and particulars thereof? whether were the same laden and put on board the said schooner in one port, or at one time, or in several ports and places, and how many by name, and at how many several times, and what particulars and what quantity at each port? who by name were the several laders or owners thereof, and what countrymen are they? where were the said goods to be delivered, and for whose account, and to whom by name did they then really belong?

12. How many bills of lading were signed for the goods seized on board the said schooner? whether were the same colourable, and whether were any bills of lading signed, which were of a different tenor with those which were on board the said schooner at the time she was seized and taken? and what were the contents of such other bills of lading, and what are become thereof?

13. What bills of lading, invoices, letters, or any instruments in writing, or papers, have you to prove your own property, or the property of any other person, and of whom in the schooner and goods, concerning which you are now examined? produce the same, and set forth the par-

ticular

ticular times when, and how, and in what manner, and upon what account, and for what consideration you became possessed thereof?

14. In what particular port or place, and in what degree of latitude were or was the schooner, concerning which you are now examined, taken and seized? at what time, and upon what day of the month, and in what year, was or were the said schooner so taken and seized?

15. Whether was there any charter party signed for the voyage, wherein the schooner, concerning which you are now examined, was taken and seized? what is become thereof? when, where, and between whom was the same made? what were the contents thereof?

16. What papers, bills of lading, letters, or other writings, any way concerning or relating to the schooner concerning which you are now examined, were on board the said schooner at the time of the seizure of the said schooner? were any of the papers thrown overboard by any person, and whom, and when, and by whose orders?

17. What loss or damage have you sustained, by reason of the seizing and taking of the said schooner concerning which you are now examined? to what value does such loss or damages amount? and how and after what manner do you compute such loss and damage? have you received any and what satisfaction for such the loss and damage which you have sustained, and when and from whom did you receive the same?

ANTIGUA.
In the Court of Vice Admiralty. }

The EXAMINATION of WITNESSES touching the Seizure of the Schooner Poiſſon Volant, and the Goods and Merchandiſes on board her, made by the private Schooner of War Mary, Edward Richards Commander.

To the 1ſt Interrogatory, this Deponent ſaith, That he was born in Genoa, and that he is a ſubject of that republic, and a mariner; that he has no particular place of reſidence, but is employed ſometimes by one nation, and ſometimes by another, wherever he can get a livelihood.

To the 2d Interrogatory, this Deponent ſaith, That the ſchooner Le Poiſſon Volant, concerning which he is now examined, was ſeized and taken by the private ſchooner of war Mary, on Friday the 13th of this inſt. Auguſt, within a reef near the Iſland of Guadaloupe; and that the ſaid ſchooner, ſo ſeized and taken, was brought into the port of St. John's in the Iſland of Antigua; and this Deponent further ſaith, there was no reſiſtance made by the ſaid ſchooner which was ſo taken and ſeized.

To the 3d Interrogatory, this Deponent ſaith, That he was one of the mariners on board the ſaid Schooner Le Poiſſon Volant, at the time ſhe was ſo ſeized and taken; and that the Schooner Le Poiſſon Volant, as this Deponent believes, is owned by Monſ. Moreau of St. Euſtatius, who this Deponent believes is a Frenchman: and this Deponent ſaith, that the lading on board was taken in at Guadaloupe, and conſiſts of ſugar, ginger, and coffee and farine; and is, as this Deponent believes, the returns of a cargo the ſaid ſchooner

ſchooner carried up from St. Euſtatia to Guadaloupe: and this Deponent ſaith, That at the time the ſaid Schooner Le Poiſſon Volant was taken, ſhe had no colours hoiſted; but that before ſhe was boarded ſhe hoiſted Dutch colours.

To the 4th Interrogatory, this Deponent ſaith, That the maſter of the ſaid Schooner Le Poiſſon Volant, at the time ſhe was taken, was a Dutchman named Gaſper, and that he is a Creole of Curacow, and generally lives at St. Euſtatia, and took poſſeſſion of the ſaid ſchooner at St. Euſtatia.

To the 5th Interrogatory, this Deponent ſaith, That there were ſeven mariners belonging to the ſaid Schooner Le Poiſſon Volant, including the ſaid Maſter, *viz.* two Portugueſe, one Frenchman, two Spaniards, and the ſaid Maſter, and this Deponent, and a free Negroe; and this Deponent ſaith, that he was no way concerned in the ſaid Schooner Le Poiſſant Volant, or her lading.

To the 6th Interrogatory, That the Schooner Le Poiſſon Volant, has been always called by that name, ever ſince he has been aboard her, and that ſhe was hailed by that name, and anſwered to it as ſuch; and does not know ſhe was ever called by any other name.

To the 7th Interrogatory, this Deponent ſaith, That the ſaid Schooner Le Poiſſon Volant was to return to St. Euſtatia, after ſhe had taken in her lading at Gaudaloupe, and that the lading ſhe carried to Guadaloupe conſiſted of mackrel and ſalt fiſh; and at the time ſuch ſchooner was taken, ſhe had no prohibited goods on board.

To the 8th Interrogatory, ſays, He knows of no bills of lading that were ſigned for the goods and merchandiſes now on board the Schooner Le Poiſſon Volant.

To

To the 9th Interrogatory, ſays, He expects to loſe nothing but his wages, if the veſſel be adjudged as lawful prize.

The Mark of
+
JOSEPH LOPEZ.

Sworn before me this 16th of Auguſt 1756, by the interpretation of PETER GUICHENET;
ROBERT CHRISTIAN.

To the 1ſt Interrogatory, this Deponent ſays, He was born at Bourdeaux, and is a ſubject of the French King; and is a mariner, and hath uſed the ſea for about ſix years.

To the 2d Interrogatory, That the ſchooner and lading concerning which he is now examined, were ſeiſed and taken by the private ſchooner of war Mary, on Friday the 13th inſt. within a reef near Guadaloupe; and that ſuch ſchooner, ſo taken, was brought into the harbour of St. John; and ſays there was no reſiſtance made by ſuch ſchooner at the time ſhe was taken.

To the 3d Interrogatory, ſays, He was one of the mariners on board the ſaid ſchooner ſo taken, at the time ſhe was ſo ſeized and taken; and that the lading now on board her, conſiſts of ſugar, coffee, ginger, and farine, and was taken in at Guadaloupe; and that when ſhe was boarded, ſhe had Dutch colours hoiſted, and at the time ſhe brought to.

To the 4th Interrogatory, ſays, The Maſter of the ſaid ſchooner ſo taken was a Dutchman named Gaſper, and believes he is a Dutchman.

To the 5th Interrogatory, ſays, There were ſeven mariners on board the ſchooner ſo ſeized and taken, including the Maſter, two of which were

were Portuguese, one Frenchman, two Spaniards, and the Master, and a Genoese.

To the 6th Interrogatory, says, The said schooner so seized and taken has, ever since he has been aboard her, which is about a month, been called by the name of Le Poisson Volant, and has been always hailed by that name, and answered to such name; and does not know she was ever called by any other name.

To the 7th Interrogatory, says, The said schooner Le Poisson Volant was to return to St. Eustatia, after she had taken in her lading at Guadaloupe; and says the same schooner took aboard at Guadaloupe, a trunk belonging to some of the inhabitants of that Island to be carried to another place in that Island, which trunk was aboard at the time of the capture; and that at such time she had no contraband goods aboard: And this Deponent says, That at the time of the capture, such schooner had not completed her lading, but was going to Grand Ance in Guadaloupe, to take in six hogsheads of sugar, which would have completed her lading.

To the 9th Interrogatory, says, He expects to lose nothing but his wages, if the vessel be adjudged as lawful prize.

Sworn before me this 16th of August 1756, by the interpretation of PETER GUICHENET.

The mark of
+
JEAN ANDRE.

ROBERT CHRISTIAN.

To the 1st Interrogatory, this Deponent saith, That he was born in the Province of Biscay in France, and is a subject of the French King; and that

that he has no particular place of refidence, his employment being a mariner.

To the 6th Interrogatory, fays, The fchooner Le Poiffon Volant, concerning which he is now examined, has been ufually called by that name; but that Monf. Moreau told this Deponent fhe was called the Princefs of Orange.

To the 7th Interrogatory, fays, The fchooner Le Poiffon Volant took in a trunk at Lamantin in Guadaloupe, which was to be delivered at Grand Ance in the faid Ifland; which trunk was aboard at the time fhe was feized and taken by the fchooner Mary.

To the 8th Interrogatory, fays, That he was a mariner aboard the fchooner Le Poiffon Volant at the time fhe was taken; and that fhe was owned by a French merchant in Guadaloupe, whofe name he does not recollect, fome time before the feizure thereof; and that the lading now aboard was taken in at Guadaloupe, and confifts of fugar, ginger, coffee and farine, and believes the fame is the returns for a cargo fent up from St. Euftatia to Guadaloupe.

To the 9th Interrogatory, fays, He expects to lofe nothing but his wages, if the fchooner Le Poiffon Volant be adjudged as lawful prize.

Sworn before me this 16th of Auguft 1756, by the interpretation of Peter Guichenet.

The mark of
+
Jean De la Croix.

There were alfo produced and read the following Exhibits:

Antigua.—In the Court of Vice-Admiralty.

James King of the Ifland of Antigua, fecond Lieutenant on board the private fchooner of war Mary,

Mary, being duly ſworn upon the Holy Evangeliſts of Almighty God, maketh oath, That the papers now produced and delivered to Robert Chriſtian, Eſq; Judge Surrogate of the Court of Vice-Admiralty of the ſaid Iſland, are all the papers that were on board the ſchooner Le Poiſſon Volant at the time ſhe was ſeized and taken by the ſaid private ſchooner of war Mary; which papers were delivered to this Deponent by the Maſter of the ſaid ſchooner at the time he went on board her, when ſhe was ſeized and taken by the ſaid private ſchooner of war Mary.

Sworn before me this 14th August 1756. JAMES KING.

ROBERT CHRISTIAN.

ANTIGUA.—In the Court of Vice-Admiralty.

The Affirmation of Jonathan Atkinſon, touching the ownerſhip of the Poiſſon Volant, or the Princeſs of Orange, taken and ſeized by the private ſchooner of war Mary, Edward Richards Commander.

JONATHAN ATKINSON of the Iſland of Antigua, merchant, being one of the people called Quakers, doth ſolemnly declare and affirm, That on the twenty-firſt inſtant, this Deponent was at the Iſland of St. Euſtatia, in company with Mr. Moreau of St. Euſtatius, and this Affirmant then congratulated him, in a jocular manner, of a ſchooner of his named the Poiſſon Volant, or the Prince of Orange, being taken by an Engliſh privateer, owned by Mr. John Yeamans and others, and carried into the Iſland of Antigua; upon which Mr. Moreau told this Affirmant, that he did not own the ſaid ſchooner Poiſſon Volant, or Princeſs of Orange, though he heard ſhe had been

been fathered upon him; nor was he then any way concerned in the ſaid ſchooner: and this Affirmant further ſaith, That the ſaid Moreau told him, this Affirmant, that the loading of the ſaid ſchooner Poiſſon Volant, might be conſigned to the ſaid Moreau by Frenchmen; but that he did not know it was.

JONATHAN ATKINSON.

Affirmed to before me this 24th
day of Auguſt 1756,
ROBERT CHRISTIAN.

In the Court of Vice-Admiralty.	The private ſchooner of war the Mary, againſt The ſchooner Le Poiſſon Volant, and her cargo, &c.

ANTIGUA.

MILES BURKE, late of the Iſland of St. Euſtatia, but now of the Iſland of Antigua, merchant, being duly ſworn on the holy Evangeliſts of Almighty God, depoſeth and ſaith, That he lived in St. Euſtatia for ſome years paſt, and is well acquainted with Meſſrs Moreau and Marcells of the ſame place, merchants and partners in trade; and ſaid, that not long ſince he had a call to Antigua on the buſineſs, where he reſides at preſent, and being informed that the ſchooner Le Poiſſon Volant, which he knew by the name of the Princeſs of Orange in St. Euſtatia, was brought into this Iſland by the privateer ſchooner called the Mary; and being alſo informed that the ſame ſchooner Le Poiſſon Volant, otherwiſe the Princeſs of Orange, belonged to the ſaid Meſſrs Moreau and Marcells, he wrote them word to St. Euſtatia, that their ſaid ſchooner was brought in here as a prize, that they might come up to claim her if they

they thought proper, as ſubjects to the States of Holland; and ſaith, That he received an anſwer thereto, the letter marked (A) now produced to him. And further depoſeth, That he hath often ſeen the hand-writing of the ſaid Moreau, in the way of buſineſs in St. Euſtatia; and believes that the names Moreau and Marcells, ſubſcribed to the ſaid letter marked (A) directed to this Deponent, and received by him as aforeſaid, are of the proper hand-writing of the ſaid Mr. Moreau. And further depoſeth, That the paper-writing marked (B) produced to him at the ſame time, importing to be a letter, but without any direction, was incloſed in the ſaid letter marked (A) contained, and deſired to be delivered to the Dutch ſchooner formerly called the Princeſs of Orange; by which poſtſcript this Deponent ſuppoſes it is intended, that he ſhould deliver it to the Captain of the ſaid prize ſchooner, whoſe name is Gaſper, as this Deponent hath heard and believes.

MYLES BURKE.

Sworn before me Auguſt
31ſt 1756.

ROBERT CHRISTIAN.

(In the original here followed the letters of Moreau, and Moreau and Marcell, which it is uſeleſs to inſert.)

ALL which having been read and conſidered, his Honour the Judge proceeded to pronounce the following ſentence:

IN THE NAME OF GOD, Amen. I Robert Chriſtian, Judge Surrogate of the Court of Vice-Admiralty of the Iſland of Antigua, being ſpecially conſtituted and appointed to hear and determine all and all manner

manner of cauſes and complaints, as to ſhips and goods ſeized and taken as prize, having ſeen, heard, and underſtood, and fully and maturely diſcuſſed the merits and circumſtances of a certain buſineſs of taking and ſeizing a certain ſchooner named Le Poiſſon Volant, whereof Gaſper was maſter, her tackle, apparel and furniture, and the goods taken therein by a private ſchooner of war called the Mary, whereof Edward Richards was Commander, by virtue of a Commiſſion or Letter of Marque lawfully granted to the ſaid Edward Richards, and brought into the port of St. John's in the Iſland of Antigua, which was lately and is ſtill depending before me, on the part and behalf of the ſaid Captain Edward Richards, againſt the ſaid ſchooner Le Poiſſon Volant, her tackle, apparel and furniture, and the goods taken therein, and againſt all perſons in general, who have or pretend to have, any right, title, or intereſt in the ſaid ſchooner Le Poiſſon Volant or goods; and I rightly and duly proceeding therein, and the ſaid Captain Edward Richards appearing before me by his proctor Thomas Warner, who prayed ſentence to be given, and juſtice to be done to his party, and all others in general having, or pretending to have, any right, title, or intereſt in the ſaid ſchooner Le Poiſſon Volant or goods, being duly and legally cited, intimated, called, and not appearing, but contumaciouſly abſenting themſelves, and pronounced contumacious, in pain of the contempt of the parties cited and not appearing, having firſt enquired into and duly conſidered the whole proceedings had and done before me in the ſaid buſineſs; and having obſerved what by law ought to be obſerved in this behalf, have thought fit, and do think fit thus to proceed to the giving and promulging of my definitive

finitive ſentence, or final decree in the ſaid buſineſs, in manner and form following: (that is to ſay,) Foraſmuch as I have, by the acts alleged, pleaded, propounded, and proved in the ſaid buſineſs, found and clearly diſcovered, that the proctor of the ſaid Edward Richards, hath ſufficiently founded his intention deduced in a certain allegation given and admitted on his behalf in the ſaid buſineſs, and now remaining in the regiſtry of this Court; which ſaid allegation, and other matters propounded, exhibited, and admitted, I take and will have taken, as if here read and inſerted for me, to pronounce for the condemnation of the ſaid ſchooner Le Poiſſon Volant, her tackle, apparel, and furniture, and the goods in the ſame, as the ſchooner and goods belonging to the French King, his vaſſals or ſubjects, or others inhabiting within any of his countries, territories, or dominions, enemies of the Crown of Great Britain, as hereafter mentioned: Therefore I Robert Chriſtian, Judge Surrogate, firſt calling upon the name of CHRIST, and having GOD alone before my eyes, and having heard learned Counſel in the law thereupon, do hereby pronounce, decree, and declare, That the ſaid ſchooner Le Poiſſon Volant, whereof the ſaid Gaſper was maſter, and her tackle, apparel, and furniture, and the goods taken therein, were rightly and duly taken and ſeized by the private ſchooner of war called the Mary by virtue of the ſaid Letter of Marque granted to the ſaid Edward Richards; and that the ſaid ſchooner Le Poiſſon Volant, her tackle, apparel, and furniture, and the goods taken therein did, at the time of the capture and ſeizure thereof (as far as appears to me) belong to the French King, his vaſſals or ſubjects, or others inhabiting within his countries, territories,

or

or dominions, enemies of the Crown of Great Britain, and as ſuch ought to be accounted and reputed liable and ſubject to a confiſcation, and to be adjudged and condemned as and for good and lawful prize to the ſaid Captain Edward Richards; and I do adjudge and condemn the ſaid ſchooner Le Poiſſon Volant, her tackle, apparel, and furniture, and the goods therein taken, as and for good and lawful prize to the ſaid Edward Richards, as being a ſchooner and goods of the enemies of the Crown of Great Britain, or otherwiſe liable to confiſcation, by this my definitive ſentence or final decree, which I read and promulge by theſe preſents.

COPY *of the Proceedings in the Court of Vice-Admiralty in Antigua, in the Caſe of a Britiſh Veſſel that was taken by the French, and afterwards retaken by two Engliſh Ships of War.*

At a Court of Vice-Admiralty held for this Iſland, on Tueſday the 31ſt day of Auguſt 1756,

P R E S E N T;

The Honourable Robert Chriſtian, Eſq; Judge Surrogate.

His Majeſty's ſhip of war Edinburgh, William Langdon, Eſq; Commander; His Majeſty's ſhip Auguſta, John Wickham, Eſq; Commander;
against
The ſchooner Betty, and her lading.

PROCLAMATION being made, and the Court called and ſat, Thomas Warner, Eſq; Advocate for the Libellants, and prayed that the Libel might be read, which was accordingly read in the words and figures following:

ANTIGUA.

ANTIGUA.
In the Court of Vice-Admiralty. } Monday the 30th day of August 1756.

The schooner Betty, whereof James Nichols was master,—William Langdon, Esq; Commander of his Majesty's ship of war called the Edinburgh; and John Wickham, Esq; Commander of his Majesty's ship Augusta;

against

The said Schooner, her Tackle, Apparel, and Furniture, and the goods therein taken and seized.

On which day Thomas Warner, as lawful Proctor of the said William Langdon, Commander of the said ship of war the Edinburgh, and of the said John Wickham, Commander of the said ship of war Augusta, by all lawful ways and means, and to all effects of law whatsoever, alleged, pleaded, and articulately propounded as follows (to wit);

1st, THAT on or about the 18th day of May 1756, war and hostilities were declared by his Majesty King George the Second, against the French King, his subjects and vassals, ; and this was and is true, public and notorious; and the party proponent doth allege and propound of any other time, and all and every thing jointly and severally.

2d, That the said schooner the Betty, whereof the said James Nichols was master, on or about the 26th day of this instant August, being a French schooner, belonging to the French King, his vassals or subjects, was, by the said ship of war called the Edinburgh, whereof the said William Langdon

don is Commander, and the ſaid ſhip of war Auguſta, whereof the ſaid John Wickham is Commander, taken and ſeized as lawful prize, and afterwards carried into the port of St. John's in Antigua; and the party proponent doth allege and propound as before.

3d. That the ſaid ſchooner and goods were and are the ſchooner and goods belonging to the French King, his vaſſals or ſubjects, or others inhabiting within his countries, territories, or dominions, and ought to be confiſcated, condemned, and adjudged to be good and lawful prize, as being the ſchooner and goods of the enemies of the Crown of Great Britain; and the party proponent doth propound and allege as before.

4th, That all and ſingular the premiſſes were and are true, public, and notorious, and thereof there was and is a public voice, fame, and report, of which legal proof being made, the party proponent prays you, Robert Chriſtian, Eſq; Judge Surrogate of the Court of Vice-Admiralty, held for Antigua aforeſaid, that right and juſtice be duly adminiſtered to him and his party in the premiſſes; and that the ſaid ſchooner, her tackle, apparel, and furniture, and the goods taken therein, be pronounced to belong, at the time of the capture of the ſame, to the French King, his vaſſals, ſubjects, or others inhabiting within his countries, territories, or dominions, and as ſuch liable and ſubject to confiſcation, and to be adjudged and condemned as and for good and lawful prize by you, and your definitive ſentence to be given in this behalf.

The Libel being read, proclamation was made, to ſee if any perſon would come in to claim the ſaid ſchooner, her tackle, apparel and furniture, and

and lading; and Charles Wager Man, Esq; coming in according to the said proclamation, interposed the following claim, as proctor of Andrew Lessly the younger, of the said Island, merchant, on behalf of Henry Baker and Richard Patten of Charlestown, in the Province of Maryland, merchants, sole owners of the said schooner, and also on behalf of the several owners of the goods taken therein, which he prayed might be read.

ANTIGUA.—In the Court of Vice-Admiralty.

William Langdon, Esq; Commander of his Majesty's ship Edinburgh, and John Wickham, Esq; Commander of his Majesty's ship Augusta;

against

The schooner Betty, her Tackle, Apparel, and Furniture, and her Lading.

CHAS. W. MAN.

The Claim of Andrew Lessly the younger, of the said Island, merchant, for and on behalf of Henry Baker and Richard Patten of Charlestown, in the Province of Maryland, merchants, sole owners of the said schooner Betty, and also for and on behalf of the several owners of the goods therein taken.

THE said Andrew Lessly the younger doth, on behalf of Henry Baker and Richard Patten, sole owners of the said schooner Betty, now under prosecution, claim the said schooner, with her tackle, apparel, and furniture; and also claim her cargo, consisting of one hundred and thirty barrels of flour, and fifty-two barrels of fish, for and on behalf of the said Henry Baker, Hansey Dolph, John Rusden Reid, and Thomas Palmer, all of

the

the Province of Maryland aforesaid, as owners thereof; and that he hath been informed, and believes, that the said schooner Betty, with her tackle, apparel, and furniture, are the property of the said Henry Baker and Richard Patten, and that the said cargo of flour and fish is the property of the said Henry Baker, Hansey Dolph, John Rusden Reid, and Thomas Palmer: wherefore the said Andrew Lessly the younger prays, That the said schooner Betty, and her tackle, apparel, and furniture, and her said cargo of flour and fish, may be adjudged to be restored to him for the benefit of the said several owners, according to their respective interests and properties therein, upon his paying to the captors thereof such salvage as, by the Act of Parliament in such case made and provided, is directed to be paid.

ANDREW LESSLY, *jun.*

Sworn this 31st day of August
1756, before me
ROBERT CHRISTIAN.

Which being read, the following Depositions taken on the part of the Libellants, were ordered to be read:

ANTIGUA.—In the Court of Vice-Admiralty.

PERSONALLY appeared John Lindsay, master's mate of his Majesty's ship the Edinburgh, and being duly sworn upon the Holy Evangelists of Almighty God, maketh oath, That the papers now produced by this Deponent, and delivered to Robert Christian, Esq; Judge Surrogate of the said Court of Vice-Admiralty, are all the papers that were found on board the said schooner Betty,

Betty, John Nichols master, at the time she was taken by his Majesty's said ship Edinburgh.

JOHN LINDSAY.

Sworn before me this 30th
August 1756.

ROBERT CHRISTIAN.

ANTIGUA.
In the Court of Vice-Admiralty.

The Examination of JEAN BOUCHE, touching the recapture of the schooner Betty, and her Lading, by his Majesty's ship Edinburgh.

THIS Deponent being duly sworn on the Holy Evangelists, deposeth and saith, That he was born at Martinique, and that he is a subject of the French King: And this Deponent further saith, That on Tuesday the twenty-fourth instant, about half an hour after eleven o'clock at noon, the schooner Betty and her lading, concerning which he is now examined, were taken by Les Deux Amis, a French privateer, commanded by Michael Revost, belonging to the Island of Martinique, to the northward of Antigua, about a mile and a half distant from the land; and that this Deponent was put on board the said schooner, and was carrying her to Guadaloupe: And this Deponent saith, That about seven o'clock in the morning of the twenty-sixth instant, the said schooner Betty, and her lading, concerning which he is now examined, were retaken by his Majesty's ship the Edinburgh, William Langdon, Esq; Commander, in sight of Guadaloupe: And this Deponent further saith, That the printed paper now produced and shewn to him, marked letter (A),

(A), is a true copy of the Commiſſion of the ſaid privateer Les Deux Amis.

Sworn before me the 30th August 1756. J. BOUCHE.

ROBERT CHRISTIAN.

(The printed paper marked letter (A), and referred to in the foregoing Depoſition; and the Copy of the French privateer's Commiſſion, are not neceſſary to be ſet out.)

Then were alſo read the following Depoſitions, taken on the part of the Claimant:

ANTIGUA.
In the Court of Vice-Admiralty.

John Wickham, Eſq; Commander of his Majeſty's ſhip Auguſta, and William Langdon, Eſq; Commander of his Majeſty's ſhip Edinburgh;

AGAINST

The ſchooner Betty, her Tackle, Apparel, and Furniture.

The Claim of Andrew Leſley the younger, of the ſaid Iſland merchant, for and on behalf of Henry Baker and Richard Patten of Charleſtown, in the Province of Maryland, merchants, ſole owners of the ſaid ſchooner Betty, and alſo for and on behalf of the ſeveral owners of the goods taken therein.

The depoſitions of Iſaac Dunſtan and Alexander Walker, mariners, taken before the Honourable Robert Chriſtian, Eſq; Judge Surrogate of his Majeſty's Court of Vice-Admiralty of the ſaid Iſland, concerning the capture and recapture of the ſaid ſchooner called

called the Betty, lately retaken from the French by John Wickham, Esq; Commander of his Majesty's ship Augusta; and William Langdon, Esq; Commander of his Majesty's ship Edinburgh, and brought into the harbour of St. John in Antigua, and now under prosecution in the said Court of Vice-Admiralty held for Antigua.

The said Deponents being duly duly sworn on the Holy Evangelists of Almighty God, severally make oath, That the said schooner Betty, belonging to Henry Baker and Richard Patten, resident merchants in Charlestown, in the Province of Maryland, sailed from Charlestown aforesaid about the latter end of July last, being laden with one hundred and thirty barrels of flour, and fifty-two barrels of fish; and that the said Henry Baker and Richard Patten are the sole owners of the said schooner: that eight barrels of fish on board her belong to the said Henry Baker, and the other forty-four barrels belong to one Hansey Dolph, an inhabitant of Maryland: that eighty-seven barrels of flour on board belong to John Rusden; thirty one barrels of flour to one Reid, a merchant in Maryland; and the remaining twelve belong to one Thomas Palmer; and that the said schooner Betty was commanded by James Nichols, to whom the said schooner and her cargo was consigned; and these Deponents say, That all and every the above-named persons are subjects to the Crown of Great Britain; and these Deponents further say, that they were bound for this Island of Antigua, and on the twenty-fourth day of this instant August, about noon, the said schooner was taken by a French privateer sloop, mounting twelve carriage guns: that the Frenchmen took the

the Captain, and all the veſſel's papers, one mariner, and a paſſenger, on board the privateer, and left theſe Deponents on board the ſchooner; and that the ſaid ſchooner was retaken on the twenty-ſixth day of Auguſt inſt. by his Majeſty's ſhips Auguſta and Edinburgh, off Deſeada, having then on board the ſaid ſchooner ſix Frenchmen, and theſe Deponents; and that the ſaid ſchooner was brought into the Road of St. John, where ſhe now lays.

The mark of + ISAAC DUNSTAN.
The mark of ┐ ALEX. WALKER.

Sworn this 31ſt day of Auguſt,
1756. before me,
Robt. Christian.

All which having been read, and duly weighed and conſidered, his Honour the Judge did, and hereby doth declare, That the ſaid ſchooner Betty, and her lading, doth belong to his Majeſty's ſubjects, and that the ſame ſchooner and her lading were taken upon the 24th day of Auguſt inſt. by the French ſhip of war Les Deux Amis, and were retaken by his Majeſty's ſhips Edinburgh, William Langdon, Eſq; Commander, and Auguſta, John Wickham, Eſq; Commander; therefore his Honour doth hereby adjudge and pronounce as his definitive ſentence, that the ſaid ſchooner Betty and her lading be reſtored to the ſaid Andrew Leſsly, on behalf of the owners thereof, and that the ſaid Andrew Leſsly do pay to William Langdon, Eſq; and John Wickham, Eſq; one-eighth part of the true value of the ſaid ſchooner and her lading, free from all deductions whatever, to be diſtributed as directed by his Majeſty's Proclamation; and for the better aſcertaining

taining the value thereof, the Captors and Claimants are to appoint each an Appraiſer to be approved of by this Court, and a Writ of Appraiſement is to iſſue for that purpoſe, and the ſaid Claimant is to pay all coſts to the Recaptors, to be taxed by the Court: and it is further ordered and decreed, That the ſaid Andrew Leſsly do give bond, with good ſecurity, to be approved of by this Court, to reſtore the ſeven-eighth parts of the ſaid ſchooner Betty and her lading, after ſuch deductions as aforeſaid to the owners thereof, according to their reſpective intereſts therein.

ANTIGUA. Know all men by theſe preſents, that we the Honourable Andrew Leſsly, of the Iſland of Antigua, Eſq; and Andrew Leſsly the younger of the ſaid Iſland, merchant, are held and firmly bound unto the Honourable Robert Chriſtian, Eſq; Judge Surrogate of the Court of Vice-Admiralty of the ſaid Iſland, in the ſum of 2000l. current gold and ſilver money of the ſaid Iſland, to be paid to the ſaid Robert Chriſtian, or to his certain Attorney, Executors, Adminiſtrators, or Aſſigns, for the which payment well and truly to be made, we bind ourſelves, and each of us, our and each of our Heirs, Executors, and Adminiſtrators, jointly and ſeverally, firmly by theſe preſents, ſealed with our Seals, and dated the 1ſt day of September, 1756.

WHEREAS

Whereas the ſchooner Betty, whereof James Nichols was Commander, belonging to Henry Baker and Richard Patten, merchants in Charleſtown, in the Province of Maryland, in North America, ſailed from Charleſtown aforeſaid the latter end of July laſt, being laden with the following merchandiſe: that is to ſay, Eight barrels of fiſh, belonging to the ſaid Henry baker; forty-four barrels of fiſh, belonging to one Hanſey Dolph; eighty-ſeven barrels of flour, belonging to John Ruſden; thirty-one barrels of flour, belonging to one Reid; and twelve barrels of flour, belonging to Thomas Palmer; all which perſons are inhabitants of Maryland, and ſubjects to the Crown of Great Britain: and whereas the ſaid ſchooner, on the 24th day of Auguſt laſt, was taken by a French privateer, and on the 26th day of the ſame month was retaken by his Majeſty's ſhips Edinburgh and Auguſta, and brought into the harbour of St. John's in this Iſland, and the Recaptors cauſed the ſaid ſchooner and her cargo to be proſecuted in due form, in the Court of Vice-Admiralty in the ſaid Iſland; and thereupon the above bound Andrew Leſsly the younger, on behalf of the ſaid owners of the ſaid ſchooner and her cargo, did claim the ſame; and the ſaid cauſe coming on to be heard on the 31ſt day of Auguſt laſt, his Honour the Judge Surrogate was pleaſed to declare, That the ſaid ſchooner Betty and her lading did belong to his Majeſty's ſubjects, and that the ſame ſchooner and her lading were taken upon the 24th day of Auguſt laſt, by the French privateer ſhip of war Les Deux Amis; and that the ſaid Betty and her lading were retaken by his Majeſty's ſhip Edinburgh, William Langdon, Eſq; Commander; and his Majeſty's ſhip Auguſta, John Wickham, Eſq; Commander:

Commander: therefore his Honour did order, decree, and adjudge, That the ſaid ſchooner Betty and her lading ſhould be reſtored to the ſaid Andrew Leſsly the younger, on behalf of the owners thereof; and that the ſaid Andrew Leſsly the younger ſhould pay to William Langdon, Eſq; and John Wickham, Eſq; one-eighth part of the true value of the ſaid ſchooner and her lading, free from all deductions whatſoever, to be diſtributed as directed by his Majeſty's Proclamation; and for the better aſcertaining the value thereof, the Captors and Claimants were to appoint each an Appraiſer to be approved of by this Court; and a Writ of Appraiſement was to iſſue for that purpoſe, and the ſaid Claimants were to pay all coſts to the Recaptors, to be taxed by the Court; and it was further ordered and decreed, That the ſaid Andrew Leſsly the younger ſhould give bond, with good ſecurity, to be approved of by this Court, to reſtore the ſaid ſchooner Betty and her lading, after ſuch deductions as aforeſaid, to the owners thereof, according to their reſpective intereſts therein, as in and by the ſaid recited ſentence relation thereto being had, will more fully appear. Now therefore the condition of the above written obligation is ſuch, that if the above bounden, Andrew Leſsly the younger, or his heirs, executors, adminiſtrators, or Aſſigns, do and ſhall well and truly and faithfully reſtore the ſeven-eighth parts of the ſaid ſchooner Betty and her lading, after ſuch deductions thereout made as mentioned in the ſaid recited ſentence to the owners thereof, according to their reſpective intereſts therein, or ſhall well and truly pay the full value and amount of ſuch ſeven-eighth parts of the ſaid ſchooner Betty and her lading, after ſuch deductions as aforeſaid to the ſaid owners, in man-

ner

ner as aforeſaid, then the above written obligation to be void, or elſe to be and remain in full force and virtue.

ANDREW LESSLY, (L. S.)
ANDREW LESSLY, Jun. (L. S.)

Sealed and delivered in
the preſence of
CHAS. W. MAN.

A MONITION *in the* ADMIRALTY.

ANTIGUA.

GEORGE the Second, &c. To Alexander Crawford, Eſq; Deputy Provoſt Marſhal of our Court of Vice-Admiralty held for our ſaid Iſland, greeting: Whereas our beloved Benjamin King, Eſq; Judge of our ſaid Court, to hear and determine all and all manner of cauſes and complaints as to ſhips and goods ſeized and taken as prize, ſpecially conſtituted and appointed, rightfully and duly proceeding, at the petition of the proctor of A. B. Commander of our ſhip C—, hath decreed all perſons in general, who have or pretend to have any right, title, or intereſt in a certain ſhip called the D—, with her tackle, apparel, and furniture, and the goods, wares, and merchandiſes laden therein, lately taken by our ſaid ſhip of war C—, and brought into the harbour of St. John in the ſaid Iſland, to be moniſhed, cited, and called to judgment at the time and place underwritten, and to the effect hereafter expreſſed, juſtice ſo requiring: we do therefore ſtrictly charge and command you, jointly and ſeverally, that you omit not by affixing of theſe preſents on the public parade of the town of St. John, in the ſaid Iſland, at the uſual time of the public reſort of of merchants thereon, to monish and cite, or cause to be monished and cited peremptorily all persons in general, who have or pretend to have any right, title, or interest in the said ship D—, and her tackle, apparel, and furniture, and the goods, wares, and merchandises taken therein, to appear before us, or our aforesaid Judge, or his Surrogate, in the Court-house in the town of St. John, upon the day of between the hours of nine and twelve in the forenoon of the same day, to shew and allege, in due form of law, a reasonable and lawful cause, if any they have, why the said ship D— and her tackle, apparel, and furniture, and the goods, wares, and merchandises taken therein, should not be pronounced to belong, at the time of the capture of the same, to our enemies, and as goods of our enemies, or otherwise liable and subject to confiscation and condemnation, to be adjudged and condemned as good and lawful prize, and further to do and receive in this behalf as to justice shall appertain. And that you duly intimate moreover, or cause to be intimated peremptorily to all persons aforesaid, to whom we, by the tenor of these presents, do also intimate, that if they shall not appear at the time and place above-mentioned, or appearing, shall not shew a reasonable and lawful cause to the contrary, our aforesaid Judge, or his Surrogate doth intend, and will proceed to the pronouncing of the said ship D—, with her tackle, apparel, and furniture, and the goods, wares, and merchandises taken therein, to belong, at the time of the capture of the same, to our enemies, and as goods of our enemies, or otherwise liable to confiscation and condemnation, for good and lawful prize, the absence or other contumacy of the persons so cited

cited and intimated in any ways notwithſtanding; and that you duly certify our aforeſaid Judge or his Surrogate, what you do in the premiſes, together with theſe preſents. Given at the town of St. John, in our aforeſaid Court, under the Seal of the ſame for cauſes, the day of in the year of our Lord and of our reign the

Paſſed the office
N. G.

COPY *of a* SENTENCE *in the* COURT *of* VICE-ADMIRALTY *in* ANTIGUA.

ANTIGUA. At a Court of Vice-Admiralty held for the ſaid Iſland, on Monday the 29th day of May, 1758,

PRESENT:

The Honourable Robert Chriſtian, Eſq; Judge Surrogate.

His Majeſty's ſloop Weazel Bowles, Eſq; Commander,

AGAINST

The ſhip La Demoiſelle Alida and her lading.

PROCLAMATION being made, and the Court called and ſat, the execution of a Monition duly iſſued being proved by the Marſhal of the ſaid Court, and the ſubſtance of the libel being opened by Mr. Warner and Mr. Man, a claim was interpoſed by Mr. Horne, on behalf of the owners of the ſaid ſhip La Demoiſelle Alida and her lading: whereupon, and upon reading in Court the ſeveral depoſitions *in preparatorio*, and alſo the depoſitions taken in ſupport of the ſaid claim, and the

the several exhibits produced in the said cause; and after hearing what could be said by Counsel on both sides upon debate of the matter, his Honour the Judge proceeded to pronounce sentence of condemnation in the usual manner, assigning such additional causes as are assigned in the preceding causes; whereupon Mr. Horne prayed an Appeal, which was granted upon giving the usual security.

A true COPY *of another* SENTENCE *in the* COURT *of* VICE-ADMIRALTY *in* ANTIGUA.

ANTIGUA. At a Court of Vice Admiralty, held for the said Island, on Saturday the 29th April, 1758,

P R E S E N T:

The Honourable Robert Christian, Esq; Judge Surrogate.

The private Sip of war Charles, Robert Patten, Commander,

AGAINST

The sloop Endraght and her lading.

PROCLAMATION being made, and the Court called and sat, and the execution of a Monition duly issued being proved by the Marshal of this Court, the substance of the libel was opened by Mr. Conyers. Then Mr. Horne interposed a claim on behalf of the owners of the said sloop and her cargo: whereupon, and upon reading in Court the several depositions taken *in preparatorio*, and also the depositions taken in support of the said claim, and the several exhibits produced in the said cause, and after hearing what could be said

ſaid by Counſel on both ſides upon debate of the matter, his Honour the Judge proceeded to pronounce ſentence of condemnation in the uſual manner, aſſigning additional cauſes for pronouncing ſuch ſentence of condemnation: whereupon Mr. Horne prayed an Appeal from the ſaid ſentence; which was granted upon the ſaid Claimant giving ſecurity as the law directs. Then Mr. Man exhibited an allegation or libel on behalf of the Captain, Officers, and Mariners of the private brigantine of war Prince of Wales; which allegation came on to be argued: whereupon it is ordered and decreed, that the libel on behalf of the ſaid Robert Patten be diſmiſſed. Then Mr. Warner, Attorney to his Majeſty's Caſual Receiver, interpoſed a claim for the ſaid ſloop and her lading on behalf of his Majeſty; whereupon it was ordered and decreed, that the ſame ſloop Endraght and her lading be divided between his Majeſty and the ſaid brigantine of war Prince of Wales ſhare and ſhare alike, ſubject nevertheleſs to ſuch gratuity as his Honour the Judge Surrogate ſhall order and appoint for the Charles, upon the final determination of the ſaid Appeal.

The Form of a CAUTION *or* SECURITY *entered into on the granting the* COMMISSION *of a Private Ship of War.*

ST. CHRISTOPHER'S.

IN the Court of Vice-Admiralty, on the twenty-ſixth day of October, in the third year of the reign of our Sovereign Lord George the Third, by the Grace of God, of Great Britain, France, and Ireland, King, Defender of the Faith, &c. On which day, time, and place, perſonally appeared William

William Webley, Commander of the private ſchooner of war called the Pelican, and A. J. and J. P. of the Iſland of St. Chriſtopher, Gentlemen, who ſubmitting themſelves to the juriſdiction of the High Court of Admiralty of England, obliged themſelves, their heirs, executors, and adminiſtrators, to our Sovereign Lord the King in the ſum of 1500 l. of lawful money of Great Britain. To this effect, that is to ſay, That whereas the ſaid William Webley is authoriſed by Letters of Marque, or a Commiſſion for a private man of war, to arm, equip, and ſet forth to ſea the ſaid ſchooner called the Pelican, of the burthen of about thirty tons, whereof he the ſaid William Webley goeth Captain, with men, ordnance, ammunition, and victuals, to ſet upon by force of arms, and to ſubdue, ſeize, and take the men of war ſhips, and other veſſels whatſoever, together with the goods, monies, and merchandiſes belonging to the French King, or any of his vaſſals and ſubjects, or others inhabiting within any of the countries, territories, or dominions whatſoever, and ſuch other ſhips, veſſels, and goods as are or ſhall be liable to confiſcation, excepting only within the harbours or roads within ſhot of the cannon of any Princes and States in amity with his Majeſty; and whereas he the ſaid William Webley has a copy of certain inſtructions approved of, and paſſed by his Majeſty in Council, delivered to him to govern himſelf therein, as by the tenor of the ſaid Commiſſion, and of the inſtructions thereto relating more at large appeareth. If therefore nothing be done by the ſaid William Webley, or any of his Officers, Mariners, or Company, contrary to the true meaning of the ſaid Inſtructions, but that the Commiſſion aforeſaid, and the ſaid Inſtructions

ſtructions ſhall in all particulars be well and truly performed and obſerved as far as they ſhall the ſaid ſchooner, Captain, and Company, any way concern; and if they or any of them ſhall give full ſatisfaction for any damage or injury which ſhall be done by them, or any of them, to any of his Majeſty's ſubjects, allies, or neuters, or their ſubjects, and alſo ſhall duly and truly pay, or cauſe to be paid to his Majeſty, or to the Cuſtomers or Officers appointed to receive the ſame for his Majeſty the uſual cuſtoms due to his Majeſty, of and from ſhips and goods ſo as aforeſaid taken and adjudged for prize: and moreover, if the ſaid William Webley ſhall not take any ſhip or veſſel, or any goods or merchandiſes belonging to the enemy, or otherwiſe liable to confiſcation, through conſent or clandeſtinely, or by colluſion, by virtue, colour, or pretence of his ſaid Commiſſion, that then this bail ſhall be void, and of none effect; and unleſs they ſhall ſo do, they do all hereby ſeverally conſent that execution ſhall iſſue forth againſt them, their heirs, executors, and adminiſtrators, goods and chattels, whereſoever the ſame ſhall be found, to the value of the ſaid ſum of 1500 l. before-mentioned; and in teſtimony of the truth thereof, they have hereunto ſubſcribed their names.

WM. WEBLEY.
A J.
J. P.

Taken and acknowledged before me Judge of his Majeſty's Court of Vice-Admiralty of the Iſland of St. Chriſtopher, the 26th day of October, in the year of our Lord 1762.

CRAISTER GREATHEED.

Form

Form of an INHIBITION *from the* HIGH COURT *of* APPEALS *for* PRIZES.

GEORGE the Third, by the Grace of God, of Great Britain, France, and Ireland, King, Defender of the Faith, &c. To all and singular our Officers and Ministers, and other our liege subjects, being literate persons, whomsoever and throughout our kingdom of Great Britain, and other our foreign Plantations and dominions, greeting: Whereas in a certain business of prize concerning the ship Neptune (William Callow, master) and goods therein taken by the private ship of war the Juno (James Amoss, Commander), which was moved and prosecuted before our beloved Abraham Chalwill, Esq; Judge of our Vice-Admiralty Court of Tortola, an Appeal and Complaint hath been made and interposed by the Proctor of the said William Callow, our subject, the Master and Claimant of the said ship Neptune and goods therein, from part of a sentence or decree made and interposed by the said Judge; and more especially from that part of the said sentence or decree, whereby he did decree, that the Captor should only pay the costs of suit, and not be liable or subject to any damages in consequence of his detaining the said brigantine the Neptune, and from his refusing to condemn the said Captor in all losses, damages, Demurrage, costs, charges, and expences whatsoever, which the said brigantine Neptune, the cargo on board, or the owners thereof, had or might suffer or sustain, as well in the hull, rigging, and cargo, as in the loss of markets at the Island of Jamaica, in consequence of such detention and illegal proceedings to us, and to our High Court of Admiralty

Admiralty of Great Britain: And whereas we have granted our Commiſſion under our Great Seal of Great Britain for the hearing and final determination of all Cauſes of Appeal as to prizes to certain moſt noble and Right Honourable perſons in our ſaid Commiſſion named: And whereas our beloved Andrew Coltee Ducarel, Doctor of Laws, their Surrogate, hath, at the petition of the Proctor of the party Appellant, decreed an inhibition, citation, and monition for the underwritten proceſs, in manner and form hereafter expreſſed (juſtice ſo requiring): we do therefore ſtrictly charge and command you, jointly and ſeverally, that you peremptorily inhibit, or cauſe to be inhibited, the aforeſaid Judge of our ſaid Court, the Judge from whom the Appeal in this behalf is made, his Surrogate or Surrogates, and Regiſter or Actuary; and alſo the ſaid James Amoſs, Commander of the ſaid private ſhip of war the Juno in ſpecial, and all other in general, who are by law to be inhibited in this behalf (all and every of whom we do alſo by the tenor of theſe preſents inhibit), that they do not, or attempt or cauſe or procure to be done or attempted, any thing to the prejudice of the ſaid party Appellant, or of his ſaid Appeal, or our juriſdiction pending this buſineſs of Appeal and Complaint, and ſo long as the ſame ſhall remain undecided before the ſaid moſt noble and Right Honourable perſons, ſo that the ſaid party Appellant may have free liberty and power (as in juſtice he ought) to proſecute this his buſineſs of Appeal and Complaint, under pain of the law and contempt thereof; and further, that you cite or cauſe to be cited, peremptorily, the ſaid James Amoſs to appear before the ſaid moſt noble and Right Honourable perſons, or any three or more of them in the

the Privy Council Chamber at the Cockpit, on the hundredth day after ſervice of theſe preſents, if it be a Court day, or elſe upon the next Court day following, between the uſual hours for hearing of cauſes, there to anſwer to the aforeſaid party Appellant in this his buſineſs of Appeal and Complaint; and further to do and receive in this behalf as to juſtice ſhall appertain; and that you moniſh moreover, or cauſe to be moniſhed peremptorily the Judge aforeſaid, his Surrogate or Surrogates, and alſo his Regiſter, Actuary or Actuaries, that they may tranſmit, or cauſe to be tranſmitted, the whole and entire proceſs had and done before the ſaid Judge, or his Surrogates, in the ſaid buſineſs, in a proper and authentic form, or in their original forms, within one hundred days after ſervice of this Monition, under pain of law and the peril which will fall thereon; and that you duly certify the ſaid moſt noble and Right Honourable perſons, or any three or more of them, what you ſhall do in the premiſes, together with theſe preſents. Given at London, under the Seal of our High Court of Delegates, the 26th Day of April, in the year of our Lord 1762, and of our reign the ſecond.

GODF. L. FARRANT, Reg.
of his Majeſty's High Court
of Appeals for Prizes.

INSTRUCTIONS

INSTRUCTIONS *for executing an* INHIBITION.

Lords Commiſſioners of Appeals.

The Neptune, William Callow, Maſter. } Appeal from Tortola.

Inſtructions for the execution of the Inhibition, Citation, and Monition, iſſued under the Seal of his Majeſty's High Court of Delegates, in the Cauſe of Appeal brought before the Lords Commiſſioners for hearing Appeals in Prize Cauſes, from the Judge of the Vice-Admiralty Court of Tortola, refuſing to decree damages to the Claimant of the ſaid Ship Neptune, in conſequence of the unjuſt ſeizure and detention thereof by James Amoſs, Commander of the private Ship of War the Juno, the pretended Captor.

THE inſtrument herewith ſent, contains an Inhibition againſt the Judge of the Vice-Admiralty Court of Tortola, againſt the Regiſter of the ſaid Court, and againſt the aforeſaid James Amoſs, Commander of the ſaid private ſhip of war the Juno, the pretended captor of the ſaid ſhip and goods, and the promoter of the cauſe below, ſtrictly commanding and enjoining them, and every of them, in his Majeſty's name, not to do or attempt any thing to the prejudice of the ſaid William Callow, the Claimant and Party Appellant, during this his Appeal; and alſo a citation againſt the ſaid James Amoſs, to appear and anſwer to the ſaid William Callow in his ſaid cauſe of Appeal; and likewiſe a monition againſt the ſaid Judge and Regiſter to tranſmit to the Lords of Appeals copies of all and every the proceedings had in this cauſe, &c. duly authenticated under

under the hand of the Regifter and Seal of the faid Vice-Admiralty Court, if not heretofore tranfmitted.

Therefore this inftrument, containing the faid inhibition, citation, and monition, muft be ferved on the faid feveral perfons: (to wit)

1ft, On the Judge of the Vice-Admiralty Court of Tortola.

2dly, On the Regifter of the faid Court.

That they may be thereby inhibited from doing any thing further in the caufe pending the Appeal, and that they do tranfmit the procefs as above.

3dly, On the faid Captain James Amofs, the Captor and Refpondent on the Appeal.

4thly, On the Proctor acting for Capt. James Amofs, in the firft inftance of this caufe.

That they may be alfo inhibited, and likewife cited to appear and anfwer to the Party Appellant as therein contained.

The fame muft be ferved perfonally on them, and each and every of them, by fhewing them the original inftrument under feal, and at the fame time leaving with each of them a copy thereof.

The perfon who ferves the fame, muft, after he has fo done, fill up the feveral blanks left, in the form of the underwritten Certificate, which muft be indorfed on the inftrument, for the times and places of fervice, &c. and then fign the fame; which done, he muft make and fubfcribe an affidavit, to be annexed to the faid inftrument, and be fworn thereto, before the Mayor or other Chief Magiftrate of the place. The purport or effect of which affidavit muft be as follows:

Form

Form of AFFIDAVIT *of* SERVICE.

On the day of 1763, appeared perſonally A. B. of and made oath on the Holy Evangeliſts as followeth; (to wit) That he this Deponent perſonally ſerved the inhibition, citation, and monition hereto annexed, on Abraham Chalwill, Eſq; the Judge of the Vice-Admiralty Court of Tortola, and on John Beaver, N. P. the Regiſter of the ſaid Court, and on the Proctor in the firſt inſtance of this cauſe, at the ſeveral times and places, and in manner and form mentioned in the Certificate indorſed thereon, to which Certificate the Deponent's name is ſubſcribed; which name, he ſaith, is of his own handwriting, and that the contents of the ſaid Certificate were and are all true.

The Magiſtrate muſt ſubſcribe the Affidavit, certifying that the ſame were ſworn before him, and the ſame muſt be authenticated under ſome public ſeal, and then, together with the original inhibition, returned by the firſt opportunity, and with all expedition to Mr. Puget.

If it ſo happens that any of the parties cannot be met with, ſo as to be perſonally ſerved with the ſaid inhibition, then let the copy be left at their uſual place of habitation, and the original ſhewn to ſome one of their family, agent, clerk, or ſervant, ſo that they may have notice thereof; and in that caſe, the Certificate and Affidavit muſt be altered, and made accordingly: ſetting forth, That ſuch party was, at ſuch times and places, ſought after, but could not be met with, ſo as to be perſonally ſerved, and that therefore the original was at ſuch time ſhewn to ſuch a perſon (mentioning his name and the relation

lation he bears to the party) and a copy thereof left with him, and that he was desired by the person serving the same, to acquaint the party therewith.

But if it be possible, let all the parties themselves be personally served.

Form of the CERTIFICATE.

This inhibition, citation, and monition, was personally served on Abraham Chalwill, Esq; the Judge of the Vice-Admiralty Court of Tortola, at   on the   day of   1763, and on John Beavor, Notary Public, the Register of the said Court, at   on the   day of   1763, and on the within-named Captain James Amoss, the Respondent, at   on the   day of   1763, and on   his Proctor in the first instance of this cause, at   on the   day of   1763, by shewing to them, and each and every of them, the same under seal; and at the same time leaving with them, and each and every of them, a true copy thereof. By me,

A. B.

Doctors Commons, 16th March 1763.

PHILIP CRESPIGNY, Jun.
Proctor for the Appellant.

Affirmance

Affirmance by the King in Council, of a Sentence given in the Vice Admiralty Court of the Island of St. Christopher.

At the Court at St. James's, the 26th day of July 1765.

PRESENT:

Sigil. Priv. Concilii.

The KING's Most Excellent Majesty,

Archbishop of Canterbury,
Lord President,
Marquis of Rockingham,
Lord Steward,
Earl of Huntingdon,
Earl of Albemarle,
Earl of Dartmouth,
Earl of Ashburnham,
Earl of Egmont,
Viscount Falmouth,
Viscount Howe,
Viscount Villiers,
Lord Edgcumbe,
Lord Grantham.

UPON reading at the Board a report from the Right Honourable the Lords of the Committee of Council for hearing Appeals from the Plantations, dated the 16th of this instant, in the words following, viz.

" Your Majesty having been pleased, by your " order in Council of the 12th of December " last, to refer unto this Committee, the humble " Petition and Appeal of John Barker, Esq. late " Commander of your Majesty's Ship Culloden, " against A—— S———, Commander of the " Privateer Mary Ann Elizabeth, and others, " from a sentence in the Vice-Admiralty Court of " the Island of St. Christopher, on the 5th of " March 1761, in relation to the Ship Elizabeth, " Sacker Peters Master, upon a question of " collusive capture; and humbly praying, that, " upon hearing the said Appeal, your Majesty " will

"will be graciously pleased to pronounce and de-
"clare, that the said Ship Elizabeth and her
"cargo, were collusively taken by the said pri-
"vate ship of war the Mary Ann Elizabeth, and
"thereupon to reverse so much of the said sen-
"tence as dismisses the Petitioner's libel, and
"condemns the said Ship Elizabeth and her
"cargo to the said A—— S———, his officers
"and mariners, or owners; and instead thereof,
"that your Majesty will be further pleased to
"pronounce for the right of your Majesty and
"the Petitioner, agreeable to the prayer of the
"Petitioner's libel, by ordering the said Ship
"Elizabeth and her cargo, or the full value
"thereof, together with the tackle, furniture,
"ammunition, and apparel of the said private
"ship of war the Mary Ann Elizabeth, to be di-
"stributed moietively between your Majesty and
"the Petitioner; or that your Majesty will be
"pleased to make such further or other order in
"the premises, as the nature and circumstances
"of the case may require, and as the Court be-
"low ought to have made. The Lords of the
"Committee, in obedience to your Majesty's
"said order of reference, this day took the said
"Petition and Appeal into their consideration;
"and having heard all the parties therein con-
"cerned, by their Counsel learned in the law, do
"agree humbly to report, as their opinion, to
"your Majesty, that the sentence given in the
"Vice-Admiralty Court of the Island of St. Chri-
"stopher's, on the 5th of March 1761, should
"be affirmed, and the said Petition and Appeal
"therefrom dismissed."

His Majesty this day took the said report into consideration, and was pleased, with the advice of of his Privy Council, to approve of what is therein proposed to be done; and to order, as it is hereby ordered, that the same be duly and punctually complied with, and carried into execution.—Whereof the Governor, Lieutenant Governor, or Commander in Chief of his Majesty's Leeward Charibbee Islands for the time being, and all others whom it may concern, are to take notice and govern themselves accordingly.

W. SHARPE.

ADMIRALTY PRECEDENTS *in the Course of the late War.*

Orders for Reprisals by the Court of London.

At the Court at St. James's, the 18th of June 1779.

PRESENT:

The King's most Excellent Majesty in Council.

WHEREAS the Ambassador of the King of Spain, has, by order of his Court, delivered to Lord Viscount Weymouth a paper, in which it is declared, that his Catholic Majesty intends to have recourse to arms, under the groundless pretence of obtaining reparation for injuries supposed to have been received; and whereas the said Ambassador has received orders to retire from this kingdom without taking leave, his Majesty being determined to take such measures as are necessary for vindicating the honour of his Crown, is pleased, by and with the advice of his Privy Council, to order, and it is hereby ordered, that general reprisals be granted against the ships, goods, and subjects of the King of Spain, so that

as

as well his Majesty's fleet and ships, as also all other ships and vessels that shall be commissionated by letters of marque or general reprisals, or otherwise, by his Majesty's Commissioners for executing the office of Lord High Admiral of Great Britain, shall and may lawfully seize all ships, vessels, and goods, belonging to the King of Spain or his subjects, or others inhabiting within any the territories of the King of Spain, and bring the same to judgment in any of the Courts of Admiralty within his Majesty's dominions; and to that end, his Majesty's Advocate General, with the Advocate of the Admiralty, are forthwith to prepare the draught of a Commission, and present the same to his Majesty at this board, authorising the Commissioners for executing the office of Lord High Admiral, or any person or persons by them empowered and appointed, to issue forth and grant letters of marque and reprisal to any of his Majesty's subjects or others, whom the said Commissioners shall deem fitly qualified in that behalf, for the apprehending, seizing, and taking the ships, vessels, and goods belonging to Spain, and the vassals and subjects of the King of Spain, or any inhabitants within his countries, territories, or dominions, and that such powers and clauses be inserted in the said Commission as have been usual, and are according to former precedents; and his Majesty's said Advocate General, with the Advocate of the Admiralty, are also forthwith to prepare the draught of a Commission, and present the same to his Majesty at this board, authorising the said Commissioners for executing the office of Lord High Admiral, to will and require the High Court of Admiralty of Great Britain, and the Lieutenant and Judge of the said Court, his Surrogate or Surrogates, as also the several

Courts

Courts of Admiralty within his Majesty's dominions, to take cognizance of, and judicially proceed upon all and all manner of captures, seizures, prizes, and reprisals of all ships or goods that are or shall be taken, and to hear and determine the same; and according to the course of Admiralty, and the laws of nations, to adjudge and condemn all such ships, vessels, and goods as shall belong to Spain, or the vassals and subjects of the King of Spain, or to any others inhabiting within any of his countries, territories, and dominions, and that such powers and clauses be inserted in the said Commission as have been usual, and are according to former precedents; and they are likewise to prepare and lay before his Majesty at this board, a draught of such instructions as may be proper to be sent to the Courts of Admiralty in his Majesty's foreign governments and plantations for their guidance herein, as also another draught of instructions for such ships as shall be commissionated for the purposes aforementioned.

Copy of his Majesty's Commission of 2d of May 1776, to the High Admiral of Great Britain, &c. and the Commissioners for executing the office of High Admiral, authorising and enjoining them to will and require the High Court of Admiralty of England, and the several Courts of Admiralty within the King's Dominions, judicially to proceed upon all captures, &c. belonging to the inhabitants of the Rebellious Colonies, and other vessels liable to confiscation, in pursuance of the Act of the 16th of George the Third, by which all manner of trade and commerce is prohibited with the Colonies of New Hampshire, Massachusett's Bay, Rhode Island, &c. during the continuance of the Rebellion within the said Colonies:

GEORGE the Third, by the grace of God, of Great Britain, France, and Ireland King, Defender of the Faith, &c. To our High Admiral of Great Britain and Ireland, and dominions thereunto belonging, for the time being, and to our right trusty and right well beloved Cousin and Counsellor John Earl of Sandwich, our trusty and well beloved John Buller, Esq; our right trusty and well beloved Cousin Henry Lord Viscount Palmerston, of our kingdom of Ireland, our right and well beloved Counsellor Charles Spencer, Esq. commonly called Lord Charles Spencer, our right trusty and well beloved Cousin Wilmot, Lord Viscount Lisburne of our said kingdom of Ireland, and our trusty and well beloved Henry Penton, Esq; and Sir Hugh Palliser, Baronet, our Commissioners for executing the office of our High Admiral of Great Britain and Ireland, and dominions thereunto belonging, and to our Commissioners for executing that office for the time being, greeting: Whereas by an Act passed in this present Session of Parliament, all manner of trade and commerce is prohibited with the Colonies of New Hampshire, Massachusett's Bay, Rhode Island, Connecticut, New York, New Jersey, Pennsylvania, the three lower Counties on Delaware, Maryland, Virginia, North Carolina, South Carolina, and Georgia, during the continuance of the present Rebellion within the said Colonies respectively; and that all ships and vessels of or belonging to the inhabitants of the said Colonies, together with their cargoes, apparel, and furniture, which shall be found trading in any port or place of the said Colonies, or going to trade or coming from trading in any such port or place, shall be forfeited to us, as if they were the ships and effects of of open enemies, and ſhall be ſo adjudged, deemed, and taken in all Courts of Admiralty, and in all other Courts whatſoever. Theſe are therefore to authoriſe, and we do hereby authoriſe and enjoin you our High Admiral of Great Britain and Ireland, and dominions thereunto belonging, for the time being, and you our ſaid Commiſſioners for executing the office of our High Admiral of Great Britain and Ireland, and dominions thereunto belonging, and the Commiſſioners for executing the ſaid office for the time being, or any three or more of you, to will and require our High Court of Admiralty of England, and the Lieutenant and Judge of the ſaid Court, and his Surrogate or Surrogates, as alſo the ſeveral Courts of Admiralty within our dominions; and they are hereby authoriſed and required to take cognizance of, and judicially to proceed upon all and all manner of ſeizures, forfeitures, captures, recaptures, prizes, and repriſals, of all ſhips and goods already ſeized and taken, or which ſhall hereafter be ſeized and taken, to hear and determine the ſame according to the courſe of Admiralty, and to adjudge and condemn all ſuch ſhips, veſſels, and goods, their tackle, apparel, and furniture, as belong to the inhabitants of the ſaid Rebellious Colonies; and alſo ſuch other ſhips, veſſels, and goods, as are or ſhall be liable to confiſcation by the ſeveral ſtatute laws of the realm, or purſuant to the reſpective treaties between us and other Princes, States, and Potentates, or the law and uſage of nations. In witneſs whereof, we have cauſed theſe our Letters to be made Patent. Witneſs ourſelf at Weſtminſter, the ſecond day of May, in the ſixteenth year of our reign.

By the King himſelf,

YORKE.

Warrant from the Commiſſioners for executing the Office of High Admiral of Great Britain, &c. to the Vice-Admiralty Court of the Province of Georgia, in purſuance of his Majeſty's Commiſſion immediately preceding.

Seal of the ADMIRALTY.

By the Commiſſioners for executing the office of Lord High Admiral of Great Britain and Ireland, &c.

WHEREAS by an Act paſſed in the ſixteenth year of his Majeſty's reign, it is declared, That all manner of trade and commerce is and ſhall be prohibited with the Colonies of New Hampſhire, Maſſachuſett's Bay, Rhode Iſland, Connecticut, New York, New Jerſey, Pennſylvania, the three lower Counties on Delaware, Maryland, Virginia, North Carolina, South Carolina, and Georgia, ſo long as the ſaid Colonies reſpectively ſhall remain in a ſtate of Rebellion; and that all ſhips and veſſels of or belonging to the inhabitants of the ſaid Colonies, together with their cargoes, apparel, and furniture, and all other ſhips and veſſels whatſoever, which ſhall be found trading in any port or place of the ſaid Colonies, or going to trade, or coming from trading in any ſuch port or place, ſhall become forfeited to his Majeſty, as if the ſame were the ſhips and effects of open enemies: We do, in purſuance of his Majeſty's Commiſſion under the Great Seal of Great Britain, bearing date the 2d of May 1776 (a copy whereof is hereunto annexed), hereby will and require the Vice-Admiralty Court of the Province of of Georgia, and the Vice-Admiral, or his Deputy or Judge of the ſaid Court, or his Deputy now and for the time being, to take cognizance of and judicially to proceed upon all and all manner of ſeizures, captures, recaptures, prizes, and repriſals of all ſhips and goods already ſeized and taken, or which ſhall be hereafter ſeized and taken, to hear and determine the ſame, according to the courſe of Admiralty, and to adjudge and condemn all ſuch ſhips, veſſels, and goods, their tackle, apparel, and furniture, as belong to the inhabitants of the Colonies abovementioned, during the continuance of the preſent Rebellion within the ſaid Colonies reſpectively; and alſo ſuch other ſhips, veſſels, and goods, as are or ſhall be liable to confiſcation by the ſeveral ſtatute laws of the realm, or purſuant to the reſpective treaties between his Majeſty, and other Princes, States, and Potentates, or the law and uſage of nations, which ſhall be brought before you for trial and condemnation.

And his Majeſty having been pleaſed, by his order in Council of the 25th of April 1776, to approve of a ſet of ſtanding Interrogatories, prepared by his Advocate General and the Advocate of the Admiralty, to be adminiſtered to all commanders, maſters, officers, mariners, and other perſons found on board any ſhip or veſſel which hath been or ſhall be ſeized or taken as prize by any of his Majeſty's ſhips or veſſels of war, concerning ſuch captured ſhips, veſſels, or any goods, wares, and merchandiſes on board the ſame; and to ſuch other perſons as ſhall be brought to be examined as witneſſes in preparatory, in conſequence of the before-mentioned Act of Parliament; and to order that the ſaid Interrogatories ſhould be tranſmitted to the ſeveral Courts of Admiralty in his

his foreign governments and plantations, for their guidance, we do, in pursuance of his Majesty's said order in Council, herewith send a copy of the said Interrogatories to the Vice-Admiralty Court of the Province of Georgia, and the Vice-Admiral, or his Deputy or Judge of the said Court, or his Deputy now and for the time being, for their guidance accordingly; and do hereby will and require them to cause the same to be duly administered to the persons for whom they are intended as aforesaid; for doing of all which this shall be their sufficient warrant. Given under our hands, and the seal of the office of Admiralty, the 28th of April 1779.

LISBURNE.
W. PENTON.
R. MAN.

To the Vice-Admiralty Court of the Province of Georgia, and the Vice-Admiral, or his Deputy or Judge of the said Court, or his Deputy now and for the time being.

By Command of their Lordships,
PHILIP STEPHENS.

Copy of standing INTERROGATORIES *transmitted by the Admiralty in England, together with the above Warrant.*

Standing Interrogatories to be administered in behalf of our Sovereign Lord George the Third, by the Grace of God, of Great Britain, France, and Ireland, King, Defender of the Faith, to all commanders, masters, officers, mariners, and other persons found on board any ship or vessel which hath been or shall be seized, or taken as prize

prize by any of his Majeſty's ſhips or veſſels of war, concerning ſuch captured ſhips, veſſels, or any goods, wares, and merchandiſes on board the ſame; and to ſuch other perſons who ſhall be brought to be examined as witneſſes in preparatory, in conſequence of an Act paſſed in the preſent Seſſion of Parliament, prohibiting all trade and commerce with the Colonies of New Hampſhire, Maſſachuſett's Bay, Rhode Iſland, Connecticut, New York, New Jerſey, Pennſylvania, the three Lower Counties on Delaware, Maryland, Virginia, North Carolina, South Carolina, and Georgia, during the continuance of the preſent Rebellion within the ſaid Colonies.

Let each witneſs be interrogated to every of the following queſtions, and their anſwer to each ſeverally written down.

1. Where were you born, and where have you lived for theſe ſeven years laſt paſt? where do you now live, and how long have you lived in that place? to what Prince or State, or to whom are you, or have ever been a ſubject, and of what cities or towns have you been admitted a burgher or freeman, and at what time were you ſo admitted?

2. Interrogate, Were you preſent at the time of taking and ſeizing the ſhip or her lading, or any of the goods or merchandiſes concerning which you are now examined? if not, how and when were you firſt made acquainted therewith? and had the ſhip, concerning which you are now examined, any commiſſion, what, and from whom?

3. Interrogate, In what place, latitude, or port, and in what year, month, and day, were the ſhip and

and goods concerning which you are now examined, taken and ſeized, upon what pretence, and for what reaſons were they ſeized, into what place or port were they carried, and under what colours did the ſaid ſhip ſail? was any reſiſtance made at the time when the ſaid ſhip was taken? and if yea; how many guns were fired, and by whom and by what ſhip or ſhips were you taken? was ſuch veſſel a ſhip of war, or a veſſel acting without any commiſſion, as you believe?

4. Interrogate, What is the name of the maſter or commander of the ſhip or veſſel taken? how long have you known the ſaid maſter, and who appointed him to the command of the ſaid ſhip? where did ſuch maſter take poſſeſſion of her, and what was the name of the perſon who delivered the poſſeſſion to the ſaid maſter? where doth he live? where is the ſaid maſter's fixed place of abode? if he has no fixed place of abode, then let him be aſked where was his laſt place of abode, and where doth he generally reſide? how long has he lived there? where was he born, and of whom is he now a ſubject? is he married? if yea, where doth his wife and family reſide?

5. Interrogate, Of what tonnage or burthen is the ſhip which has been taken? what was the number of the mariners, and of what country were the ſaid ſeamen or mariners? did they all come on board at the ſame port, or different ports, and who ſhipped or hired them, and when and where?

6. Interrogate, Had you, or any of the officers or mariners belonging to the ſhip concerning which you are now examined, any and what part, ſhare, or intereſt in the ſaid ſhip, or in any of her lading? if yea, ſet forth who and what goods or intereſt you or they have? did you belong to the ſaid

ſaid ſhip or veſſel at the time ſhe was ſeized and taken? in what capacity did you belong to her? how long have you known her? when and where did you firſt ſee her, and where was ſhe built?

7. Interrogate, What is the name of the ſaid ſhip? how long has ſhe been ſo called? do you know of any other name or names by which ſhe hath been called? if yea, what were they? had ſhe any paſſport or ſea-brief on board, and from whom? to what ports and places did ſhe ſail during her ſaid voyage, before ſhe was taken? where did her laſt voyage begin, and where was the ſaid voyage to have ended? Set forth the quality of every cargo the ſhip has carried to the time of her capture, and what port ſuch cargoes have been delivered at.

8. Interrogate, What lading did the ſaid ſhip carry, at the time of her firſt ſetting ſail in her laſt voyage, and what particular ſort of lading and goods had ſhe on board at the time ſhe was taken? in what year, and in what month, was the ſame put on board? Set forth the different ſpecies of the lading, and the quantities of each ſort.

9. Interrogate, Who were the owners of the ſhip or veſſel concerning which you are now examined, at the time ſhe was ſeized? how do you know that they were the owners of the ſaid ſhip at that time? of what nation or country were ſuch owners by birth, where do they reſide, and where do their wives and families reſide? to whom are they ſubject?

10. Interrogate, Was any bill of ſale made to the aforeſaid owners of the ſaid ſhip; and if any ſuch was made, in what month and year? where, and in the preſence of what witneſſes was ſuch bill of ſale made? where did you laſt ſee it? and what is become of it?

11. In-

11. Interrogate, Was the ſaid lading put on board in one port, and at one time; or at ſeveral ports, and at ſeveral times; and at what ports by name? Set forth what quantities of each ſort of goods were ſhipped at each port.

12. Interrogate, What are the names of the reſpective laders, or owners, or conſignees of the ſaid goods? what countrymen are they? where do they now live and carry on their buſineſs or trade, and where were the ſaid goods to be delivered, and for whoſe real account, riſk, or benefit? can you take upon yourſelf to ſwear, that you believe that at the time of the lading the cargo, and at this preſent time, and alſo if the goods ſhall be reſtored and unladen at the deſtined port, the goods did, do, and will belong to the ſame perſons, and to none others?

13. Interrogate, How many bills of lading were ſigned for the goods ſeized on board the ſhip? were any of thoſe bills of lading falſe or colourable, or were any bills of lading ſigned which were different in any reſpect from thoſe which were on board the ſhip the time ſhe was taken? what were the contents of ſuch other bills of lading, and what became of them?

14. Interrogate, Are there in Great Britain any bills of lading, invoices, letters, or inſtruments relative to the ſhip or goods concerning which you are now examined? if yea, ſet forth where they are, and in whoſe poſſeſſion, and what is the purport thereof, and when were they brought or ſent to this kingdom?

15. Interrogate, Was there any charter-party ſigned for the voyage in which the ſhip concerning which you are now examined was ſeized and taken? and what became thereof? when, where, and

and between whom was ſuch charter-party made, and what were the contents of it?

16. Interrogate, What papers, bills of lading, letters, or other writings, were on board the ſhip the time ſhe took her departure from the laſt clearing port before her being taken as prize? were any of them burnt, torn, thrown overboard, deſtroyed, or cancelled, concealed, or attempted to be concealed, and when and by whom? and who was then preſent?

17. Interrogate, Has the ſhip concerning which you are now examined been at any time, and when, ſeized as prize, and condemned as ſuch? if yea, ſet forth into what port ſhe was carried, and by whom, or by what authority, and on what account ſhe was condemned?

18. Interrogate, Have you ſuſtained any loſs by the ſeizing and taking the ſaid ſhip concerning which you are examined? if yea, in what manner do you compute ſuch your loſs? have you already received any indemnity, ſatisfaction, or promiſe of ſatisfaction, for any part of the damage which you have or may ſuſtain by this capture and detention, and when and from whom?

19. Interrogate, Is the ſaid ſhip or goods, or any, and what part inſured? if yea, for what voyage is ſuch inſurance made, and at what premium, and when, and by what perſons, and in what country, was ſuch inſurance made?

20. Interrogate, In caſe you had arrived at your deſtined port, would your cargo, or any part thereof, on being unladen, have immediately become the property of the conſignee, or any other perſon, and whom? or was the lader to take the chance of the market for the ſale of his goods?

In caſe of recapture of ſhip and goods, or of recapture of a hoſtage and ranſom bill for Britiſh ſhip and goods, or foreign ſhip in his Majeſty's ſervice, beſides the above interrogatories,

21. Interrogate every witneſs preciſely as to the true place and circumſtances of the capture and recapture, ſo that it may appear with certainty what number of hours the prize or hoſtage and ranſom bill were in the cuſtody of the enemy, and their treatment of the hoſtages; and particularly where a hoſtage is retaken, let him be examined fully as to every circumſtance of the capture and recapture.

And in caſe of a ranſom, beſides the above interrogatories,

22. Interrogate the hoſtages particularly into the reaſons and conditions of the ranſom, and be very circumſpect as to the number of priſoners which may have been releaſed; the place where the ſhip was diſcharged, the quality of her cargo, and the time of her being releaſed, and the neceſſity for releaſing the priſoners.

COPY *of a Commiſſion to cruiſe againſt all Ships and Veſſels belonging to the Thirteen American Colonies.*

GEORGE the Third, by the Grace of God, of Great Britain, France, and Ireland, King, Defender of the Faith, &c. To all to whom theſe preſents ſhall come, greeting: Whereas by a ſtatute made and paſſed in the ſixteenth year of our reign, intituled, An Act to prohibit all trade and intercourſe with the Colonies of New Hampſhire, Maſſachuſett's Bay, Rhode-Iſland, Connecticut,

necticut, New Jerfey, Pennfylvania, the three lower Counties on Delaware, Maryland, Virginia, North Carolina, South Carolina, and Georgia, during the continuance of the prefent rebellion within the faid Colonies refpectively; for repealing an Act made in the fourteenth year of the reign of his prefent Majefty, to difcontinue the landing and difcharging, lading or fhipping of goods, wares, and merchandize, at the town and within the harbour of Bofton, in the Province of Maffachufett's Bay; and alfo two Acts made in the laft Seffion of Parliament, for reftraining the trade and commerce of the Colonies, in the faid Acts refpectively mentioned, and to enable any perfon or perfons appointed and authorized by his Majefty, to grant pardons, to iffue proclamations, in the cafes and for the purpofes therein mentioned (it is amongft other things enacted), That all fhips and veffels of, or belonging to the inhabitants of the Colonies, herein above mentioned, together with their cargoes, apparel and furniture, and all other fhips and veffels whatfoever, together with their cargoes, apparel and furniture, which fhall be found trading in any port or place of the faid Colonies, or going to trade, or coming from trading in any fuch port or place, fhall become forfeited to us, as if the fame were the fhips and effects of open enemies, and fhall be fo adjudged, deemed, and taken in all Courts of Admiralty, and in all other Courts whatfoever: And whereas, by a certain other ftatute made and paffed in the feventeenth year of our reign, intituled, An Act for enabling the Commiffioners for executing the office of Lord High Admiral of Great Britain, to grant Commiffions to the Commanders of private fhips and veffels employed in trade, or retained in his Majefty's fervice, to take and make prize of all fuch fhips ſhips and veſſels, and their cargoes, as are therein mentioned, for a limited time; reciting, as therein it is recited; it is among other things enacted, That the Lord High Admiral of Great Britain, or the Commiſſioners for executing the office of Lord High Admiral of Great Britain for the time being, or any three or more of them, or any perſon or perſons by him or them empowered and appointed, ſhall and may, from and after the twentieth day of February one thouſand ſeven hundred and ſeventy-ſeven, at the requeſt of any merchant or merchants, being owner or owners of any ſhip or veſſel employed in trade, or retained in his Majeſty's ſervice, giving ſuch bail and ſecurity as is therein after mentioned and expreſſed, cauſe to be iſſued forth one or more commiſſion or commiſſions, to any perſon or perſons whom ſuch merchant or merchants ſhall nominate to be Commander, or in caſe of death ſucceſſively, Commanders of ſuch ſhip or veſſel, for the attacking, ſurpriſing, ſeizing, and taking, by and with ſuch ſhip or veſſel, or with the crew thereof, all ſhips and veſſels, goods, wares, and merchandizes, chattels, and effects whatſoever, belonging to the inhabitants of the ſaid Colonies now in rebellion, and all ſhips and veſſels, with their cargoes, apparel and furniture, belonging to our ſubjects in Great Britain and Ireland, which ſhall be found trading to or from the ſaid Colonies, contrary to the proviſions of the ſaid Act of Parliament, herein before firſt above in part recited. And whereas three of our Commiſſioners for executing the office of Lord High Admiral of Great Britain, by their warrant under their hands, and the ſeal of the office of Admiralty, bearing date the fourth day of June, in the year of our Lord one thouſand ſeven hundred and ſeventy-eight,

eight, reciting, as therein it is recited, have duly empowered and appointed our trusty and well-beloved JAMES ROBERTSON, Esq; our Captain-General and Governor in Chief in and over our Province of New-York, and the territories depending thereon in America, Chancellor and Vice-Admiral of the same, to cause to be issued forth, pursuant to the said Act of the seventeenth year of our reign, by warrant under his hand, and the seal of the said Province of New-York, directed to the Judge of the Admiralty of the said Province (such warrant to be made severally from time to time), at the request of any merchant or merchants, being owner or owners of any ship or vessel employed in trade, or retained in our service, one or more commission or commissions to the effect aforesaid, to any person or persons whom such merchant or merchants shall nominate to be Commander; or in case of death, successively Commanders of such ship or vessel, and to cause such bail and security to be taken, as is directed by the said Act; and moreover to cause, that in granting such commissions, all other things be had and done conformable to, and as the said Act requires. And Whereas J—— M—— of the city of New-York, merchant, principal owner of a certain boat or vessel, called the K——, hath made application in writing to our said Captain-General and Governor in Chief, and therein set forth a particular description of the said vessel, specifying the cargo and burthen thereof, the number and nature of the guns on board the same, to what place the said vessel belongs, and on what voyage she is bound, that he is the principal owner thereof, and the number of men intended to be put on board the same, to the effect herein after at large expressed; and thereby requested

queſted our ſaid Captain-General and Governor in Chief, to cauſe a commiſſion to be iſſued, for the purpoſe aforeſaid, unto J—— K——, whom he hath nominated Commander of the ſaid veſſel, and in caſe of his death, unto R—— D——, and in caſe alſo of his death, unto J—— W——, whom, in the order they are herein before mentioned, the ſaid owner hath nominated ſucceſſively Commanders thereof, in caſe of death as aforeſaid. And whereas our ſaid Captain-General and Governor in Chief, hath thereupon iſſued his warrant, under his hand and the ſeal of our ſaid Province of New-York, bearing date the twelfth day of June inſtant, to Robert Bayard, Eſq; Judge of our Court of Vice-Admiralty, for the ſaid Province of New-York directed, willing and requiring the ſaid Judge to cauſe a commiſſion to be accordingly iſſued out of the ſaid Court, unto the ſaid J—— K——, and in caſe of his death, unto the ſaid R—— D——, and in caſe alſo of his death, unto the ſaid J—— W——, for the ſetting forth the ſaid boat or veſſel in a warlike manner, with the powers and authorities, and to the intents and purpoſes in the ſtatute, laſt above mentioned, directed and expreſſed. And whereas the ſaid J—— M—— hath given ſufficient bail, with ſureties to us, in our ſaid Court of Vice-Admiralty for the Province of New-York, purſuant to the ſaid ſtatute, and according to the effect and form ſet down in our inſtructions for the better guidance and governance of the Commanders of ſuch ſhips and veſſels, iſſued under our Royal Signet and Sign Manual, bearing date at St. James's the twenty-ſeventh day of March one thouſand ſeven hundred and ſeventy-ſeven, a copy of which inſtructions is delivered with theſe preſents to the ſaid J—— K——, at preſent Commander of the

ſaid

ſaid boat or veſſel K——. Know ye therefore, That we do, by theſe preſents, grant Commiſſion to, and do licenſe, authoriſe, and empower the ſaid J—— K——, and in caſe of his death the ſaid R—— D——, and in caſe alſo of his death, the ſaid J—— W——, nominated in the order aforeſaid, to be in caſe of death, ſucceſſively Commanders thereof, to ſet forth, in a warlike manner, the ſaid boat or veſſel called the K——, the ſame being a boat employed in trade, laden with ballaſt, of the burden of ten tons, having on board two guns carrying ſhot of ſix pounds weight, two howitzers, and ſix ſwivels, belonging to the port of New-York, bound on a voyage to the Iſland of Bermuda, and intended to be manned with forty men; and by or with ſuch boat or veſſel, or the crew thereof, to attack, ſurprize, ſeize and take, all ſhips and veſſels, goods, wares, and merchandizes, chattels and effects whatſoever, belonging to the inhabitants of the ſaid Colonies now in rebellion, and all ſhips and veſſels, with their cargoes, apparel, and furniture, belonging to our ſubjects in Great Britain or Ireland, which ſhall be found trading to or from the ſaid Colonies, contrary to the proviſions of the herein before mentioned ſtatute, made in the ſixteenth year of our reign as aforeſaid, the ſame being made liable to ſeizure by merchant ſhips employed in trade, or retained in our ſervice, being thereunto commiſſioned, according to the ſaid ſtatute, made in the ſeventeenth year of our reign as aforeſaid, and to bring the ſame to ſuch port as ſhall be moſt convenient, and to which the ſame may be lawfully brought, in order to have the ſame legally adjudged in our High Court of Admiralty of England, or before the Judge of ſuch other Admiralty Court within our dominions

as

as ſhall be lawfully authorized to hear and determine concerning the ſame; which being condemned, it ſhall and may be lawful to and for the ſaid J—— K——, and the ſaid other perſons herein before nominated to be ſucceſſively Commanders, as aforeſaid, when they ſhall reſpectively, according to the true intent and meaning of theſe preſents, ſo command the ſaid boat or veſſel to ſell and diſpoſe of ſuch ſhips, veſſels, and goods ſo adjudged and condemned, in ſuch ſort and manner as, by the courſe of Admiralty, hath been accuſtomed, except in ſuch caſes where it is otherwiſe directed by our ſaid inſtructions: Provided that nothing be done by the ſaid J— K—, or any of his officers, mariners and company, contrary to the true meaning of our inſtructions delivered unto him herewith as aforeſaid; but that the ſaid inſtructions, and each and every of them, as far as they, or any of them, are therein concerned, ſhall, in all particulars, be well and duly performed and obſerved: and we pray and deſire all Kings, Princes, Potentates, States, and Republics, being our friends and allies, and all others to whom it ſhall appertain, to give the ſaid J—— K—— all aid, aſſiſtance, and ſuccour in their ports, with the ſaid boat or veſſel, company and prizes, without doing, or ſuffering to be done to him or them, any wrong, trouble or hindrance, we offering to do the like when we ſhall be by them thereunto deſired; and we will and require all our officers whatſoever, to give him and them ſuccour and aſſiſtance as occaſion ſhall require. In Teſtimony whereof we have cauſed the Seal of our Court of Vice-Admiralty for our ſaid Province of New-York to be hereunto affixed. Witneſs our truſty and well-beloved Robert Bayard, Eſq; Judge of our Court of Vice-Admiralty for our ſaid

Province

Province of New-York, at the city of New-York in our said Province, the twelfth day of June, in the twenty-second year of our reign.

ROB^T. BAYARD.

By order of his Honour the Judge,
D. MATTHEWS, Reg.

(L. S.)

I do hereby certify that the above is a true copy of my Commission, and I do authorise W—— G——, prize-master, to take charge of the schooner America, laden with tobacco, taken near the mouth of Rappahannock, in the State of Virginia, bound to H——, to proceed to New-York as quick as possible, and deliver her up to J—— M—— agent.

(Signed) J—— K——, Commander of the K—— privateer barge.

July 31st 1782.

GEORGE R.

(L. S.)

INSTRUCTIONS *for the Commanders of such Merchant Ships or Vessels, who shall have Letters of Marque and Reprisals for private Men of War, against the French King, his Vassals and Subjects, or others inhabiting within any of his countries, territories, or dominions, by virtue of our Commission granted under our Great Seal of Great Britain, bearing date the fifth day of August* 1778. *Given at our Court at St. James's, the fifth day of August* 1778, *in the eighteenth year of our reign.*

Art.

Art. 1. THAT it ſhall be lawful for the Commanders of ſhips, authorized by Letters of Marque and Repriſals, for private men of war, to ſet upon by force of arms, and ſubdue and take the men of war, ſhips and veſſels, goods, wares, and merchandizes of the French King, his vaſſals and ſubjects, and others inhabiting within any of his countries, territories, and dominions; but ſo as that no hoſtility be committed, nor prize attacked, ſeized, or taken, within the harbours of Princes and States in amity with us, or in their rivers or roads within the ſhot of their cannon, unleſs by permiſſion of ſuch Princes or States, or of their Commanders or Governors in Chief in ſuch places.

Art. 2. That the Commanders of ſhips and veſſels ſo authorized as aforeſaid, ſhall bring all ſhips, veſſels, and goods which they ſhall ſeize and take, into ſuch port of this our realm of England, or ſome other port of our dominions not in rebellion, as ſhall be moſt convenient for them, in order to have the ſame legally adjudged in our High Court of Admiralty of England, or before the Judges of any other Admiralty Court lawfully authorized, within our dominions.

Art. 3. That after ſuch ſhips, veſſels and goods, ſhall be taken and brought into any port, the taker, or one of his chief officers, or ſome other perſon preſent at the capture, ſhall be obliged to bring or ſend, as ſoon as poſſibly may be, three or four of the principal of the company (whereof the maſter, mate, or boatſwain to be always two), of every ſhip or veſſel ſo brought into port, before the Judge of our High Court of Admiralty of England, or his Surrogate, or before the Judges of ſuch other Admiralty Court within our dominions, lawfully authorized as aforeſaid, or ſuch

as

as ſhall be lawfully commiſſioned in that behalf, to be ſworn, and examined upon ſuch interrogatories as ſhall tend to the diſcovery of the truth, concerning the intereſt or property of ſuch ſhip or ſhips, veſſel or veſſels, and of the goods, merchandizes, or other effects found therein; and the taker ſhall be farther obliged, at the time he produceth the company to be examined, and before any monition ſhall be iſſued, to bring and deliver into the hands of the Judge of the High Court of Admiralty of England, his Surrogate, or the Judge of ſuch other Admiralty Court within our dominions, lawfully authoriſed, or others commiſſioned as aforeſaid, all ſuch papers, paſſes, ſea-briefs, charter-parties, bills of lading, cockets, letters, and other documents and writings as ſhall be delivered up, or found on board any ſhip; the taker, or one of his chief officers, or ſome other perſon who was preſent at the capture, and ſaw the ſaid papers and writings delivered up, or otherwiſe found on board at the time of the capture, making oath, that the ſaid papers and writings are brought and delivered in as they were received and taken, without any fraud, addition, ſubduction, or embezzlement, or otherwiſe to account for the ſame upon oath, to the ſatisfaction of the Court.

Art. 4. That the ſhips, veſſels, goods, wares, merchandizes, and effects, taken by virtue of letters of marque and repriſals as aforeſaid, ſhall be kept and preſerved, and no part of them ſhall be ſold, ſpoiled, waſted, or diminiſhed, and that the bulk thereof ſhall not be broken, before judgment be given in the High Court of Admiralty of England, or ſome other Court of Admiralty lawfully authorized in that behalf, that the ſhips, goods, and merchandizes are lawful prize.

Art.

Art. 5. That if any ſhip or veſſel belonging to us, or our ſubjects, ſhall be found in diſtreſs, by being in fight ſet upon, or taken by the enemy, or by reaſon of any other accident, the Commanders, Officers, and Company of ſuch merchant ſhips or veſſels, as ſhall have letters of marque and repriſals as aforeſaid, ſhall uſe their beſt endeavours, and give aid and ſuccour to all ſuch ſhip and ſhips, and ſhall, to the utmoſt of their power, labour to free the ſame from the enemy, or any other diſtreſs.

Art. 6. That the Commanders or Owners of ſuch ſhips and veſſels, before the taking out letters of marque and repriſals, ſhall make application in writing, ſubſcribed with their hands to our High Admiral of Great Britain, or our Commiſſioners for executing that office for the time being, or the Lieutenant or Judge of the ſaid High Court of Admiralty, or his Surrogate, and ſhall therein ſet forth a particular, true, and exact deſcription of the ſaid ſhip or veſſel for which ſuch letter of marque and repriſal is requeſted, ſpecifying the burthen of ſuch ſhip or veſſel, and the number and nature of the guns, and what other warlike furniture and ammunition are on board the ſame, to what place the ſhip belongs, and the name or names of the principal owner or owners of ſuch ſhip and veſſel, and the number of men intended to be put on board the ſame, and for what time they are victualled, alſo the names of the Commander and Officers.

Art. 7. That the Commanders of ſhips and veſſels having letters of marque and repriſals, as aforeſaid, ſhall hold and keep, and are hereby enjoined to hold and keep, a correſpondence, by all conveniencies, and upon all occaſions, with our High Admiral of Great Britain, or our Commiſſioners

missioners for executing that office for the time being, or their Secretary, so as from time to time to render and give him or them, not only an account or intelligence of their captures and proceedings, by virtue of such commissions, but also of whatsoever else shall occur unto them, or be discovered and declared to them, or found out by them, by examination of, or conference with any mariners or passengers of or in the ships or vessels taken, or by any other ways and means whatsoever, touching or concerning the designs of the enemy, or any of their fleets, ships, vessels or parties, and of the stations, sea-ports, and places, and of their intents therein, and of what ships or vessels of the enemy, bound out or home, or where cruizing, as they shall hear of, and of what else material in these cases may arrive at their knowledge, to the end such course may be thereupon taken, and such orders given as may be requisite.

Art. 8. That no Commander of any ship or vessel, having a letter of marque and reprisal as aforesaid, shall presume, as they will answer it at their peril, to wear any jack, pennant, or other ensign or colours usually borne by our ships, but that, besides the colours usually borne by merchant ships, they do wear a red jack, with the union jack, described in the canton, at the upper corner thereof, near the staff.

Art. 9. That no Commander of any ship or vessel, having a letter of marque and reprisal as aforesaid, shall ransom, or agree to ransom or quit, or set at liberty, any ship or vessel, or their cargoes, which shall be seized and taken.

Art. 10. That all Captains or Commanding Officers of ships having letters of marque or reprisals, do send an account of, and deliver over, what

what prisoners shall be taken on board any prizes, to the Commissioners appointed, or to be appointed, for the exchange of prisoners of war, or the persons appointed in the sea-port towns to take charge of prisoners, and that such prisoners be subject only to the orders, regulations, and directions of the said Commissioners, and that no Commander, or other Officer of any ship, having a letter of marque and reprisal as aforesaid, do presume, upon any pretence whatsoever, to ransom any prisoners.

Art. 11. That in case the Commander of any ship, having a letter of marque and reprisal as aforesaid, shall act contrary to these instructions, or any such further instructions of which he shall have due notice, he shall forfeit his commission to all intents and purposes; and shall, together with his bail, be proceeded against according to law, and be condemned in costs and damages.

Art. 12. That all Commanders of ships and vessels having letters of marque and reprisal, shall, by every opportunity, send exact copies of their journals to the Secretary of the Admiralty, and proceed to the condemnation of their prizes, as soon as may be, and without delay.

Art. 13. That Commanders of ships and vessels having letters of marque and reprisal, shall, upon due notice being given to them, observe all such other instructions and orders as we shall think fit to direct from time to time, for the better carrying on this service.

Art. 14. That all persons who shall violate these or any other of our Instructions, shall be severely punished, and also required to make full reparation to persons injured contrary to our Instructions, for all damages they shall sustain by

any

any capture, embezzlement, demurrage, or otherwise.

Art. 15. That before any Letter of Marque and Reprisals for the purpose aforesaid shall issue under Seal, bail shall be given, with sureties before the Lieutenant and Judge of our High Court of Admiralty of England, or his Surrogate, in the sum of three thousand pounds Sterling, if the ship carries above one hundred and fifty men; and if a less number, in the sum of fifteen hundred pounds Sterling; which bail shall be to the effect, and in the form following:

"WHICH day, time, and place, personally appeared A. B, &c.

and C. D. &c.
who submitting themselves to the jurisdiction of the High Court of Admiralty of England, obliged themselves, their heirs, executors, and administrators, in the sum of
pounds, of lawful money of Great Britain, to this effect: that is to say, That whereas E. F. &c.

is duly authorised by Letters of Marque and Reprisals with the ship called the G——— of the burden of about
tons, whereof he the said E. F. goeth Master, by force of arms to attack, surprise, seize, and take all ships and vessels, goods, wares, and merchandises, chattels, and effects belonging to the French king, or to any of his vassals and subjects, or others, inhabiting within any of his countries, territories, or dominions whatsoever, excepting only within the harbours or roads within shot of the cannon of Princes and States

States in amity with his Majesty: And whereas he the said E. F. hath a copy of certain instructions approved of, and passed by his Majesty in Council, as by the tenor of the said Letters of Marque and Reprisals, and instructions thereto relating, more at large appeareth. If therefore nothing be done by the said E. F. or any of his Officers, Mariners, or Company, contrary to the true meaning of the said Instructions, and of all other Instructions which may be issued in like manner hereafter, and whereof due notice shall be given him; but that the Letters of Marque and Reprisals aforesaid, and the said Instructions shall, in all particulars, be well and duly observed and performed, as far as they shall the said ship, Master, and Company any way concern; and if they shall give full satisfaction for any damage or injury which shall be done by them, or any of them, to any of his Majesty's subjects, or of foreign States in amity with his Majesty, and also shall duly and truly pay, or cause to be paid to his Majesty, or the Customers or Officers appointed to receive the same for his Majesty, the usual customs due to his Majesty, of and for all ships and goods so as aforesaid taken and adjudged for prize: and moreover, if the said E. F. shall not take any ship or vessel, or any goods or merchandises belonging to the enemy, or otherwise liable to confiscation, through consent or clandestinely, or by collusion, by virtue, colour, or pretence of his said Letters of Marque and Reprisals: that then this bail shall be void, and of none effect; and unless they shall so do, they do all hereby severally consent, that execution shall issue forth against them, their

heirs,

heirs, executors, and adminiſtrators, goods and chattels, whereſoever the ſame ſhall be found, to the value of the ſum of pounds before-mentioned: and in teſtimony of the truth thereof, they have hereunto ſubſcribed their names, &c."

By his Majeſty's Command.

WEYMOUTH.

George R.

L. S.

Additional Instructions to ſuch Commanders of private ſhips and veſſels employed in trade, or retained in our ſervice, who ſhall or may have Commiſſions, purſuant to an Act of Parliament of the ſeventeenth year of our reign, for ſeizing and taking the ſhips and goods belonging to the inhabitants of the Colonies now in rebellion, as alſo for ſuch merchant ſhips who ſhall have Letters of Marque and Repriſals againſt the French King, his vaſſals and ſubjects, or others, inhabiting within any of his countries, territories, or dominions, by virtue of our Commiſſion, dated the 5th of Auguſt, 1778. Given at our Court at St. James's, the 18th day of November, 1778, and in the nineteenth year of our reign.

WHEREAS information has been received, that ſeveral of the ſeamen belonging to veſſels employed in our ſervice have been induced to deſert from the ſaid veſſels, and to enter on board privateers by the offer of large bounties, and other advantages, held out to them by the Commanders of ſuch privateers; in conſequence of which the ſaid veſſels have been detained in port, to the great detriment and diſtreſs of our ſervice: for the avoiding ſuch inconvenience for the future: We do hereby ſtrictly charge and enjoin all Commanders of privateers and merchant ſhips having Letters of Marque, that they do upon no account receive and detain on board their ſhips any ſeamen belonging to any of our ſhips of war, or any other veſſels employed in our ſervice, either as tranſports, ſtore-ſhips or victuallers; and that if they ſhould, at any time, undeſignedly have received any ſuch ſeamen, they do immediately deliver him up upon application made by, or on behalf of the Captain or Commander of ſuch ſhip of war, or other ſhip employed in our ſervice, to which he belonged before he entered on board ſuch privateer or commiſſioned ſhip, under pain of our higheſt diſpleaſure, and ſuch penalty as by law may be inflicted.

By his Majeſty's Command.

GEO. GERMAINE.

[The Copies of the Depoſitions, and of ſome other of the Vice-Admiralty Precedents which I got at Antigua, were ſo looſe and incorrect, that I found it neceſſary to alter them in different places to make ſenſe of them; and ſeveral ungrammatical and other inaccurate expreſſions which were in the manuſcript yet remain, from my overlooking them in the proof-ſheets. I am alſo to apologize to the Purchaſer, for my inatten-

tion

tion in lengthening the Proceedings in the Caufe of the Schooner Poiffon Volant, by fuffering the Depofitions of three Witneffes of the fame purport to ftand in the manufcript, when the infertion of one of thefe Depofitions would have anfwered the purpofe. However, with all their imperfections, thofe Antigua Precedents may have their ufe, as there are no other Vice-Admiralty forms in print.]

3dly, The Court of Vice-Admiralty in the Colonies has a concurrent jurifdiction with the Courts of Record there, in the cafe of forfeitures and penalties incurred by the breach of any Act of Parliament relating to the trade and revenues of the Britifh Colonies in America; for the Informer or Profecutor hath the election of proceeding either in any Court of Record in the Colonies where fuch offence is committed, or in the Court of Vice-Admiralty there, for the recovery of fuch penalties and forfeitures.

By the 4 Geo. III. c. 15. f. 41. it is enacted, That all the penalties and forfeitures inflicted by that or any other Act or Acts of Parliament, relating to the trade and revenues of the faid Britifh Colonies or Plantations in America, which fhall be incurred there, fhall and may be profecuted, fued for, and recovered in any Court of Record, or in any Court of Admiralty in the faid Colonies or Plantations where fuch offence fhall be committed, or in any Court of Vice-Admiralty which may or fhall be appointed over all America (which Court of Admiralty or Vice-Admiralty are hereby refpectively authorifed and required to proceed, hear, and determine the fame) at the election of the Informer or Profecutor.

And

And by ſ. 42. it is enacted, That all penalties and forfeitures ſo recovered there, under that or any former Act of Parliament, ſhall be divided, paid, and applied as follows; that is to ſay, after deducting the charges of proſecution from the groſs produce thereof, one-third part of the nett produce ſhall be paid into the hands of the Collector of his Majeſty's Cuſtoms at the port or place where ſuch penalties or forfeitures ſhall be recovered, for the uſe of his Majeſty, his heirs and ſucceſſors; one-third part to the Governor or Commander in Chief of the ſaid Colony or Plantation; and the other third part to the perſon who ſhall ſeize, inform, and ſue for the ſame, excepting ſuch ſeizures as ſhall be made at ſea by the Commanders or Officers of his Majeſty's ſhips or veſſels of war duly authoriſed to make ſeizures; one moiety of which ſeizures, and of the penalties and forfeitures recovered thereon, firſt deducting the charges of proſecution from the groſs produce thereof, ſhall be paid as aforeſaid to the Collector of his Majeſty's Cuſtoms, to and for the uſe of his Majeſty, his heirs and ſucceſſors, and the other moiety to him or them who ſhall ſeize, inform, and ſue for the ſame: any law, cuſtom, or uſage to the contrary, notwithſtanding; ſubject nevertheleſs to ſuch diſtribution of the produce of the ſeizures ſo made at ſea, as well with regard to the moiety herein before granted to his Majeſty, his heirs and ſucceſſors, as with regard to the other moiety given to the Seizor or Proſecutor, as his Majeſty, his heirs and ſucceſſors ſhall think fit to order and direct by any * order or orders of Coun-

* On the 12th of October 1764, an order of Council was made for the diſtribution of his Majeſty's ſhare of ſeizures amongſt the Captors, in the proportions therein ſet forth.

cil,

cil, or by any Proclamation or Proclamations to be made for that purpoſe.

And in ſ. 46. of the ſame Act, it is enacted, That in caſe any information ſhall be commenced and brought to trial in America, on account of any ſeizure of any ſhip or goods as forfeited by this or any other Act of Parliament relating to his Majeſty's cuſtoms, wherein a verdict or ſentence ſhall be given for the Claimer thereof, and it ſhall appear to the Judge or Court before whom the ſame ſhall be tried, that there was a probable cauſe of ſeizure, the Judge or Court before whom the ſame ſhall be tried, ſhall * certify on the Record or other proceedings, that there was a probable cauſe for the Proſecutor's ſeizing the ſaid ſhip or goods; and in ſuch caſe the Defendant ſhall not be intitled to any coſts of ſuit whatſoever; nor ſhall the perſons who ſeized the ſaid ſhip or goods be liable to any action, or other ſuit or proſecution on account of ſuch ſeizure; and in caſe any action, or other ſuit or proſecution ſhall be commenced and brought to trial againſt any perſon or perſons whatſoever, on account of the ſeizing any ſuch ſhip or goods, where no information ſhall be commenced or brought to trial to condemn the ſame, and a verdict or ſentence ſhall be given upon ſuch action or proſecution againſt the Defendant or Defendants, if the Court or Judge before whom ſuch action or proſecution ſhall certify in like manner as aforeſaid, that there was a probable cauſe for ſuch ſeizure, then the Plaintiff, beſides his ſhip or goods ſo ſeized, or the value thereof, ſhall not be entitled to above twopence damages, nor to any coſts of ſuit; nor

† By a deciſion of the Court of King's Bench in England, this Certificate may be made at any time.

ſhall

ſhall the Defendant, in ſuch proſecution, be fined above one ſhilling.

And by the 47th ſection of the ſame Act, it is enacted, That if any action or ſuit ſhall be commenced either in Great Britain or America, againſt any perſon or perſons for any thing done in purſuance of this or any other Act of Parliament relating to his Majeſty's Cuſtoms, the Defendant or Defendants in ſuch action or ſuit may plead the general iſſue and give the ſaid Acts, and the ſpecial matter in evidence at any trial to be had thereupon; and that the ſame was done in purſuance and by the authority of ſuch Act; and if it ſhall appear ſo to have been done, the Jury ſhall find for the Defendant or Defendants; and if the Plaintiff ſhall be non-ſuited, or diſcontinue his action after the Defendant or Defendants ſhall have appeared, or if judgment ſhall be given upon verdict or demurrer againſt the Plaintiff, the Defendant or Defendants ſhall recover treble coſts, and have the like remedy for the ſame as Defendants have in other caſes by Law. By 8 Geo. III. c. 22. all forfeitures and penalties inflicted by any Acts relating to the trade or revenues of the Britiſh Colonies in America, may be ſued for and recovered in any Court of Vice-Admiralty, having juriſdiction within the Colony or place where the cauſe of ſuit ſhall have ariſen; and either party may appeal from ſuch determination to any Court of Vice-Admiralty appointed to hear and determine ſuch Appeals.

In proſecutions in the Court of Vice-Admiralty in the Colonies for the breach of any Act of Parliament relating to the trade and revenues of the Colonies, all queſtions, as well of fact as of law, are decided by the Judge alone, without the intervention of a Jury; for ſuch was the inclination

of

of the Coloniſts in many Provinces to carry on a contraband trade, that, to try the fact of an information by a Jury would be almoſt equivalent to the repealing the Act of Parliament on which ſuch information was grounded. In other reſpects, I apprehend the proceedings ſhould be conducted, as near as may be, to the practice of the Court of Exchequer in England; and thoſe who have acted otherwiſe have committed ſtrange miſtakes. Some years ago, the Judge of the Court of Vice-Admiralty in a Colony on the Continent demanded *ex officio* from, and adminiſtered the Oath of Calumny to an Officer of the Cuſtoms there, who proſecuted in that Court for a ſeizure, under the Laws of Trade; which ſurpriſed me the more, as that Judge was bred to the law.

FORM *of an* INFORMATION *in a Court of Vice-Admiralty in the Colonies, in the Caſe of a Veſſel and Cargo ſeized for a Breach of the Acts of Trade.*

A—, in the Court of Vice-Admiralty. } Before the Honourable W. M. Eſq; Judge of his Majeſty's Court of Vice-Admiralty, held for the Iſland of A—.

BE it remembered, that F. G. Eſq; Maſter and Commander of his Majeſty's ſloop of war the Merlin (being a perſon duly and legally authoriſed and impowered to make ſeizures, and to inform againſt and proſecute the ſame), who, as well for our Sovereign Lord the King as for himſelf, proſecutes, comes into this Court on this 21ſt day of March, in the year of our Lord 1765, in his proper perſon, and as well for our ſaid Lord

Lord the King as for himself, gives this Court to understand and be informed, that between the 1st day of the month of December last past, and the day of exhibiting this Information, he the said F. G. on the high seas, and within the jurisdiction of this Court, did seize and arrest the schooner or vessel called the Queen of Stars (whereof J. B. D. was Master), with her apparel and furniture, and the goods, wares, and merchandises on board her, being the goods, wares, and merchandises of merchants unknown; for this, to wit, that the said goods, wares, and merchandises were between the said 1st day of the month of December last past and the day of exhibiting this Information exported in the said schooner or vessel out of some Colony or Plantation in America, then and now belonging to, and in the possession of our present Sovereign Lord the King by way of merchandise, the aforesaid schooner or vessel at the aforesaid time of the exportation of the said goods, wares, and merchandises, not being a schooner or vessel wholly owned by the people of Great Britain, or of the Dominions and Plantations thereunto belonging, or any of them, and navigated with the Master and three-fourths of the mariners of the said places only against the form of the Statute in such case made and provided: Wherefore the said F. G. as well for our said Sovereign Lord the King as for himself, prays the advice of this Court in the premises and due process against the said schooner or vessel; and that the said schooner or vessel, with her apparel and furniture, and the goods, wares, and merchandises aforesaid, for the causes aforesaid, may, by the definitive sentence of this Court, remain and be adjudged, forfeited, and may be divided in such manner as is directed by the late Statute made

made in the fourth year of his said present Majesty's reign with regard to seizures made at sea by the Commanders or Officers of his Majesty's ships or vessels of war duly authorised to make seizures; subject nevertheless to such distribution as is directed by his said present Majesty's order in Council, made the 12th day of October, in the year of our Lord 1764: and the said F. G. further giveth this Court to understand and be informed, That between the 1st day of the month of December last past and the day of exhibiting this Information, he the said F. G. on the high seas, and within the jurisdiction of this Court, did seize and arrest the said schooner or vessel called the Queen of Stars, with her apparel and furniture, and the goods, wares, and merchandises on board her, being the goods, wares, and merchandises of merchants unknown; for this, to wit, that the said schooner or vessel between the said 1st day of December last past, and the day of exhibiting this Information, did load certain goods, wares, and merchandises in one of his Majesty's Plantations in America, before the Master or person having a charge of the said schooner or vessel did make such oath or affirmation before the Governor or Collector of the Customs of such his Majesty's Plantation in America where the said schooner or vessel did arrive, as is directed in and by a certain Statute made in the fifteenth and sixteenth years of the reign of his late Majesty King George the Second; whereupon the said schooner or vessel became forfeited and lost, as if she had not been registered in pursuance of a certain Act of Parliament made in the seventh and eighth years of the reign of King William the Third: Wherefore the said F. G. as well for our said Sovereign Lord the King

King as for himſelf, prays the advice of this Court in the premiſes and due proceſs againſt the ſaid ſchooner or veſſel, and that the ſaid ſchooner or veſſel, with her apparel and furniture, for the cauſe laſt aforeſaid, may, by the definitive ſentence of this Court, remain and be adjudged, forfeited, and may be divided in ſuch manner as is directed by the ſaid late Statute made in the fourth year of his preſent Majeſty's reign, with regard to ſeizures made at ſea by the Commanders or Officers of his Majeſty's ſhips or veſſels duly authoriſed to make ſeizures; ſubject nevertheleſs to ſuch diſtribution as is directed by his ſaid preſent Majeſty's order in Council, made the 12th day of October, in the year of our Lord 1764; and the ſaid F. G. further giveth this Court to underſtand, and be informed, that between the 1ſt day of the month of December laſt paſt and the day of exhibiting this Information, he the ſaid F. G. on the high ſeas, and within the juriſdiction of this Court, did ſeize and arreſt divers goods, wares, and merchandiſes on board the ſaid ſchooner or veſſel, being the goods, wares, and merchandiſes of merchants unknown; for this, to wit, that between the ſaid 1ſt day of December laſt paſt and the day of exhibiting this Information, the ſaid goods, wares, and merchandiſes were ſhipped and laden on board the ſaid ſchooner or veſſel in one of the Britiſh Colonies or Plantations in America, to be carried from thence to ſome other Britiſh Colony or Plantation, without a ſufferance or warrant, firſt had and obtained from the Collector, or other proper Officer of the Cuſtoms at the port or place where ſuch goods were put on board; and for that the Maſter of the ſaid ſchooner or veſſel did not, before the ſame were removed or carried out from the port or place where he took in his lading,

lading, take out a cocket or cockets expreſſing the quantity and quality of the goods and marks of the package ſo laden, with the merchants names, by whom ſhipped, and to whom conſigned, againſt the form of the Statute in ſuch caſe made and provided; wherefore the ſaid F. G. as well for our ſaid Sovereign Lord the King as for himſelf, prays the advice of this Court in the premiſes, and due proceſs againſt he ſaid laſt mentioned goods, wares, and merchandiſes; and that the ſaid goods, wares, and merchandiſes, for the cauſes laſt aforeſaid, may, by the definitive ſentence of this Court, remain and be adjudged, forfeited, and may be diſtributed in ſuch manner as is directed by the ſaid late Statute made in the fourth year of his preſent Majeſty's reign, with regard to ſeizures made at ſea by the Commanders or Officers of his Majeſty's ſhips or veſſels duly authorized to make ſeizures; ſubject nevertheleſs to ſuch diſtribution as is directed by his ſaid preſent Majeſty's order in Council, made the 12th day of October, in the year of our Lord 1764.

Another FORM *of an* INFORMATION.

St. C——, in the Court of Vice-Admiralty. } Before the Honourable J—— K——, Eſq; Judge of his Majeſty's Court of Vice-Admiralty held for the Iſland of St. C—.

BE it remembered, that F. G. Eſq; Maſter and Commander of his Majeſty's ſloop of war the Merlin (being a perſon duly and legally authoriſed and impowered to make ſeizures, and to inform againſt, and proſecute the ſame), who, as well for

for our Sovereign Lord the King as for himself, prosecutes, comes into this Court on this day of April, in the year of our Lord 1765, in his proper person, and as well for our said Lord the King as for himself, gives this Court to understand and be informed, that between the 1st day of August last past, and the day of exhibiting this Information, he the said F. G. on the high-seas, and within the Jurisdiction of this Court, did seize and arrest the sloop or vessel called the Catherine (whereof A. G. was Master), with her apparel and furniture, and the goods, wares, and merchandises on board her, being the goods, wares, and merchandises of merchants unknown; for this, to wit, That the said sloop or vessel, between the said 1st day of August last past, and the day of exhibiting this Information, did load certain goods, wares, and merchandises in one of his Majesty's Plantations in America, before the master or person having charge of the said sloop or vessel did make such oath or affirmation, before the Governor or Collector of the Customs of such his Majesty's Plantations in America, where the said sloop or Vessel did arrive, as is directed in and by a certain Statute made in the 15th and 16th years of the reign of his late Majesty King George the Second; whereupon the said sloop or vessel became forfeited and lost, as if she had not been registered, in pursuance of a certain Act of Parliament made in the 7th and 8th years of the reign of King William the Third: Wherefore the said F. G. as well for our said Sovereign Lord the King as for himself, prays the advice of this Court in the premises and due process against the said sloop or vessel; and that the said sloop or vessel, with her apparel and furniture, for the cause aforesaid, may, by the definitive

finitive ſentence of this Court, remain and be adjudged forfeited, and may be divided in ſuch manner as is directed by the ſaid late Statute made in the fourth year of his preſent Majeſty's reign with regard to ſeizures made at ſea by the Commanders or Officers of his Majeſty's ſhips or veſſels, duly authoriſed to make ſeizures; ſubject nevertheleſs to ſuch diſtribution as is directed by his ſaid preſent Majeſty's Order in Council, made the 12th day of October, in the year of our Lord 1764: and the ſaid F. G. further giveth this Court to underſtand and be informed, That between the 1ſt day of Auguſt laſt paſt, and the day of exhibiting this Information, he the ſaid F. G. on the high ſeas, and within the juriſdiction of this Court, did ſeize and arreſt the ſaid ſloop or veſſel called the Catherine, with her apparel and furniture, and the goods, wares, and merchandiſes on board her, being the goods, wares, and merchandiſes of merchants unknown; for this, to wit, That the ſaid ſloop or veſſel between the ſaid 1ſt day of Auguſt laſt paſt, and the day of exhibiting this Information, did unload certain goods, wares, and merchandiſes in one of his Majeſty's Plantations in America, before the Maſter or perſon having charge of the ſaid ſloop or veſſel did make ſuch oath or affirmation before the Governor or Collector of the Cuſtoms of ſuch his Majeſty's Plantation in America, where the ſaid ſloop or veſſel did arrive, as is directed in and by a certain Statute made in the 15th and 16th years of the reign of his late Majeſty King George the Second: whereupon the ſaid ſloop or veſſel became forfeited and loſt, as if ſhe had not been regiſtered, in purſuance of a certain Act of Parliament made in the ſeventh and eighth years of the reign of King William the Third: Wherefore

fore the said F. G. as well for our said Sovereign Lord the King as for himself, prays the advice of this Court in the premises, and due process against the said sloop or vessel; and that the said sloop or vessel, with her apparel and furniture, for the cause last aforesaid, may, by the definitive sentence of this Court, remain and be adjudged, forfeited, and may be divided in such manner as is directed by the said late Statute made in the fourth year of his present Majesty's reign, with regard to seizures made at sea by the Commanders or Officers of his Majesty's ships or vessels duly authorised to make seizures; subject nevertheless to such distribution as is directed by his said present Majesty's order in Council, made the 12th day of October, in the year of our Lord 1764.

An Appeal lies from the sentence or judgment of this Court in matters relating to the trade or revenues of the Colonies to his Majesty in Council; but, if the matter in question does not exceed the sum or value of 500 l. Sterling, then the party who is desirous of appealing must first prefer a Petition to his Majesty for leave to appeal from such judgment or sentence; and if the prayer of such Petition is granted, then an order of Council is drawn up in the following form:

Sigillum privati concilii.

At the Court at St. James's, the 6th day of September, 1765.

PRESENT:

The King's Most Excellent Majesty,

Lord President	Earl of Litchfield
Lord Chamberlain	Earl of Egmont
Duke of Grafton	Earl of Besborough
Marquis of Rockingham	Lord Grantham
Earl of Huntingdon	Mr. Comptroller.

UPON reading at the Board a Report from the Right Honourable the Lords of the Committee of Council for hearing Appeals from the Plantations, dated the 14th of last month, in the words following, *viz.*

" Your Majesty having been pleased by your " Order in Council of the 1st of this instant, to " refer unto this Committee the humble Petition " of J— P——, of the Island of Antigua, vint- " ner; humbly praying, That he may be admit- " ted to an Appeal from a Sentence given in the " Vice-Admiralty Court of the said Island of " Antigua, on the 22d of February 1765, in " favour of W—— A——, Esq; Commander " of your Majesty's ship the B——, where- " by a small schooner or boat called the Free " Mason, belonging to the Petitioner, was " condemned, for having taken goods, wares, " and merchandises on board before the Master " of her had made such oath or affirmation as is " directed by the Statute; and further praying, " that the Governor of the Leeward Islands may " be permitted to put the Great Seal to the pro- " ceedings upon the said seizure, that the same

" may

" may be transmitted and brought before your
" Majesty in Council.—The Lords of the Com-
" mittee, in obedience to your Majesty's said
" order of Reference, this day took the said Pe-
" tition into their consideration, and heard the
" Petitioner by his Solicitor thereupon, and do
" agree humbly to report to your Majesty as their
" opinion, that the Petitioner should be admit-
" ted to an Appeal to your Majesty in Council
" from the said Sentence given in the Vice-Ad-
" miralty Court of the Island of Antigua, on the
" 22d of February 1765, upon entering into the
" usual security here for prosecuting the same to
" effect within a year and a day, and abiding the
" determination of your Majesty in Council
" thereupon:—and that the Petitioner should be
" allowed copies of all the proceedings in the said
" cause, properly authenticated under the Seal
" of the Leeward Islands, upon paying the usual
" fees for the same."

His Majesty this day took the said report into consideration, and was pleased, with the advice of his Privy Council, to approve thereof, and to order, as it is hereby ordered, That the said J— P—— be admitted to appeal to his Majesty in Council from the said Sentence given in the Vice-Admiralty-Court of the Island of Antigua on the 22d of February 1765, upon entering into the usual security here for prosecuting the same to effect within a year and a day, and abiding the determination of his Majesty in Council thereupon, and paying such costs as shall be awarded by his Majesty in Council, in case the said Appeal be dismissed: and it is hereby further ordered, That the Petitioner be allowed copies of all the proceedings in the said cause, properly authenticated

cated under the Seal of the Leeward Iſlands, upon paying the uſual fees for the ſame: whereof the Governor or Commander in Chief of his Majeſty's Leeward Charibbee Iſlands for the time being, and all others whom it may concern, are to take notice, and govern themſelves accordingly.

W. SHARPE.

Council Chamber, Whitehall,
the 18th day of Sept. 1765.

This day R—— O—— of Gould's Square, merchant; and M—— L—— of the ſame place, Gentleman, entered into the ſecurity required by the above Order.

W. SHARPE.

CHAP. XIV.

The method of authenticating LETTERS *of* ATTORNEY, *and* AFFIDAVITS *in Great Britain, for the Recovery of Debts in the Colonies in America, with Forms of both ſorts.*

BEFORE the fifth year of King George the Second, the Legiſlatures of ſome Colonies had paſſed Acts of Aſſembly to make lands and Negroes there liable to the payment of debts, whilſt others refuſed ſo to do:— on which ſeveral merchants in England that traded to the Colonies preferred a Petition to Parliament, and complained that in Virginia and Jamaica, a privilege was claimed to exempt their houſes, lands and tenements, and their negroes alſo from being extended for debt; and the Lords of Trade repreſented, that the Aſſemblies of thoſe Colonies could never be induced to diveſt themſelves of theſe privileges by any Act of their own. In conſequence of this Petition, the Statute of

5 Geo.

5 Geo. II. c. 7. intitled, " An Act for the more " easy recovery of debts in his Majesty's Plantations " and Colonies in America," was made; by which it is enacted, That in any action or suit then depending, or thereafter to be brought in any Court of Law or Equity in any of the said Plantations, for or relating to any debt or account, wherein any person residing in Great Britain shall be a party, it shall and may be lawful to and for the Plaintiff or Defendant, and also to and for any witness to be examined or made use of in such action or suit, to verify or prove any matter or thing by affidavit or affidavits in writing upon oath; or in case the person making such affidavit be one of the people called Quakers, then upon his or her solemn affirmation, made before any Mayor or other Chief Magistrate of the city, borough, or town corporate in Great Britain, where, or near to which, the person making such affidavit or affirmation shall reside, and certified and transmitted under the Common Seal of such city, borough, or town corporate, or the Seal of the Office of such Mayor, or other Chief Magistrate; which oath and solemn affirmation, every such Mayor and Chief Magistrate shall be and is hereby authorised and impowered to administer; and every affidavit or affirmation so made, certified, and transmitted, shall, in all such actions and suits be allowed to be of the same force and effect, as if the person or persons making the same upon oath or solemn affirmation as aforesaid, had appeared and sworn or affirmed the matters contained in such affidavit or affirmation *viva voce* in open Court, or upon a Commission issued for the examination of witnesses, or of any party in any such action or suit respectively; provided that in every such affidavit and affirmation there shall be ex-

pressed

preſſed the addition of the party making ſuch affidavit or affirmation, and the particular place of his or her abode.

And by ſect. 2. of the ſame Act, it is enacted, That in all ſuits then depending, or thereafter to be brought in any court of law or equity by or in behalf of his Majeſty, his heirs and ſucceſſors in any of the ſaid Plantations, for or relating to any debt or account, that his Majeſty, his heirs and ſucceſſors, ſhall and may prove his and their debts and accounts, and examine his or their witneſs or witneſſes by affidavit or affirmation, in like manner as any ſubject or ſubjects is or are impowered, or may do by this preſent act.

And by ſect. 3. of the ſame act, it is enacted, That if any perſon making ſuch Affidavit, upon oath or ſolemn Affirmation, as aforeſaid, ſhall be guilty of falſely and wilfully ſwearing or affirming any matter or thing in ſuch Affidavit or Affirmation, which if the ſame had been ſworn upon an examination in the uſual form, would have amounted to wilful and corrupt perjury, every perſon ſo offending, being thereof lawfully convicted, ſhall incur the ſame penalties and forfeitures, as by the laws and ſtatutes of this realm are provided againſt perſons convicted of wilful and corrupt perjury.

And by ſect. 4. of the ſame Act, it is enacted, That the houſes, lands, negroes, and other hereditaments and real eſtates, ſituate or being within any of the ſaid Plantations belonging to any perſon indebted, ſhall be liable to and chargeable with all juſt debts, duties, and demands of what nature or kind ſoever, owing by any ſuch perſon to his Majeſty, or any of his ſubjects, and ſhall and may be aſſets for the ſatisfaction thereof, in like

like manner as real eſtates are by the law of England liable to the ſatisfaction of debts due by bond or other ſpecialty, and ſhall be ſubject to the like remedies, proceedings, and proceſs in any Court of Law or Equity, in any of the ſaid Plantations reſpectively, for ſeizing, extending, ſelling, or diſpoſing of any ſuch houſes, lands, negroes, and other hereditaments and real eſtates, towards the ſatisfaction of ſuch debts, duties, and demands, and in like manner as perſonal eſtates in any of the ſaid Plantations reſpectively, are ſeized, extended, ſold or diſpoſed of, for the ſatisfaction of debts.

A LETTER *of* ATTORNEY *and an* AFFIDAVIT *certified under the Seal of the City of London, for the purpoſe of recovering a Debt in one of the Colonies, due to a Perſon in Great Britain.*

TO all to whom theſe preſents ſhall come, I William Bridgen, Eſq. Lord Mayor of the City of London, in purſuance of an Act of Parliament made and paſſed in the 5th year of the reign of our late Sovereign Lord King George the Second, intituled, An Act for the more eaſy recovery of debts in his Majeſty's Plantations and Colonies in America, do hereby certify, That J—— B—— of Upper Thames-ſtreet, London, Clerk to J—— R——— of L———ſtreet, London, Attorney at Law, being a perſon well known and worthy of good credit, did by ſolemn oath, which he took upon the Holy Evangeliſts of Almighty God, ſolemnly declare, teſtify, and depoſe to be true, the ſeveral matters and things contained in the Affidavit hereunto annexed.

In

Seal of the City of LONDON.

In Faith and Teſtimony whereof, I the ſaid Lord Mayor have cauſed the Seal of the Office of Mayoralty of the ſaid City of London to be hereunto put and affixed, and the Bill or Account, and Deed, Poll, or Letter of Attorney, mentioned in the ſaid Affidavit, to be alſo hereunto annexed. Dated in London the 15th day of March, in the 4th year of the Reign of our Sovereign Lord George the Third, by the Grace of God, King of Great Britain, France and Ireland, Defender of the Faith, and in the year of our Lord 1764.

HODGES.

J—— B———— of Upper Thames-ſtreet, London, Clerk to J—— R———— of L——-ſtreet, London, Attorney at Law, maketh oath, That the Bill or Account hereunto annexed, ſigned by the ſaid J—— R——, is a juſt and true copy of a Bill or Account, as entered in the books of the ſaid J—— R—— by this Deponent: and this Deponent further ſaith, That he did on the 3d of May 1762, deliver a copy of the ſaid bill to Mr. J—— Y————, perſonally, at the houſe of Mr. W—— L——, Merchant, in Brabant Court, Philpot-lane, London: and this Deponent further ſaith, That he verily believes that the ſum of 10*l.* 6*s.* 6*d*, the amount of the ſaid bill or account is now juſtly due and owing from the ſaid J—— Y——— to the ſaid J—— R————: and this Deponent further ſaith, That he was preſent, and did ſee the ſaid J—— R———— duly ſign, ſeal, and

and as his act and deed, deliver the Deed, Poll or Letter of Attorney hereunto alſo annexed; and that the name J—— B———, thereunto ſubſcribed as a witneſs, is the proper hand-writing of this Deponent; and that the name W—— E——, thereunto alſo ſubſcribed as a witneſs, is the proper handwriting of the ſaid W——— E——.

Sworn at the Guildhall, London, the 15th day of March 1764, before me, J—— B——.

W. BRIDGEN, Mayor.

* Mr. J—— Y——. Dr. to J—— R——.

1761.		£.	s.	d.
Aug. 6.	Drawing and ingroſſing Power of Attorney from you to Meſſ. H——, and others, of Antigua, generally to ſell eſtates, and tranſact all your affairs, -	0	10	6
	Drawing and ingroſſing Affidavit of the due execution thereof before my Lord Mayor, -	0	5	6
	Attending at the Manſion Houſe to ſwear the ſame, and paid ſwearing	0	8	0
	Paid for the City Seal	0	18	8
	Many attendances procuring the ſame, -	0	6	8
28.	Drawing and ingroſſing Affidavit, proving you to			

* It is hoped the Editor will be excuſed for ſetting out this ſhort Bill of Coſts, as it contains the expence of the City Seal, &c. But the ſtamps are, in ſome inſtances, increaſed ſince the year 1762.

Aug. 28.	be the only ſurviving Guardian of the perſon and eſtate of S——— G——, -	0	5	6
Sept. 23.	To your proportion of three ſets of Arbitration Bonds between you and Mr. S—— ; and for my trouble and many attendances on you both, and Mr. D——, one of the Arbitrators, to fix him, -	2	2	0
25.	Drawing Affidavit relating to the Privateer Schooner Sally, having loſt her maſts, &c. in a gale of wind, -	0	5	0
	Copy thereof for Mr. B——'s peruſal,	0	2	6
	Ingroſſing and ſtamps	0	4	0
Oct. 24.	Drawing Affidavit for Captain P——, late Maſter of the True Friend, to prove the capture of the veſſel, -	0	5	0
	Fair copy thereof for your and Capt. S——'s peruſal, -	0	2	6
1762. Jan. 19.	Ingroſſing thereof, and ſtamps, -	0	4	0
	Freſh ingroſſment of the ſame, with further proof, and ſtamps, -	0	4	6
	Letter and Meſſenger to Mr. R—— S———, threatening to ſue him for refuſing to ſettle the			

loss upon a policy underwrote by him, upon which he immediately settled, -	0	6	8
Letter and Messenger to the Master of the Swan with Two Necks, about a parcel left there for Liverpool, which was not forwarded according to the direction, and advising you thereon,	0	6	8
You having been arrested at the suit of your Taylor, attending you at your lodgings; when I prevailed upon E—— the officer to discharge you, upon your depositing in his hands two Bills of Exchange as a security; which he at first objected to, they being noted for non-acceptance; but he at last accepted the same, upon my assurance to him that they were ample security for the debt - -	0	6	8
Attending you taking instructions, and advising relating to W——'s affairs; when you directed me to proceed against him, and retain the Solicitor General,	0	6	8
Retaining fee to Mr. Solicitor General, -	1	1	0
His Clerk, -	0	2	6

Attending him ſearching his books, and retaining him, - -	0	6	8

HILARY VACATION 1762.

Y—— against W——. { Warrant to ſue	0	1	0
Latitat	0	11	0
Copy and ſervice	0	5	0
Letters and Meſſengers, &c.	0	5	0
Searching for common bail	0	3	4
	10	6	6

This is my Bill.
(Signed) J—— R——.

TO all to whom theſe preſents ſhall come, J—R———, of L———ſtreet, London, Gentleman, ſendeth greeting: Whereas G. H. of the Iſland of Antigua in the Weſt Indies, drew a Bill of Exchange, dated at Antigua, the 18th day of April laſt, upon Mr. J—— M——, Merchant, Lombard-ſtreet, London, and thereby directed him at ſixty days ſight to pay unto Mr. T—— T—— or order, ſeventy eight pounds ſixteen ſhillings and eight pence ſterling, for value received. And whereas the ſaid T—— T—— duly indorſed the ſame to Meſſ. H——— and A———, who directed the contents thereof to be paid to M—— G——, Eſq; or order. And whereas the ſaid bill has been noted and proteſted in due form for non-acceptance and non-payment thereof, as by the proteſt or duplicate thereof may appear. And whereas the ſaid M—— G—— hath, in conſideration of the like ſum of 78*l.* 16*s.* 8*d.* paid him by the ſaid J—— R——, duly

duly indorſed the ſaid bill to the ſaid J—— R———. And whereas ſeveral perſons in the ſaid Iſland of Antigua alſo ſtand indebted to the ſaid J—— R——— in divers ſums of money; now know ye, That the ſaid J—— R—— hath made, ordained, authoriſed, conſtituted, and appointed, and by theſe preſents doth make, ordain, authoriſe, conſtitute, and appoint S—— M———, of Antigua aforeſaid, Merchant, and R—— W——, of Antigua aforeſaid, Eſq; and each of them, his true and lawful Attorney and Attornies for him, and in his name and ſtead, and to and for his uſe, to aſk, demand, ſue for, levy, recover, and receive of and from the drawer of, and the indorſers on the ſaid Bill of Exchange, and every, or any, or either of them, either ſeparately or jointly, as they the ſaid S—— M—— and R—— W——, or either of them ſhall think proper; and alſo of and from all and every other perſon or perſons whomſoever, whom the ſame doth, ſhall, or may concern, all ſum and ſums of money whatſoever now due or owing, or that ſhall or may at any time or times hereafter be due or owing, for or on account of the ſaid Bill of Exchange, or for or on account of any coſts, charges or expences, intereſt or damages due or hereafter to be due, or accrue for the ſame; and alſo to aſk, demand, compound, ſue for, levy, recover, and receive by all lawful ways and means whatſoever, of and from all and every perſon and perſons aforeſaid, and all and every other perſon or perſons whomſoever, whom it doth, ſhall, or may concern, all and every debt and debts, dues, demands, ſum and ſums of money, and other effects, which now are, or hereafter ſhall be due, owing, payable, or belonging to him, the ſaid J—— R———, upon, or by virtue

virtue of any bond, judgment, bill, debt, or upon any other account, or by any other ways or means whatsoever or howsoever; and upon receipt or recovery thereof, or of any part thereof, receipts, acquittances, and other good and sufficient discharges for the same, for and in the name of him the said J—— R——, to make, give, sign, seal, and execute; and generally to do, manage, transact, and perform all such acts, matters, and things whatsoever, in and about the premises, as fully and effectually as he the said J—— R—— might or could do, were he personally present, and did the same himself, hereby ratifying and confirming all and whatsoever the said S—— M—— and R—— W——, or either of them, shall or lawfully may do or cause to be done in and about the premises, by virtue of these presents. In witness whereof, the said J—— R—— hath hereunto set his hand and seal, this 9th day of March, in the year of our Lord 1764, and in the 4th year of the reign of King George the Third.

J—— R——.

Sealed and delivered, being first duly stampt in the presence of,

W—— E——.
J—— B——.

Another Letter *of* Attorney *and* Affidavit, *certified under the Seal of the City of London.*

TO all to whom these presents shall come, I Sir William Stephenson, Knight, Lord Mayor of the City of London, in pursuance of an Act of Parliament made and passed in the 5th year of the reign of his late Majesty King George the Second,

cond, intituled, An Act for the more eaſy recovery of debts in his Majeſty's Plantations and Colonies in America, do hereby certify, that on the day of the date hereof, perſonally came and appeared before me J. L. the Deponent named in the Affidavit hereunto annexed, being a perſon well known and worthy of good credit, and by ſolemn oath, which the Deponent then took before me, upon the Holy Evangeliſts of Almighty God, did ſolemnly and ſincerely declare, teſtify, and depoſe to be true, the ſeveral matters and things mentioned and contained in the ſaid annexed Affidavit.

Seal of the City of LONDON.

In Faith and Teſtimony whereof, I the ſaid Lord Mayor have cauſed the Seal of the Office of Mayoralty of the ſaid City of London to be hereunto put and affixed, and the Letter of Attorney mentioned and referred to in and by the ſaid Affidavit to be hereunto alſo annexed. Dated in London the 26th day of October, in the year of our Lord 1765.

HODGES.

London to wit.

I. L. Clerk or Book-keeper to J. D. Eſq. of London, Merchant, maketh oath and ſaith, That G. V. of London, Merchant, heretofore Clerk to the ſaid J. D. is now juſtly and truly indebted unto the ſaid J. D. in the ſum of 500 *l.* ſterling, and upwards, for monies received of ſundry perſons indebted to the ſaid J. D. and for his account; and for which ſaid ſum or any part thereof,

thereof, this Deponent ſaith, That the ſaid J. D. hath received no ſecurity or ſatisfaction whatſoever, this Deponent giving for reaſons of his knowledge and belief in the premiſes, for that he hath been Clerk or Book-keeper to the ſaid J. D. for the ſpace of five years laſt paſt and upwards, been privy to all his dealings and tranſactions in trade, and that he is very well acquainted with the ſeveral perſons from whom the ſaid G. V. received the money on account of the ſaid J. D. and that he very well knows the ſaid G. V. hath not accounted with or paid the ſaid J. D. the ſame or any part thereof: and further this Deponent ſaith, That he was preſent and did ſee the ſaid J. D. (by the name and addition of J. D. Eſq; of London, Merchant), ſign, ſeal, and as his act and deed, in due form of law, execute and deliver the original Letter of Attorney hereunto annexed, for the uſes, intents, and purpoſes therein mentioned; and that he this Deponent, and J. K. who was alſo preſent at the execution of the ſaid Letter of Attorney, are ſubſcribing witneſſes to the ſame.

J. L.

Sworn the 26th day of October
1765, before me,
W. Stephenson, Mayor.

KNOW all men by theſe preſents, That I, J. D. Eſq; of London, Merchant, have made, ordained, conſtituted, and appointed, and by theſe preſents, do make, ordain, conſtitute, and appoint M. L. and U. L. of the Iſland of St. Chriſtopher's, Merchants, my true and lawful Attornies; giving and by theſe preſents granting unto my ſaid Attornies, jointly and ſeverally, full power and lawful authority for me the ſaid conſtituent,

tuent, and in my name and behalf, to ſeize, attach, ſequeſter, and condemn to my uſe, all ſuch goods and merchandiſe as now are or ſhall hereafter be found in the hands, cuſtody, or poſſeſſion of any perſon or perſons whatſoever belonging to G. V. of London, Merchant, or ſuch part thereof as will be ſufficient to pay and ſatisfy a debt due and owing to me the conſtituent from the ſaid G. V. to the amount of 500*l.* ſterling, and upwards, and upon receipts, to give one or more acquittances or other ſufficient diſcharges in due form of law; but in caſe of refuſal or delay by any perſon or perſons whom it doth or may concern, to make and render a juſt and true account, payment, delivery, and ſatisfaction in the premiſes, him, them, and every of them, thereunto to compel, and for that purpoſe to appear before all Lords Judges, and Juſtices, in any court or courts, there to anſwer, defend, and reply in all matters and cauſes touching or concerning the premiſes, and to do, ſay, ſue, purſue, ſequeſter, attach, impriſon, and condemn, and out of priſon again to deliver; alſo, if need be, to compound, compromiſe, conclude, and agree by arbitration or otherwiſe; and generally in the premiſes, to do, perform, tranſact, and accompliſh all and whatever ſhall be requiſite and neceſſary, as fully and effectually to all intents and purpoſes as I the ſaid conſtituent might or could do, being perſonally preſent, with power to my ſaid Attornies to ſubſtitute one or more perſon or perſons to act under them, and the ſame at pleaſure to revoke; and I the ſaid conſtituent do hereby promiſe to ratify and confirm all and whatever my ſaid Attornies jointly or ſeverally, or their or either of their ſubſtitutes ſhall lawfully do or cauſe to be done in the premiſes, by virtue of theſe preſents. In witneſs

witneſs whereof I have hereunto ſet my hand and ſeal, the 26th day of October 1765.

J. D. (L. S.)

Sealed and delivered
in the preſence of

J. L.
J. K.

A Letter of ATTORNEY *and* AFFIDAVIT, *certified under the Seal of the City of Briſtol.*

J—— L——, of the City of Briſtol, Gentleman, maketh oath, That on this 20th day of Auguſt, in the year of our Lord 1763, he, this Deponent, did ſee J—— B—— of the ſaid City, Merchant, ſign, ſeal, and as his act and deed deliver the Deed, Poll, or Letter of Attorney hereto annexed: and this Deponent ſaith, That the names J. C—— and J—— L——, ſigned as witneſſes to the execution of the ſaid Letter of Attorney, are of the proper hands-writing reſpectively of J—— C—— of the ſaid City, Gentleman, and him this Deponent.

J—— L——.

City and County of Briſtol, } To wit.

Seal of the City of BRISTOL.

To all to whom theſe preſents ſhall come, I, John Noble, Eſq; Mayor of the City of Briſtol (by virtue of an Act of Parliament, paſſed in the fifth year of the reign of his late Majeſty King George the Second, for the more eaſy recovery of debts in his Majeſty's Plantations and Colonies in America), do hereby certify,

tify, That on the day of the date hereof, the above named J—— L—— appeared perſonally before me, and made oath on the Holy Evangeliſts of Almighty God, that the contents of his Affidavit above written were and are true. In teſtimony whereof, I the ſaid Mayor have hereunto ſet my hand, and the ſeal of my office of Mayor, the 20th day of Auguſt, in the year of our Lord 1763.

John Noble, Mayor.

KNOW all men by theſe preſents, that I, J—— B——— of the City of Briſtol, Merchant, have made, ordained, conſtituted, and appointed, and by theſe preſents do make, ordain, conſtitute, and appoint R—— N———, of the ſaid City of Briſtol, Merchant, my true and lawful Attorney, for me, and in my name, and for my uſe, to aſk, demand, and receive of and from B—— D—— and C—— S———, both of the Iſland of Antigua in America, Merchants and Copartners, and H—— T———, of the ſame Iſland, Merchant; and alſo of and from all and every perſon and perſons whatſoever, reſiding in or belonging to the ſame Iſland, all and every debt and debts, dues, ſum and ſums of money, merchandiſe and effects, and all accounts of ſales, accounts current, and other accounts, notes, bills, bonds, warrants for confeſſing judgments, and other ſpecialties and ſecurities for monies whatſoever, due, owing, or belonging to me, or which I am or may be intitled unto upon any account whatſoever; and to ſettle, balance, and adjuſt all accounts

accounts and reckonings touching the premiſes, and to receive what ſhall appear to be due or belonging to me, or which I am or may be intitled unto thereon; and to make any compoſition or agreement for taking leſs than the whole, and to ſubmit any diſpute or diſputes to arbitration; and in caſe of non-payment, non-delivery, or in default of giving a juſt account, or making ſatisfaction in the premiſes to my ſaid Attorney, to make uſe of and proſecute all ſuch legal methods by action, ſuit, or otherwiſe, againſt the perſon or eſtates, whether real or perſonal, of the ſaid B——, D——, C——, S——, H—— T——, or other perſon or perſons aforeſaid, their or any of their heirs, executors, adminiſtrators, or other repreſentatives, as my ſaid Attorney ſhall think proper, or be adviſed; and on receipt, delivery, or ſatisfaction made in the premiſes to my ſaid Attorney, to give and execute all proper releaſes, acquittances, and diſcharges therefore, and one or more Attorney or Attornies under him from time to time to conſtitute, and at pleaſure to revoke. Giving, and by theſe preſents granting unto my ſaid Attorney and his ſubſtitute, my full power in the premiſes, for the aſking, demanding, receiving, ſettling, adjuſting, compounding, referring, ſuing for, and diſcharging the ſame, and doing, ſigning, ſealing, and executing whatſoever may be needful or expedient to be done in or about the premiſes, as fully and effectually to all intents and purpoſes as I myſelf might or could do, if perſonally preſent, ratifying and holding firm all and whatſoever my ſaid Attorney or his ſubſtitutes ſhall lawfully do or cauſe to be done in or about the premiſes, by virtue hereof; and I do hereby revoke and make void all other powers of Attorney by me heretofore

fore given in respect of the premises. In witness whereof, I have hereunto set my hand and seal, the 20th day of August, in the year of our Lord 1763.

S—— B————. (L. S.)

Sealed and delivered in
the presence of

J. C——.
J—— L——, Notary Public.

An AFFIDAVIT *under the Seal of the City of London, for the purpose of recovering a Debt in one of the Colonies.*

TO all to whom these presents shall come, I William Beckford, Esq. Lord Mayor of the City of London, in pursuance of an Act of Parliament, made and passed in the fifth year of the reign of his late Majesty King George the Second, intituled, an Act for the more easy recovery of debts in his Majesty's Plantations and Colonies in America, do hereby certify, That on the day of the date hereof, personally came and appeared before me J—— W————, the Deponent named in the Affidavit hereunto annexed, being a person well known, and worthy of good credit, and by solemn oath, which the said Deponent then took before me upon the Holy Evangelists of Almighty God, did solemnly and sincerely declare, testify, and depose to be true, the several matters and things mentioned and contained in the said annexed affidavit.

In

Seal of the City of LONDON.

In Faith and Teſtimony whereof, I the ſaid Lord Mayor have cauſed the Seal of the Office of Mayoralty of the ſaid City of London to be hereunto put and affixed, and the ſeveral accounts mentioned and referred to in and by the ſaid Affidavit to be hereunto alſo annexed. Dated in London the 13th day of June, in the year of our Lord 1763.

HODGES.

LONDON, ſcil.

J—— W———, Clerk or Book-keeper to E—— C——— and J—— M———, of London, Merchants and Partners, maketh oath, That he hath lived with the ſaid E—— C——— and J—— M——, for the ſpace of three years and upwards, and ſaith, That the accounts hereunto annexed, intitled W—— K——'s diſburſements, purporting to be an account for the Snow Elizabeth from St. Kitts, and the Portlage Bill for the ſaid Snow Elizabeth from Antigua to London; and alſo the account hereunto alſo annexed, intitled debtor, the owners of the Snow Elizabeth in account with W—— K——, creditor, is a true extract or copy of the ſame accounts as delivered in, and ſettled and adjuſted by the ſaid W—— K——, and that the ſum of 87 *l.* 1 *s.* 10 *d.* appearing to be the balance of the ſaid laſt mentioned account, was well and truly paid to the ſaid W—— K—— by the ſaid E—— C——— and J—— M——, and that the receipt was duly ſigned by the ſaid W—— K—— on the original account now in the cuſtody of the ſaid C——— and M——: And this Deponent further ſaith, That he hath carefully peruſed and examined

examined the account hereunto alſo annexed, intitled Debtor, the owners of the Elizabeth, W——K—— Commander, in account current with C——— and M——, creditors, with the books of account of the ſaid E—— C——— and J—— M——, and that the ſame is a true extract or copy of the ſame account taken from the ſaid books, and doth agree therewith: and this Deponent ſaith, by means of his ſaid employment, he knows the ſeveral ſums of money in the ſaid laſt account mentioned to be paid to W—— S——, and the ſeveral other perſons therein named, and for poſtage of letters, and ſuch other purpoſes as therein is ſpecified, were all well and truly paid and diſburſed by the ſaid E—— C——— and J—— M——; and that he, this Deponent, hath carefully computed and examined the ſeveral ſums charged in the ſaid annexed account for intereſt and commiſſion, and that the ſame are rightly charged and computed, and are the ſame as uſually charged and allowed in the like caſes: and this Deponent further ſaith, That he hath alſo peruſed and examined the account hereunto annexed, intitled Debtors, N— R—— and Mr. R—— B——, junior, in account current with C——— and M——, creditors with the books of account of the ſaid E—— C——— and J—— M——, and that the ſame is a true extract or copy of the ſame account taken from the ſaid books, and doth agree therewith: and this Deponent further ſaith, He knows alſo that the ſeveral ſums in the ſaid annexed account, mentioned to be paid to J—— C——, and the ſeveral other perſons therein named, for the ſeveral purpoſes therein mentioned, were well and truly paid by the ſaid E—— C——— and J—— M—— accordingly: and that he, this Deponent, hath

hath computed and examined the ſeveral ſums charged in the annexed account for intereſt and commiſſion, and that the ſame are rightly computed and juſtly charged: and laſtly, this Deponent ſaith, That to the beſt of this Deponent's knowledge and belief, the ſaid E—— C—— and J—— M—— have, in the ſaid two laſt mentioned accounts, brought to account and given credit for all monies and effects received by them on the ſaid accounts reſpectively.

J—— W——.

Sworn at London, the 13th
day of June 1763, before
me,

William Beckford, Lord Mayor.

An Affidavit *under the Seal of the City of Briſtol, for the purpoſe of recovering a Debt in one of the Colonies.*

B—— H——, of the City of Briſtol, Plumber, maketh oath, That on or about the firſt day of March 1763, he this Deponent agreed with R—— P——, Commander of the Brig Flora, then bound from the port of Briſtol to Antigua (on account of T—— H——, jun. as he could not appear perſonally at that time for fear of arreſts) for the paſſage of T—— H——, E—— his wife, one child, and a negro ſervant, from the ſaid port of Briſtol to Antigua, at the price of fifty pounds ſterling, one half of which to be paid at the port of Briſtol before the ſailing of the ſaid brig (which was paid accordingly), and the other half to be paid by the ſaid T—— H—— on his arrival at Antigua in the ſaid brig: and this Deponent further ſaith, That the ſaid T—— H—— was to find himſelf, wife, child, and negro ſervant,

vant, with ſuch proviſions during ſuch ſaid paſſage, as is uſual for paſſengers: and this Deponent further ſaith, That the ſaid T—— H——, E—— his wife, and their family, were in conderation of ſuch ſaid 50 *l.* ſo to be paid as aforeſaid, to have the uſe of part of the cabbin in the ſaid brig, during ſuch their ſaid paſſage; and that the above is the whole agreement ſo made by this Deponent, for or on account of the ſaid T—— H——, for ſuch his ſaid paſſage to Antigua in the ſaid brig as aforeſaid.

B—— H——.

Seal of the City of BRISTOL.

I Richard Farr, Eſq; Mayor of the City of Briſtol, within which city the above B—— H—— reſides, do certify that the above named B—— H—— came before me this 24th day of March 1764, and after he had ſubſcribed the above written Affidavit, made oath of the truth thereof on the Holy Evangeliſts of Almighty God. In teſtimony whereof, I the ſaid Mayor have cauſed the Seal of Office of Mayor of the ſaid City to be hereunto put and affixed the day and year above written.

RICHARD FARR, Mayor.

By an Act of Aſſembly of the Iſland of Antigua, the method of proving debts due to perſons reſiding in Great Britain, introduced by the 5 Geo. II. c. 7. is extended to debts due from perſons in Antigua, to creditors reſiding in Ireland, the continent of America, or in any other of of his Majeſty's Colonies or Plantations, provided that in every Affidavit and Affirmation, there ſhall be expreſſed the addition of the party making the ſame, and the particular place of the witneſſes abode; and that before ſuch examination, nine months notice be given in writing to the adverſe party or his counſel, of the names of the witneſſes, and the time and place of the examination, which Affidavit or Affirmation may be made before, and certified under the ſeal of office, or under the private ſeal of the Chief Governor, or the perſon in command for the time being, Mayor, or Juſtice.

And by another ſection of the ſame Act of Aſſembly, Conveyances and Deeds, Letters of Attorney, Procurations, and other Powers in Writing, made out of the Iſland, with a depoſition proving the ſame, ſworn before the Lord Mayor of London, York, or Dublin, or any other Mayor, or chief Officer of any City or Town Corporate, within Great Britain or Ireland, atteſted under the Public Seal of ſuch City or Town Corporate, or under the Hand and Public Seal of any Chief Governor or Magiſtrate, Lieutenant Governor, or Preſident of the Council of any Colony in his Majeſty's dominions, and annexed to the thing proved, ſhall be as ſufficient evidence in law and equity, as if the witneſſes therein named made ſuch proof *viva voce*, provided that ſuch deed, if concerning lands and ſlaves, be recorded in the Regiſter's office of Antigua, as the laws of that Iſland require.

Similar Acts of Aſſembly have paſſed in ſome other Colonies.

CHAP.

CHAP. XV.

The Method of authenticating LETTERS *of* ATTORNEY, *which are to be transmitted without Affidavits of Debt; together with* FORMS *of* LETTERS *of* ATTORNEY, *adapted to various Cases.*

ALL Affidavits transmitted to the Colonies, for the purpose of recovering debts, must be authenticated in the manner directed by the statute of 5 Geo. II. c. 7. above recited; and when a Letter of Attorney is transmitted at the same time with an Affidavit, they are both annexed together, and certified under the Common Seal of the City, Borough, or Town corporate, where, or next to which, the person making the Affidavit or Affirmation happens to reside; but where a Letter of Attorney is transmitted without an Affidavit, it may then either be certified under such Common Seal as aforesaid, or (which is the easiest and least expensive method) it may be executed in the presence of persons who are going to the Colony to which the Letter of Attorney is to be transmitted: and then one of the subscribing witnesses may prove the execution of the Letter of Attorney, before a Judge of the Colony in which such Letter of Attorney is to be made use of:—I shall give the Reader different forms of each sort.

A LETTER *of* ATTORNEY *certified under the Seal of the City of London*

TO all to whom these presents shall come, I Sir Samuel Fluyder, Knight and Baronet, Lord Mayor of the City of London, in pursuance of an Act of Parliament made and passed in the fifth year

year of the reign of his late Majeſty King George the Second, intituled, An Act for the more eaſy recovery of Debts in his Majeſty's Plantations and Colonies in America, do hereby certify, That on the day of the date hereof, perſonally came and appeared before me B—— H——, the Deponent named in the Affidavit hereunto annexed, being a perſon well known, and worthy of good credit; and by ſolemn oath, which the ſaid Deponent then took before me upon the Holy Evangeliſts of Almighty God, did ſolemnly and ſincerely declare, teſtify, and depoſe to be true, the ſeveral matters and things mentioned and contained in the ſaid annexed Affidavit.

SEAL of the City of LONDON.

In faith and teſtimony whereof, I the ſaid Lord Mayor have cauſed the Seal of the Office of Mayoralty of the ſaid City of London to be hereunto put and affixed, and the Letter of Attorney mentioned and referrred to in and by the ſaid Affidavit to be hereunto alſo annexed, dated in London, the 16th day of April, in the year of our Lord 1762.

HODGES.

LONDON, to wit,

B—— H——, Clerk to W—— T—— of the pariſh of St. Edmund the King and Martyr, London, Notary Public, maketh oath, That on the 15th day of April inſtant, he this Deponent was preſent, and did ſee A—— J—— (by the name, ſtyle, and title of A—— J——— of Pall Mall, in the County of Middleſex, taylor) ſign, ſeal, and as his act and deed, in due form of law, execute and

and deliver the original paper, writing, procuration, or Letter of Attorney hereunto annexed, bearing date the ſaid 15th day of April inſtant, to and for the uſes, intents, and purpoſes therein mentioned. And that in teſtimony of ſuch execution, he this Deponent and R—— P——, alſo Clerk to the ſaid W—— T——, ſeverally ſet or ſubſcribed their names as witneſſes thereto, as thereby may appear.

Sworn the 16th day of April, in the year 1762, before me at the Manſion Houſe,
S. FLUDYER, Mayor.

B—— H——.

On the 15th day of April, in the year of our Lord 1762, before me W—— T——, Notary and Tabellion Public in London, duly admitted and ſworn, and witneſſes, perſonally appeared A—— J—— of Pall Mall, in the County of Middleſex, taylor, who declared to have made, ordained, conſtituted, authoriſed, and appointed, and by theſe preſents doth make, ordain, conſtitute, authoriſe and ordain J—— H——, of the Iſland of Antigua, Eſq; his true and lawful Attorney, giving and hereby granting unto his ſaid Attorney, full power and lawful authority for him the ſaid conſtituent, in his name and for his uſe, to aſk, demand, levy, ſue for, and by all lawful ways and means recover and receive, of and from all and every, or any perſon or perſons whatſoever whom it ſhall or may concern, inhabiting or being in the Iſland of Antigua aforeſaid, or any other of the Leeward Iſlands, all ſuch ſum and ſums of money, goods, wares, merchandize, effects, eſtate and things which now are, or ſhall or may hereafter be due, owing, payable, belonging, or in any wiſe appertaining unto him

the

the ſaid Conſtituent, whether by bond, note, bill, book, debt, account, conſignment, contract, agreement, decree, ſentence, judgment, execution, extent, or for, by, or upon any other account, way, reaſon, or means ſoever, nothing in law or equity excepted or reſerved; and to that end, with all and every or any perſon or perſons whatſoever whom it ſhall or may concern, inhabiting or being in the Iſland of Antigua aforeſaid, or any other of the Leewards Iſlands, to account and to view, ſtate, ſettle, and adjuſt all accounts, and the balance thereof to receive, and upon recovery and receipts, to give one or more acquittances, or other ſufficient diſcharges, in due form of law; but in caſe of refuſal or delay, by all and every, or any perſon or perſons whatſoever whom it ſhall or may concern, to make and render juſt and true account, payment, delivery and ſatisfaction in the premiſſes, him, her, them, any or either of them, thereunto to compel, by all lawful ways and means whatſoever; alſo (if need be) to appear before all or any Lords Judges, and Juſtices, in any Court or Courts, there to anſwer, defend and reply, in all matters and cauſes touching or concerning the premiſes, to do, ſay, purſue, implead, ſeize, ſequeſter, attach, arreſt, impriſon, and to condemn, and out of priſon again to deliver; alſo to compound, conclude, and agree, by arbitration or otherwiſe, as his ſaid Attorney ſhall think fit: and generally in and concerning the premiſes to do, perform, and execute, all and whatſoever ſhall be requiſite and neceſſary, as fully, amply, and effectually, to all intents, conſtructions, and purpoſes, as he the ſaid Conſtituent might or could do if perſonally preſent. With power to ſubſtitute one or more Attornies under him, with like or limited power, and

and the ſame again to revoke, he the ſaid A— J— hereby ratifying, confirming, and holding for good and valid, all and whatſoever the ſaid J— H—, or his ſubſtitutes, ſhall lawfully do, or cauſe to be done, in or about the premiſes, by virtue of theſe preſents; thus done and paſſed in London aforeſaid, in the preſence of the underwritten witneſſes.

Sealed and delivered (being firſt duly ſtamped) in the preſence of
B—— H——
R—— P——.

A—— J——. (L.S.)

SEAL.

In præmiſſorum fidem
W—— T——, Not. Pub.
1762.

A SUBSTITUTION *under the laſt mentioned* LETTER *of* ATTORNEY.

ANTIGUA.

KNOW all men by theſe preſents, That I J—H— of the Iſland of Antigua aforeſaid, Eſq; the lawful Attorney of A—— J—— of Pall Mall, in the County of Middleſex, and Kingdom of Great Britain, taylor, have made and ordained, and by theſe preſents (by virtue of the power and authority to me in that behalf given by the ſaid A—J—, by a certain writing, or Letter of Attorney under his hand and ſeal, dated the 15th day of April 1762), do make, ordain, conſtitute and appoint R—— K——, of the ſaid Iſland of Antigua, merchant, to be my true, certain, and lawful Attorney; and I do hereby authoriſe and empower him to act as, and to be the Attorney of the ſaid A—— J——, in his name to demand, ſue for, recover

recover and receive, of and from all and every perſon or perſons whatſoever, whom it doth and ſhall concern, as well in his Majeſty's Iſland of * Dominica, as in all other his Majeſty's Charibbee Iſlands in America, all ſuch ſum and ſums of money, goods, wares, merchandize, effects, eſtate, and things which now are, or ſhall or may hereafter be due, owing, payable, belonging, or in any wiſe appertaining unto him the ſaid A—— J——, whether by bond, note, bill, book, debt, account, conſignment, contract, agreement, decree, ſentence, judgment, execution, extent, or for, by, and upon any other account, way, reaſon, or means whatſoever, nothing in law or equity excepted or reſerved. And I the ſaid J—— H—— do hereby give and grant unto the ſaid R— K—, all my full power and authority, as Attorney of the ſaid A—— J——, and otherwiſe in and touching the premiſes, to uſe, have, and take all lawful ways and means, in and for recovering and receiving of all ſum and ſums of money, goods, wares, merchandiſes, effects, eſtate, and things, or any part thereof, as well in his Majeſty's ſaid Iſland of Dominica, as in all other his Majeſty's Charibbee Iſlands in America, and to do and perform all other matters and things in and to the premiſes requiſite and neceſſary, as fully as I myſelf might or could do, by virtue of the power to me given by the ſaid A—— J—— or otherwiſe: and I do hereby ratify and confirm all and whatſoever my ſaid Attorney ſhall legally do or procure to be done, in and touching the premiſes.

* The Attorney exceeded the power delegated to him; for his authority extended only to the Leeward Iſlands, and Dominica was not one of them: the ſubſtitution was therefore void as to Dominica, and ſuch of the Charibbees as were not in the government of the Leeward Iſlands.

In

In witneſs whereof I have hereunto ſet my hand and ſeal, this day of December 1764.

Sealed and delivered in the preſence of J—— H——. (L. S.)

L—— M——.

A LETTER *of* ATTORNEY *certified by the Lord Provoſt of Glaſgow, under the Common Seal of that City.*

KNOW all men by theſe preſents, That I J—J—, poſtmaſter of Glaſgow, and merchant, for divers good cauſes and conſiderations me thereunto moving, have made, conſtituted, and appointed, and by theſe preſents do make, conſtitute, and appoint C—— J—— of St. John's in Antigua, merchant, my true and lawful Attorney, for me and in my name, and for my uſe, to aſk, demand, ſue for, recover and receive, of all and whoever are or may be indebted to me, in any of the Weſt India or American Iſlands belonging to Great Britain, France, Spain, Denmark, and Holland, all ſuch ſum and ſums of money, debts and duties whatſoever, which now are or may be due and owing to me the ſaid J— J——, by all and whoever are or may be indebted to me, belonging to the above mentioned Iſlands, and to have, uſe, and take all lawful ways and means in my name, for recovery thereof by attachment, arreſt, diſtreſs, or otherwiſe, and to make and give acquittances, or other diſcharges, in my name, and generally to do and execute in the premiſes, as fully in every reſpect as I myſelf might or could do, being perſonally preſent, and to make Attornies, one or more of them under him, for the purpoſes aforeſaid, and at his pleaſure to revoke the ſame; ratifying, confirming, and allowing all and whatſoever my ſaid Attorney ſhall lawfully do or cauſe to be done therein by virtue of theſe preſents.

In

In witneſs whereof I have hereunto ſet my hand and ſeal, this 21ſt day of September, in the year of our Lord 1763.

Signed, ſealed, and delivered in preſence of J—— J——. (L. S.)

J—— G——.
D—— W——.

At Glaſgow the 5th day of October ſeventeen hundred and ſixty-three years, in preſence of Archibald Ingram, Eſq; Lord Provoſt and Chief Magiſtrate of the ſaid City, one of his Majeſty's Juſtices of Peace for the County of Lanerk, appeared J—— G—— of ſaid City, merchant, who upon his great and ſolemn oath, taken by him before the ſaid Provoſt, upon the Holy Evangeliſts of Almighty God, depoſes and ſays, That he, this Deponent, was preſent and did ſee the within J—— J—— ſign, ſeal, and for and as his true and genuine act and deed, deliver the Letter of Attorney within written, upon the day of the date thereof; and that D—— W—— of ſaid City, merchant, was alſo then preſent, and that the name J—— J——, appearing at ſaid Letter of Attorney as granter thereof, and ſeal thereto adhibited, is the proper hand-writing and ſeal of J—— J—— aforeſaid; and that the names J—— G—— and D—— W——, alſo appearing at ſaid Letter of Attorney, as witneſſes thereto, are of the reſpective proper hand-writings of this Deponent, and of D— W—— aforeſaid.

(L. S.) In teſtimony whereof theſe preſents are ſubſcribed by the ſaid Deponent, and by the ſaid Lord Provoſt, who has cauſed the Common Seal of the ſaid City to be hereto affixed, date above.

ARCH. INGRAM. J—— G——.

LET-

Letter *of* Attorney *executed by a Gentleman in England, impowering his Friend in Nevis to appoint Persons to take an Inventory and Appraisement of Negroes, &c. on the Expiration of a Lease.——The Execution of this Letter of Attorney was proved before a Judge in Nevis, by one of the subscribing Witnesses, who saw the same executed in England.*

TO all to whom these presents shall come, I T—— B—— of Darking, in the County of Surry, Esq; send greeting, Whereas by an Indenture of Lease, bearing date the 14th day of June, in the year of our Lord 1753, made between the said T— B— of the one part, and W— W— of the said Island of St. Christopher, Esq; of the other part, to commence from the 1st day of August then next ensuing, for the term of ten years, it is therein, amongst other things, mutually covenanted and agreed, by and between both the said parties, That at the end, expiration, or other sooner determination of the said term of ten years, a new Appraisement or Valuation shall be made and taken, of all the negroe-slaves, horses, mules, cattle, and of the issue and increase thereof, which shall then be, and of all the Plantation utensils and implements thereby demised, and in the schedule or inventory thereunto annexed, contained, as also of all canes which shall be then standing and growing, and of all the buildings upon the said demised lands, and that such new Valuation and Appraisements shall be made and taken, by two indifferent persons, of good reputation and competent judgment in that behalf, one of them to be named and chosen by the said T—— B——, his heirs or assigns, and the other by the said W—— W——, his executors, administrators, or assigns; and in case such

Appraisement

Appraiſement ſo to be made, at the end of the ſaid term, ſhall, upon the valuation thereof, exceed the ſum of 10,356*l.* 5*s.* 10*d.* current money of Nevis, that then and in ſuch caſe, he the ſaid T——— B———, his heirs or aſſigns, ſhall and will pay unto the ſaid W——— W———, his executors, adminiſtrators, or aſſigns, ſo much money as the ſurplus or exceſs thereof (if any be) ſhall amount to, over and above the ſum of 10,356*l.* 5*s.* 10*d.* current money of Nevis; and in caſe the ſaid new Appraiſement, ſo to be made at the end of the ſaid term thereby demiſed, ſhall fall ſhort of, and be leſs in value than the ſaid ſum of 10,356*l.* 5*s.* 10*d.* that then the ſaid W— W—, his executors, adminiſtrators, or aſſigns, ſhall and will pay unto the ſaid T—— B——, his heirs or aſſigns, ſuch ſum, and ſo much money, whatſoever the ſame be, as ſuch future Valuation and Appraiſement, ſo to be made and taken as aforeſaid, ſhall amount to. Now know ye, That I the ſaid T—— B——, for the end and purpoſe aforeſaid, have conſtituted and appointed, and by theſe preſents do conſtitute and appoint H—— H——, of the Iſland of Nevis, Eſq; to be my true and lawful Attorney, for me, and on my behalf, to nominate and appoint one or more perſon or perſons, to take an account of all the negro ſlaves, and all other things contained in the ſchedule or inventory annexed to the ſaid leaſe, that are now, or ſhall be remaining and being on the demiſed premiſes; and to make and take a new Inventory and Appraiſement thereof; which Inventory and Appraiſement ſo to be made and taken, between the ſaid T—— B—— and W—— W——, it is hereby declared and agreed ſhall ſtand and be binding on them, the ſaid T——— B——— and H——— H———, and be annexed to, and comprized

prized in the schedule of the lease of the said premises now granted by the said T——— B——— to the said H——— H———, which bears date the 3d day of this instant May, to commence from the 1st day of August now next ensuing; and to do, execute, and perform all and every other act and acts, thing and things whatsoever, which shall be thought necessary and convenient to be done, in or about the premises, hereby ratifying and confirming all and whatsoever my said Attorney shall lawfully do, or cause to be done, in, about, or touching the same. In witness whereof I the said T—— B——— have hereunto set my hand and seal, this 9th day of May 1763.

Sealed and delivered by the above named T— B—, in the presence of us, T— B——. (L. S.)

W—— M———, *jun.*
J—— W———, *jun.*

BEFORE Joseph Herbert, Esq; Chief Justice, &c. personally appeared Mr. W—— M———, *jun.* and made oath on the Holy Evangelists of Almighty God, That he was present and did see the within named T—— B——, Esq; sign, seal, and deliver the within Letter of Attorney to H—— H——, Esq; and that he did also see J—— W——, *jun.* subscribe his name to the same, together with this Deponent, as witness thereto.

Sworn before me, August 27th 1763. W—— M——, *jun.*

JOSEPH HERBERT.

The

The above Affidavit ſeems to have been drawn in a hurry; had it been drawn at leiſure, it would perhaps have been ſomething in the following form, which may ſerve as a precedent in ſimilar caſes:

Before the Honourable JOSEPH HERBERT, *Eſq; Chief Juſtice of his Majeſty's Court of King's Bench and Common Pleas of the Iſland of Nevis.*

PERSONALLY appeared A— B—, late of C—, in the Kingdom of Great Britain, but now of the ſaid Iſland of Nevis, Eſq; who being duly ſworn on the Holy Evangeliſts of Almighty God, maketh oath, That he this Deponent is one of the ſubſcribing witneſſes to the above Inſtrument of Writing, bearing date the ninth day of May one thouſand ſeven hundred and ſixty-three, and purporting to be a Letter of Attorney from D— E— of F——, in the County of Surry, Eſq; to G—— H—— of Nevis, Eſq; and this Deponent ſaith, That he was preſent and did ſee the above named D—— E—— ſign, ſeal and deliver the above written Inſtrument, or Letter of Attorney, as his act and deed, at F—— in the County of Surry, in the Kingdom of Great Britain aforeſaid; and that the name or letters D—— E—— ſet and ſubſcribed at the foot or bottom of the above Inſtrument of Writing or Letter of Attorney, as the perſon executing the ſame, are of the proper hand-writing of the ſaid D—— E——: And laſtly, this Deponent ſaith, That the name or letters A—— B——, and the name or letters J—— K——, appearing to be ſet and ſubſcribed as witneſſes atteſting the execution of the above Inſtrument of Writing or Letter of Attorney, are of the reſpective proper hands writing of this Deponent,

ponent, and of J— K—— late of M—, in the ſaid Kingdom of Great Britain, but now of the Iſland of Nevis aforeſaid, Eſq.

Sworn at the Iſland of Nevis, the 27th day of Auguſt 1763, before me
JOSEPH HERBERT.

A—— B——.

This form of an Affidavit is ſuppoſed to be written under the Letter of Attorney, and on the ſame ſheet of paper; but when it is written on the back of the Letter of Attorney, it muſt be varied accordingly, by ſaying, the "*within*" Inſtrument of Writing, inſtead of the "*above*" Inſtrument, &c.

A POWER *of* ATTORNEY *from the Aſſignees of a Bankrupt in Briſtol, to recover a Debt from his Partner in Antigua.*

TO all to whom theſe preſents ſhall come, J—— P—— and W—— B——, merchants, and T—— M——, apothecary, all of the City of Briſtol, ſend greeting, Whereas B—— S——, late of the Iſland of Antigua, but now of the City of Briſtol, merchant, and partner with G— R— of Antigua aforeſaid, merchant, is lately become bankrupt, and a commiſſion of bankruptcy under the Great Seal of Great Britain, bearing teſt at Weſtminſter the 4th day of February laſt, hath been awarded againſt him, which commiſſion hath been carried into execution, and the ſaid B— S— thereupon adjudged a bankrupt, and the ſaid J—— P——, W—— B—— and T—— M—— have been duly choſen aſſignees of the eſtate and effects of the ſaid B—— S——; and thereupon an aſſignment of ſuch eſtate and effects hath, by indenture,

indenture, bearing date the twenty-ſixth day of February laſt, been made and executed by the Commiſſioners, in the ſaid commiſſion named to them, the ſaid J—— P——, W—— B—— and T—— M——, as in and by the ſaid indenture, reference thereto being had, will more fully and at large appear. And whereas there are ſundry goods, wares, and merchandiſes, and alſo ſeveral debts and ſums of money due, owing and belonging to the eſtate of the ſaid B—— S——, jointly with the ſaid G—— R——, and on his own ſeparate account in Antigua aforeſaid, and other places beyond ſea, and alſo in the hands of the ſaid G—— R——. Now know ye, That we the ſaid J—— P——, W—— B——, and T—— M——, have, and each and every of us hath made, ordained, conſtituted, authorized, impowered, appointed, and deputed, and by theſe preſents do, each and every of us doth make, ordain, conſtitute, authorize, impower, appoint, and depute R—— N———, of the ſaid City of Briſtol, mariner, our and each and every of our true and lawful Attorney, for us the ſaid Aſſignees, and in our or any of our names, to aſk, demand, levy, ſue for, take, recover and receive, of and from the ſaid G—— R———, and all and every other perſon and perſons whomſoever, in Antigua aforeſaid, or elſewhere, his, their, or any of their executors, adminiſtrators, or aſſigns, all and all manner of goods, wares, and merchandiſes, debts, ſum and ſums of money whatſoever, due, owing, or in any manner belonging to the eſtate of the ſaid B— S—, either as partner with the ſaid G—— R———, or in his own private or ſeparate capacity, and to call to account and bring to reckoning the ſaid G—— R———, and ſuch other perſon and perſons, his, her, and their executors and adminiſtrators,

ſtrators, and to ſtate, ſettle, and finally adjuſt all accounts, reckonings, and demands whatſoever relating thereto; and if it ſhall be thought neceſſary to refer any diſputes touching the ſame to arbitration, and for that purpoſe, for us and in our names to enter into and duly execute any bond or bonds of arbitration, for the ſubmitting ſuch diſputes to be ſettled and adjuſted by referees to be choſen for the purpoſe; and alſo, if he ſhall ſee occaſion to take and accept of a compoſition or compoſitions, in lieu of and for ſuch goods, wares, and merchandizes, debts, ſum or ſums of money; and upon receipt of ſuch goods, wares, and merchandizes, debts, ſum or ſums of money, or any compoſition, or any ſecurity or ſatisfaction for the ſame, for us and in our names to ſign, ſeal, and duly execute and deliver ſuch receipts, acquittances, releaſes, or other diſcharges, as the nature of the caſe ſhall require, and on non-payment or non-delivery of ſuch goods, wares, and merchandizes, debts, ſum or ſums of money, to bring, commence, and effectually proſecute ſuch ſuit or ſuits, either in law or equity, for the recovery thereof, as our ſaid Attorney ſhall judge neceſſary or be adviſed, and in ſuch ſuit or ſuits to proceed to judgments, decrees, and executions, and ſuch ſuit or ſuits to diſcontinue, or therein to become nonſuit, and commence others as occaſion ſhall require; and likewiſe one or more Attorney or Attorneys under him the ſaid R— N—, for the purpoſes aforeſaid, to ſubſtitute and appoint, and the ſame at pleaſure to revoke, and to ſubſtitute other or others in his or their ſtead or ſteads, and generally to do, perform, and execute, all and every ſuch farther act and acts, thing and things whatſoever, for the recovering, receiving, compounding, and diſcharging the ſaid goods,

goods, wares, and merchandizes, debts, ſum and ſums of money, as ſhall be, or by our ſaid Attorney ſhall be thought to be requiſite and neceſſary, in as full and effectual manner, to all intents and purpoſes, as we ourſelves, or either of us, could or might do if perſonally preſent; and all and whatſoever our ſaid Attorney, or his ſubſtitutes, ſhall lawfully do or cauſe to be done, in any of the premiſes aforeſaid, by virtue of theſe preſents, we do hereby agree to allow, ratify, and confirm for valid. In witneſs whereof we have hereunto ſet our hands and ſeals, the 16th day of March, in the 5th year of the reign of our Sovereign Lord George the Third, by the Grace of God of Great Britain, France, and Ireland King, Defender of the Faith, and ſo forth, in the year of our Lord 1765.

Sealed and delivered by the
within named J— P——,
T— M—, and W— B—,
in the preſence of
P— D——, *jun.*
S— W——.

POWER *of* SUBSTITUTION.

St. CHRISTOPHER'S.

KNOW all men by theſe preſents, That I J— O——, Eſq; at preſent in the Iſland of St. Chriſtopher, but about to depart to the Iſland of St. Vincent, the lawful Attorney of D— O-—, now or late reſiding in the County of Middleſex, in the Kingdom of Great Britain, Eſq; have made, ordained, conſtituted, and by theſe preſents (by virtue of the power and authority to me in that behalf given, by the ſaid D— O——, by by a certain Writing or Letter of Attorney under his hand and seal, dated the fifth day of April 1768), do make, ordain, constitute, and appoint W— P———, of the said Island of St. Christopher, merchant, to be my true, certain, and lawful Attorney: and I do hereby authorize and impower him, the said W— P———, to act as, and to be the Attorney of the said D— O———, and in his name, place and stead, and to and for his use, to ask, demand, and by all lawful ways and means whatsoever to recover and receive, of and from all and every person or persons whatsoever, in the said Island of Saint Christopher or elsewhere, in his Majesty's Leeward Charibbee Islands in America, whom it doth, shall, or may concern, all and every sum and sums of money, debts, dues, goods, chattels, effects, and other things which is or are, and which shall or may grow and become due, owing, payable, or belonging to him the said D— O———, upon or by virtue of any mortgage, bond, judgment, or other specialty, or upon any bill of exchange, promissory note, or other simple contract, or by virtue of any deed or will, or upon any account, or by any ways or means whatsoever or howsoever, and upon receipt or recovery thereof, or of any part thereof, for him the said D— O———, and in his name, from time to time to make, give, and execute, good and sufficient acquittances and discharges for the same, and for him the said D— O—, and in his name, or in the name of him my said Attorney, as and for his the said D——— O———'s act and deed, or acts and deeds, to sign, seal, and deliver any deed or deeds, conveyances and assurances, good, valid, and sufficient in the law for reconveying or assigning and assuring any Plantations, lands, tenements, negroes, hereditaments, and

and chattels, which he the ſaid D— O—— now hath or may have, in mortgage for any ſum or ſums of money, upon payment of the principal money and intereſt due on ſuch mortgage or mortgages, and to give good and ſufficient acquittances and diſcharges for the conſideration or mortgage money, and all or every or any ſuch deed or deeds, conveyances and aſſurances, to acknowledge as for his the ſaid D— O——'s act and deed, or acts and deeds, before any Judge, or other Magiſtrate or Officer appointed, or to be appointed, to take the acknowledgment of deeds, ſo that the ſame may be recorded and perfected in due form of law; and to call to account and bring to a reckoning all and every perſon and perſons concerned in the premiſes, and to ſettle and adjuſt all accounts now or hereafter depending between him the ſaid D— O——, and all or any perſon or perſons whomſoever, upon ſuch terms, and in ſuch manner, and with ſuch allowances therein, as the ſaid W— P—— ſhall think fit and adviſeable for his the ſaid D— O——'s intereſt; and in caſe any difference or diſpute ſhall ariſe concerning the premiſes, to refer the ſame to arbitration, if the ſaid W— P—— ſhall ſo think fit, and for the ſaid D— O——, and on his behalf, to abide by and perform ſuch award as ſhall be made, in purſuance of ſuch reference; and alſo, if need be, to compound and take leſs than the whole of, and for any debt or debts, ſum or ſums of money, or other matter or thing which is or are, and which ſhall become due and payable or belonging to him the ſaid D— O——, by or from any perſon or perſons whomſoever: and I the ſaid J—— O—— do hereby authorize and impower my ſaid Attorney, as and when he ſhall think proper, to commence, ſue, and proſecute or or defend, any action or suit, actions or suits, at law or in equity, and to pursue all or any legal or equitable means, as occasion shall be and require, for touching or concerning all, every, or any the matters aforesaid, in any wise howsoever, and for him the said D—— O——, and in his name, and to and for his use, to accept and take any security or securities, for any debt or debts due to him, as my said Attorney shall think fit and approve; and generally to do and perform all other acts, deeds, matters, and things needful or requisite in and about all and singular the premises, as fully and effectually, to all intents and purposes whatsoever, as I myself might or could do, by virtue of the power to me given by the said D—— O—— or otherwise; and I do hereby ratify, allow, and confirm, all and whatsoever my said Attorney shall lawfully do or cause to be done in and about the premises, by virtue of these presents. In witness whereof I have hereunto set my hand and seal, the 20th day of May, in the year of our Lord 1769.

Sealed and delivered, &c.

CHAP.

CHAP. XVI.

Of the NEGROES *in the Colonies, and the Mode of conveying and manumitting them.*

TO enumerate the ſeverities that are exerciſed by ſome Planters in the Sugar and Rice Colonies on their Negroes, would exceed the bounds of this deſign. I ſhall at preſent content myſelf with obſerving, that in the Sugar Colonies the lands in which they plant canes are not ploughed, but hoed up by Negroes, who have no preſcribed taſk, but are followed up by drivers with whips. Their food is either Indian corn, rice, yams, Potatoes, or horſe-beans, in much ſmaller quantities than are neceſſary for people who work hard; and theſe unhappy people are often laid down and ſeverely whipped for ſlight offences. Whilſt I was in the Weſt Indies, a man of good credit told me, he was preſent at a Planter's houſe there, when one of the Negroes complained to his maſter that his allowance of corn was too ſmall, and the land allowed him ſo trifling, that he had not enough to live on. The maſter ſaid he would not increaſe his allowance: whereupon the Negro aſked, " What muſt I do?" To which the maſter replied, Why, d—n you, ſteal!" In St. Kitt's, the Negroes are worſe off than in moſt of the other Sugar Colonies, becauſe that Iſland is ſmall, and the land ſo fertile, that they allow their Negroes very little ground to plant for themſelves. The ſlender allowance made the Negroes in the Iſlands in general is not only a circumſtance of great cruelty to them, but is productive of very diſagreeable conſequences to the white people who live in the towns; for hunger compels the Negroes to ſteal;

and

and they frequently not only rob the yards of the ſtock, but even break open ſtores, and carry off proviſions to a large amount. Theſe depredations are ſenſibly felt in a country where the lands, though fertile, are chiefly employed to raiſe ſugar canes; ſo that proviſions and ſtock are laid in at a great expence, and the ſupply is precarious, particularly in time of war. But there are two evils attending the enſlaving the Negroes in the Colonies, which muſt induce every good man to condemn it: the one is, the neglecting to inſtruct them in the principles of the Chriſtian religion; nay, I have heard men, who ought to have known better, ridicule ſuch an attempt: the other is, that from cruelty, hard labour, and a want of ſufficient food, the number of Negroes that die exceeds the number that are born in moſt if not in all the Iſlands; ſo that an annual ſupply from the Coaſt of Guinea is neceſſary to keep up their quota.

In the Rice Colonies, the caſe is not quite ſo bad as in the Sugar Iſlands; for, in the Rice Colonies the Negroes in general have rice, Indian-corn, potatoes, or black-eyed peaſe, ſufficient to ſubſiſt them, and land enough to plant for themſelves; they have alſo a certain limited taſk every day, be their work either that of planting, or ſawing lumber; and this taſk in general is not too hard. Their numbers alſo do not decreaſe on the Indigo Plantations and Lumber Eſtates; but then in the Rice Plantations they are frequently obliged to get up in the winter before day, and work in the barn; and when they are heated with labour in a cloſe building, warmed with a fire, they are then turned out to work in the Rice Swamps, half leg deep in water, which brings on pleuriſies and peripneumonies, and deſtroys numbers of them; and in the Summer,

mer, the quantity of water let into the Rice-fields makes it very ſickly.

The pretence that ſugar canes and rice could not be raiſed without the labour of Negroes, is erroneous. The White Creoles of Anguilla and Tortola, and the Ten Acre men in Barbadoes, who have been bred up in active life, and not debauched with eaſe and luxury, are a brave hardy people, and prove that White men can cultivate lands in a tropical climate; and many of the poor White people in Carolina and Georgia raiſe grain without the aſſiſtance of Negroes. A white man, with a light plough drawn by two horſes, will cultivate as much land as ſeven Negroes with hoes.

If the Reader ſhould aſk what ſhare I have had in the traffic of human fleſh, I ſmite my breaſt, and ſay, "God be merciful to me a ſinner!" When I went to the Weſt Indies, they told me I could not do without Negroes; and a gentleman bought one, ſent her home, and told me he had given a bond for me, which I muſt take up. For want of reflection, I bought others from time to time; and when I went to North America, I had nine. There I planted Indigo; and at one time I had thirty-four Negroes. In the different countries where I reſided, many ſaid that I ſpoiled my Negroes with indulgence. Eight were killed at the ſiege of Savannah, and ſeven others I manumitted; ſo that I have not benefited by my dealing in Negroes. For ſome time I have been very uneaſy at having ever purchaſed a Negro; and I heartily pray to be forgiven for the ſhare I have had in enſlaving my fellow-creatures.

The old ſettled Iſlands in the Weſt Indies become every day more weak and defenceleſs; for the great planters buy up all the ſmall tracts of land owned by the poorer white people, and

plant

plant them with ſugar canes; by which means the number of Negroes daily increaſes, and the number of Whites decreaſes. Many white families were formerly ſettled at the windward end of St. Kitt's, which is called the Salt Ponds; a country fit only for the raiſing of ſtock and proviſions, with which, as alſo with fiſh, they ſupplied the town of Baſſeterre. Theſe white people added greatly to the ſtrength of the Iſland, and, as they occupied a part of the country unfit for ſugar canes, it was adviſeable, both from humanity and policy, to ſuffer them to remain undiſturbed. But in a former reign, a gentleman obtained a grant of that part of the country, and he and another divided theſe lands between them. Part of theſe lands have ſince been converted into Sugar Plantations, and the white people turned off; but they produce little: and the ſalt pond has yielded little ſalt ſince the white people were moved away. Had Negroes never been introduced into the Weſt Indies, the Iſlands would have been divided amongſt a number of white people, who might have been able to defend themſelves againſt foreign invaſions; and as every one would have made ſome rum and ſugar, or elſe have planted cotton, cocoa, pimento, ginger, or aloes, they would have conſumed a much greater quantity of Britiſh manufactures than thoſe countries do in their preſent ſtate. At this time all the old ſettled Iſlands, except Jamaica, have fewer inhabitants than they had fifty years ago; and the number is daily decreaſing. In proceſs of time, moſt of the Sugar Iſlands will probably become the property of a few over-grown planters, who may perhaps carry matters with a high hand over their inferiors. In my time there were leading men on many of the Iſlands, who kept the inferior people in a ſtate of great dependency; and in one

of

of the Iſlands, I well remember an Ariſtocracy carried all before them.

In all the Colonies, Negroes, on their firſt importation from Guinea, are abſolutely perſonal eſtate; they are carried on ſhore from the ſhip to ſome yard, and ſold there like cattle in a fair. The wife is often ſeparated from the huſband, and the child from its parent. No deed or writing is neceſſary for the conveyance of them from the Guinea Factor to the purchaſer. When an agreement is made for the price, the purchaſer takes them away, and pays down the purchaſe money; or, which is more uſually the caſe, he gives a bond for payment at a future day; but if, after Negroes are ſold in the Guinea Yard, the purchaſer does not carry them out of the Iſland or Province forthwith, but works and employs them there; then they are either real or perſonal eſtate, according to the laws of that Colony in which they continue. In Antigua, Barbadoes, and Jamaica, ſeaſoned Negroes are real eſtate, ſubject nevertheleſs to be extended and ſold as perſonal eſtate for the ſatisfaction of debts, by the Stat. of the 5 Geo. II. c. 7. above mentioned, and alſo by the Provincial laws of moſt of the Colonies. They were alſo real eſtate in Virginia before the civil war. In ſome of the Plantations, Negroes are, in all reſpects, perſonal eſtate; in others they are of a mixed nature; for in the Iſland of Nevis in particular, Negroes are perſonal eſtate, until they have been once worked on lands there; and from that time they ever afterwards become real eſtate, and follow the ſame courſe of deſcent, unleſs they are extended and ſold for payment of debts. In all the Colonies where Negroes are real eſtate, they muſt be conveyed by deed; and that deed muſt be regiſtered in the Office. In ſome of the Colonies

Colonies where they are perfonal eftate (particularly in the Ifland of Montferrat), feafoned Negroes cannot be conveyed without a bill of fale regiftered in the Office.

A Feoffment *of a Negro Woman and her Daughter, a Mulatto, in the Ifland of Antigua, where Slaves are Real Eftate.*

Antigua.

THIS Indenture was made the day of June, in the year of our Lord 1763, between E. C. of the town of St. John in the Ifland of Antigua, fpinfter, of the one part, and D. H. of the parifh of St. John in the Ifland of Antigua aforefaid, of the other part, witneffeth, That for and in confideration of the fum of 65 l. of good current money of the faid Ifland of Antigua to the faid E. C. in hand, well and truly paid by the faid D. H. at or before the fealing and delivery of thefe prefents, the receipt whereof fhe the faid E. C. doth hereby acknowledge, and thereof and of every part thereof doth acquit, releafe, and difcharge the faid D. H. his executors, adminiftrators, and affigns, and every of them, for ever, by thefe prefents, fhe the faid E. C. hath granted, bargained, fold, aliened, enfeoffed, releafed, and confirmed; and by thefe prefents doth grant, bargain, and fell, alien, enfeoff, releafe, and confirm unto the faid D. H. his heirs and affigns for ever, one Negro woman flave, named Queen, with her child Margaret, a Mulatto girl, together with the iffue and increafe of the faid flaves hereafter to be born; and the reverfion and reverfions, remainder and remainders, of the faid flaves, and each of them, and all the eftate, right, title, intereft, truft, property, claim, and demand whatfoever, whatſoever, both at law and in equity of her the ſaid E. C. of, in, or to the ſaid ſlaves, and each of them, to have and to hold the ſaid ſlaves, and each of them, unto the ſaid D. H. his heirs and aſſigns for ever, to and for the only proper uſe and behoof of him the ſaid D. H. his heirs and aſſigns for ever: and the ſaid E. C. doth hereby for herſelf, her heirs, executors, and adminiſtrators, covenant, promiſe, grant, and agree to, and with the ſaid D. H. his heirs and aſſigns, that the ſaid D. H. his heirs and aſſigns, ſhall and may from time to time, and at all times hereafter peaceably and quietly have, hold, occupy, poſſeſs, and enjoy the ſaid ſlaves hereby or mentioned, or intended to be hereby granted and conveyed, and each of them, without the lawful let, ſuit, trouble, denial, eviction, or interruption of or by the ſaid E. C. her heirs, executors, adminiſtrators, or aſſigns, or of or by any other perſon or perſons whomſoever, and that free and clear, and freely and clearly acquitted, exonerated, and diſcharged, or otherwiſe, by the ſaid E. C. her heirs, executors, and adminiſtrators, well and ſufficiently ſaved, defended, kept harmleſs and indemnified of, from, and againſt all and all manner of former and other gifts, grants, bargains, ſales, leaſes, mortgages, jointures, dowers, titles of dower, uſes, truſts, wills, entails, ſtatutes, recognizances, judgments, extents, executions; and of, from, and againſt all and ſingular other eſtates, titles, troubles, charges, and incumbrances whatſoever, had, made, done, committed, occaſioned, or ſuffered, or to be had, made, done, committed, occaſioned or ſuffered by the ſaid E. C. her heirs, executors, adminiſtrators, or aſſigns, or any of them, or by any other perſon or perſons whomſoever; and alſo that ſhe the ſaid

ſaid E. C. is rightfully and abſolutely ſeized in her demeſne, as of fee, of and in the ſaid ſlaves, of a good, ſure, lawful, and indefeaſible eſtate of inheritance in fee ſimple to her and her heirs for ever, without any reverſion or remainder, truſt, limitation, power of revocation, uſe or uſes, or any other matter, reſtraint, or thing whatſoever, to alter, change, charge, revoke, make void, leſſen, incumber or determine the ſame; and that ſhe the ſaid E. C. at the time of the ſealing and delivery hereof, hath in herſelf good right, full power, and lawful and abſolute authority to grant, bargain, ſell, alien, enfeoff, releaſe, and confirm the ſaid ſlaves unto the ſaid D. H. his heirs and aſſigns for ever: And laſtly, that ſhe the ſaid E. C. and her heirs, and all and every other perſon and perſons having or lawfully claiming, or which ſhall or may have or lawfully claim any eſtate, right, title, truſt or intereſt at law or in equity, of, in, or to the ſaid ſlaves hereby or mentioned or intended to be hereby granted and conveyed, or either of them, ſhall and will from time to time, and at all times hereafter, upon every reaſonable requeſt, and at the proper coſts and charges in the law of the ſaid D. H. his heirs or aſſigns, make, do, acknowledge, and execute, or cauſe or procure to be made, done, acknowledged and executed all and every ſuch further and other lawful and reaſonable acts, deeds, and and things, devices, conveyances, and aſſurances in the law whatſoever, for the further, better, more perfect, and abſolute granting, conveying, and aſſuring of the ſaid ſlaves hereby or mentioned or intended to be hereby granted and conveyed, and each of them unto, and to the uſe of him the ſaid D. H. his heirs and aſſigns for ever, as by the ſaid D. H. his heirs or aſſigns, or his or their

Counſel

Counſel learned in the law, ſhall be reaſonably adviſed or deviſed and required, ſo as ſuch further aſſurances contain in them no further or other warranty or covenants than againſt the perſon or perſons, his or their heirs, who ſhall make or do the ſame; and ſo as the party or parties who ſhall be requeſted to make ſuch further aſſurances, be not compelled or compellable for making or doing thereof, to go or travel above ten miles from his or their then reſpective dwellings or places of abode. In witneſs whereof, the ſaid parties to theſe preſents have hereunto ſet their hands and ſeals the day and year firſt above-written.

E. C. (L. S.)

Sealed, delivered, and acknowledged this day of June 1763, in the preſence of
E. G. Reg.

Received on the day of the date of the above-written Indenture of the above-named D. H. the ſum of 65 l. of good, current, and lawful money of the ſaid Iſland of Antigua, being the full conſideration money above mentioned to be paid to me.

E. C.

Witneſs, E. G. Reg.

By an Act of Aſſembly of the Iſland of Antigua, the regiſtering a deed in the Regiſter's Office is equivalent to livery and ſeiſin. This law has occaſioned their frequently uſing the Deed of Feoffment in preference to any other mode of conveyance.

And by the laws of that Iſland, thoſe parties to a Deed, from whom the intereſt paſſes, muſt either acknow-

acknowledge ſuch Deed before the Regiſter in perſon; or elſe they muſt, by a Letter of Attorney, inſerted in the Deed, impower ſome perſon or perſons to acknowledge it for them before the Regiſter. The introduction of this ceremony has frequently occaſioned miſtakes in the conveyances ſent out from England: but in moſt of the other Iſlands, an Affidavit proving the execution of a conveyance is ſufficient for the purpoſe of having it regiſtered. I need ſay no more at preſent, becauſe moſt of the Forms of Deeds hereafter inſerted being authenticated according to the laws of thoſe Iſlands reſpectively, for which they are intended, will ſpeak for themſelves.

A FEOFFMENT *of a Slave in Antigua from a Man and his Wife, and the Truſtee of the Wife, in which caſe the Wife was privately examined before a Judge to bar her of Dower.*

ANTIGUA.

THIS Indenture Tripartite, made the day of in the year of our Lord 1765, between W. H. D. late of the Iſland of Antigua, Eſq; (by R. B. of the ſaid Iſland of Antigua, Eſq; his Attorney by Deed, poll bearing date the day of 17 duly conſtituted and appointed) of the firſt part, E. P. of the ſaid Iſland of Antigua, Gentleman; and Ann his wife, late Ann H. ſpinſter, of the ſecond part; and C. B. of the ſaid Iſland of Antigua, Eſq; of the third part: Whereas by Indenture Tripartite, made or mentioned to be made the 11th day of December, in the year of our Lord 1751, between Ann M. of the ſaid Iſland, widow and relict of C. M. of the ſaid Iſland, deceaſed, and reſiduary, deviſee,

visee, and legatee of his Last Will and Testament of the first part; J. D. of the same place, Esq; of the second part; and C. H. and A. H. nephew and niece of the said A. M. of the third part. It is witnessed, that for and in consideration of the natural love and affection which she the said A. M. had and bore to and for the said C. and A. H. her nephew and niece; and also for and in consideration of the sum of 5s. current money of the said Island, to her in hand paid by the said J. D. the receipt whereof is thereby acknowledged, she the said A. M. did give, grant, bargain, sell, alien, enfeoff, release, and confirm unto the said J. D. his heirs and assigns for ever, all those the following slaves; that is to say, a Negro woman named Dinah, and her daughter Mary, and a Negro woman named Letitia, and her two daughters named Rose and Phillis, with all the future issue and increase of the said female slaves; and also all the estate, right, title, interest, property, claim and demand whatsoever of her the said A. M. of, in, and to the said slaves, or any or either of them, and the reversion and reversions, remainder and remainders, rents, services, and profits, of all and every the said slaves, to hold the said Negro woman named Dinah, and her said daughter Mary, and the said Negro woman named Letitia, and her said two daughters named Rose and Phillis, together with all their future issue and increase, unto the said J. D. his heirs and assigns for ever, to the only proper use and behoof of the said J. D. his heirs and assigns for ever: In trust neverthelefs, and to and for such uses, intents, and purposes, only as are therein after expresfsly declared, *viz.* As for touching and concerning the said Negro woman named Dinah, and her said daughter Mary, with their

their future iſſue and increaſe, in truſt, and to and for the uſe and behoof of the ſaid C. H. his heirs and aſſigns for ever: but in caſe he the ſaid C. H. ſhould happen to die under the age of twenty-one years, and without iſſue lawfully begotten, then in truſt for and to the uſe and behoof of the ſaid A. H. her heirs and aſſigns for ever; and as for touching and concerning the ſaid Negro woman named Letitia, and her ſaid two daughters named Roſe and Phillis, with their future iſſue and increaſe, in truſt to and for the uſe and behoof of the ſaid A. H. her heirs and aſſigns for ever: but in caſe the ſaid A. H. ſhould happen to die under the age of twenty-one years, and without iſſue lawfully begotten, then in truſt for and to the uſe and behoof of the ſaid C. H. his heirs and aſſigns for ever, and to and for no other uſe, intent, or purpoſe whatſoever, as in and by the ſaid Indenture duly recorded in the Regiſter's Office of the ſaid Iſland of Antigua, relation being thereunto had, may more fully and at large appear: And whereas the ſaid J. D. hath ſince departed this life, leaving the ſaid W. H. D. his eldeſt ſon and heir at law; and the ſaid A. P. hath attained her age of twenty-one years, and hath intermarried with the ſaid E. P.: And whereas the ſaid C. B. hath agreed with the ſaid E. P. and A. his wife, for the purchaſing of the aforeſaid Negro girl ſlave named Phillis; NOW THEREFORE, to the intent and for making the ſale thereof accordingly, THIS INDENTURE WITNESSETH, That the ſaid E. P. and Ann his wife (by and with the conſent and approbation of the ſaid S. H. D. teſtified by his being a party to, and ſigning and ſealing theſe preſents) for and in conſideration of the ſum of   current money of the ſaid Iſland of Antigua to the ſaid E. P. in hand

hand well and truly paid by the ſaid C. B. at or before the ſealing and delivery of theſe preſents, (the receipt whereof the ſaid E. P. doth hereby acknowledge, and thereof and of every part thereof doth acquit, releaſe, and diſcharge the ſaid C. B. his executors, adminiſtrators, and aſſigns, and every of them, for ever, by theſe preſents) have, and each of them hath granted, bargained, ſold, aliened, enfeoffed, releaſed, and confirmed, and by theſe preſents, do, and each of them doth grant, bargain, and ſell, alien, enfeoff, releaſe, and confirm unto the ſaid C. B. his heirs and aſſigns for ever, the ſaid Negro girl ſlave named Phillis, together with the iſſue and increaſe of the ſaid ſlave hereafter to be born; and the reverſion and reverſions, remainder and remainders of the ſaid ſlave, and all the eſtate, right, title, intereſt, truſt, property, claim and demand whatſoever, both at law and in equity of them the ſaid E. P. and Ann his wife, of, in, or to the ſaid ſlave, TO HAVE AND TO HOLD the ſaid ſlave unto the ſaid C. B. his heirs and aſſigns for ever, to and for the only proper uſe and behoof of him the ſaid C. B. his heirs and aſſigns for ever; and the ſaid E. P. doth hereby for himſelf and for the ſaid Ann his wife, and for their reſpective heirs, executors, and adminiſtrators, covenant, promiſe, grant, and agree to and with the ſaid C. B. his heirs and aſſigns; that he the ſaid C. B. his heirs and aſſigns, ſhall and may from time to time, and at all times hereafter, peaceably and quietly have, hold, occupy, poſſeſs, and enjoy the ſaid ſlave hereby or mentioned or intended to be hereby granted and conveyed, without the lawful let, ſuit, trouble, denial, eviction, or interruption of or by the ſaid E. P. and Ann his wife, or either of them, their, or either of their heirs, executors, adminiſtrators

tors

tors or aſſigns, or of or by any other perſon or perſons whomſoever; and that free and clear, and freely and clearly acquitted, exonerated, and diſcharged, or otherwiſe, by the ſaid E. P. and Ann his wife, and each of them, their and every of their heirs, executors, and adminiſtrators, well and ſufficiently ſaved, defended, kept harmleſs, and indemnified of, from, and againſt all and all manner of former and other gifts, grants, bargains, ſales, leaſes, mortgages, jointures, dowers, titles of dower, uſes, truſts, wills, entails, ſtatutes, recognizances, judgments, extents, executions, and of, from, and againſt all and ſingular other eſtates, titles, troubles, charges, and incumbrances whatſoever, had, made, done, committed, occaſioned or ſuffered by the ſaid Ann while ſhe was ſole, or by the ſaid E. P. and Ann his wife ſince their intermarriage, or to be had, made, done, committed, occaſioned, or ſuffered by the ſaid E. P. and Ann his wife, their heirs, executors, adminiſtrators, or Aſſigns, or any or either of them, or by any other perſon or perſons whomſoever: And alſo that they the ſaid E. P. and Ann his wife are, or one of them is rightfully and abſolutely ſeized in his, her, or their demeſne as of fee, of and in the ſaid ſlave, of a good, ſure, lawful, and indefeaſible eſtate of inheritance, in fee ſimple to them and their heirs for ever, without any reverſion or remainder, truſt, limitation, power of revocation, uſe or uſes, or any other matter, reſtraint, or thing whatſoever, to alter, change, charge, revoke, make void, leſſen, incumber, or determine the ſame; and that they the ſaid E. P. and Ann his wife, at the time of the ſealing and delivery hereof, have in themſelves good right, full power, and lawful and abſolute authority, to grant, bargain, ſell, alien, enfeoff, releaſe, and confirm

confirm the ſaid ſlave unto the ſaid C. B. his heirs and aſſigns for ever: And laſtly, That they the ſaid E. P. and Ann his wife, and their heirs, and all and every other perſon and perſons having or lawfully claiming, or which ſhall or may have or lawfully claim any eſtate, right, title, truſt, or intereſt, at law or in equity, of, in, or to the ſaid ſlave hereby or mentioned or intended to be hereby granted and conveyed, ſhall and will from time to time, and at all times hereafter, upon every reaſonable requeſt, and at the proper coſts and charges in the law of the ſaid C. B. his heirs or aſſigns, make, do, acknowledge, and execute, or cauſe or procure to be made, done, acknowledged and executed all and every ſuch further and other lawful and reaſonable acts, deeds, and things, devices, conveyances, and aſſurances in the law whatſoever, for the further, better, more perfect and abſolute granting, conveying, and aſſuring of the ſaid ſlave hereby or mentioned or or intended to be hereby granted and conveyed, unto and to the uſe of him the ſaid C. B. his heirs and aſſigns for ever, as by the ſaid C. B. his heirs or aſſigns, or his or their Counſel learned in the law, ſhall be reaſonably adviſed, or deviſed and required; ſo as ſuch further aſſurances contain in them no further or other warranty or covenants than againſt the perſon or perſons, his or their heirs, who ſhall make or do the ſame, and ſo as the party or parties who ſhall be requeſted to make ſuch further aſſurances be not compelled or compellable for making or doing thereof, to go or travel above ten miles from his or their then reſpective dwellings or places of abode. In witneſs whereof, the ſaid parties to theſe preſents have

have hereunto set their hands and seals the day and year first above written.

Sealed, delivered, and acknowledged, this day of 1765, in the presence of	W. H. D. (L. S.) By his Attorney R. B.
	E. P. (L. S.)
	A. P. (L. S.)
L— M— Reg.	C. B. (C. B.)

Received on the day of the date of the within written Indenture of the within named C. B. the sum of of good current and lawful money of the said Island of Antigua, being the full consideration money to be paid to me

E. P.

Witness, L— M—, Reg.

Memorandum, that this day of 1765, before me S—— T——, one of the Justices of his Majesty's Court of Common Pleas, held for the said Island of Antigua, personally appeared A. P. party to the within Indenture, who being by me privately and apart examined, declared, that she voluntarily, and of her own free will and consent, executed the within indenture, without any threats, fear, dread, or compulsion, of the said E. P. her husband, certified in my capacity aforesaid, the day and year last above written.

S— T—, Judge.

A FEOFFMENT *by the Acting Provost Marshal of Antigua, of several Slaves that were sold by him under Execution, to the highest Bidder at Public Sale.*

ANTIGUA.

THIS Indenture, made the day of in the year of our Lord 1765, between Samuel Henry

Henry Warner, Esq; Deputy Provost Marshal of the Island of Antigua, of the one part, and R. F. of the said Island of Antigua, Esq; of the other part. Whereas at a Court of Common Pleas held for the said Island of Antigua, on the 5th day of June, in the year of our Lord 1764, judgment was obtained against J. G. and J. W. of the said Island, merchants, at the suit of J. D. and B. C. of the said Island, merchants, for the sum of 3560l. 12s. 8d. halfpenny, Sterling money of Great Britain, with costs; upon which said judgment execution issued on the 14th day of the said month of June, and was delivered into the hands of the Deputy Provost Marshal at twenty-four minutes after one o'clock of the same day: And whereas also, at a Court of Common Pleas held for the said Island of Antigua on the said 5th day of June, judgment was obtained against the said J. G. at the suit of S. B. and W. W. of the said Island, merchants, for the sum of 3400 l. Sterling, money of Great Britain, with costs, upon which said judgment execution issued on the 14th day of the same month of June, and was delivered into the hands of the Deputy Provost Marshal, at thirty-eight minutes past one o'clock of the same day: And whereas also at a Court of Common Pleas held for the said Island of Antigua on the said 5th day of June, judgment was obtained against the said J. G. at the suit of A. D. and K. M. of the said Island, merchants, for the sum of 637l. 13s. 7d. halfpenny current gold and silver money of Antigua, with costs, upon which said judgment execution issued on the said 14th day of June, and was delivered into the hands of the Deputy Provost Marshal, at thirty-five minutes after two o'clock of the same day: And whereas also a Court of Common Pleas held for

for the said Island of Antigua, on the said 5th day of June, judgment was obtained against the said J. G. at the suit of J. B. of the said Island, Esq; for the sum of 1136 l. 2 s. Sterling money of Great Britain, with costs; upon which said judgment execution issued on the said 14th day of June, and was delivered into the hands of the Deputy Provost Marshal at eleven minutes after three o'clock of the same day: And whereas also at a Court of Common Pleas held for the said Island of Antigua, on the 3d day of July, in the said year of our Lord 1764, judgment was obtained against the said J. G. at the suit of J. T. senior, B. T. J. T. junior, and J. A. all of the city of London, merchants, for the sum of 4227 l. 19 s. 8 d. Sterling money of Great Britain, with costs; upon which said judgment execution issued on the said 3d day of July, and was delivered into the hands of the Deputy Provost Marshal, at fifty-five minutes after six o'clock in the morning of the same day: And whereas also at a Court of Common Pleas held for the said Island of Antigua, on the 7th day of August, in the said year of our Lord 1764, judgment was obtained against the said J. G. at the suit of J. L. and B. L. for the sum of 178 l. 12 s. 10 d. current gold and silver money of the said Island, with Costs; upon which said judgment execution issued on the same day, and was delivered into the hands of the Deputy Provost Marshal, at thirty-five minutes past nine o'clock of the same day: And whereas also at a Court of Common Pleas held for the said Island of Antigua, on the second day of April, in the year of our Lord 1765, judgment was obtained against the said J. G. at the suit of R. S. the elder, T. S. and R. S. the younger, of the city of London, merchants, for the sum of

5988 l.

5988l. 1s. 4d. lawful money of Great Britain, with costs; upon which said judgment execution issued on the 5th day of the same month of April, and was delivered into the hands of the Deputy Provost Marshal, at twenty-three minutes past eight o'clock of the same day: And whereas also at a Court of Common Pleas held for the said Island of Antigua, on the said 2d day of April, judgment was obtained against the said J. G. at the suit of S. R. executor of the Last Will and Testament of J. H. deceased, for the sum of 199l. 14s. good and lawful money of Antigua, with costs; upon which said judgment execution issued on the 20th day of the same month of April, and was delivered into the hands of the Deputy Provost Marshal, at thirty minutes past eleven o'clock of the same day; all which said executions were duly levied upon the following Negro men slaves, *viz.* Low, Hum, Quaw, Tom, Punch, Alarm, Gift, and London; which said slaves were, after proper advertisements and publications for sale thereof, put up to be sold upon the 8th day of May last, upon the Public Parade, in the town of St. John; which said sale was continued to the setting of the sun on the same day, and at sunset thereof the same sale was finished; and the said R. F. was then and there declared to be the best bidder for the said slaves so levied on as aforesaid, he having bid for them as follows, *viz.* for the said Negro man slave named Low, 100l. gold and silver money of the said Island of Antigua; for the said Hum, 101l. like money; for the said Quaw, 62l. like money; for the said Tom, 84l. like money; for the said Punch, 90l. like money; for the said Alarm, 82l. like money; for the said Gift, 61l. like money; and for the said London, 91l. like money; amounting in the whole

whole to the sum of 671 l. gold and silver money of the said Island of Antigua, as by the said recited judgments remaining of record in the Secretary's Office; and the said recited writs of execution, levy, publication, and sale, all filed in the Marshal's Office of Antigua, or contained in his Office Book, relation being thereto had, may more fully and at large appear. NOW THEREFORE THIS INDENTURE WITNESSETH, That as far forth as the said Samuel Henry Warner, by his said Office of Deputy Provost Marshal, can or may do, by virtue of all or any Statutes of Great Britain, or any act or acts, law or laws of the said Island of Antigua, he the said Samuel Henry Warner, for and in consideration of the said sum of 671 l. to him in hand well and truly paid by the said R. F. at or before the sealing and delivery of these presents, the receipt whereof he the said Samuel Henry Warner doth hereby acknowledge, and thereof and of every part thereof, doth acquit and discharge the said R. F. his heirs and assigns for ever, by these presents, hath granted, bargained, sold, aliened, enfeoffed, released, and confirmed, and by these presents doth grant, bargain, and sell, alien, enfeoff, release, and confirm unto the said R. F. his heirs and assigns for ever, the said eight Negro men, slaves of him the said J. G. so levied on and sold as aforesaid, and all such estate, right, title, and interest, both in law and equity, as he the said J. G. hath in them, TO HAVE AND TO HOLD all and singular the said slaves so levied on and sold as aforesaid; and all such estate, right, and title and interest both at law and equity, as he the said J. G. hath in them unto the said R. F. his heirs and assigns for ever, to the only proper use and behoof of him the said R. F. his heirs and assigns for ever, and

and for no other uſe, intent, or purpoſe whatſoever, in the moſt full and ample manner, that he the ſaid Samuel Henry Warner can or may grant and convey the ſame ſlaves by virtue of his ſaid Office of Deputy Provoſt Marſhal as aforeſaid. In witneſs whereof, he the ſaid Samuel Henry Warner hath hereunto ſet his hand and ſeal the day and year firſt above written.

Sealed and delivered, &c.

A Mortgage *of Negroes for Five hundred Years, to ſecure the Repayment of* 256 l. *and Intereſt.*

Antigua.

THIS Indenture, made the third day of November, in the year of our Lord 1764, between J. L. of the ſaid Iſland of Antigua, Gent. of the one part; and R. B. of the ſaid Iſland of Antigua, Eſq; and J. H. of the ſaid Iſland, Gent. of the other part, witneſſeth, That the ſaid J. L. for and in conſideration of 256l. current money of the ſaid Iſland of Antigua, to him in hand paid by the ſaid R. B. and J. H. at or before the ſealing and delivery of theſe preſents, the receipt whereof the ſaid J. L. doth hereby acknowledge, and thereof and of every part and parcel thereof doth freely, clearly, and abſolutely acquit, exonerate, and diſcharge the ſaid R. B. and J. H. their executors, adminiſtrators, and aſſigns, by theſe preſents hath demiſed, granted, and to farm let, and by theſe preſents, doth demiſe, grant, and to farm let, unto the ſaid R. B. and J. H. their executors, adminiſtrators, and aſſigns, as tenants in common, and not as joint tenants, all thoſe ſeveral Negroes following: (that is to ſay) one Negro man ſlave, named James; one Negro woman ſlave, named Iſabella; and one other Negro

woman

woman slave, named Phillis; together with the future issue and increase of the females of the said slaves; and the reversion and reversions, remainder and remainders of the said slaves; and all the estate right, title, interest, property, claim, or demand whatsoever, of him the said J. L. of, in, and to the same slaves, and each and every of them, to have and to hold all and singular the said slaves herein before named, together with the future issue and increase of the females of the said slaves hereby demised, or meant, mentioned, or intended to be hereby demised unto the said R. B. and J. H. their executors, administrators, and assigns, from the date hereof, for and during, and unto the full end and term of five hundred years from hence next ensuing, and fully to be complete and ended, yielding and paying therefore yearly, and every year during the said term, unto the said J. L. his heirs or assigns, the yearly rent of one pepper corn, on the feast of St. Michael the Archangel, if the same shall be lawfully demanded; provided always, and these presents are upon this express condition, that if the said J. L. his heirs, executors, and administrators do and shall well and truly pay, or cause to be paid unto the said R. B. and J. H. their executors, administrators, and assigns, the sum of 256l. current money of the said Island, on or before the 3d day of November, which will be in the year of our Lord 1766, together with lawful interest for the same, at and after the rate of 6l. by the hundred by the year; that then this present Indenture, and every matter, clause, and thing herein contained, shall cease, determine, and be void, and of none effect, to all intents and purposes whatsoever; any thing herein contained to the contrary thereof notwithstanding: And the said J. L. for himself, his

his heirs, executors, and adminiſtrators, and for every of them, doth hereby covenant, promiſe, grant, and agree to and with the ſaid R. B. and J. H. their executors, adminiſtrators, and aſſigns, in manner and form following: that is to ſay, That he the ſaid J. L. now is true and lawful owner of the ſaid ſeveral Negroes hereby demiſed, or mentioned or intended to be hereby demiſed, and each and every of them, and is rightfully and abſolutely ſeized of the ſaid Negro ſlaves, and each and every of them, of a good, ſure, abſolute, and indefeaſible eſtate of inheritance in fee ſimple, without any manner of condition, truſt, covenant, proviſo, or limitation of uſe or uſes, or other reſtraint, matter, or thing whatſoever, to alter, change, charge, determine, incumber, defeat, or evict the ſame: And that the ſaid J. L. now hath in himſelf good right, full power, and lawful and abſolute authority to demiſe all and ſingular the ſaid ſeveral Negroes hereby demiſed, or mentioned or intended to be hereby demiſed, as aforeſaid, and each and every of them unto the ſaid R. B. and J. H. their executors, adminiſtrators, and aſſigns, in manner and form aforeſaid: And alſo that they the ſaid R. B. and J. H. their executors, adminiſtrators, and aſſigns, ſhall and may, from time to time, and at all times after default ſhall be made in payment of the ſaid principal ſum of 256 l. current money of the ſaid Iſland, together with lawful intereſt thereon, to grow due and payable, peaceably and quietly to take poſſeſſion of, and have, hold, occupy, and enjoy the ſaid ſeveral Negroes before named, together with the future iſſue and increaſe of the females of the ſaid Negroes, without the let, ſuit, trouble, hindrance, moleſtation, interruption, or denial of him the ſaid J. L. his heirs and aſſigns, or either

either of them, or of any other person or persons lawfully claiming or to claim, by, from, or under him, them, or any or either of them: And it is hereby declared and agreed by and between the said parties to these presents, That in the mean time, and until default shall happen to be made of, or in payment of the said principal sum, or of the interest that shall grow due thereon, it shall and may be lawful to and for the said J. L. his heirs and assigns, peaceably and quietly to have, hold, and enjoy all and singular the said slaves herein before named, and to receive and take the rents and profits of them and every of them, to and for his own use and benefit, without the lawful let, suit, trouble, or interruption of or by the said R. B. and J. H. their executors, administrators, and assigns, or of or by any other person or persons lawfully claiming, or to claim from, by, from or under him, them, or any or either of them. In witness whereof, the said parties to these presents have hereunto set their hands and seals the day and year first above written.

J— L— (L. S.)
L— B— (L. S.)
J— H— (L. S.)

Sealed, delivered, and acknowledged this 3d day of November, 1764, before the

L— M— Reg.

Received the day of the date of the above written Indenture from the above named R. B. and J. H. the sum of 256l. current money of the the said Island of Antigua, being the full consideration money mentioned to be paid to me

J— L—

Witness, L— M— Reg.

BILL *of* SALE *of two* NEGROES *in the Iſland of St. Chriſtopher, where Negroes are perſonal Eſtate, and the Inſtrument by which they are conveyed, need not be regiſtered.*

ST. CHRISTOPHER'S.

KNOW all men by theſe preſents, that I G— C——, of the Iſland of St. Chriſtopher, Widow and Executrix of the laſt Will and Teſtament of T—— C——, late of the ſaid Iſland, Eſq; deceaſed, for and in conſideration of the ſum of 120*l.* current money of the ſaid Iſland to me in hand, paid by W—— W—— of the ſaid Iſland of St. Chriſtopher, Merchant, at or before the ſealing and delivery of theſe preſents, the receipt whereof I do hereby acknowledge, have bargained, ſold, releaſed, granted, and confirmed, and by theſe preſents do bargain, ſell, releaſe, grant, and confirm unto the ſaid W—— W—— the two Negro Slaves following: That is to ſay, a Negro Woman Slave, named Suſannah, and a Negro Girl Slave, named P——, daughter of the ſaid S——, to have and to hold the ſaid Slaves, and each of them, by theſe preſents bargained, ſold, releaſed, granted, and confirmed, together with the iſſue and increaſe of the ſaid Slaves, and each of them hereafter to be born, unto and to the only proper uſe, benefit, and behoof of the ſaid W—— W——, his executors, adminiſtrators, and aſſigns for ever, freely, quietly, peaceably, and intirely, without any contradiction, claim, diſturbance, or hindrance of any perſon whatſoever, and without any account to me or to any other perſon whomſoever, to be made, anſwered, or hereafter to be rendered, ſo that neither I the ſaid G—— C——, nor any perſon for me or in my name, or as repreſenta-

tive

tive of the ſaid T—— C——, deceaſed, or otherwiſe, ſhall or will at any time or times hereafter exact, challenge, claim, or demand any right, title, or intereſt of, in, to, or out of the ſaid Slaves hereby bargained and ſold, or either of them; or of, in, to, or out of the future iſſue and increaſe of the ſaid ſlaves, or either of them; but that I the ſaid G—— C——, and all perſons claiming under me, or under the ſaid T—— C——, deceaſed, or otherwiſe howſoever, ſhall be wholly barred and excluded, by force and virtue of theſe preſents, from all action, right, eſtate, title, claim, demand poſſeſſion, and intereſt, of, in, to, and out of the ſaid ſlaves, and each of them, of, in, to, and out of the future iſſue and increaſe of the ſaid Slaves, and each of them. And I the ſaid G—— C—— for myſelf, my executors, and adminiſtrators, the ſaid Slaves, and each of them, together with their and each of their future iſſue and increaſe unto the ſaid W——— W———, his executors, adminiſtrators, and aſſigns, againſt me the ſaid G——— C——— my executors, adminiſtrators, and aſſigns, and againſt the repreſentatives of the ſaid T—— C——, deceaſed, and all and every other perſon and perſons whatſoever, ſhall and will warrant, and for ever defend by theſe preſents, of which Slaves I the ſaid G—— C—— have put the ſaid W—— W—— in full poſſeſſion, by delivering them unto him at the ſealing and delivery hereof. In witneſs whereof, I the ſaid G—— C—— have hereunto put my hand and ſeal this 25th day of September, in the year of our Lord 1766.

G—— C——. (L. S)

Sealed and delivered, and livery and ſeiſin of the ſaid Slaves, above bargained and ſold, deli-

vered

vered by the ſaid G——
C——, delivering the
ſaid Slaves unto the ſaid
W—— W——, in the
preſence of us, the day
and year above written.

R—— T——.
R—— S——.

ST. CHRISTOPHER'S.

Received on the day of the date of the above written Deed Poll, the ſum of 120*l.* being the full conſideration money within mentioned, to be paid to me.

G—— C——.

Witneſs,

R—— T——.
R—— S——.

MANUMISSION *of two* NEGROES, *with an* AFFIDAVIT *proving the Execution thereof.*

ST. CHRISTOPHER'S.

TO all people to whom theſe preſents ſhall come, I W—— W—— of the Iſland of Saint Chriſtopher, Merchant, do ſend greeting:— Whereas G—— C——, late of the ſaid Iſland of St. Chriſtopher, Widow and Executrix of the laſt Will and Teſtament of T—— C——, late of the ſaid Iſland, Eſq; deceaſed, by deed-poll, or bargain and ſale, bearing date the 25th day of September, which was in the year of our Lord 1766, in conſideration of 120*l.* current money of the ſaid Iſland, did bargain, ſell, releaſe, grant, and confirm unto me the ſaid W—— W——, the two Negro Slaves following; that

that is to ſay, a Negro Woman Slave, named Suſannah, and a Negro Girl Slave, named Penelope, daughter of the ſaid Suſannah; to hold the ſaid Slaves, and each of them, together with the iſſue and increaſe of the ſaid Slaves, and each of them thereafter to be born, to the only proper uſe, benefit, and behoof of me the ſaid W—— W——, my executors, adminiſtrators, and aſſigns for ever, as by the ſaid deed-poll, or bargain and ſale, relation being thereunto had, will appear. And whereas the ſaid 120*l.* the conſideration money in the ſaid deed-poll mentioned, were the proper monies of the ſaid Suſannah; and I the ſaid W—— W——, the bargainee named in the ſaid recited deed-poll, or bargain and ſale, acted merely as a truſtee for the ſaid Suſannah, in order that the ſaid Suſannah, and her ſaid daughter Penelope, might be duly manumitted and made free: NOW THEREFORE KNOW YE, That I the ſaid W—— W——, in purſuance of the ſaid truſt in me repoſed, and in diſcharge thereof, have manumitted, enfranchiſed, made free, and from every tie of ſervitude abſolved; and by theſe preſents do for myſelf, my heirs, executors, and adminiſtrators, and each and every of them, manumit, enfranchiſe, make free, and from every tie of ſervitude abſolve the ſaid Negro Woman Slave named Suſannah, and the ſaid Negro Girl Slave named Penelope, reſpectively; and alſo the iſſue and increaſe of the ſaid Suſannah, and of the ſaid Penelope, and of each of them now born or hereaſter to be born, ſo that neither I the ſaid W—— W——, nor my heirs, executors, or adminiſtrators, or any or either of them, ſhall from thenceforth have, claim, challenge, or demand any right or title, by reaſon of

any

any ſlavery or villenage in the ſaid Suſannah and the ſaid Penelope, or either of them, or in their or either of their iſſue, now born or hereafter to be born; but that the ſaid Suſannah and the ſaid Penelope, and each of them, their, and each of their iſſue, now born or hereafter to be born, ſhall from henceforth for ever hereafter be as free to all intents, conſtructions, and purpoſes whatſoever, as any other ſubject of his Majeſty King George the Third. In witneſs whereof, I the ſaid W—— W—— have hereunto ſet my hand and ſeal this 2d day of November, in the year of our Lord 1767.

W—— W——. (L. S.)

Sealed and delivered
in the preſence of

J—— M——.
B—— B——.

ST. CHRISTOPHER'S. Before the Honourable Craiſter Greatheed, Eſq; Chief Juſtice of his Majeſty's Court of King's Bench and Common Pleas held for the ſaid Iſland of Saint Chriſtopher.

PERSONALLY appeared J. M. of the pariſh of Saint George, Baſſeterre, in the ſaid Iſland of Saint Chriſtopher, Gentleman, who being duly ſworn on the Holy Evangeliſts of Almighty God, maketh oath and ſaith, That he this Deponent was preſent, and did ſee W. W. of the ſaid Iſland of Saint Chriſtopher, Merchant, the donor in the paper writing or deed-poll before-written (purporting to be a deed-poll executed by the ſaid W. W. for the purpoſe of manumitting a Negro Woman

Woman Slave, named Susannah, and a Negro Girl Slave, named Penelope) sign, seal, and as his act and deed deliver the said paper-writing or deed-poll: and this Deponent further saith, That the name W. W. appearing to be set or subscribed to the said paper-writing or deed-poll, is of the proper hand-writing of the said W. W. and this Deponent (together with B. B.) did subscribe his name as a witness to the due execution of the said paper-writing or deed-poll: and lastly, this Deponent saith, That the names J. M. and B. B. appearing to be subscribed as witnesses to the due execution of the said paper-writing or deed-poll, are of the respective proper hand-writing of the said B. B. and of him this Deponent.

J. M.

Sworn this day of November 1767, before me,

C. G.

In every Colony, the execution of a Manumission ought to be proved before one of the Judges, and then registered in the office. In some Colonies, the proper place for registering deeds is the Secretary's Office; in other Colonies, there is a Register's Office, established by Act of Assembly for that purpose. When the Manumission is registered, the officer will deliver it back, and the person manumitted ought to take great care of it, for in the Colonies every Negro *primâ facie*, is supposed to be a Slave, and the proof of freedom lies on the Negro. I am afraid there have been too many base white men, who, after destroying the Manumission, have endeavoured to enslave those unhappy people. If the Manumission is registered, they are not remediless. I mention these cautions, for the sake of those Negroes

groes who are happy enough to get their freedom.

CHAP. XVII.

Of the Manner of docking Estates Tail, Reversions, and Remainders; and of barring Dower in the Colonies; with Directions for authenticating and registering Deeds there, and Abstracts from several Acts of Assembly relating thereto.

THE mode of conveying real and personal property in the British West India Islands, is similar to that used in England, except that in the Colonies they do not use fines and recoveries; but instead thereof, an Estate Tail, Reversion, or Remainder, is docked, and destroyed by an acknowledgment made before a Judge; and Dower is barred by the private examination of a feme covert, by a Judge who certifies the same on the back of the conveyance. This cheap and concise method of effecting those purposes, is preferable to the tedious and expensive process of fines and recoveries in England. See the 2d Black. Com. 361.

By an Act of Assembly of the Island of Barbadoes, which was passed in the year 1649, and revived in 1661, soon after the Restoration of King Charles the Second, by a law, intitled, "An Act "concerning the conveyance of Estates;" which (after reciting that the King's writs did not run there, whereby fines and recoveries could not be there had and levied, as in England, &c.) enacts, "That a Deed made in due form of law, "and acknowledged within three months after "the date of it, before the resident Governor for "the

" the time being, or a chief Judge of one of the " Courts within the Island, by all the parties that " pass, or grant away, or lease (for above three " years) any freehold or inheritance by such " Deed; or by so many of the parties as shall be " then living; or by any person lawfully autho- " rised by them, under hand and seal to convey " or grant the same, shall be valid to pass the " same, without livery, attornment, or any other " act or ceremony whatsoever, provided such " deed be recorded at length in the Secretary's " Office of Barbadoes, within three months after " the date thereof; and no deed, without such " acknowledgment and enrollment, shall pass any " estate of freehold or inheritance, or any lease " for more than three years.

" And if any married woman be minded to " alien her jointure, dower, or other estate of " freehold or inheritance in Barbadoes, whether " it be joint or in severalty, she must convey the " same by writing, under her hand and seal, and " acknowledge it before the Governor, or the " chief Judge of some Court within the Island, " who is to acquaint her what she is to convey by " that writing, and for what estate; and he shall " demand of her, in private, whether she is will- " ing to do the same, and doth it freely and vo- " luntarily, and not for fear, or by reason of any " threats or menaces. And if she then confess, " that she doth it freely, and uncompelled by " fear or otherwise, then her acknowledgment of " the said writing shall be received, and the day " of such acknowledgment, with the Governor or " chief Judge's name, before whom such ac- " knowledgment was taken, shall be endorsed " and subscribed; and, from thenceforth, such " writing shall become valid and firm against her,

" and

" and all that ſhall claim the lands, tenements, " or hereditaments therein mentioned to be " granted for, or under her, or in right of her.

" And a fine levied in England by a married " woman of her jointure, or title of dower, or " other freehold or inheritance in Barbadoes, be- " ing carried over, and entered on record there, " ſhall be as valid as if the ſame were of lands in " England. Immediately after the death of the " huſband, the wife (that hath not a jointure " made before coverture in Barbadoes, or elſe- " where) ſhall be endowed of one third part of " all the lands, tenements, and hereditaments, " whereof the huſband died ſeiſed in Barbadoes, " according to the laws of England; and in like " manner as ſhe would have been, if her huſband " had died ſeiſed of any lands within the king- " dom of England. But ſhe ſhall be endowed " only of ſuch lands, tenements, or heredita- " ments in Barbadoes, whereof her huſband died " actually, and ſolely ſeiſed in fee ſimple, or fee- " tail general. And by another Act of Aſſembly " of Barbadoes, made in the year 1670, intitled, " An additional Act to the Act concerning the " Conveyance of Eſtates," a man and his wife " of full age, or woman ſole, if reſiding in Eng- " land, Scotland, or Ireland, or any other his " Majeſty's dominions, may, by deed of ſale or " other inſtrument, acknowledged before a Judge " of any Court of Law, Mayor of a City or Cor- " poration, or Chief Governor of an Iſland or " place where they inhabit, convey away their " land in Barbadoes; in which acknowledgment " the woman muſt declare her voluntary and free " conſent, without threats or force of her huſ- " band; but the deed muſt be ſent over to Bar- " badoes, truly certified under the ſeal of the

" Judge

" Judge, Mayor, Corporation, or Governor, and " recorded at length in the Secretary's Office, " within twelvemonths next after the acknow- " ledgment, and then shall be as effectual to con- " vey the land therein contained, as if executed " in Barbadoes."

The above recited Acts are inserted at length in the collection of the Acts of Assembly of Barbadoes, printed in the year 1721, and I apprehend are now in force.

By an Act of Assembly of Jamaica, made in the year 1681, intitled, " An Act for registering of Deeds and Patents," it is enacted, That a deed made in due form of law, and acknowledged within three months after the date, by the party or parties that grant the same, or proved by the oath of one sufficient witness, or more, before the Governor, or some one of the Judges of the Courts of Jamaica, and recorded at length in the Office of Enrollments at Saint Jago de la Vega, within three months after the date, shall be valid, without livery, seisin, attornment, or any other act or ceremony in the law whatsoever; and no deed, without such acknowledgment, or proof and enrollment, shall be sufficient to pass away any freehold or inheritance, or to grant any lease for more than three years. And a conveyance made out of Jamaica, if remitted thither, and proved before the Governor or any Judge of the Common Pleas there, as aforesaid; or if personally acknowledged by the grantor, before the Court of the Lord Mayor and Aldermen of the City of London, and attested under the City Seal, and recorded in the said office of Enrollments at St. Jago de la Vega, within six months after the arrival of the ship that brought the same, shall, to all intents and purposes whatsoever, be as valid, as if it had been made

made in the Iſland, and acknowledged, proved, and recorded, according to the form and time before appointed.

By another Act of Aſſembly of Jamaica, made in the year 1681, intitled, " An Act for prevention of law ſuits," it is enacted, " That all bills " of ſale and conveyances whatſoever, thereto- " fore made, or thereafter to be made by huſ- " band and wife, and acknowledged before the " Judge of any Court of Record within Jamaica, " and duly recorded, ſhall be good and valid in " law, againſt all perſons whatſoever, that can " or may pretend to claim any eſtate in the lands " or tenements ſo conveyed, to all intents and " purpoſes whatſoever, as if the ſame had paſſed " by fine and recovery in his Majeſty's Courts of " Weſtminſter."

By a third Act of Jamaica, made in the year " 1711, intitled, " An Act for the further quiet- " ing poſſeſſions, and preventing vexatious ſuits, " at law," it is enacted, " That all bills of ſale, " deeds, and other conveyances whatſoever, at " any time theretofore made, and duly executed, " acknowledged, proved, and recorded, purſuant " to the true intent and meaning of an Act of " Jamaica, intitled, " An Act for prevention of " law ſuits," although no valuable conſideration " be reſpectively inſerted; and all deeds and other " conveyances whatſoever, thereafter to be made " for valuable conſideration, of any lands, tene- " ments, negroes, and hereditaments within Ja- " maica (excepting ſuch as have been or ſhall " be made by infants during their infancy, and " perſons of nonſane memory, during the time " they continue ſo), ſuch lands, tenements, ne- " groes, and hereditaments, are thereby enacted " and declared, *to have paſſed, and to be conveyed* by " the

" the ſame as fully, to all intents and purpoſes, " of any real eſtate in the kingdom of Great Bri- " tain *might or could paſs*, by fine and recovery, in " his Majeſty's Court of Common Pleas in Weſt- " minſter Hall."

By a fourth Act of Aſſembly of the Iſland of Jamaica, paſſed in the year 1731, " The record " of any deeds duly executed (and proved or ac- " knowledged) and enrolled in the office of en- " rollments; and the record or enrollment of any " laſt wills and teſtaments duly executed accord- " ing to law, and proved before the Governor, " or Commander in Chief, by one or more of the " ſubſcribing witneſſes thereto, ſhall be ſufficient " evidence of the titles to any lands, tenements, " negroes, hereditaments, or eſtate whatſoever, " real or perſonal, claimed under ſuch deeds, " conveyances, or wills; and ſhall be read and " allowed in all courts of law and equity in Ja- " maica, as if the originals were produced, " proved, and read.

" And the exemplification of all wills made in " Great Britain or Ireland, or any other of his " Majeſty's Colonies or Dominions, and ſent to " Jamaica, atteſted as ſuch (after probate thereof " made according to law, in the ſaid ſeveral do- " minions and Colonies reſpectively) under the " ſeal of the Prerogative Court of Canterbury, or " under the ſeal of the Archbiſhop or Lord " Mayor of Dublin, or any other Archbiſhops in " their reſpective dioceſes in England or Ireland, " or the Mayor, Provoſts, or Bailiffs of any Cor- " poration, or Body Politic, or under the ſeal of " any of the ſaid Dominions or Colonies reſpec- " tively, and afterwards recorded or enrolled in " Jamaica, ſhall be good and ſufficient evidence " in all courts of law and equity there.

" But

" But all deeds executed in Jamaica, of any " lands, tenements, negroes, or hereditaments " whatſoever, muſt be duly proved or acknow- " ledged, and recorded within ninety days after " the date thereof, and if executed out of Ja- " maica, they muſt be duly proved or acknow- " ledged, and recorded or enrolled in the office " of enrollments in Jamaica, within ſix calendar " months after the date, and within ninety days " after the arrival of the ſhip that carries them " to Jamaica, otherwiſe they are void againſt " other purchaſers or mortgagees *bona fide*, for " valuable conſideration; but good againſt the " vendor or mortgagor, and his heirs, in caſe " they are proved and recorded, or enrolled be- " fore a ſecond conveyance."

The above in part recited Acts, are inſerted at full length in the collection of the Acts of Aſſembly of Jamaica, printed in the year 1738, and I apprehend are now in force. I ſpeak with diffidence of Jamaica and Barbadoes, as I have not the laſt editions of their laws, and I never was in either of thoſe Iſlands.

But when the Leeward Charibbee Iſlands (where I reſided ſeveral years) had but one Council and Aſſembly, an Act was paſſed at Nevis, in the year 1705 (which was the 4th of Queen Anne) by the Commander in Chief of the Leeward Charibbee Iſlands in America, and the General Council and General Aſſembly of thoſe Iſlands, which enacts, " That a deed or deeds, in " due form of law, made and executed by the " huſband and wife, of the plantations, lands, " and tenements, negroes, and other heredita- " ments of the wife, or of any plantations, lands, " and tenements, Negroes, and other heredita- " ments, whereof the huſband was ſolely and in " his own right ſeiſed, at any time during the

" coverture;

" coverture; or whereof the husband or husbands, " and wife were seised, in right of the wife, or " the husband jointly with the wife, or by tenant " in tail general or special, and by the party or " parties, and each of them, from whom the in- " terest passes, acknowledged before some of her " Majesty's Justices of the Court of Common " Pleas in the kingdom of England or Ireland, " or of any of her Majesty's Leeward Charibbee " Islands, wherein such plantation, lands, tene- " ments, negroes, and other hereditaments do " lie, shall to all intents and purposes be as ef- " fectual and valid in the law, to pass all the " estate, right, title, interest, and claim of the " party or parties, and of each of them, to such " deed or deeds, in or to all, or any the planta- " tion or plantations, lands, tenements, negroes, " or other hereditaments, by such deed or deeds " granted, conveyed, or made over, or thereby " intended to be granted, conveyed, or made " over, to the person or persons, bargainee " or bargainees, grantee or grantees, in the " said deed or deeds mentioned, their heirs " and assigns for ever; to whom, or to whose use, " any estate in such plantation or plantations, " lands, tenements, negroes, or other heredita- " ments, is by the said deed or deeds limited, " bargained, sold, granted, or conveyed, ac- " cording to the several limitations in the said " deed or deeds contained, as if the party or " parties to the said deed or deeds from whom " the interest moves, had levied a fine or fines " with proclamations, or suffered a common re- " covery or recoveries of such plantation or plant- " ations, lands, tenements, negroes, and other " hereditaments, in any of her Majesty's Courts " of Record at Westminster, and duly executed " deeds, leading the uses of such fine or fines, or

" declaring

" declaring the uſes of ſuch recovery or recove-
" ries, to be to ſuch bargainee or bargainees,
" grantee or grantees, their heirs and aſſigns for
" ever, to whom, or to whoſe uſe, ſuch planta-
" tion or plantations, lands, tenements, negroes,
" and other hereditaments, are by the deed or
" deeds ſo to be executed and acknowledged,
" as is abovementioned, limited, and conveyed;
" or that the ſame, and every part thereof, had
" been bargained, ſold, conveyed, or ſet over,
" by any the firmeſt deed or deeds, conveyance
" or conveyances, aſſurance or aſſurances in the
" law, that could be adviſed or deviſed by Coun-
" ſel learned in the law.

" Sect. 4. Provided that the wife, who is party
" to any ſuch deed or deeds, be of full age at the
" time of the execution thereof, and be privately
" and apart examined by the Judge before
" whom ſuch deed or deeds is acknowledged,
" whether ſhe do execute the ſame freely, vo-
" luntarily, and without fear, threats, or com-
" pulſion, of or by her huſband uſed; which exa-
" mination of the wife ſhall be indorſed, together
" with the acknowledgment of the party or par-
" ties, from whom the intereſt by the ſaid deed
" or deeds paſs; and ſuch acknowledgments ſhall
" be ſubſcribed by the Judge, before whom the
" acknowledgments of ſuch deed or deeds is
" taken, and by and before whom ſuch wife is
" privately examined.

" Sect. 5. And that all, and every deed or
" deeds ſo executed and acknowledged as afore-
" ſaid, ſhall be enrolled at length in the Secre-
" tary's or Regiſter's Office of that Iſland,
" wherein the eſtate ſo granted or conveyed lies
" (if the ſaid deed or deeds be executed and ac-
" knowledged

" knowledged in any of these her Majesty's Lee-
" ward Charibbee Islands), within six calendar
" months after the acknowledgment of such deed
" or deeds; and in case the said deed or deeds
" shall be executed and acknowledged within
" either of her Majesty's kingdoms of England or
" Ireland, that the same shall be enrolled at
" length in the High Court of Chancery of that
" kingdom, wherein the same was executed and
" acknowledged, within six calendar months after
" the acknowledgment thereof; and that the ac-
" knowledgment of such deed or deeds so sub-
" scribed by the Judge before whom the same
" was taken (as before is directed), shall be a suf-
" ficient proof of the due execution of the said
" deed or deeds; and the record, or an exempli-
" fication or attested copy of such deed or deeds,
" shall be admitted and allowed to be given in
" evidence, upon any trial at law, or hearing in
" equity, where the original deed or deeds is or
" are mislaid, and cannot be produced."

This Act of Assembly is now in force in Antigua, Montserrat, Nevis, and St. Christopher's, and is the law by which they regulate their proceedings in such cases.

By an Act of Assembly of Antigua, passed the 13th of April 1668, a Register's Office is established, and all patents, deeds of sale, leases of land, and mortgages, must be recorded therein at large. By another Act of Assembly of Antigua, passed the 9th of January 1676, "for confirming the inhabitants titles to their lands," all deeds and conveyances of and relating to lands in Antigua, if made by such as are resident in the Island, must be enrolled and recorded in the Register's Office, within twenty days after the execution

cution of them; and if made in Europe, muſt be inrolled, &c. within one year after execution, or elſe ſhall be utterly void.

By another Act of Aſſembly of Antigua, paſſed the 3d of November 1698, "For the better re-"gulation and ſettlement of the Regiſter's Of-"fice," no conveyance of lands is good, unleſs acknowledged by the vendor, donor, leſſor, or other perſon conveying or transferring the ſame (or by ſome perſon lawfully impowered to acknowledge the ſame before the Regiſter or his Deputy) which acknowledgment muſt be indorſed on the back of the conveyance, with the day of the month and year of our Lord, in words at large, and afterwards ſigned by the Regiſter or his Deputy, who is to enter the ſame at large in a book kept for that purpoſe, before he parts with it out of his office; and the time of the acknowledgment is deemed to be the time of the entry or regiſtry thereof.

No will, whereby any eſtate in lands is deviſed, ſhall be evidence in law or equity, unleſs proved before the Governor in Chief, Lieutenant, or Deputy Governor, Preſident of the Council, or other perſon, having the power to take probate of wills, and entered at large in the Regiſter's Office; and copies of all deeds, wills, &c. entered in the Regiſter's Office, and atteſted by him, are as good evidence in any Court, as if the originals were there exhibited; and the recording a deed in the Regiſter's Office, is equal to livery and ſeiſin. And by another Act of Aſſembly of Antigua, paſſed the 28th day of July 1764, intitled, "An Act for the ſupplying the ſeveral "defects in the laws of that Iſland, concerning "conveyances and aſſurances of lands, tene-"ments, ſlaves, and other freeholds and inherit-"ances

" ances, lying and being in Antigua, and the " Iſlands thereto adjacent and belonging; and " for making the probate of the execution of " deeds in parts beyond ſeas, relating to ſuch " lands, tenements, ſlaves, and other freeholds " and inheritances effectual, without an acknow- " ledgment thereof before the Regiſter of that " Iſland or his Deputy:" It is enacted, that all deeds, conveyances, and aſſurances, which ſhall be executed in any parts beyond the ſeas, of and concerning lands, tenements, ſlaves, rents, and other freeholds and inheritances, lying and being in Antigua, or the Iſlands adjacent and thereto belonging, ſhall be good and effectual to paſs eſtates and intereſts, rights and titles, of and in ſuch lands, tenements, ſlaves, rents, and other freeholds and inheritances in Antigua, or the Iſlands thereto adjacent and belonging, according to the purport, words, and lawful intention of the ſame deeds, without livery or ſeiſin, or attornment. It being thereby declared, that livery of ſeiſin or attornment, were never required in any ſuch deeds, by the conſtant uſage, laws, and practice of Antigua; and that all and every ſuch deeds, conveyances, and aſſurances, having ſufficient words to paſs the fee ſimple of ſuch lands, tenements, ſlaves, rents, and other freeholds and inheritances, and duly recorded as the laws of Antigua direct and require, ſhall be to all intents and purpoſes as effectual to bar, diſcontinue, dock, extinguiſh, cut off, and deſtroy all eſtates tail, rights to eſtates tail, remainders, veſted and contingent, and all reverſions, rights, charges, powers, and authorities, dowers and thirds eſtates, and rights of femes covert, of and in, touching and concerning all and every ſuch lands, tenements, ſlaves, rents, and other free-

holds

holds and inheritances as a fine with Proclamations, according to the laws of that part of Great Britain called England, duly levied in the Court of Common Pleas at Weſtminſter, or a common recovery ſuffered with due execution, returned and made in the ſame Court of Common Pleas at Weſtminſter, or both, ſuch fine and recovery, with deeds properly executed, to lead and declare the uſes of both, or either, ſuch fine and recovery are or is by law in that part of Great Britain called England, of, for, touching and concerning lands, tenements, rents, and other freeholds and inheritances lying and being in that part of Great Britain called England, and all rights, charges, powers, authorities, touching and concerning the ſame, ſo always that all parties ſo granting, conveying, or paſſing, ſhall be of full age of one and twenty years: PROVIDED ALWAYS, That all deeds, conveyances, and aſſurances, bargains and agreements, of and concerning lands, tenements, ſlaves, rents, and other freeholds and inheritances, lying and being in Antigua, or the Iſlands adjacent and thereto belonging, executed in any part of his Majeſty's dominions in Europe or elſewhere (except Antigua), or any other place of the world not belonging to or under the Crown of Great Britain, ſhall be inrolled, regiſtered, and recorded in the Regiſter's Office of Antigua, within two years after the execution thereof: and provided alſo, That wherever any eſtates tail, rights to eſtates tail, remainders veſted or contingent, reverſions, rights, charges, powers and authorities, dowers and thirds-eſtates, and rights of femes covert, are to be barred, diſcontinued, docked, extinguiſhed, cut off, or deſtroyed, that the deed or deeds ſo paſſing or conveying, if executed in that

part

part of Great Britain called England, or in Ireland, ſhall in all reſpects be executed and acknowledged by the party and parties granting and conveying, and married women be thereon privately examined, and be certified, inrolled, and regiſtered, as directed and required in and by a certain general Act of the Leeward Charibbee Iſlands in America, made at Nevis, intituled, An Act for the ſupplying the want of fines and recoveries in theſe Iſlands, and for making any deed or deeds duly executed and acknowledged before any of her Majeſty's Juſtices of the Court of Common Pleas in the kingdom of England or Ireland, or of any of theſe Iſlands, equivalent to a fine and recovery, or fines and recoveries, duly and regularly levied and ſuffered in any of her Majeſty's Courts of Record at Weſtminſter, dated in Nevis the 21ſt day of June, Anno Domini 1705, and in the fourth year of her late Majeſty's reign: and if executed in Antigua, to be alſo acknowledged by the party and parties granting and conveying, and married women thereon privately examined, and be certified and regiſtered as the particular laws and acts of Antigua do require; and if executed in that part of Great Britain called Scotland, then to be acknowledged by ſuch parties granting and conveying, and married women to be privately examined before one of the Lords of Seſſion, or any Sheriffs of any County or Stewarty, and ſuch acknowledgment and examination, with the name of the place, and day and year of our Lord, or the King's reign, ſhall be certified upon the ſame deed and deeds, under the hand and ſeal of ſuch Lord of Seſſion, or ſuch Sheriff, and if executed in Barbadoes, or in any of the Leeward Charibbee Iſlands in America, or in any other Colony, territory, or dominion, in Europe, Aſia, Africa, or or America, belonging or to belong to the Crown of Great Britain, then to be acknowledged by ſuch parties, and married women to be privately thereon examined, before ſome Judge of his Majeſty's Court of Common Pleas, or of ſome other Court of Record, or where no ſuch Court of Common Pleas, or other ſuch Court of Record is eſtabliſhed, then before the perſon who ſhall exerciſe and execute the chief Command there, and ſuch acknowledgment and examination, with the name of the place, and day and year of our Lord, or the King's reign, ſhall be certified upon the ſame deed and deeds, under the hand and ſeal of ſuch Judge or Commanding Officer, and if the ſame ſhall be executed in any foreign kingdom, territory, Colony, or place in the world, not belonging to, or under the dominion of the Crown of Great Britain, then ſuch acknowledgment and examination, if taken in Europe, ſhall be taken before the Chief Officer of, and ſhall be certified under the public Seal of ſome City or Town corporate, or City or Town being in nature of a Corporation, having a public Chief Officer, and uſing a public Seal, in any part of Europe; and if ſuch acknowledgment and examination ſhall be taken in any foreign Colony in Aſia, Africa, or America, the ſame ſhall be taken before the perſon there in chief command, and be certified under his hand, and ſuch Seal as ſuch perſon there in chief command ſhall uſe as his public Seal; and touching and concerning the proof, and further authenticating ſuch deeds and conveyances, it is enacted, That no ſuch deeds, conveyances, or aſſurances, executed any where beyond ſea, out of Antigua, ſhall be pleadable in law or equity, or given or admitted to be proved or read in evidence in law or equity, until the ſame, with the

the acknowledgment, examination, and certificate thereon, ſhall be all recorded at length in the Regiſter's Office by law appointed, or to be appointed, in Antigua, for regiſtering deeds relating to lands in Antigua, and that where any ſuch deed ſhall be produced, in any ſuch manner as aforeſaid acknowledged and certified, the ſame, without any further acknowledgment or proof, ſhall be received and recorded in the ſaid Regiſter's Office of Antigua; and after being ſo recorded, ſhall need no further proof, but be admitted as evidence in law and equity, and copies atteſted from the ſaid Office of all ſuch deeds, ſhall be as good evidence as allowed and practiſed with relation to copies of deeds there regiſtered in other caſes in law and equity in Antigua, and ſhall have priority as in other caſes directed; and the very day and year of our Lord, in words at length, when ſuch deeds reſpectively firſt ſhall be brought to the ſaid Regiſter's Office to be recorded, ſhall be truly and immediately indorſed on ſuch deeds, and atteſted under the hand of the Regiſter, or his Deputy executing the ſaid Office, and ſhall be duly regiſtered and entered in the ſaid Office, with the reſpective deed, and ſuch time when ſuch deeds ſhall be firſt brought to the Regiſter's Office to be recorded, ſhall be deemed, eſteemed, and taken to be the time of the entry or regiſtery thereof.

By an Act of Aſſembly of the Iſland of Saint Chriſtopher, made in the year 1727 (with a clauſe ſuſpending the execution thereof until his then Majeſty declared his Royal aſſent thereto, and which Act was confirmed by the King in 1728), intituled, "An Act againſt covinous and fraudulent conveyances, and for a public Regiſtry in the Iſland

Iſland of St. Chriſtopher," an Office is eſtabliſhed to be kept in the Town of Baſſeterre in the ſaid Iſland of St. Chriſtopher, for entering and regiſtering all deeds and conveyances, gifts, grants, and aſſurances, wills, and deviſes in writing, whereby any meſſuages, lands, tenements, hereditaments, negroes, or other ſlaves whatſoever in St. Chriſtopher's may be any way affected in law or in equity; by that Act, all ſuch conveyances, if executed in St. Chriſtopher's, are to be entered and regiſtered in the Regiſter's Office, within three calendar months after the execution thereof, and if executed beyond the ſeas, then within two years after the execution thereof, otherwiſe they are to be adjudged fraudulent and void againſt ſubſequent purchaſers, for a valuable conſideration, who regiſtered their conveyances before them.

And all wills are to be regiſtered within three calendar months after the death of the deviſor or teſtator, if he died in St. Chriſtopher's, and within two years if he died beyond the ſeas. And every deviſe of lands, negroes, &c. regiſtered after thoſe times reſpectively, are to be fraudulent and void againſt ſubſequent purchaſers, for valuable conſideration.

A ſecond mortgage or ſale, if executed in St. Chriſtopher's, is to be regiſtered in one calendar month after execution, and if executed beyond the ſeas, within one year after execution.

All gifts and grants of Negroes, and other ſlaves, in conſideration of blood or natural affection, are declared void, unleſs put into writing, and regiſtered within ſuch times as other conveyances are directed to be regiſtered.

The Regiſter is to indorſe a certificate on every conveyance and will, mentioning the day, hour, and

and time when entered and regiſtered, and the ſame is to be allowed as evidence of ſuch regiſtries in all Courts of Record in St. Chriſtopher's. This Act was explained and amended in ſome particulars by another made the 21ſt of June 1758, which recites it, and then enacts, That all Letters Patent, bargains, ſales, feoffments, grants, mortgages, and other conveyances whatſoever, of lands, tenements, hereditaments, Negroes, and other ſlaves in St. Chriſtopher's, ſhall be adjudged fraudulent againſt any ſubſequent purchaſer or mortgagee, for valuable conſideration, unleſs ſuch conveyances are regiſtered in the Office before the regiſtering the deed or conveyance under which ſuch ſubſequent purchaſer or mortgagee claims; but all ſuch conveyances, whether abſolute or conditional, which are entered and regiſtered in the Regiſter's Office, after the expiration of the time limited in the Act for regiſtering them, are as valid and effectual againſt the grantors, mortgagors, and other perſons therein named, only from whom the intereſt paſſes, as if entered and regiſtered within the times limited by the recited Act; however, ſuch conveyances ſhall not deſtroy or weaken any right, title, or intereſt to any lands, Negroes, &c. therein mentioned, which any perſons claim under any ſubſequent conveyance, which was duly entered and regiſtered within the time limited by the recited Act; and where any original will or conveyance, duly entered and regiſtered, purſuant to the Act, and atteſted by the Regiſter or his Deputy, is proved on oath to be loſt or miſlaid, a copy thereof, under the hand of the Regiſter or his Deputy, is as good evidence in all the Courts of St. Chriſtopher's, as if the original was exhibited.

I have

I have not the laws of Nevis by me, but if I am not miſtaken, their Regiſter's Act is ſimilar to thoſe of St. Chriſtopher's.

The edition of the laws of Montſerrat, which I have, comes no lower than the year 1740. I find no Regiſters Act in it but in the year 1669. There was an Act of Aſſembly paſſed with a very extraordinary clauſe, which enacted, That all writings made upon the Iſland by the inhabitants, except only bills, obligations, or acquittances, that were not made in the Secretary's Office of that Iſland, by him or his Subſtitute, or by his allowance, ſhould be of no effect, and the parties who preſumed to draw them were liable to be fined, as the Governor ſhould ſee convenient. I make no doubt but that this law has been long obſolete. I was at Montſerrat two ſeveral times for weeks together on viſits, and I well remember they had a law which required, that all ſales of Negroes (except thoſe ſold in a Guinea-yard), ſhould be in writing, and regiſtered in the Secretary's Office. I alſo know, that all conveyances of land there muſt be regiſtered, but whether that is done in conſequence of an Act of Aſſembly of Montſerrat, made for that purpoſe, or of the above mentioned Act of the Leeward Charibbee Iſlands, made in the year 1705, for the ſupplying the want of fines and recoveries, &c. I cannot take upon me to ſay.

Soon after Legiſlatures were eſtabliſhed in the ceded Iſlands, they paſſed Acts of Aſſembly there, for ſupplying the want of fines and recoveries, and for regiſtering conveyances. I have not thoſe Acts by me, but I apprehend their Acts for ſupplying the want of fines and recoveries, were chiefly copied from that of the Leeward Charibbee Iſlands, and thoſe for regiſtering conveyances from

from the laws of Antigua, the legal Conſtitution of which Iſland they affected to adopt in moſt inſtances, as there were many adventurers from Antigua who ſettled in the ceded Iſlands, and amongſt them ſome Gentlemen of the profeſſion of the law.

Plantations in the Sugar Iſlands being of great value, the deeds conveying them are generally ſettled with good advice; and many of them are drawn by able conveyancers in England. But the lands in the Colonies on the Continent, being of much leſs value, the deeds (before the Civil War) were generally drawn in a ſlovenly manner; and in the Southern Provinces on the Continent they were ſo inaccurate, that they did not even annex their deeds properly; for in common ſenſe, where a deed conſiſts of ſeveral ſkins of parchment, or ſheets of paper, which are annexed at the bottom, the firſt ſkin or ſheet, which begins with "This Indenture, &c." ſhould be on the outſide, and the laſt ſheet, which concludes with "In witneſs, &c." ſhould be next to the ſeals: but in Carolina and Georgia, they frequently reverſed the natural order of the ſkins or ſheets; and on opening a deed, the firſt ſheet, which began with "This Indenture, &c." was in front, and came next to the ſeals.

Fines are frequently levied in the Court of Common Pleas in Weſtminſter Hall, of lands lying in the Weſt Indies, by ſuppoſing the Iſland in which the lands lie to be in ſome Pariſh and County in England; ſee 1. Barnes's Notes, 146. Wilſon on Fines, 57. When I was in the Weſt Indies, a Gentleman at Nevis had a mortgage on an eſtate there, for a conſiderable ſum of money, which eſtate was claimed by a man as tenant in tail: on looking over the mortgagee's papers, the

Chirograph

Chirograph or Indenture of a Fine of the lands, in Latin, was discovered, by which means he saved his principal and interest.

In South Carolina they have an Act of Assembly, which enumerates what English statutes shall be in force there, the statute of Westminster 2. the 13 Ed. I. c. I. (commonly called the statute *de Donis*), not being enumerated in that Act of Assembly, is not in force in that Province; and therefore, all estates there are fee-simple, conditional at Common Law; but their conveyances frequently have such terms in them, as are applicable only to estates tail, which is absurd.

The Constitution of the State of Georgia now directs, that an estate shall not be entailed.

But (before the Civil War), the private examination of a feme covert, in order to bar dower, was entered on a sheet of paper separate from the deed, and then signed by the Chief Justice of the Province, or the Assistant Judge who took it. It was then carried to the Office of the Prothonotary of the General (or Superior Common Law Court), who put the Seal of the Court to it. The private examination was then entered on Record in the Prothonotary's Office, and afterwards returned to the purchaser or mortgagee. If the feme covert lived at a distance from the seat of government, a *Dedimus Potestatem* issued to Commissioners, to take her private examination, and they returned the *Dedimus*, with the private examination annexed, which were both registered in the Prothonotary's Office. The *Dedimus Potestatem* was issued from the Prothonotary's Office, and tested by the Chief Justice.—I apprehend the practice in such cases was exactly the same in South Carolina, and all the other Southern Provinces.

CHAP. XVIII.

CONVEYANCES *of* LANDS *and* NEGROES *in Barbadoes, Antigua, St. Christopher's, and Jamaica.*—

A CONVEYANCE *by Lease and Release of Lands in Barbadoes, with the* POWER *of* ATTORNEY, *&c. this being the Release.*

THIS Indenture, made the 20th day of July, *anno Domini* 1728, and in the second year of the reign of our Sovereign Lord King George the Second, *&c.* between Sir Abel Ash of Bardon, in the county of Cornwall, Bart. eldest surviving son and heir of Sir David Ash late of the same place, Bart. and of Dame Eliza Ash, his late wife, both deceased, and also brother and heir of Sir David Ash, late of the same place, Bart. also deceased, who, whilst living, was eldest son and heir of the said Sir David Ash the father, and of the said Dame Eliza, of the one part; and Francis Ash of Bardon aforesaid, Esquire, younger brother of the said Sir Abel Ash, and Gilbert Gill and Henry Hart, both of the Island of Barbadoes in America, Esquires, of the other part. Whereas the said Sir David Ash the father, in and by his Last Will and Testament in writing, by him duly published, bearing date on or before the 10th day of April 1716, did (among other things) give to his then wife, the said Dame Eliza Ash, her heirs, executors, and assigns, all his Plantations, houses, buildings, mills, Negroes, and all other his real and personal estate whatsoever in the said Island of Barbadoes upon trust, to sell and dispose of the same, and every

every of them, as ſoon as conveniently might be after his deceaſe; and, with the money ariſing by ſale or ſales thereof, in the firſt place to pay all his juſt debts, and afterwards the legacies and ſums of money in his ſaid Will mentioned and expreſſed; and if his ſaid then wife ſhould die before the ſeveral eſtates were ſold that were deviſed to her for that purpoſe, then the ſaid teſtator gave ſuch of thoſe eſtates as remained unſold at her death, to the ſaid Sir David Aſh his eldeſt ſon, then David Aſh, Eſq; his heirs, executors, and aſſigns, to be by him or them ſold for the performance of his ſaid Will; and the ſaid Sir David Aſh the teſtator, did thereby conſtitute the ſaid Dame Eliza, his then wife, ſole executrix of his ſaid Will: And whereas the ſaid Dame Eliza Aſh died inteſtate ſoon after the death of the ſaid Sir David Aſh her late huſband, and before ſhe had proved his ſaid Will, or ſold or diſpoſed of the ſaid truſt-eſtate and premiſes, or any part thereof, and ſoon after her deceaſe Letters of Adminiſtration of her goods and chattels, and alſo Letters of Adminiſtration of the goods and chattels of the ſaid Sir David Aſh the father, with his ſaid Will annexed, were granted by the Prerogative Court of Canterbury unto the ſaid David Aſh the ſon, who ſome years ſince alſo departed this life without iſſue, and without having ſold or diſpoſed of the ſaid truſt-eſtate and premiſes, or any part thereof, upon whoſe deceaſe the ſaid truſt-eſtate and premiſes deſcended, or otherwiſe legally came to and veſted in the ſaid Sir Abel Aſh, upon the truſt, and for the purpoſes aforeſaid, and the ſaid Sir Abel Aſh, ſoon after the deceaſe of the ſaid Sir David Aſh, obtained Letters of Adminiſtration out of the ſaid Prerogative Court of Canterbury of the goods and chattels, with

with the Will annexed of the ſaid Sir David Aſh, the father, unadminiſtered by the ſaid Sir David Aſh the ſon; and alſo Letters of Adminiſtration of the goods and chattels of the ſaid Dame Eliza Aſh, unadminiſtered as aforeſaid: And whereas the ſaid Francis Aſh hath contracted and agreed with the ſaid Sir Abel Aſh for the abſolute purchaſe of the meſſuages, buildings, Plantations, lands, Negroes, and other hereditaments herein after mentioned, to be hereby granted and releaſed, being part and parcel of the ſaid truſt-eſtate, and premiſes ſo given to the ſaid Dame Eliza Aſh in truſt, to be ſold as aforeſaid; and alſo of all the crop of ſugars and other the produce of or upon the ſame Plantation, lands, and premiſes, or which hath ariſen from, or been produced upon the ſame premiſes, or any part thereof, from and after the Feaſt of St. Michael the Archangel laſt paſt, before the date hereof, for the ſum or price of 10,000 l. of lawful money of Great Britain. NOW THIS INDENTURE WITNESSETH, That in purſuance and performance of the ſaid recited agreement, and for and in conſideration of the ſum of 10,000 l. of lawful money of Great Britain to the ſaid Sir Abel Aſh, in hand, well and truly paid by the ſaid Francis Aſh, at or before the enſealing and delivery of theſe preſents, to be by him the ſaid Sir Abel Aſh applied and diſpoſed of for the purpoſes in the ſaid recited Will in that behalf mentioned and directed, the receipt and payment of which ſaid ſum of 10,000 l. he the ſaid Sir Abel Aſh doth hereby acknowledge, and thereof, and of every part thereof, doth acquit, releaſe, and diſcharge the ſaid Francis Aſh, his heirs, executors, adminiſtrators, and aſſigns, and every of them, for ever, by theſe preſents; and in conſideration of the ſum of 5 s.

of

of like money to the ſaid Sir Abel Aſh, in hand paid by the ſaid Gilbert Gill and Henry Hart, at or before the enſealing and delivery of theſe preſents, the receipt whereof is hereby acknowledged: he the ſaid Sir Abel Aſh hath granted, bargained, ſold, aliened, releaſed, and confirmed, and by theſe preſents doth grant, bargain, ſell, alien, releaſe, and confirm unto the ſaid Francis Aſh, Gilbert Gill, and Henry Hart, and the heirs and aſſigns of the ſaid Francis Aſh, all that the Upper Plantation land or ground of him the ſaid Sir Abel Aſh, commonly called or known by the name of Jag Hall, ſituate, lying, and being in the pariſh of Knowt, in the ſaid Iſland of Barbadoes, and containing by eſtimation three hundred and ninety-ſix acres, or thereabouts, be the ſame more or leſs; and alſo all meſſuages, tenements, edifices, erections, buildings, houſes, ſtore-houſes, ſugar-houſes, boiling-houſes, curing-houſes, ſtill-houſes, mills and kilns, erected, built, ſtanding, or being; or to be erected, built, ſtanding, or being in or upon the ſaid Plantation, land, ground, hereditaments, and premiſes, every or any part thereof, with their and every of their rights, privileges, members, and appurtenances; and alſo all Negroes and ſlaves, men and women, and children, and the increaſe and progeny of the ſame Negroes and ſlaves; and alſo all horſes, cows, oxen, ſheep, and other cattle whatſoever; and all coppers, ſtews, ladles, ſkimmers, potting-baſons, ſugar-pots, ſtills, ſtill-heads, worms, worm-tubs, coolers, ciſterns, Plantation tools, and all other implements, goods and chattels whatſoever, to the ſaid meſſuages, buildings, Plantation, land, ground, hereditaments, and premiſes hereby or mentioned and intended to be hereby granted and releaſed, every or any of them, or any part thereof, belonging

longing or in any wise appertaining, or with them or any of them used, occupied, possessed, or enjoyed; and also other the messuages, buildings, lands, ground, and hereditaments whatsoever, of him the said Sir Abel Ash, situate, lying, or being in the said parish of Knowt, in the said Island of Barbadoes, with their and every of their appurtenances (except and always reserved out of these presents, and the grant or conveyance hereby made or intended to be made, all that small slip or parcel of ground of him the said Sir Abel Ash, lying and being in the said parish of Knowt, but being part of and used and enjoyed with the lower Plantation, lying in the parish of Loke, in the said Island of Barbadoes, and all erections, buildings, hereditaments, Plantations, tools, implements and appurtenances whatsoever, upon the said excepted small slip or parcel of ground, or any part thereof, now being thereunto belonging or appertaining, or therewith used or enjoyed), all which said messuages, buildings, Plantation, lands, grounds, Negroes, slaves, cattle, utensils, hereditaments, and other the premises hereby or mentioned or intended to be hereby granted and released (except before excepted), are now in the actual possession of the said Francis Ash, Gilbert Gill, and Henry Hart, by virtue of a bargain and sale to them thereof, made by the said Sir Abel Ash for the term of one whole year, in consideration of 5 s. to him paid by the said Francis Ash, Gilbert Gill, and Henry Hart, in and by one Indenture, bearing date the day next before the day of the date hereof, and by force of the Statute for transferring uses into possession, made and provided; and the reversion and reversions, remainder and remainders, rents, issues, and profits, and produce thereof, and of every part and parcel thereof; and alſo all the eſtate, right, title, intereſt, truſt, property, claim, and demand whatſoever, both at law and in equity of him the ſaid Abel Aſh, of, into, or out of the ſaid meſſuages, buildings, Plantation lands, grounds, Negroes, ſlaves, cattle, utenſils, hereditaments, and other the premiſes hereby or mentioned or intended to be hereby granted and releaſed, or any of them, or any part or parcel thereof (except before excepted); and alſo all deeds, evidences, writings, and records whatſoever, touching, or in any wiſe concerning the ſame premiſes, or any part thereof, which he the ſaid Sir Abel Aſh now hath in his cuſtody, or can come by without ſuit in law, TO HAVE AND TO HOLD the ſaid meſſuages, buildings, Plantations, lands, grounds, Negroes, ſlaves, cattle, utenſils, hereditaments, and all and ſingular other the premiſes hereby or mentioned or intended to be hereby granted and releaſed, with their and every of their appurtenances (except before excepted) unto the ſaid Francis Aſh, Gilbert Gill, and Henry Hart, and the heirs and aſſigns of the ſaid Francis Aſh, to the uſe and behoof of them the ſaid Francis Aſh, Gilbert Gill, and Henry Hart, and of the heirs and aſſigns of the ſaid Francis Aſh for ever; in truſt as to the eſtate of the ſaid Gilbert Gill and Henry Hart, for and for the only benefit of the ſaid Francis Aſh, and of his heirs and aſſigns for ever, and to, for, or upon no other uſe, truſt, intent, or purpoſe whatſoever; and the ſaid Sir Abel Aſh doth hereby, for himſelf, his heirs, executors, and adminiſtrators, covenant, promiſe, grant, and agree to and with the ſaid Francis Aſh, his heirs and aſſigns, in manner following; that is to ſay, That (for and notwithſtanding any Act, matter, or

thing

thing whatsoever by him the said Sir Abel Ash, or by the said Sir David Ash his late brother, or by the said Sir David Ash his late father, and Dame Eliza his late wife, mother of him the said Sir Abel Ash, or by Sir David Ash, Bart. his late grandfather deceased, or any of them, done, committed, or wittingly or willingly suffered to the contrary) he the said Sir Abel Ash now is and standeth lawfully, rightfully, and absolutely seized of and in the said messuages, buildings, Plantation, lands, grounds, Negroes, slaves, utensils, hereditaments, and premises hereby or mentioned or intended to be hereby granted and released of a good, sure, lawful, absolute, and indefeasible estate of inheritance in fee simple, to him and his heirs, without any reversion, remainder, trust, limitation, power of revocation, use or uses, or other matter, restraint, or thing whatsoever, to alter, change, charge revoke, make void, lessen, incumber, or determine the same: And also that he the said Sir Abel Ash, for and notwithstanding any such Act, matter, or thing as aforesaid, hath, at the time of the sealing and delivery of these presents, in himself good right, full power, and lawful and absolute authority to grant and convey the said messuages, buildings, Plantation, lands, ground, and Negroes, slaves, utensils, hereditaments, and premises hereby mentioned or intended to be hereby granted and released, with their appurtenances, unto and to the use of the said Francis Ash, Gilbert Gill, and Henry Hart, and the heirs and assigns of the said Francis Ash, in manner aforesaid, and according to the purport, true intent and meaning of these presents; and further, that it shall and may be lawful to and for the said Francis Ash, his heirs and assigns, from time to time, and at all times hereafter, peaceably

peaceably and quietly to enter into, have, hold, occupy, poſſeſs, and enjoy the ſame meſſuages, buildings, Plantation, lands, grounds, Negroes, ſlaves, utenſils, hereditaments, and premiſes hereby or mentioned or intended to be hereby granted and releaſed, and to receive and take the rents, profits, crop, and produce thereof, and of every part thereof, from and after the ſaid feaſt of St. Michael the Archangel laſt paſt, before the date hereof, to and for his and their own uſe and benefit, without the lawful let, ſuit, trouble, denial, eviction, or interruption, of or by the ſaid Sir Abel Aſh, his heirs or aſſigns, or of or by any other perſon or perſons lawfully claiming, or to claim any eſtate, right, title, truſt, or intereſt at law or in equity, of, in, to, or out of the ſaid hereby, or mentioned or intended to be hereby, granted and releaſed meſſuages, buildings, Plantation, lands, grounds, negroes, ſlaves, utenſils, hereditaments, and premiſes, or any of them, or any part or parcel thereof, from, by, or under, or in truſt for him, them, or any of them, or from, by, or under the ſaid Sir David Aſh, his late brother Sir David Aſh and Dame Eliza Aſh, his late father and mother, and Sir David Aſh his late grandfather, or any of them, and that free and clear, and freely and clearly acquitted, exonerated and diſcharged, or otherwiſe, by the ſaid Sir Abel Aſh, his heirs, executors, and adminiſtrators, well and ſufficiently ſaved, defended, and kept harmleſs and indemnified of, from, and againſt all and all manner of former and other gifts, grants, bargains, ſales, leaſes, mortgages, jointures, dowers, uſes, truſts, wills, entails, ſtatutes, recognizances, judgments, extents, executions, and of, from, and againſt all and ſingular eſtates, titles, troubles, charges, and incumbrances whatſoever, had,

had, made, done, committed, occaſioned, or ſuffered, or to be had, made, done, committed, occaſioned or ſuffered by the ſaid Sir Abel Aſh, Sir David Aſh his late brother, Sir David Aſh and Dame Eliza Aſh his late father and mother, and Sir David Aſh his late grandfather, or any of them, their, or any of their heirs or aſſigns, or by any other perſon or perſons lawfully claiming, or to claim from, by, or under, or in truſt for them, or any of them, or from, by, or under their or any of their Act, means, aſſent, conſent, or procurement: And moreover, that he the ſaid Sir Abel Aſh, and his heirs, and all other perſons having or lawfully claiming, or which ſhall or may have, or lawfully claim any eſtate, right, title, truſt, or intereſt of, into, or out of the ſaid meſſuages, buildings, Plantation, lands, grounds, Negroes, ſlaves, utenſils, hereditaments, and premiſes hereby mentioned or intended to be hereby granted and releaſed, or any of them, or any part thereof, from, by, or under, or in truſt for him, them, or any of them, or from, by, or under his ſaid anceſtors herein before named, or any of them, ſhall and will from time to time, and at all times hereafter, during the ſpace of ten years next enſuing the date hereof, upon every reaſonable requeſt, and at the proper coſts and charges in the law of the ſaid Francis Aſh, his heirs or aſſigns, make, do, acknowledge, levy, ſuffer, and execute, or cauſe or procure to be made, done, acknowledged, levied, ſuffered, and executed, all and every ſuch further and other lawful and reaſonable Acts, deeds, and things, devices, conveyances and aſſurances in the law whatſoever, for the further, better, more perfect, and abſolute granting, conveying, and aſſuring of the ſaid meſſuages, buildings, Plantation, Lands, grounds, Negroes, ſlaves, and utenſils, ſiis, hereditaments, and premiſes hereby mentioned or intended to be hereby granted and releaſed, with their appurtenances unto, and to the uſe of the ſaid Francis Aſh, Gilbert Gill, and Henry Hart, and to the heirs and aſſigns of the ſaid Francis Aſh in truſt as aforeſaid, as to the eſtate of the ſaid Gilbert Gill and Henry Hart, be the ſame by fine, feoffment, common recovery, deed, inrolled or not inrolled, the inrollment of theſe preſents, or otherwiſe, howſoever, as by the ſaid Francis Aſh, his heirs, or aſſigns, or his or their Counſel learned in the law, ſhall be reaſonably adviſed or deviſed, and required, ſo as ſuch further aſſurances contain in them no other or further warranty or covenants than againſt the perſon or perſons, his or their heirs, who ſhall make or do the ſame, and ſo as the party or parties who ſhall be requeſted to make ſuch further aſſurances be not compelled or compellable for making or doing thereof, to go or travel above five miles from his or their then reſpective dwellings or places of abode; and for the conſideration aforeſaid; the ſaid Sir Abel Aſh doth hereby for himſelf, his heirs, executors, and adminiſtrators, further covenant, promiſe, grant, and agree to and with the ſaid Francis Aſh, his executors, adminiſtrators, and aſſigns, that he the ſaid Francis Aſh, his executors, adminiſtrators, and aſſigns, ſhall and may immediately enter upon and have, receive, take, retain, and and convert to and for his and their own uſe and benefit, all the crop of ſugars and all other the goods, chattels, and produce of or upon the ſaid Plantation, lands, hereditaments, and premiſes hereby or mentioned or intended to be hereby granted and releaſed every or any part thereof, from and after the ſaid feaſt of St. Michael the Archangel laſt paſt, before the date hereof: And the

the ſaid Sir Abel Aſh doth hereby accordingly grant, bargain, ſell, aſſign, and ſet over the ſaid crop of ſugars, and all other the ſaid goods, chattels, and produce of or upon the ſame Plantation, lands, hereditaments, and premiſes, every or any part thereof, and all the benefit and advantage thereof, unto the ſaid Francis Aſh, his executors, adminiſtrators, and aſſigns, to have, hold, receive, perceive, retain, take, and enjoy the ſaid hereby aſſigned premiſes, and every part thereof, and all the benefit and advantage thereof unto him the ſaid Francis Aſh, his executors, adminiſtrators, and aſſigns, to and for his and their uſe and benefit, and as his and their own goods and chattels abſolutely and for ever with warranty againſt all men. In witneſs, &c.

The Manner of executing DEEDS OF CONVEYANCE *of a* PLANTATION *in Barbadoes, by a Perſon impowered by a Letter of Attorney; and the Letter of Attorney. The Deed is to conclude thus:*

IN witneſs whereof to one part of theſe preſents the ſaid Abel Archer, by Barnard Bray of &c. in the Iſland of Barbadoes, Gent. his Attorney, hereunto lawfully authoriſed by a certain power of Attorney hereon indorſed, hath ſet his hand and ſeal, and to the other part of theſe preſents, the ſaid Caleb Coates hath ſet his hand and ſeal, the day and year above written.

To be indorſed thus:

The within written Deed was ſigned, ſealed, and delivered by Barnard Bray, named in the Inſtrument or Power of Attorney written on this ſide of this ſkin of parchment, as the Attorney of the within named Abel Archer, for and in the name, and as the act and deed of the ſaid Abel Archer, in the preſence of us.

To

To be indorsed again thus:

Received before the day of the date of the within written Indenture, namely on the 20th day of May 1731, of and from the within Caleb Coates, by the hands of David Dent and Edmond Dent of London, merchants, the sum of 4200 *l.* of lawful money of Great Britain, being the consideration money within mentioned to have been actually paid in hand to me. I say received.

Witness to the signing thereof by Barnard Bray, of the parish of, &c. in Barbadoes, as the Attorney of the within named Abel Archer, for and in the name, and as the act of the said Abel Archer.

A Third Indorsement *thus, being the Power of Attorney.*

KNOW all men by these presents, that I Abel Archer of the City of Bath, in the Kingdom of Great Britain, Esq; for divers good and valuable causes and considerations me hereunto moving, and more particularly for and in consideration of the sum of 4200 *l.* of lawful money of Great Britain, to me in hand paid at or before the sealing and delivery of this present Instrument by Caleb Coates of the Island of Barbadoes, Planter (by the hands of David Dent and Edmond Dent of London, Merchants) and of the further sum of 7800 *l.* of like lawful money, agreed and secured according to my good liking and approbation, to be paid unto me, my executors, administrators,

miniſtrators or aſſigns, at ſeveral times hereafter, making together the ſum of 12,000 *l.* of lawful money of Great Britain, and being in full for the intire and abſolute purchaſe of the fee-ſimple, inheritance, and full propriety of all and ſingular the lands, plantations, ſugar works, hereditament, ſlaves, ſtock, utenſils, and other things in the within written writing mentioned or deſcribed, and thereby intended to be hereafter granted and conveyed, and to the end, intent and purpoſe, that the ſame premiſes may be legally, ſufficiently and effectually granted, conveyed and aſſured unto and upon the ſaid Caleb Coates, his heirs and aſſigns, for ever diſcharged of all eſtates tail and remainders whatſoever, have made, ordained, authorized, conſtituted and appointed, and by theſe preſents do make, ordain, authorize, conſtitute and appoint Barnaby Bray, of, &c. Gent. and Fulk Flint, of, &c. Gent. jointly and each one of them ſeparately my true and lawful Attornies and Attorney, irrevocable for me and in my name, and as my act and deed, forthwith and as ſoon as conveniently may be after this preſent Inſtrument ſhall arrive in the ſaid Iſland of Barbadoes, to fill up, or cauſe to be filled up, the blanks at the top or beginning of the writing or deed within written, with the day of the month, and month whereon the ſame writing or deed ſhall be executed, purſuant to the further power hereafter in theſe preſents given, or with any other proper date alſo to fill up, or cauſe to be filled up, the blanks at the bottom or end of the writing or deed within written, by and with the name, deſcription and addition of ſuch one of my ſaid Attornies, as ſhall act by virtue of theſe preſents, and of the power hereby given. And after thoſe blanks ſhall be be ſo filled up, then at the foot of the ſaid Deed to ſubſcribe the name Abel Archer, by virtue of theſe preſents, and to ſeal and deliver the ſaid writing or deed for me, in my name and as my act and deed, to the uſe of the ſaid Caleb Coates, his heirs and aſſigns for ever, and that in the preſence of any competent number of witneſſes. And alſo for me to ſubſcribe to the receipt written on this ſide of this ſkin of parchment, the name Abel Archer; and further, to appear for me within three months next after the date which ſhall be ſo filled up in the ſaid within written deed or writing, and after the execution of the ſame writing, and to acknowledge ſuch deed before the reſident Governor of the ſaid Iſland, or before ſome other of the chief Judges for the time being, of ſome one of the Courts of Juſtice within the ſaid Iſland. And to do for me and in my name, and as my act and deed, but to the uſe of the ſaid Caleb Coates, his heirs and aſſigns, all and every other act, matter and thing whatſoever, which ſhall be neceſſary, fitting, or expedient, to the full, legal, effectual and complete execution, acknowledgment and inrolment, or recording in due time of the deed or writing within written, or of any other deed or deeds of the like tenor or purport to the like uſes, and of the ſame premiſſes therein mentioned, although the ſame ſhould be conveyed in other or different forms or terms; and although the premiſſes in ſuch other deed or deeds ſhould be differently or otherwiſe deſcribed, the better to aſcertain the ſame as fully, amply, and beneficially to all intents, conſtructions and purpoſes whatſoever, as I myſelf might or could do, if preſent, and did the ſame perſonally, ſo that there may be made a good

good and perfect title and conveyance unto the ſaid Caleb Coates, his heirs and aſſigns for ever in fee-ſimple, of all and ſingular the premiſes in and by the within mentioned deed or writing meant or mentioned, or intended to be hereafter paſſed or granted away, hereby giving unto my ſaid Attornies or Attorney my full and whole power and authority in the premiſes, and ratifying and confirming, and promiſing to hold for good, firm, valid and effectual, all that my ſaid Attornies or Attorney ſhall lawfully do, or cauſe to be done in the premiſſes by virtue of theſe preſents. Provided always, That theſe preſents, or the power hereby given, ſhall in no wiſe extend, or to be conſtrued to extend, to repeal, revoke, determine or make void any former or other power or powers of attorney by me at any time heretofore given, or appointed to any other perſon or perſons whatſoever, for any diſtinct or other purpoſes, but that ſuch other power and powers of attorney ſhall ſtill, notwithſtanding theſe preſents, and the power hereby given, remain, continue and be of the ſame authority, validity, force and effect, as if theſe preſents had never been made or executed. Provided alſo, That theſe preſents, or the power hereby given, ſhall in no wiſe extend, or be conſtrued to extend, to appoint the ſaid Barnaby Bray and Fulk Flint, every, either, or any of them, my Attornies or Attorney, to or for any other act, intent or purpoſe whatſoever, but ſolely and only for the making, executing, perfecting and completing unto the ſaid Caleb Coates, his heirs and aſſigns, ſufficient and proper deeds, writings and titles, whereby to paſs, grant away and aſſure unto him, his heirs and aſſigns for ever, the free and clear fee-ſimple, inheritance and abſolute propriety of and in all

and

and ſingular the premiſes in the within written deed or writing deſcribed, mentioned, or expreſſed, and thereby meant and intended to be hereafter granted, bargained, ſold, releaſed, and confirmed. In witneſs, &c *.

Signed, ſealed, and delivered
by the above-named G——
S——, in the preſence of
us.

A CONVEYANCE *by Leaſe and Releaſe of Lands and Negroes in* Antigua.

LEASE *for a* YEAR.

THIS Indenture, made the 7th day of March, in the third year of the reign of our Sovereign Lord George the Third, by the Grace of God, of Great Britain, France, and Ireland, King, Defender of the Faith, &c. and in the year of our Lord 1763, between the Honourable A—— L—— late of the iſland of Antigua, but now of Youngſbury, in the county of Hertford, in the kingdom of Great Britain, Eſquire; and S—— his wife, of the one part, and W—— L—— late of the ſaid Iſland of Antigua, but now of Gerard Street Soho, in the county of Middleſex, in the ſaid kingdom of Great Britain, Eſquire, of the other part, witneſſeth, That for and in conſideration of the ſum of five ſhillings, a piece of lawful money of Great Britain, to the ſaid A—— L——, and S—— his wife, in hand, well and truly paid by the ſaid W—— L——, at and before the ſealing and delivery of theſe preſents (the receipt whereof is hereby acknowledged). They, the ſaid A—— L—— and S—— his wife, have, and

* See the ſecond Volume of Horſman's Conveyancer, from 768 to 773.

each

each of them hath granted, bargained, and ſold, and by theſe preſents do, and each of them doth grant, bargain, and ſell, unto the ſaid W—— L——, ALL THAT PLANTATION, or parcel of land, of him the ſaid A—— L——, ſituate, lying, and being in the pariſh of St. Mary, and diviſion of Bermudian Valley, in the ſaid Iſland of Antigua, containing, by eſtimation, four hundred and fifty acres of land, be the ſame more or leſs butted and bounded to the north with the eſtates, late of J—— F—— deceaſed, and F—— F—— eaſt, with Dark Valley, now in the poſſeſſion of J—- W——, and J—- F—— ſouth, with the eſtate of E—— J—— deceaſed, and lands of W—— B——, and with part of the lands of A—— P—— and Weſt, with part of the eſtate of J—— F——, the Pond; and part with the lands of A—— P——, or however otherwiſe the ſame is butted or bounded, lying or being; and alſo the dwelling-houſe and out-houſes thereto belonging; and the windmill, boiling-houſe, curing-houſe, ſtill-houſe, and all other buildings whatſoever, erected upon the ſaid Plantation: and alſo, all ſugar coppers, ſtills, ſtill-heads, worms, worm tubs, carts, carriages, and all other plantation utenſils of what nature or kind ſoever to the ſame plantation belonging, or in anywiſe appertaining: And alſo, all that other plantation, or parcel of land, of him the ſaid A—— L——, called S—— V——, and G—— ſituate in the ſame diviſion and pariſh, containing, by eſtimation, thirty-five acres, or thereabouts, be the ſame more or leſs butted and bounded to the weſt by the ſea, to the eaſt with land of A——P——, to the north with the Pond, and to the ſouth with other lands of the ſaid A—— L——, at the pitch of Crab-hill; or however

however otherwiſe the ſame is butted, bounded, lying, or being: And alſo, all that other Plantation, or parcel of land, of him the ſaid A—— L——, called C—— V——, and C——, ſituate in the diviſion of Old Road, and Pariſh of St. Mary, in the ſaid iſland, containing, by eſtimation, one hundred and ten acres of land, or thereabouts, be the ſame more or leſs butted and bounded to the weſt with the ſea; to the eaſt partly with lands of J—— D——, and partly with lands of W—— B——, to the ſouth with lands of the ſaid J——D——, and to the north with the lands of T—— U——, lands of P—— D———, and other lands of the ſaid A—— L———, or however otherwiſe the ſame is butted or bounded, lying or being: And alſo, all thoſe the Negroe ſlaves following (that is to ſay), Peter, Dickey, French, Pero (with ſeventy nine others named in the deed), being men; Sidney, Treſe, Quaſheba, Cecil (with eighty-four others named in the deed) being women; Iſaac, Valentine, Quaſhey, Frederick (with twenty-one others named in the deed), being boys; and Sam Picart a Muſtee boy; Nanny, Hannah, Little Betty, Violet (with thirty-nine others named in the deed), being girls; and Bonnée a Muſtee girl; or ſuch of the ſaid Negro ſlaves as are now living, together with all the iſſues, and increaſe of all and every the ſaid female Negroe ſlaves, now born, or hereafter to be born; and alſo two bulls named Creole and March; and alſo all thoſe the following oxen (that is to ſay), Tom, Butcher, Spaniard, Aberdeen (with thirty-three others named in the deed); and alſo all thoſe the following cows (that is to ſay), Beſs, Torey, Sabella, Mirah (with twenty-nine others named in the deed); and alſo, all thoſe the following ſteers (that

(that is to ſay), Duke, Man of War, Swagger (with ten others mentioned in the deed); and alſo, all thoſe the following bull calves (that is to ſay), Sunday, Monday, Harry, Bright, and Dramer; and alſo, all thoſe the following cow calves (that is to ſay), Peggy, Maltain, Sukey, Handſome, and Hannah; and alſo, all thoſe the following horſes (that is to ſay), Gunthorpe, Brown, Gatley, Squirrel, and Button; and alſo, all thoſe the following mares (that is to ſay), Jenny, Muggy, Phillis, Florenda, Europa, and her colt, and Guadaloupe; and alſo a colt, named Sarah, or ſuch of the ſaid cattle, horſes, and mares, as are now living; together alſo, with all horſes, cattle, mules, and ſtock, on the ſaid Sugar-work, Plantation; and alſo, all the coppers, ſtills, coolers, ciſterns, worms, worm-tubs, pots, drips, ſkimmers, ladles, waggons, carts, and other utenſils, and appurtenances to the ſaid Sugar-work Plantation belonging, or in anywiſe appertaining; and all other the lands, tenements, or eſtate whatſoever, of him the ſaid A—— L——, party hereto, and S—— his wife, or either of them, in the ſaid Iſland of Antigua, and all ways, waters, water-courſes, woods, trees, paſtures, feedings, ground, foil, profits, perquiſites, royalties, freedoms, franchiſes, privileges, hereditaments, and appurtenances, to the ſaid premiſes, or any of them, in any way belonging, or appertaining, or therewith now, or heretofore uſed, occupied, or enjoyed, or accepted, reputed, taken, or known to be part, parcel, or member thereof, or of any part of the ſame, and the reverſion and reverſions, remainder and remainders, rents, iſſues, and profits thereof. TO HAVE AND TO HOLD the ſaid Plantations, or Sugar-works, houſes, buildings,

lands,

lands, Negroes, slaves, cattle, horses, mules, and plantation-utensils, and other the hereditaments and premisses whatsoever herein-before mentioned, with their and every of their appurtenances unto the said W—— L——, his executors, administrators, and assigns, from the day next before the day of the date of these presents, for and during, and unto the full end and term of one whole year from thence next ensuing, and fully to be complete and ended; YIELDING and PAYING therefore at the end and expiration of the said term, unto the said A—— L——, and S—— his wife, their executors, administrators, and assigns, the rent of one pepper-corn, if the same shall be lawfully demanded, to the intent that, by virtue of these presents, and by force of the statute for transferring uses into possession, he, the said W—— L——, may be in the actual possession of all and singular the premises aforesaid, with their appurtenances; and may thereby be enabled to take and accept of a grant and release of the reversion and inheritance thereof, to him and his heirs, to the only proper use and behoof of him the said W—— L——, his heirs and assigns for ever, as in and by a certain indenture, intended to bear date the day next after the day of the date of these presents, and to be made between the same parties, the same shall be granted and released. And to the intent these presents may be duly recorded, acknowledged, and registered, and take effect according to the laws of the said Island of Antigua; they, the said A—— L—— and S—— his wife, have made, ordained, constituted, and appointed, and by these presents do, and each of them doth make, ordain, constitute, and appoint, the Honourable T—— J—— Esquire, S—— B—— Esquire, and T—— W—— Esquire, now resident in the

the ſaid Iſland of Antigua, jointly and ſeverally, to be their true and lawful attorney and attornies, for them, and in either of their name or names, to appear before the Secretary or Regiſter of the ſaid Iſland of Antigua, or his lawful deputy, or any other proper officer of the ſaid Iſland, to acknowledge theſe preſents to be the acts and deeds of them the ſaid A—— L——— and S—— his wife, and the names and ſeals thereto ſubſcribed and affixed to be the hands and ſeals of them the ſaid A—— L——— and S—— his wife; and further, to do and perform every or any other act, matter, or thing in the like caſes accuſtomed, or which ſhall be neceſſary for the making theſe preſents valid and effectual in the law, according to the true intent and meaning hereof. In witneſs whereof, the ſaid A—— L—— and S—— his wife, have hereunto, and to one other part hereof, of the ſame tenor and date, ſet their hands and ſeals the day and year firſt above written.

A—— L———. (L. S.)
S—— L———. (L. S.)

Sealed and delivered (being firſt duly ſtamped) in the preſence of us,

J—— P———.
G—— H———.

In CHANCERY,

J—— P———, of the pariſh of St. Giles in the Fields, in the county of Middleſex, Gentleman, maketh oath and ſaith, That he, this deponent, is one of the ſubſcribing witneſſes to a certain deed or writing hereunto annexed, bearing date the 7th day of March, in the year of our Lord 1763, and made between the Hon. A— L— late

late of the Island of Antigua, but now of Youngsbury in the County of Hertford, in the kingdom of Great Britain, and S——, his wife, of the one part, and W—— L——, late of the said Island of Antigua, but now of Gerard-street, Soho, in the county of Middlesex, in the said kingdom of Great Britain, Esquire, of the other part, purporting to be a Lease for a year of certain lands and premises in the parish of St. Mary, and division of Bermudian Valley, in the said Island of Antigua: and this Deponent further saith, That the said A—— L—— and S—— L——, did sign, seal, and deliver the said deed or writing as their act and deed, in the presence of this Deponent, and of G—— H——, the other subscribing witness to the said deed or writing; and that the names A— L—— and S— L——, thereunto set and subscribed, are of the respective proper hands-writing of them the said A— L—— and S— L——: and this Deponent further saith, That the name J—— P—— appearing to be set and and subscribed as one of the witnesses to the said deed or writing, is the proper hand-writing of this Deponent; and that the name G—— H—— also appearing to be set and subscribed as the other witness to the said writing, is of the proper hand-writing of the said G— H——.

J—— P——.

Sworn at the public office,
the 16th of August 1763,
before me,

SAMUEL PECHELL.

16th August 1763. This deed or parchment writing was produced, and shewn to J—— P——, and is the same mentioned and referred to in his Affidavit this day sworn to by him, before me,

SAMUEL PECHELL.

INROLLED in his Majesty's High Court of Chancery, the 16th day of August, in the year of our Lord 1763 (being first duly stamped), according to the tenor of the statute, made in the 6th year of the reign of their late Majesties King William and Queen Mary, by

HUMPH. HACKSHAW.

MEMORANDUM. The within Indenture was acknowledged by T—— W———, Esq; as the respective acts and deeds of A—— L———, Esq; and S—— his wife, by virtue of a Power of Attorney, the 9th day of February 1764, before me, EDWARD GAMBLE, Reg.

RELEASE.

THIS Indenture, made the 8th day of March, in the 3d year of the reign of our Sovereign Lord George the Third, by the Grace of God of Great Britain, France, and Ireland King, Defender of the Faith, &c. and in the year of our Lord 1763, between the Honourable A—— L—— late of the Island of Antigua, but now of Youngsbury, in the County of Hertford, in the Kingdom of Great Britain, Esq; and S—— his wife, of the one part, and W—— L———, late of the said Island of Antigua, but now of Gerrard Street, Soho, in the County of Middlesex, in the said Kingdom of Great Britain, Esq; of the other part: WHEREAS the said A—— L—— being justly indebted to J—— B——, late of the Island of Antigua, but now of Grosvenor Street, in the said County of Middlesex, Esq; in the sum of 3604*l*. lawful money of Great Britain, heretofore secured upon the Plantations or sugar-works, lands, and hereditaments herein after mentioned, to be hereby released, or some part thereof, by the

the ſaid A— L—— to F— D—— and P— C—, by way of mortgage for a term of 500 years, by Indenture bearing date the 19th day of September 1753, which ſaid mortgage was afterwards, on the 19th day of September 1756, aſſigned to the ſaid J—— B——, the ſaid W—— L—— hath, at the requeſt, and by and with the conſent and direction of the ſaid A—— L——, paid to the ſaid J—— B—— the ſaid ſum of 3604*l.* and all intereſt due thereon; in conſideration whereof, the ſaid J—— B—— hath agreed to aſſign his intereſt in the ſaid mortgaged premiſes to the ſaid W—— L——, or to ſuch perſon as he ſhall direct: AND WHEREAS, on the 10th of September 1754, the ſaid A—— L—— confeſſed adjudgment in the Court of Common Pleas in the ſaid Iſland of Antigua, to D—— O—— the elder, and W—— O——, in an action of debt upon bond, of the penalty of 8072*l.* of lawful money of Great Britain, and there remaining due from the ſaid A—— L——, on the ſaid judgment, the ſum of 3341*l.* 5*s.* 1*d.* of like lawful money, the ſaid W—— L—— hath, at the requeſt, and by and with the conſent and direction of the ſaid A—— L——, paid the ſum of 3341*l.* 5*s.* 1*d.* and hath taken an aſſignment thereof to himſelf, or ſome perſon in truſt for him: AND WHEREAS the ſaid A—— L—— is alſo juſtly indebted to the ſaid W—— L—— in the ſum of 6000*l.* of like lawful money of Great Britain, together with an arrear of intereſt, in reſpect thereof ſecured to the ſaid W—— L——, upon the ſaid Plantations or ſugar-works, lands, and hereditaments, by way of mortgage thereof in fee, by virtue of certain Indentures of Leaſe and Releaſe, bearing date reſpectively the 17th and 18th days of July, in the year of our Lord 1759, and made, or mentioned

tioned to be made, between the ſaid A— L—— of the one part, and the ſaid W—— L—— of the other part: AND WHEREAS the ſaid W—— L—— hath advanced and lent to the ſaid A—— L——, the ſum of 60 *l.* 10 *s.* over and beſides the three ſeveral ſums before mentioned: AND WHEREAS there now remains due to the ſaid W—— L—— from the ſaid A—— L——, for principal and intereſt to the day of the date hereof, on the three ſeveral ſecurities herein before mentioned, together with the ſaid ſum of 60 *l.* 10 *s.* the ſum of 13,380 *l.* of like lawful money of Great Britain: AND WHEREAS the ſaid A—— L—— is likewiſe juſtly indebted to the ſeveral perſons herein after named, in the ſeveral ſums of money upon the ſeveral ſecurities herein after mentioned or expreſſed (that is to ſay) to R—— G—— of London, merchant, in the ſum of 2663 *l.* of like lawful money of Great Britain, for ſecuring the payment whereof, with intereſt, the ſaid A—— L—— hath executed a Warrant of Attorney, to confeſs judgment to the ſaid R—— G—— in the ſaid Court of Common Pleas in the ſaid Iſland of Antigua, bearing date the 5th day of November, in the year of our Lord 1762, which ſaid Warrant of Attorney hath been tranſmitted by the ſaid R—— G—— to the ſaid Iſland of Antigua, in order to enter up judgment thereon: To J—— B—— of the pariſh of Stepney, in the ſum of 992 *l.* of like lawful money, for part of which ſaid ſum of 992 *l.* being the ſum of 775 *l.* 13 *s.* 4 *d.* the ſaid J—— B—— hath recovered a judgment againſt the ſaid A— L——, and for the remainder thereof, being the ſum of 216 *l.* 6 *s.* 8 *d.* the ſaid A—— L—— hath given his note of hand to the ſaid J—— B——; To R—— K—— of the ſaid Iſland of Antigua, Gentleman,

Gentleman, in the ſum of 690 *l.* of like lawful money of Great Britain, for ſecuring the payment whereof, the ſaid A—— L——— hath entered into a bond or obligation to the ſaid R— K——, bearing date the 28th day of April, in the year of our Lord 1760, in the penalty of 1262 *l.* 2 *d.*: To J—— D——— in the ſum of 485 *l.* of like lawful money, for ſecuring the payment whereof, the ſaid A—— L—— hath entered into a bond or obligation, bearing date the 3d day of June, in the year of our Lord 1760: To R— M—— of London, merchant, in the ſum of 325 *l.* of like lawful money, for ſecuring the payment whereof, the ſaid A—— L—— hath given his note of hand to the ſaid R—— M——, which ſaid ſeveral debts, ſo due from the ſaid A—— L—— to R—— G——, J—— B———, R—— K———, J—— D——, and R—— M——, amount in the whole, with intereſt computed thereon as aforeſaid, to the day of the date of theſe preſents, to the ſum of 5155 *l.* AND WHEREAS there are ſeveral rents charge, or yearly ſums iſſuing and payable out of the ſaid Plantations and hereditaments herein after mentioned, to the ſeveral perſons herein after named (that is to ſay) To C—— J—— and A—— J—— his wife, during their joint lives, and the lives of the ſurvivor, the yearly ſum of 100 *l.* of lawful money of Great Britain: To C—— B—— for her life, the yearly ſum of 22 *l.* of like lawful money: To A— L— for her life, the yearly ſum of 75 *l.* of like lawful money: To the ſaid A—— L——, ſhe having ſurvived her huſband T—— L——, a further annuity of 80 *l.* *per annum*, of like lawful money of Great Britain, and to J—— L———, if ſhe ſurvives her huſband A—— L—— the younger, the yearly ſum of 200 *l.* of like lawful money of Great

Great Britain; and C—— B—— is entitled to a grofs fum of 800*l.* Antigua currency, if fhe fhall furvive her hufband J— B——, and to the intereft thereof after the rate of 6*l. per cent. per annum*, Antigua currency, in the mean time refpectively charged on the fame Plantation and hereditaments: AND WHEREAS the faid feveral rents, charge, or yearly fums, together with the faid grofs fum of 800*l.* payable upon the contingency aforefaid, with fuch intereft for the fame in the mean time, as herein before is mentioned, have been eftimated and valued by the faid A—— L——, party hereto, and W—— L——, at the fum of 3439*l.* of lawful money of Great Britain: AND WHEREAS there is now due to the faid C—— J——, for his faid annuity, from the faid A—— L——, the fum of 100*l.* of like lawful money of Great Britain, and to the faid C—— B——, the fum of 50*l.* of like lawful money, which the faid W—— L—— hath, at the requeft of the faid A—— L——, agreed to pay for him: AND WHEREAS the faid W—— L—— hath contracted with the faid A— L——, party hereto, for the abfolute purchafe of the inheritance in fee fimple, and equity of redemption of the faid Plantation or fugar-work, lands, and hereditaments herein after mentioned, to be hereby releafed, fubject to, and charged and chargeable with the payment of the faid feveral debts herein before mentioned to amount to the fum of 18,535*l.* and of the faid feveral rents, charge, and grofs fum of 800*l.* payable upon the contingency aforefaid, and with fuch intereft in the mean time, as herein before is mentioned, and of the faid two fums of 100*l.* due to the faid C—— J——, and 50*l.* due to the faid C—— B——, at or for the price or fum of 24,000*l.* of lawful

lawful money of Great Britain; and it hath been agreed between them, that the ſaid W—— L—— ſhall retain to his own uſe, out of the ſaid purchaſe-money, the ſaid ſum of 13,380 *l.* in ſatiſfaction and diſcharge of the ſeveral debts herein before mentioned, to be due and owing to him as aforeſaid. AND ALSO the ſaid ſeveral ſums of 5155 *l.* and 3439 *l.*, as a compenſation, for and towards ſatisfaction and diſcharge of the ſeveral other debts herein before mentioned, and of the ſaid ſeveral rents charge, or yearly ſums, and other money, and alſo the ſaid two ſums of 100 *l.* and 50 *l.* herein before mentioned, which the ſaid W—— L—— hath undertaken to pay. And the ſaid Plantations or ſugar-work, and hereditaments, are intended to remain ſubject to, and charged and chargeable therewith; and that the ſum of 1876 *l.*, reſidue of the ſaid ſum of 24,000 *l.*, ſhall be ſecured to be paid to the ſaid A—— L——, party hereto, by the ſaid W—— L——, by his bond or obligation, bearing even date herewith. NOW THIS INDENTURE WITNESSETH, that for and in ſatisfaction and diſcharge of the ſaid ſeveral ſums of money, and intereſt herein before mentioned, to be due and owing to the ſaid W—— L——, amounting, in the whole, to the ſum of 13,380 *l.* of lawful money of Great Britain, and agreed to be retained by him out of the ſaid 24,000 *l.*; and for and in conſideration as well of the ſaid ſeveral further ſums of 5155 *l.* and 3439 *l.*, other part of the ſaid purchaſe money, retained by the ſaid W— L—, in compenſation for, and towards ſatisfaction of, the ſaid ſeveral other debts, rents-charges, and other money, as alſo the ſaid two ſums of 100 *l.* and 50 *l.* herein before mentioned, to be due to C— J— and C— B—, which the ſaid W— L— hath undertaken

taken to pay and discharge: AND ALSO the further sum of 1876 *l.* of like lawful money of Great Britain, being the remainder of the said sum of 24,000 *l.*, secured to be paid by the said W— L— to the said A— L—, party hereto, in the manner herein before mentioned, with which said security the said A—— L—— doth hereby acknowledge himself to be satisfied and content, and doth declare the said six several sums of 13,380 *l.*, 5155 *l.*, 3439 *l.*, 100 *l.*, 50 *l.*, and 1876 *l.*—amounting together to the said sum of 24,000 *l.*—of lawful money of Great Britain, to be the full consideration for such purchase as aforesaid, and thereof, and of and from every part thereof doth acquit, release, and discharge the said W—— L——, his heirs, executors, and administrators; and also for and in consideration of the sum of 10*s.* of like lawful money by the said W—— L——, to the said A—— L——, party hereto, and S—— his wife, in hand, at or before the sealing and delivering of these presents, well and truly paid, the receipt whereof is hereby acknowledged. THEY the said A—— L——, party hereto, and S—— his wife, HAVE, and each of them HATH granted, bargained, sold, aliened, released, and confirmed, and by these presents DO, and each of them DOTH grant, bargain, sell, alien, release, and confirm unto the said W—— L—— (in his actual possession now being, by virtue of a bargain and sale to him thereof made, by the said A—— L—— and S—— his wife, for five shillings apiece consideration, by indenture bearing date the day next before the day of the date of these presents, for one whole year, commencing from the day next before the day of the date of the same indenture of bargain and sale, and by force of the statute for transferring uses ufes into poffeffion) and to his heirs and affigns, ALL THAT PLANTATION, or parcel of land, of him the faid A— L—, fituate, lying, and being in the parifh of St. Mary, and divifion of Bermudian Valley, in the faid Ifland of Antigua, containing, by eftimation, 450 acres of land, be the fame more or lefs, butted and bounded to the north with the eftate late of J— F— deceafed, and F— F—; eaft, with Dark Valley, now in poffeffion of J— W— and J— F—; fouth, with the eftate of C— J— deceafed, and lands of W— B—, and with part of the lands of A— P—; and weft, with part of the eftate of J— F—, the pond, and part with lands of A— P—; or however otherwife the fame is butted and bounded, lying or being: And alfo the dwelling-houfe and outhoufes thereto belonging, and the windmill, boiling-houfe, curing-houfe, ftill-houfe, and all other buildings whatfoever, erected upon the faid Plantation: AND alfo all fugar-coppers, ftills, ftill-heads, worms, worm-tubs, carts, carriages, and all other plantation utenfils, of what nature or kind foever, to the fame plantation belonging, or in any wife appertaining: AND ALSO all that other Plantation, or parcel of land, of him the faid A— L—, called S— V—, and G—, fituate in the fame divifion and parifh, containing, by eftimation, thirty-five acres or thereabouts, be the fame more or lefs, butted and bounded to the weft by the fea; to the eaft, with lands of A— P—; to the north, with the pond; and, to the fouth, with other lands of the faid A— L—, at the pitch of Crab Hill, or however otherwife the fame is butted and bounded, lying or being: AND ALSO all that other Plantation, or parcel of land, of him the faid A— L—, called C— V—,

V—, and C—, situate in the division of Old Road, and parish of St. Mary, in the said island, containing, by estimation, 110 acres of land, or thereabouts, be the same more or less, butted and bounded to the west with the sea; to the east, partly with lands of J— D—, and partly with lands of W— B—; to the south, with lands of the said J— D—; and, to the north, with lands of T—— U——, lands of P—— D——, and other lands of the said A— L—; or however otherwise the same is butted or bounded, lying or being: And also all those the Negroe slaves following (that is to say), Peter, Dickey, French, Pero (with seventy-nine others named in the deed), being men; Moll, Sidney, Trese, Quasheba (with eighty-four others named in the deed), being women; Isaac, Valentine, Quashey, Frederick (with twenty-one others named in the deed), being boys; and Sam, Picart, a Mustee boy; Nanny, Hannah, Little Betty, (with forty others named in the deed) being girls; and Bonney, a Mustee girl; or such of the said Negroe slaves as are now living, together with all the issues and increase of all and every the said female Negroe slaves now born, or hereafter to be born; and also two bulls, named Creole, and March; and also all those the following oxen, that is to say, Tom, Butcher, Spaniard, Aberdeen, (with thirty-three others named in the deed); and also all those the following cows (that is to say) Bess, Torey, Isabella, Mirah, (with twenty-nine others named in the deed); and also all those the following steers (that is to say) Duke, Man of War, Swagger, with ten others named in the deed); and also all those the following bull calves (that is to say), Sunday, Monday, Harry, Bright, and Drainer;

Drainer; and alſo all thoſe the following cow calves (that is to ſay), Peggy, Mattain, Sukey, Handſome, and Hannah; and alſo all thoſe the following horſes (that is to ſay) Gunthorpe, Brown, Gantley, Squirrel, and Button; and alſo all thoſe the following mares (that is to ſay) Jenny, Muggy, Phillis, Florenda, Europa and her colt, and Guadaloupe, and alſo a colt named Sarah, or ſuch of the ſaid cattle, and horſes, and mares as are now living; together alſo with all other horſes, cattle, mules, and ſtock on the ſaid Sugar-work Plantation; and alſo all the coppers, ſtills, coolers, ciſterns, worms, worm-tubs, pots, drips, ſkimmers, ladles, waggons, carts, and other utenſils and appurtenances to the ſaid Sugar-work Plantation belonging, or in any wiſe appertaining; and all other the lands, tenements, or eſtate whatſoever of him the ſaid A—— L——, party hereto, and S—— his wife, or either of them, in the ſaid Iſland of Antigua, and all ways, waters, water-courſes, woods, trees, paſtures, feedings, ground, ſoil, profits, perquiſites, royalties, freedoms, franchiſes, privileges, hereditaments, and appurtenances to the premiſes, or any of them, in any way belonging or appertaining, or therewith now or heretofore uſed, occupied, or enjoyed, or accepted, reputed, taken, or known to be part, parcel, or member thereof, or of any part of the ſame; and the reverſion and reverſions, remainder and remainders, rents, iſſues and profits thereof; and alſo, all the eſtate, right, title, inheritance, equity of redemption, uſe, truſt, intereſt, claim, or demand whatſoever, either at law or in equity, of them the ſaid A—— L——, party hereto, and S—— his wife, or either of them, of, in, to, or out of the ſaid Plantations, ſugar-works, meſſuages, lands, tenements,

ments, Negroes, ſlaves, and premiſſes, with their and every of their appurtenances, or any of them, or any part of the ſame, and all deeds, evidences, and writings whatſoever relating to the ſame ſeveral premiſes, in their or either of their cuſtody or power, to come by without ſuit at law or in equity; TO HAVE AND TO HOLD the ſaid Plantations, or ſugar-works, houſes, buildings, lands, Negroes, ſlaves, cattle, horſes, mules, and plantation utenſils, and other the hereditaments and premiſes whatſoever mentioned to be hereby granted and releaſed, with their and every of their appurtenances, unto the ſaid W—— L——, and his heirs and aſſigns, to the only proper uſe and behoof of the ſaid W—— L——, his heirs, and aſſignees for ever, and to and for no other uſe, intent, or purpoſe whatſoever; and the ſaid A—— L——, party hereto for himſelf, his heirs, executors, and adminiſtrators, DOTH covenant, promiſe and grant to and with the ſaid W—— L——, his heirs and aſſigns, by theſe preſents, in the manner following (that is to ſay) that for and notwithſtanding any act, matter, or thing whatſoever by them the ſaid A—— L——, party hereto, and S——, his wife, or either of them, heretofore done, or wittingly ſuffered to the contrary, THEY the ſaid A—— L——, party hereto, and S—— his wife, or one of them now at the time of the ſealing and delivery of theſe preſents, are and ſtand, or is and ſtandeth lawfully and rightfully ſeized of and in the ſaid Plantations, ſugar-works, meſſuages, lands, Negroes, Mulatto ſlaves, hereditaments, and premiſes, with their and every of their appurtenances, of a good, ſure, perfect, and abſolute eſtate of inheritance, without any manner of

con-

condition contingent, proviſo, power of limitation, of new, or other uſe, or uſes; or other reſtraint, matter, or thing, to alter, change, charge, or defeat the ſame; and alſo, that for and notwithſtanding any ſuch act, matter, or thing as aforeſaid, they the ſaid A—— L——, party hereto, and S—— his wife, have in themſelves good right, full power, and lawful and abſolute authority by theſe preſents, and the acknowledgment of them the ſaid A—— L—— and S—— his wife, intended to be taken in ſuch manner as the ſame is intended to be indorſed on theſe preſents, to releaſe and aſſure unto and to the uſe of the ſaid W—— L——, his heirs and aſſigns, the ſame Plantations and premiſes according to the purport, true intent, and meaning of theſe preſents. AND FURTHER, That he the ſaid W—— L——, his heirs and aſſigns ſhall, and lawfully may, from time to time, and at all times hereafter, peaceably and quietly have, hold, uſe, occupy, poſſeſs, and enjoy all the ſaid Plantations, ſugar-works, houſes, buildings, lands, Negro and Mulatto ſlaves, hereditaments, and other the premiſes whatſoever, with their and every of their appurtenances, without the let, ſuit, hindrance, interruption, or denial of them the ſaid A—— L——, party hereto, and S—— his wife, or either of them, their or either of their heirs or aſſigns, or of any other perſon or perſons whomſoever, lawfully claiming, or who ſhall or may claim by, from, or under him, her, them, or any, or either of them, or any of their anceſtors, and that free and clear, and freely and clearly acquitted, exonerated and diſcharged, or otherwiſe well and ſufficiently ſaved and kept harmleſs, and indemnified by the ſaid A—— L——, and S—— his

wife,

wife, their heirs, executors, and administrators, of and from all former and other gifts, grants, bargains, sales, mortgages, jointures, dowers, uses, intails, rents, arrears of rent, statutes merchant, and of the staple, judgments, recognizances, titles, charges, and incumbrances whatsoever, had, made, done, committed, or suffered by the said A—— L——, and S—— his wife, or either of them, or by, through, or with their or either of their act or acts, means, consent, privity, or procurement, save and except the several charges and incumbrances herein before mentioned. AND MOREOVER, That the said A—— L——, party hereto, and S—— his wife, their heirs and assigns, and all other person and persons whatsoever, now having or claiming, or which at any time hereafter shall or may have or claim any estate, right, title, trust, or interest of, in, to, or out of the said lands, plantations, sugar-works, houses, buildings, hereditaments, and other the premises, with the appurtenances, or of, in, to, or out of any part, or parcel thereof (other than and except the several persons claiming the said several debts, rents, charge, and other money, which the same several premises are intended to remain charged and chargeable with in respect thereof only), shall and will, from time to time, and at all times hereafter, at the request, and at the costs and charges in the law of the said W—— L——, his heirs or assigns, make, do, acknowledge, suffer, and execute, or cause or procure to be made, done, acknowledged, executed, and suffered, all and every such further and other reasonable act and acts, thing and things, device and devices, assurance and assurances in the law whatsoever, for the further, better, and more perfect and absolute assuring,

ſuring, ſure-making, conveying, and confirming of all the ſaid plantations, lands, hereditaments, and premiſes, with their and every of their appurtenances unto and to the uſe of the ſaid W—— L——, his heirs and aſſigns for ever, as by the ſaid W—— L——, his heirs or aſſigns, or by his or their Counſel learned in the law ſhall be reaſonably deviſed, adviſed or required, ſo as ſuch further aſſurances contain in them no further or other covenants or warranty, than againſt the perſon or perſons who ſhall be required to make and execute the ſame as his, her and their acts and deeds, and ſo as no perſon be compelled or compellable to travel, or go from the uſual place of his, her, or their habitation or abode for the doing thereof. And the ſaid A—— L——, party hereto, doth hereby for himſelf, his heirs, executors and adminiſtrators, further covenant, promiſe, and agree to and with the ſaid W—— L——, his executors, adminiſtrators and aſſigns, that the ſaid ſum of 1876l. ſecured to be paid by the ſaid W—— L—— to the ſame A—— L——, as herein before mentioned, as and for the remainder of the purchaſe-money for the premiſes, ſhall remain and continue in the hands of the ſaid W—— L—— until ſuch time as the ſaid W—— L——, his heirs or aſſigns, or ſome perſon or perſons duly authorized and impowered by and under him or them, ſhall have ſearched the Regiſter's or Secretary's Office of the ſaid Iſland of Antigua, in order to be ſatisfied what charges or incumbrances now affect the ſaid ſeveral premiſes mentioned, to be hereby releaſed, or any of them; and in caſe upon ſuch ſearch any ſuch incumbrance or charge ſhall be found, the payment whereof is not hereby provided for, that then, and in ſuch caſe, the ſaid W——

L——

L—— ſhall and may be at liberty, and is hereby impowered to pay and apply ſo much of the ſaid ſum of 1876l. in payment and ſatisfaction of ſuch charge and incumbrance as aforeſaid, PROVIDED the ſame money will extend to pay the ſame; but in caſe ſuch charge and incumbrance ſhall exceed the ſaid ſum of 1876l. now remaining in the hands of the ſaid W—— L——, THEN, and in ſuch caſe, the ſecurity ſo given by him for the payment of the ſaid ſum of 1876l. ſhall ceaſe, determine, and be void to all intents and purpoſes as if the ſame had not been made; and theſe preſents, and the grant and releaſe hereby made, ſhall from thenceforth be and enure, and the ſaid W—— L——, his heirs and aſſigns, ſhall ſtand and be ſeized of the ſaid ſeveral plantations, ſugar-works, meſſuages, lands, hereditaments, and premiſes, ſubject to redemption by the ſaid A—— L——, party hereto, his heirs, executors, or adminiſtrators, on his or their paying to the ſaid W—— L——, his executors, adminiſtrators, or aſſigns, the ſaid ſeveral debts amounting to the ſum of 13,380l. herein before mentioned to be due and owing to him, with the intereſt thereof, within three calendar months then next enſuing; and the ſaid W—— L—— doth hereby for himſelf, his heirs, executors, and adminiſtrators, covenant, promiſe and agree to and with the ſaid A—— L——, party hereto, his heirs, executors, and adminiſtrators, that in caſe upon ſuch ſearch as aforeſaid, no charge or incumbrance (other than ſuch as are hereby provided for the payment of) exceeding the reſidue of the ſaid purchaſe-money agreed to remain in the hands of the ſaid W—— L—— ſhall appear to affect the ſaid ſeveral premiſes, or or any part thereof, THEN, and in ſuch caſe,

he

he the ſaid W—— L——, his heirs, executors, adminiſtrators, and aſſigns, ſhall and will, from time to time, and at all times hereafter, bear, pay, and diſcharge all and ſingular the ſaid ſums of money, rents, charge or yearly ſums, and other charges herein before mentioned and recited to be due from, and payable by the ſaid A—— L——, party hereto, together with all intereſt that may hereafter become due thereon; and alſo ſhall and will, from time to time, and at all times hereafter, well and ſufficiently ſave harmleſs, and keep indemnified the ſaid A—— L——, his heirs, executors, and adminiſtrators, and his and their goods and chattels, lands and tenements, of, from, and againſt all ſuch coſts, charges, damages and expences as ſhall or may at any time hereafter be recovered againſt, or be ſuſtained, expended or become payable by him or them, for or by reaſon or means of the non-payment of the ſaid ſeveral ſums of money, rents charge or yearly ſums, and other charges and incumbrances herein before recited, or any part thereof. AND to the INTENT that theſe preſents may be duly recorded, acknowledged and regiſtered, and take effect according to the laws of the ſaid Iſland of Antigua, they the ſaid A—— L——, and S—— his wife, HAVE made, ordained, conſtituted and appointed, and by theſe preſents DO, and each of them DOTH make, ordain, ſtitute and appoint the Honourable T—— I——, Eſq. S——B——, Eſq. and T—— W——, Eſq. now reſident in the ſaid Iſland of Antigua, jointly and ſeverally to be their true and lawful Attorney and Attorneys for them, and in any of their name or names to appear before the Secretary or Regiſter of the ſaid Iſland of Antigua, or his lawful Deputy, or any other proper Officer of the

the ſaid Iſland, to acknowledge theſe preſents to to be the acts and deeds of them the ſaid A—— L——, party hereto, and S—— his wife, and the names and ſeals thereto ſubſcribed and affixed to be the hands and ſeals of them the ſaid A—— L——, party hereto, and S—— his wife. AND FURTHER, to do and perform every or any other act, matter, or thing in the like caſes accuſtomed, or which ſhall be neceſſary for the making theſe preſents valid and effectual in the law, according to the true intent and meaning thereof. IN WITNESS whereof, the ſaid parties have hereunto, and to one other part thereof, of the ſame tenor and date, ſet their hands and ſeals the day and year firſt above written.

A—— L——. (L. S.)
S—— L——. (L. S.)

SEALED and delivered (being firſt duly ſtampt) in the preſence of us,

J—— P——.
G—— H——.

BE IT REMEMBERED, That on the 8th day of March 1763, before me Sir Charles Pratt, Knt. Chief Juſtice of his Majeſty's Court of Common Pleas, perſonally appeared A—— L—— and S—— his wife, parties to the within written Indenture, being the grantors therein named, and did then ſeverally acknowledge before me, that the within written Indenture was their reſpective act and deed, and was by them reſpectively duly executed, in order and to the intent that the ſame Indenture, together with this preſent acknowledgment thereon had, may be effectual to bar all intails, and paſs all eſtate,

eſtate, right, title and intereſt of them the ſaid A—— L—— and S—— his wife reſpectively, of and in the Plantations or Sugar Works, Meſſuages, Lands, Hereditaments, Slaves, Cattle and other things comprized in the within written Indenture, and therein mentioned to be thereby granted and releaſed (the ſaid S—— being ſolely examined by me, and conſenting thereunto) which I atteſt under my hand the day and year above written, in my aforeſaid capacity.

C. PRATT.

In CHANCERY.

J—— P——, of the Pariſh of St. Giles in the Fields, in the County of Middleſex, Gent. maketh oath and ſaith, That he this deponent is one of the ſubſcribing witneſſes to a certain deed or writing hereunto annexed, bearing date the 8th day of March, in the year of our Lord 1763, and made between the Honourable A—— L——, late of the Iſland of Antigua, but now of Youngsbury in the County of Hertford, in the Kingdom of Great Britain, and S— his Wife, of the one part, and W— L—, late of the ſaid Iſland of Antigua, but now of Gerard-ſtreet, Soho, in the County of Middleſex, in the ſaid Kingdom of Great Britain, Eſq; of the other part, purporting to be a releaſe of certain lands and premiſes in the pariſh of St. Mary and diviſion of Bermudian Valley in the ſaid Iſland of Antigua. And this deponent ſaith, That the ſaid A—— L—— and S—— L—— did ſign, ſeal and deliver the ſaid deed or writing, as their act and deed, in the preſence of this deponent, and of G—— H——, the other ſubſcribing witneſs to the ſaid deed or writing; and that the names A—— L—— and S—— L—— thereunto ſet and ſubſcribed, are of of the reſpective proper hands-writing of them the ſaid A—— L—— and S—— L——. And this deponent further ſaith, That the name J—— P——, appearing to be ſet and ſubſcribed as one of the witneſſes to the ſaid Deed or writing, is of the proper hand-writing of this deponent. And that the name G—— H—— alſo appearing to be ſet and ſubſcribed as the other witneſs to the ſaid deed or writing, is of the proper hand-writing of the ſaid G—— H——.

J—— P——.

Sworn at the Public Office
the 16th of Auguſt 1763,
before

SAM. PECHELL.

16th of Auguſt 1763. This Deed or parchment-writing was produced and ſhewn to J—— P——, and is the ſame mentioned and referred to in his affidavit this day ſworn to by him before me,

SAM. PECHELL.

INROLLED in his Majeſty's High Court of Chancery the 16th day of Auguſt, in the year of our Lord 1763, being firſt duly ſtampt, according to the tenor of the ſtatute made in the ſixth year of the reign of their late Majeſties King William and Queen Mary, by

HUMPH. HACKSHAW.

TO all to whom theſe preſents ſhall come, I William Beckford, Eſq; Lord Mayor of the City of London, in purſuance of an Act of Parliament made and paſſed in the fifth year of the reign of his late Majeſty King George the Second, intituled, An Act for the more eaſy Recovery of Debts

Debts in his Majesty's Plantations and Colonies in America, do hereby certify, That on the day of of the date hereof, personally came and appeared before me G—— H——, the Deponent named in the affidavit hereunto annexed, being a person well known and worthy of good credit; and by solemn oath which the said deponent then took before me upon the Holy Evangelists of Almighty God, did solemnly and sincerely declare, testify, and depose to be true, the several matters and things mentioned and contained in the said annexed affidavit.

LORD MAYOR'S SEAL.

In faith and testimony whereof, I the said Lord Mayor have caused the Seal of the Office of Mayoralty of the said City of London to be hereunto put and affixed, and the lease and release mentioned and referred to in and by the said affidavit, to be hereunto also annexed. Dated in London, the 3d day of September, in the year of our Lord 1763.

HODGES.

LONDON.

G—— H——, of Great Queen-street, Lincoln's Inn Fields, Gent, maketh oath and saith, That he was present and did see the Honourable A—— L——, Esq; and S—— his wife, parties to the two parchment writings or deeds hereunto annexed (purporting to be a lease and release from the said A—— L—— and S—— his wife

to

to W——— L———, late of the iſland of Antigua, but now of Gerard-ſtreet, Soho, in the County of Middleſex, in the Kingdom of Great Britain, Eſq;) ſeverally and reſpectively ſign and ſeal, and as their ſeveral and reſpective acts and deeds, deliver the ſaid two parchment-writings or deeds. And this deponent ſaith, That the names A—— L—— and S—— L—— appearing to be ſet or ſubſcribed to each of the ſaid parchment-writings or deeds, are of the reſpective proper hands-writing of the ſaid A—— L—— and S—— his wife. And this deponent did, together with J—— P——, indorſe his name as a witneſs to the due execution of the ſaid parchment-writings or deeds. And further ſaith, That the names J—— P—— and G—— H—— appearing to be indorſed as witneſſes to the due execution of the ſaid parchment-writings or deeds, are of the reſpective proper hands-writing of the ſaid J—— P—— and him this deponent.

G—— H——.

Sworn the 3d day of Sept.
1763, before me,
WILLIAM BECKFORD, Mayor.

MEMORANDUM, the within Indenture was acknowledged by T—— W——, Eſq; as the reſpective acts and deeds of A—— L——, Eſq; and S—— his wife, by virtue of the within power of attorney, the 9th day of February 1764, before me,

EDWARD GAMBLE, Regiſter.

MORTGAGE

Mortgage *in Fee by Bargain and Sale inrolled, of a Plantation, Slaves, &c. in St. Christopher's, with the Acknowledgment of the Husband and Wife, and the private Examination of the Wife to bar Dower.*

THIS Indenture, made the fourteenth day of November, in the twenty-fourth year of the reign of our Sovereign Lord George the Second, by the Grace of God, of Great Britain, France, and Ireland King, Defender of the Faith, and so forth; and in the year of our Lord one thousand seven hundred and fifty, Between F— P—, late of his Majesty's Island of St. Christopher in America, but at present resident in the City of London, Esq; and E— his wife of the one part, and D— O— of Great James Street, in the parish of St. Andrew, Holborn, in the county of Middlesex, Esq; of the other part: Whereas the said F— P— doth allege, that he now is lawfully and solely seized and possessed in his demesne as of fee simple, of and in, and is well entitled unto the fee simple, inheritance, and absolute property of a certain sugar-work Plantation, with the lands, dwelling-house, other houses, still-houses, works, and buildings thereon being, and thereunto belonging and appertaining, situate, lying, and being in the late French part of the said Island of St. Christopher, and in or near the parish of St. Paul Capisterre in the said Island, which, as the said F— P— doth allege, contains in the whole the quantity of ninety-four acres of cane lands, and ten acres more of mountain land, or thereabouts, and that the said Plantation is commonly called or known by the name of the C——— P———, or the C——— E———, and is abutted and bounded

bounded to the eastward, with the lands now or late in the possession, tenure, or occupation of D— T—, Esq; or his lessee or lessees, or under-tenant or under-tenants, and to the northward, with lands now or late in the possession, tenure, or occupation of B— M—, Esq; or of his lessee or lessees, or under-tenant or under-tenants, and to the southward, and also to the westward, with lands now or late in the possession, tenure, or occupation of G— L—, Esq; or of his lessee or lessees, or under-tenant or under-tenants; and that there are upon, and belonging to the said Plantation, one good mansion-house or dwelling-house, a cook-room, or kitchen, with stores adjoining, a wind-mill and cattle-mill, a boiling-house, a distill-house, and a stable, together with all sorts of stills, coppers, worms, tubs, coolers, utensils, implements, and appurtenances necessary for the well carrying on of the said sugar work Plantation; and that there are a large number of horses, asses, mules, bulls, sheep, hogs, goats, and other live stock and dead stock thereon, and also one hundred and twenty in number at the least, of good and able working Negro slaves, upon and belonging and appertaining to the same; and that all the same Plantation, buildings, utensils, implements, beasts, cattle, slaves, and premises, do lawfully belong unto the said F— P—, in pure fee simple, and absolute property, and are wholly and entirely free from all wills, settlements, jointures, dowers, uses, trusts, gifts, grants, sales, mortgages, leases, debts, decrees, bonds, judgments, executions, extents, levies, forfeiture, and cause and causes of forfeiture, and of and from all other claims, demands, charges, burthens, and incumbrances whatsoever, save only the quit rent, from henceforth

forth to be payable to the Crown for the ſaid Plantation, and one ſingle debt or incumbrance of three thouſand five hundred and eighty pounds ſix ſhillings and eight pence of lawful money of Great Britain, or to that value, which is due unto A— B— and J— B, of London, merchants and partners, and which is ſome how ſecured, together with the intereſt thereof, unto or for the ſaid A— B— and J— B—, by ſome mortgage or ſecurity made and taken in the ſaid Iſland of St. Chriſtopher, in or about the month of April now laſt paſt: AND WHEREAS the ſaid F— P— hath requeſted of the ſaid D— O— the loan of a ſum of one thouſand nine hundred and nineteen pounds thirteen ſhillings and four pence, of lawful money of Great Britain, to anſwer the preſent occaſions of the ſaid F— P—, which ſum the ſaid D— O— hath agreed to lend him, and hath at the time of the execution of theſe preſents actually advanced and paid into the proper hands of the ſaid F— P—. NOW THIS INDENTURE WITNESSETH, That for the docking, barring, cutting off, defeating, and entirely deſtroying of all eſtates tail, and of all other contingent or other eſtates dependant or expectant upon any ſuch eſtates tail, and of all remainders and reverſions at any time or times heretofore made, ſettled, created, deviſed, or limited, of or concerning all and every, or any the Plantations, lands, tenements, and hereditaments herein after-mentioned, to be hereby bargained, ſold, or releaſed; or of or concerning any part or parts of the ſame (in caſe any ſuch eſtates tail, remainders, reverſions, or other eſtates there be of the ſame, or of any part or parts thereof) and for the barring the dower, and right and title of dower of the ſaid E—, the wife of the ſaid F—

P—, of, in, and to the Plantations, lands, tenements, and hereditaments herein after mentioned, to be hereby bargained, ſold, or releaſed; and for and in conſideration of the ſum of one thouſand nine hundred and nineteen pounds thirteen ſhillings and four-pence of lawful money of Great Britain by the ſaid D— O— unto the ſaid F—P— and E— his wife, or one of them in hand, well and truly paid at or before the time of the ſealing and delivery of theſe preſents; the receipt whereof the ſaid F—— P—— and E—— his wife do hereby reſpectively acknowledge, and themſelves and each of them to be therewith fully ſatisfied, contented, and paid, and thereof and therefrom do, and each of them doth acquit, releaſe, and diſcharge the ſaid D—— O——, his heirs, executors, adminiſtrators, and aſſigns, and every of them, by theſe preſents. THEY the ſaid F—— P—— and E—— his wife have, and each of them HATH granted, bargained, ſold, aliened, remiſed, releaſed, aſſigned, and confirmed, and by theſe preſents, DO and each of them DOTH fully and abſolutely grant, bargain, ſell, alien, remiſe, releaſe, aſſign, and confirm unto the ſaid D—— O——, his heirs, executors, adminiſtrators, and aſſigns (ſeverally and reſpectively as herein after-mentioned), ALL AND SINGULAR that and thoſe the herein before mentioned or deſcribed ſugar-work Plantation, lands, dwelling-houſe, other houſes, ſtill-houſes, works, buildings, cane lands, mountain land, manſion-houſe, cook-room or kitchen, ſtores, wind-mill, cattle-mill, boiling-houſe, diſtill-houſe, ſtable, ſtills, coppers, worms, tubs, utenſils, implements, appurtenances, horſes, aſſes, mules, bulls, ſheep, hogs, goats, live ſtock, dead ſtock, Negroes, and premiſes, with their and every

of

of their reſpective appurtenances in whatſoever pariſh or place within the late French part of the ſaid Iſland of St. Chriſtopher, the ſame or any part thereof, do or doth lie, or are or is ſituate, ſtanding, lying, or being; and whatever quantity or number of acres the ſame or any part thereof do or doth contain, and by what name or names ſoever the ſame, or any part thereof, now are or is, or at any time or times heretofore, have or hath been called, known, named, or diſtinguiſhed, and however the ſame and every, or any particular part or parts thereof, do or doth abut or bound, or have or hath abutted or bounded, and whatſoever other miſtake, miſinformation, or other error, defect, or imperfection there may be in the before-mentioned deſcription, or mention of the ſame: AND ALSO ALL AND SINGULAR OTHER the ſugar-work Plantations, and other Plantations, cane lands, mountain lands, and other lands and hereditaments (being parcel of the late French lands in the ſaid Iſland of St. Chriſtopher) of them the ſaid F—— P—— and E—— his wife, and of each of them; or whereof, or wherein, or whereto they, or either of them, are poſſeſſed or intitled unto any eſtate, right, title, or intereſt, ſituate, lying, or being in every and any pariſh or place in the ſaid Iſland of St. Chriſtopher, within that which was lately the French part of the ſaid Iſland, whatſoever the names, contents, quantities, qualities, numbers, ſituations, abuttals, boundaries, or other deſcriptions of the ſame may be: AND all manſion-houſes, dwelling-houſes, meſſuages, tenements, ſtill-houſes, works, edifices, erections, and buildings whatſoever, upon the ſame: AND ALL and every the ſtills, coppers, worms, tubs, coolers, utenſils, implements,

ments, and appurtenances which now are, or which at any time or times hereafter ſhall be to the ſame, or any of them belonging, or in any wiſe appertaining: AND ALL and every the horſes, aſſes, mules, bulls, ſheep, hogs, goats, cattle, beaſts, live ſtock, and dead ſtock, which now are, or which at any time or times hereafter ſhall be upon, or belonging to, or in any wiſe eſteemed, deemed, reputed, or taken to be upon or belonging to any of the premiſes: AND ALL and ſingular the Negro ſlaves, and other ſlaves, of every age, ſex, or capacity, ſort and kind belonging unto, or to belong unto, or be the property of the ſaid F—— P—— and E—— his wife, or either of them, or their or either of their heirs, executors, or adminiſtrators (how many ſoever they are, or ſhall be in number) which now do or are, or at any time or times hereafter ſhall belong or be appertaining unto, or be wrought, worked, uſed, or any way employed in, upon, about, or for the ſaid plantations, lands, tenements, houſes, or any of the premiſes aforeſaid, or any part of the ſame, or which are or ſhall be in any wiſe eſteemed, deemed, reputed, or taken to be belong or appertain unto, or to be wrought, worked, uſed, or in any way employed in, upon, about, or for the ſaid plantations, lands, tenements, houſes, or any of the premiſes aforeſaid, or any part or parts of the ſame: AND ALL iſſues, progenies, and increaſe of the ſaid ſlaves: AND ALL and ſingular other the appurtenances to any of the ſaid premiſes: AND the reverſion and reverſions, remainder and remainders yearly, and other rents, iſſues, proceeds, produce, and increaſe of all and ſingular the premiſes, and of every part and parcel thereof, with their

and

and every of their rights, members, incidents, and appurtenances: AND ALL the eſtate, right, title, intereſt, term and terms for years, inheritance, property, power, uſe, truſt, equity, and benefit of redemption, dower, right, and title of dower, and other claims and demands whatſoever of the ſaid F—— P—— and E—— his wife, and of each of them, and of their, each and every of their iſſue, and of their, each and every of their heirs, executors, adminiſtrators, and truſtees, whether at law or in equity, or otherwiſe howſoever, of, in, and to all and ſingular, or any the premiſes herein beforementioned, or any part or parts of the ſame. AND ALL AND EVERY the contracts, grants, confirmations, patents, plans, ſurveys, conveyances, deeds, ſettlements, wills, ſales, bills of ſale, mortgages, counterparts of mortgages, bonds, judgments, executions, levies, devices, aſſignments, copies of records, title deeds, and other writings, inſtruments, liſts of negroes, and evidences whatſoever, relating to the premiſes, or to any part or parts of the ſame, which the ſaid F—— P—— and E—— his wife, or either of them, or their or either of their heirs, executors, adminiſtrators, truſtees, attornies, managers, overſeers, or other agents, or any of them now have or hath, or at any time or times hereafter ſhall or may have in their or in any of their hands, poſſeſſion, cuſtody, or power, or which, he, ſhe, they, every or any of them, ſhall or may have at any time or times hereafter be able to have or come by in any way or manner, without ſuit at law or in equity for the ſame. TO HAVE AND TO HOLD ſo much, and ſo many and ſuch parts of all and ſingular the hereditaments and premiſes herein before granted, bargained, ſold, or re-

leaſed,

leafed, or meant, mentioned, or intended fo to be, as are or fhall be of the nature of real eftate or inheritance unto the faid D—— O——, his heirs and affigns from henceforth for ever, to the only proper ufe and behoof of the faid D—— O——, his heirs and affigns from henceforth for evermore, and to or for no other ufe, truft, intent, or purpofe whatfoever. AND TO HAVE AND TO HOLD fo much and fo many, and fuch parts of all and fingular the premifes herein before granted, bargained, fold, or affigned, or meant, mentioned, or intended fo to be, as are or fhall be of the nature of perfonal eftate unto the faid D—— O——, his executors, adminiftrators, and affigns, from henceforth for ever; and for and during all fuch other or leffer terms, eftates, and interefts, as the faid F—— P—— and E—— his wife have, or either of them hath therein feverally and refpectively; TO AND FOR the only proper benefit of the faid D—— O——, his executors, adminiftrators, and affigns, and as his and their own proper goods, chattels, and effects, and to and for no other truft, intent, or purpofe whatfoever; and all and fingular the fugar work plantations, other plantations, cane lands, mountain lands, other lands, hereditaments, manfion-houfes, dwelling-houfes, meffuages, tenements, ftill-houfes, works, edifices, erections, buildings, ftills, coppers, worms, tubs, coolers, utenfils, implements, horfes, affes, mules, bulls, fheep, hogs, goats, cattle, beafts, live ftock, dead ftock, Negro flaves, other flaves, iffues, progenies, increafe, reverfions, remainders yearly, and other rents, iffues, profits, proceeds, produce, rights, members, incidents, and other the premifes herein before granted, bargained, fold, aliened, remifed, releafed, affigned,

or

or confirmed, or meant, mentioned, or intended ſo to be, with their and every of their appurtenances unto the ſaid D—— O——, his heirs and aſſigns, and unto the ſaid D—— O——, his executors, adminiſtrators, and aſſigns, ſeverally and reſpectively, according to the ſeveral natures of the premiſes reſpectively, the ſaid F—— P——, his heirs, executors, and adminiſtrators, doth and hereby do warrant, and for ever defend; and by theſe preſents ſhall and will for ever warrant and defend againſt the ſaid F—— P——, his heirs, executors, adminiſtrators, and aſſigns, and againſt the ſaid E——, the wife of the ſaid F—— P——, and againſt all manner of perſon and perſons whatſoever, ſave only as againſt the ſaid A— B—— and J—— B——, and their heirs, executors, adminiſtrators, and aſſigns, in reſpect only of the ſaid debt or ſum of three thouſand five hundred and eighty pounds, ſix ſhillings, and eight pence; and in reſpect of the mortgage or ſecurity, which was made in Saint Chriſtopher's for that debt only, upon the premiſes herein before bargained or ſold, or meant, mentioned, or intended ſo to be, or upon ſome part or parts of the ſame; and the ſaid F—— P—— for himſelf, his heirs, executors, and adminiſtrators, and for each and every of them, doth covenant, promiſe, grant, and agree to and with the ſaid D—— O——, his heirs, executors, adminiſtrators, and aſſigns, and to and with each and every of them, by theſe preſents, in manner and form following: That is to ſay, that they the ſaid F—— P—— and E—— his wife now, at the time of the ſealing and delivery of theſe preſents, are and ſtand, or one of them is and ſtandeth lawfully and abſolutely ſeized in their or in his demeſne as of fee-ſimple, and in full and

abſolute

abſolute property of and in all and ſingular the ſaid ſugar work plantations, other plantations, cane lands, mountain lands, other lands, hereditaments, meſſuages, tenements, buildings, utenſils, implements, cattle, beaſts, live ſtock, dead ſtock, Negro ſlaves, other ſlaves, and all and ſingular other the premiſes herein before granted, bargained, or ſold, or meant, mentioned, or intended ſo to be, and of every part and parcel of the ſame, with their and every of their rights, members, incidents, and appurtenances, of a good, ſure, clear, perfect, abſolute, and indefeaſible eſtate of inheritance in fee-ſimple, and of the whole, full, and abſolute power, intereſt, and property in the ſame, without any condition, forfeiture, limitation of uſe or uſes, truſt, or other reſtraint, matter, cauſe, or thing whatſoever, to forfeit, determine, alter, change, charge, burthen, incumber, evict, or defeat the ſame, in any manner or wiſe. And that the ſaid F—— P—— and E—— his wife, now have, or one of them hath in themſelves, or in himſelf or herſelf, good right, true title, full power, and lawful and abſolute authority to grant, bargain, ſell, alien, remiſe, releaſe, aſſign, and confirm all and ſingular the hereditaments, and other the premiſes herein before granted, bargained, ſold, aliened, remiſed, releaſed, aſſigned, or confirmed, or meant, mentioned, or intended ſo to be, and every part and parcel of the ſame, with their and every of their appurtenances, unto and to the uſe of the ſaid D—— O——, his heirs and aſſigns, and unto the ſaid D—— O——, his executors, adminiſtrators, and aſſigns (according to the ſeveral natures of the reſpective parts of the premiſes), from time to time, and at all times hereafter to enter into, have, hold, and enjoy all and ſingular the

the ſaid hereditaments, and other the premiſes herein before granted, bargained, or ſold, or meant, mentioned, or intended ſo to be, and every part and parcel of the ſame, with their and every of their appurtenances, and the yearly and other rents, iſſues, profits, proceeds, produce, and increaſe of the ſame, to have, receive, take, and enjoy to his and their own uſe and benefit, from henceforth for evermore, without any the lawful let, ſuit, trouble, denial, hindrance, eviction, moleſtation, interruption of or by the ſaid F—— P—— and E—— his wife, or either of them, or of or by their or any of their iſſue, heirs, executors, adminiſtrators, aſſigns, truſtees, or agents, or of or by any other perſon or perſons whatſoever lawfully claiming, or to claim, by, from, under, in truſt for, or to the uſe of every and any other perſon whatſoever. AND THAT free and clear, and freely and clearly, and abſolutely freed, acquitted, exonerated, releaſed, and diſcharged, or otherwiſe upon requeſt at all times well and ſufficiently ſaved and kept harmleſs, and indemnified by the ſaid F—— P——, his heirs, executors, and adminiſtrators, or by ſome or one of them, of, from, and againſt all and all manner of former and other titles, gifts, grants, forfeitures, conditions, bargains, ſales, mortgages, aſſignments, wills, ſettlements, uſes, truſts, debts, decrees, judgments, executions, dower, right, and title of dower, charges, burthens, claims, demands, and incumbrances whatſoever, at any time or times heretofore created, incurred, charged, or ſettled, or ſecured, had, made, done, or committed, or at any time or times hereafter to be created, incurred, charged, or ſettled, or to be ſecured, had, made, done, or committed by any perſon or perſons whatſoever, of the ſame premiſes, or of any

any part or parcel thereof, in any manner or wise. And that the said F— P—— and E—— his wife, and each of them, and their and either of their heirs, executors, administrators, and assigns, and all and every person and persons whatever, any estate, right, title, trust, interest, or demand, lawfully having or claiming, or which he, she, or they shall or may at any time hereafter lawfully have or claim to have, of, in, to, upon, or out of all and every the hereditaments and premises herein before granted, bargained, or sold, or meant, mentioned, or intended so to be, or any part or parts of the same, or their or any of their appurtenances (save only the said A—— B—— and J—— B——, and their several and respective heirs, executors, administrators, assigns, trustees, attornies, and agents, for and in respect of such mortgage or security, as has been made to them, or some or one of them, in the said Island of Saint Christopher, of the said hereditaments and premises, or of some part or parts thereof, for securing the principal sum of three thousand five hundred and eighty pounds six shillings and eightpence only, and no more, with interest for the same) shall and will from time to time, and at all times hereafter, upon the request of the said D— O——, his heirs, executors, administrators, or assigns, or any of them, but at the proper costs and charges of the said F—— P——, his heirs, executors, and administrators, or of some or one of them, make, do, execute, acknowledge, and perfect, or cause or procure to be made, done, executed, acknowledged, and perfected, all and every such farther lawful and reasonable act and acts, deed and deeds, instruments, devices, conveyances, assignments, and assurances in the law whatsoever, for the further better

better and more ſure and abſolute aſſigning, conveying, aſſuring, and ſure making of all and ſingular the hereditaments and premiſes herein before granted, bargained, or ſold, or meant, mentioned, or intended ſo to be, or of any part or parts thereof, with their and every of their appurtenances, unto and to the uſe of the ſaid D—— O——, his heirs and aſſigns, and unto the ſaid D—— O——, his executors, adminiſtrators, and aſſigns (ſeverally and reſpectively, according to the ſeveral natures of the reſpective parts of the premiſes ſo to be further aſſigned, conveyed, or aſſured) in ſuch way and manner, and by ſuch ſort of deeds, inſtruments, aſſignments, aſſurances, conveyances, and other acts and matters, and attended with ſuch acknowledgments and private examinations of the parties to the ſame, and with ſuch other circumſtances and ſolemnities, as by the ſaid D—— O——, his heirs, executors, adminiſtrators, or aſſigns, or any of them, or his, their, or any of their Counſel learned in the law, ſhall be lawfully and reaſonably adviſed, or deviſed and required, ſo as ſuch further aſſignments or aſſurances contain no further or other greater warranty or covenant, than againſt the parties making and executing the ſame, and his and their anceſtors, and his or their acts and deeds, and ſo as for the making or doing thereof, no perſon ſhall be compelled or compellable to travel more than twenty miles from the place of their then preſent abode or reſidence. AND FURTHER, That the ſaid F—— P—— and E—— his wife, ſhall within three days next enſuing, the day of the date of theſe preſents, in due form of law, acknowledge their reſpective execution of this preſent indenture, and alſo of a duplicate of the ſame, before ſome of the Juſtices of his Majeſty's Court

Court of Common Pleas at Weftminfter: AND that, on fuch occafion, the faid E— fhall be privately and apart from the faid F— P—, examined before fuch Judge, and will thereon declare, that fhe executed the fame, and makes fuch acknowledgment thereof, of her own pure and free will and voluntary confent, and without any force, compulfion, menace, threat, dread, or fear of her faid hufband, in any fort or on his part ufed: AND that the faid F— P— will, within fuch three days, alfo acknowledge thefe prefents, and a duplicate thereof, and his execution of the fame, before one of the Mafters of the High Court of Chancery of Great Britain, and will confent and defire that thefe prefents, and fuch duplicate, may be enrolled at full length in the faid Court; AND will procure thefe prefents, and fuch duplicate, to be enrolled at full length, in the faid Court of Chancery, within ten days next enfuing the day of the date of thefe prefents; and alfo fhall and will forthwith hereafter caufe and procure thefe prefents, and fuch duplicate, and the execution of the fame, to be duly proved on oath before the Lord Mayor of the city of London; and fuch proof thereof, and a teftimonial or certificate of the fame to be in the ufual and proper manner annexed to thefe prefents, and to fuch duplicate, under the Seal of the faid city of London; AND forthwith hereafter will caufe thefe prefents, and the duplicate thereof, and the execution of both the fame by the faid F—— P—— and E—— his wife, to be duly acknowledged in the faid Ifland of St. Chriftopher, by fome perfon or perfons to be lawfully impowered to do the fame, before all proper perfons and officers there; and afterwards to be forthwith duly enrolled and recorded, at full

full length, in the proper offices and places in the ſaid Iſland, in order to give the utmoſt force and validity to the ſame; AND that all the ſame matters and things ſhall be done at the coſts and expences of the ſaid F—— P——, his heirs, executors, or adminiſtrators; and in the beſt manner, and with as much expedition as the ſame may reaſonably be done: AND MOREOVER the ſaid F— P— doth hereby deſire and direct all and every his preſent and future attornies, counſel, managers, overſeers, and agents, in the ſaid Iſland, immediately upon demand thereof, to deliver up, from time to time, unto the ſaid D—— O——, or his heirs, executors, and adminiſtrators, or unto his or their attornies or attorney, by liſt or ſchedule, all ſuch of the grants, deeds, copies of records, liſts of Negroes, and other writings whatſoever, relating to the premiſes, or any part of the ſame, which the ſaid F—— P—— hath herein before mentioned to bargain, ſell, or aſſign unto the ſaid D—— O——, whole, fair, and uncancelled; or ſo much and ſo many of the ſame, as ſhall be in their or any of their hands, poſſeſſion, cuſtody, or power, or which they, or any of them, may or can any way come by, without ſuit in law or equity. AND the ſaid F— P— doth hereby, for himſelf and for his heirs, executors, and adminiſtrators, and for each and every of them, covenant, promiſe, grant, and agree to, and with the ſaid D—— O——, his heirs, executors, and adminiſtrators, and to and with each and every of them, that all ſuch grants, deeds, copies of records, liſts of Negroes, and other evidences, as are herein before mentioned, to be hereby bargained, ſold, or aſſigned, ſhall from time to time be delivered, whole, fair, and uncancelled,

cancelled, unto the ſaid D—— O——, or his heirs, executors, adminiſtrators, or his or their attornies or attorney in the ſaid Iſland, purſuant to the true intent and meaning of theſe preſents: AND MOREOVER, that the ſaid F—— P——, his heirs and aſſigns, ſo long as he or they ſhall be in the poſſeſſion of the ſaid Plantations, or any of them; or if he or they ſhall not be in the ſaid Iſland, then his or their attornies or attorney, or managers or manager, in the ſaid Iſland, ſhall, once in every year, upon demand, and if demanded deliver, from time to time, unto the ſaid D—— O——, his heirs, executors, and adminiſtrators, or his or their attornies or attorney in the ſaid Iſland, a true liſt, ſigned by or in behalf of the ſaid F—— P——, his heirs and aſſigns, of all the Negroes and ſlaves which, from time to time, ſhall be upon, or belong to, all and every the ſaid plantations, and other the premiſſes, for the better information of the ſaid D—— O——, his heirs, executors, and adminiſtrators, in the premiſes: PROVIDED ALWAYS, and theſe preſents are upon this condition nevertheleſs, which is hereby agreed upon by and between the ſaid parties to theſe preſents, That, if the ſaid F—— P——, his heirs, executors, adminiſtrators, or ſome or one of them, do and ſhall well and truly pay, or cauſe to be paid unto the ſaid D—— O——, his executors or adminiſtrators, at or in the dwelling-houſe of the ſaid D—— O——, ſituate in Great James Street aforeſaid, the full ſum of two thouſand and fifteen pounds thirteen ſhillings, of lawful money of Great Britain, in manner and form following: that is to ſay, the ſum of forty-ſeven pounds, nineteen ſhillings, and ten-pence, part thereof on the fifteenth day of May next enſuing the

the day of the date of theſe preſents; and the ſum of one thouſand nine hundred and ſixty-ſeven pounds, thirteen ſhillings, and two-pence, reſidue and in full payment thereof, on the fifteenth day of November then next enſuing, and which will be in the year of our Lord, one thouſand ſeven hundred and fifty-one, without any delay, deduction or abatement, for or in reſpect of any charges, taxes, or aſſeſſments charged, taxed, or impoſed, or to be taxed, charged, or impoſed, by any Act or Acts of Parliament, or by any Act or Acts of Aſſembly, or for or in reſpect of any other matter, cauſe, or thing whatſoever; then theſe preſents, and the bargain, ſale, conveyance, and aſſignment, and every other matter and thing herein contained, ſhall ceaſe, determine, and be null and void, to all intents and purpoſes, as if the ſame had never been made or executed; theſe preſents, or any thing herein contained, in any wiſe to the contrary thereof notwithſtanding. And the ſaid F— P—, for himſelf, his heirs, executors, and adminiſtrators, and for each and every of them, doth covenant, promiſe, grant, and agree to, and with the ſaid D—— O——, his executors, adminiſtrators, and aſſigns, in manner following: that is to ſay, that he the ſaid F— P—, his heirs, executors, or adminiſtrators, ſhall and will, at or in the place herein before mentioned and appointed for ſuch payment, well and truly pay, or cauſe to be paid, unto the ſaid D—— O——, his executors, adminiſtrators, or aſſigns, the ſaid full ſum of two thouſand and fifteen pounds, thirteen ſhillings, of lawful money of Great Britain; and every part thereof, in the manner, and at the days and times in the foregoing proviſo mentioned or appointed for payment of the ſame; and

and without any delay, deduction, or abatement, for or in respect of any charges, taxes, or assessments, charged, taxed, or imposed, or to be charged, taxed, or imposed, by any Act or Acts of Parliament, or by any Act or Acts of Assembly, or for or in respect of any other matter, cause, or thing whatsoever, in full performance of the foregoing proviso or condition, and according to the true intent and meaning of these presents. AND IT IS agreed by and between the said parties to these presents, that, until some breach or default shall happen to be made in performance of the proviso or condition herein before contained, either in the whole or in a part thereof, it shall and may be lawful to and for the said F— P—, his heirs and assigns, to hold and enjoy the hereditaments and premises herein before conveyed and assigned, and every part thereof, and to receive and take the rents, issues, and profits of the same, to his and their own use and benefit, without rendering any account, or payment of or for the same, or any part thereof, unto the said D— O—, his heirs, executors, or administrators, or any of them, in any manner or wise; these presents, or any thing herein before contained, to the contrary thereof in any wise notwithstanding. AND LASTLY, the said F—— P—— and E—— his wife, and D—— O——, have, and each and every of them hath, authorized and impowered, and by these presents DO, and each and every one of them DOTH, fully authorize and impower R— P—, W— B—, J— L—, and R— P—, of the said Island of St. Christopher, Esquires, or any three or two of them jointly, and each one of them singly and separately, to appear before all proper officers and persons whatsoever, in the said Island of St. Christopher;

Chriſtopher; and to acknowledge the ſeveral and reſpective ſigning, ſealing, and delivery, by each one of them the ſaid F— P— and E— his wife, and D— O—, of theſe preſents, and their ſeveral and reſpective hands and ſeals ſet thereto; and to conſent and procure that theſe preſents be duly enrolled, regiſtered, and recorded, in all proper offices and places within the ſaid Iſland of St. Chriſtopher, according to the laws, cuſtoms, uſages, and practice, in force and obſerved in the ſaid Iſland, in order to give the utmoſt ſtrength, force, and validity hereto. In witneſs whereof the parties before named to theſe preſents their hands and ſeals have hereunto ſet, the day and year firſt above written.

F— P—. (L. S.)
the Mark of
E— + P—. (L. S.)
D— O—. (L. S.)

Signed, ſealed, and delivered by the within named F— P— and E— his wife, and D— O—, parties to the within written Indenture, in the preſence of us, the ſaid E— P— ſigning the ſame, by making her Mark on each ſide of the ſecond or middle Seal within affixed.

F— J— P—.
F— E—.

Received

RECEIVED the day and year firſt within written, of and from the within named D—— O——, the full ſum of one thouſand nine hundred and nineteen pounds, thirteen ſhillings, and four pence, of lawful money of Great Britain, being the conſideration-money within mentioned, to be by him to us paid; we ſay received by us,	*L. s. d.* 1919 13 4

F—— P——.
The Marks of
E—— +— +— P——.

WITNESSES to the payment of the ſum of one thouſand nine hundred and nineteen pounds, thirteen ſhillings, and four pence, to the within named F—— P——, and E—— his wife, or one of them, and to their ſigning this receipt for the ſame, the ſaid E—— ſigning by two marks or croſſes, inſtead of her names.

F— J — P—.
F — E——.

BE IT REMEMBERED, That on the 14th day of November, one thouſand ſeven hundred and fifty, before me Sir Thomas Birch, Knight, one of the Juſtices of his Majeſty's Court of Common Pleas at Weſtminſter, perſonally appeared F—— P——, Eſq; and E—— his wife, parties within named to the within written Indenture, and did, in purſuance of a certain Act of Aſſembly of his Majeſty's Leeward Charibbee Iſlands in America, ſeverally acknowledge, that each one of them, ſeverally and reſpectively, did ſign,

ſign, or mark and ſeal, and as his and her ſeveral act and deed deliver the ſaid within written Indenture, and that the ſeveral and reſpective names or marks, and ſeals of the ſaid F—— P—— and E—— his wife, ſet at the foot of the ſame within written Indenture, in ſuch manner as they now ſeverally and reſpectively appear thereto, was, were, and is, and are of their ſeveral and reſpective proper hand writing and ſealing: And moreover, the ſaid E—— being by me privately examined, ſeparate and apart from her ſaid huſband, did declare, That ſhe executed the ſaid Indenture, and made the before mentioned acknowledgment of the ſame of her own free will and voluntary conſent, without any force, compulſion, threat, or menace, uſed by her ſaid huſband in any ſort. All which I do hereby certify, purſuant to the above mentioned Act of Aſſembly: Witneſs my hand hereunto ſet the day and year laſt above mentioned.

THOMAS BIRCH.

INROLLED in his Majeſty's High Court of Chancery another part of this Indenture, the fifteenth day of November, in the year within written, being firſt duly ſtamped, according to the tenor of the ſtatute, made in the ſixth year of the reign of their late Majeſty's King William and Queen Mary.

By GEORGE ECKERSALL.

* I DO hereby certify, That the within Inſtrument of Writing, and annexed Atteſtation and Bond (No. 4567) were entered in the Regiſter's

* This Certificate of the Regiſter ought to have come in after the Atteſtation and Bond, p. 534.

Office

Office in St. Christopher's, on Thursday the second day of May, in the year of our Lord one thousand seven hundred and fifty-one, about five of the clock in the afternoon of the same day, in pages 191, &c.——Libri Q.

WIL. BUCKLEY, Reg.

TO all to whom these presents shall come, I Francis Cokayne, Esq; Lord Mayor of the City of London, in pursuance of an Act of Parliament made and passed in the fifth year of the reign of our Sovereign Lord King George the Second, intituled, An Act for the more easy recovery of debts in his Majesty's Plantations and Colonies in America, do hereby certify, That on the day of the date hereof, personally came and appeared before me F—— E—— of Child's Court in the Strand, in the parish of St. Martin in the Fields, in the County of Middlesex, in the Kingdom of Great Britain, Gentleman, being a person well known and worthy of good credit; and did by solemn oath, which he took upon the Holy Evangelists of Almighty God, solemnly declare, testify, and depose to be true, the several matters and things contained in the Affidavit hereunto annexed.

LORD MAYOR'S SEAL.

In faith and testimony whereof, I the said Lord Mayor have caused the seal of the Office of Mayoralty of the said City of London to be hereunto put and affixed, and the parchment Indenture and Bond mentioned in the said Affidavit to be also hereunto annexed, dated in London the nineteenth day of November, in the twenty-

twenty-fourth year of the reign of our Sovereign Lord George the Second, by the Grace of God King of Great Britain, France, and Ireland, Defender of the Faith, and in the year of our Lord one thousand seven hundred and fifty.

MAN.

F—— E—— of Child's Court in the Strand, in the parish of St. Martin in the Fields, in the County of Middlesex, in the Kingdom of Great Britain, Gentleman, maketh oath, That he was personally present as a witness, and did see and hear F—— P——, and E—— P—— his wife, and D—— O——, parties to the parchment-writing or Indenture hereunto annexed, severally and respectively sign, or mark and deliver the said Parchment-writing or Indenture hereunto annexed: AND THAT the name F— P—, set and subscribed to the same Parchment-writing or Indenture, at the foot or end thereof, at the first seal there affixed, as the name of one of the parties executing the same, in such manner as the same now appears thereto, was, and is of the proper hand-writing of the said F— P—: AND THAT the two marks or crosses appearing set and subscribed to the same Parchment-writing, at the second seal at the foot or end thereof, as the marks of the said E——, one of the parties executing the same Indenture, in such manner as the same now appears thereto, was and were, and is and are of the proper marking or signing of the said E— P—: AND THAT the name D— O——, also set and subscribed to the same Parchment-writing or Indenture, at the foot or end thereof, at the third and last seal there, as the name of the other

other of the parties executing the ſame, in ſuch manner as the ſame now appears thereto, was and is the proper hand-writing of the ſaid D—— O——: AND THAT the name F— E——, ſet and ſubſcribed to the Atteſtation written on the backſide of the ſame Parchment Indenture, as the name of one of the two witneſſes atteſting the ſigning, ſealing, and delivery thereof, by the ſaid F—— P—— and E——— his wife, and D—— O——, in ſuch manner as the ſame now appears thereto, was and is of the proper hand-writing of this Deponent: AND THAT the name F— J—— P———, alſo ſet and ſubſcribed to the ſame atteſtation, as the name of the other of the two witneſſes atteſting the execution of the ſame Indenture, in ſuch manner as the ſame now appears thereto, was and is of the proper hand-writing of F— J— P——, of Surry Street in the Strand, in the pariſh of St. Clement Danes, in the ſaid County of Middleſex, Gentleman, and was by him ſo thereunto ſet and ſubſcribed, in the preſence of this Deponent: AND this Deponent was alſo preſent, and did ſee the ſaid F— P—— ſign his name, and the ſaid E—— ſet or ſign her marks and croſſes to the receipt indorſed or written on the backſide of the ſame Parchment Indenture: AND THAT the name F— P——, ſet and ſubſcribed to the ſame receipt, in ſuch manner as the ſame now appears thereto, was and is of the proper hand-writing of the ſaid F— P—: AND THAT the two marks or croſſes appearing ſet and ſubſcribed to the ſame atteſtation, as the marks or croſſes of the ſaid E—— P———, in ſuch manner as the ſame now appears thereto, was and were, and is and are of the proper marking or ſigning of the ſaid E— P———: AND THAT the name F— E——, ſet and ſubſcribed to the ſame atteſtation, as the name of one

of

of the two witneſſes to the payment of the conſideration-money, and to the ſigning or marking the ſaid receipt, by the ſaid F—— P—— and E—— his wife, reſpectively, in ſuch manner as the ſame now appears thereto, was and is of the proper hand-writing of this Deponent: AND THAT the name F— J—— P——, ſet and ſubſcribed to the ſame receipt, as the name of the other of the two witneſſes to the ſame, in ſuch manner as the ſame now appears thereto, was and is of the proper hand-writing of the herein before-named F—— J—— P——, and was by him ſo thereunto alſo ſet and ſubſcribed, in the preſence of this Deponent: AND FURTHER, this Deponent ſaith, That he was alſo perſonally preſent as a witneſs, and did ſee and hear the ſaid F— P—— ſign, ſeal, and as his act and deed deliver the Paper-writing or Bond alſo hereunto annexed: AND THAT the name F—— E——, ſet and ſubſcribed to the atteſtation written at the end of the ſame condition, as the name of one of the two witneſſes atteſting the ſigning, ſealing, and delivery of the ſame Paper-writing or Bond, in ſuch manner as the ſame now appears thereto, was and is of the proper hand-writing of this Deponent: AND THAT the name F— J— P——, alſo ſet and ſubſcribed at the foot or end of the ſame condition, as the name of the other of the two witneſſes atteſting the execution of the ſame, in ſuch manner as the ſame now appears thereto, was and is of the proper hand-writing of the before named F— J— P—, and was by him ſo thereunto ſet and ſubſcribed, in the preſence of this Deponent,

Sworn the 19th day of November 1750, before me, in London, F—— E——.

F. COKAYNE, Mayor.

KNOW

KNOW ALL MEN by these presents, That I F—— P ——, late of his Majesty's Island of St. Christopher in America, but at present resident in the City of London, Esq; am held and firmly bound unto D—— O———, of Great James Street, in the parish of St. Andrew, Holborn, in the County of Middlesex, Esq; in the full sum of three thousand eight hundred thirty and nine pounds six shillings and eight pence, of good and lawful money of Great Britain, to be paid unto the said D— O—, his executors, administrators, or assigns, or his or their certain Attorney or Attorneys, to the which payment, well and truly to be made, I hereby bind and oblige myself, my heirs, executors, and administrators, and each and every of them firmly, by these presents, SEALED with my Seal, and dated this fourteenth day of November, in the twenty-fourth year of the reign of our Sovereign Lord George the Second, by the Grace of God of Great Britain, France, and Ireland King, Defender of the Faith, and so forth, and in the year of our Lord one thousand seven hundred and fifty.

THE condition of the above written obligation is such, That if the above bounden F—— P——, his heirs, executors, or administrators, or some or one of them, do and shall well and truly pay, or cause to be paid, unto the said D—— O——, his executors or administrators, at or in the dwelling-house of the said D—— O——, situate in Great James-street above mentioned, the full sum of two thousand and fifteen pounds

pounds and thirteen ſhillings of lawful money of Great Britain, in manner and form following: that is to ſay, the ſum of forty-ſeven pounds nineteen ſhillings and ten pence, part thereof, on the fifteenth day of May next enſuing the day of the date of the above written obligation, and the ſum of one thouſand nine hundred ſixty and ſeven pounds thirteen ſhillings and two-pence, reſidue and in full payment thereof, on the fifteenth day of November then next enſuing, and which will be in the year of our Lord one thouſand ſeven hundred fifty and one, without any delay, deduction or abatement for or in reſpect of any charges, taxes or aſſeſſments charged, taxed or impoſed, or to be taxed, charged or impoſed by any Act or Acts of Parliament, or by any Act or Acts of Aſſembly, or for or in reſpect of any other matter, cauſe or thing whatſoever. AND ALSO do and ſhall well and truly pay, perform, fulfil, obſerve and keep all and ſingular other the payments, covenants, conditions, proviſoes and agreements which, in a certain Indenture bearing even date with the before written obligation, and made or mentioned to be made between the ſaid F—— P—— (by the deſcription before mentioned) and E—— his wife of the one part, and the ſaid D—— O—— (by the deſcription alſo before mentioned) of the other part, are contained, and which on the part and behalf of the ſaid F—— P——, his heirs, executors or adminiſtrators, or of any of them, are or ought to be paid, performed, done, fulfilled, obſerved or kept. AND THAT AND THOSE in and by all things, and in every reſpect according to the purport and true intent and meaning of the ſaid Indentures, and of the covenants, conditions, proviſoes and agreements

ments therein contained; then the before written obligation to be void and of none effect, otherwise to stand and remain in full force and virtue.

F—— P—— (L. S.)

Signed, sealed and delivered by the before named F— P—, Esq; in the presence of us,

F—— J—— P——.
F—— E——.

MORTGAGE *in Fee (by Lease and Release) by Husband and Wife, of Lands and Negroes in Jamaica: The Conveyance being executed in London; the private Examination of the Wife to bar Dower, was taken before the Lord Mayor there, agreeable to the Laws of Jamaica.*

The LEASE *for a* YEAR.

THIS Indenture, made the thirteenth day of November, in the seventeenth year of the reign of our Sovereign Lord George the Third, by the Grace of God, of Great Britain, France and Ireland, King, Defender of the Faith, &c. and in the year of our Lord, one thousand seven hundred and seventy-six, between J—— N—— of the parish of T——— in the Island of Jamaica, Esq; but now in London, of the one part, and J—— M—— and T—— S—— of the City of London, merchants, of the other part, witnesseth, That the said J—— N——, for and in consideration of the sum of five shillings of lawful money of Great Britain to him in hand well and truly paid by the said J—— M—— and T—— S——, at or before the sealing and delivery of these presents, the receipt whereof is hereby acknowledged, he the said J—— N—— hath bargained and sold, and by these presents doth bargain and sell

ſell unto the ſaid J—— M—— and T—— S——, their executors, adminiſtrators and aſſigns, all that Plantation and Sugar Work, commonly called and known by the name of R——, ſituate, lying, or being at or near M——, in the ſaid pariſh of T—— in the Iſland of Jamaica, containing by eſtimation five hundred acres, be the ſame more or leſs, butting and bounding eaſterly on W—— Plantation, belonging to the heirs of J—— D——, deceaſed, weſterly on the heirs of J—— L——, deceaſed, northerly on P—— Plantation, belonging to J—— C——, and ſoutherly on S—— Plantation, belonging to the heirs of B—— B——, deceaſed, and all meſſuages, mills, mill-houſes, boiling-houſes, curing-houſes, ſtill-houſes, and all other houſes, out-houſes, edifices, erections and buildings on the ſaid Plantation and lands, or any part thereof, erected or built, and all ways, paths, paſſages, waters, water-courſes, woods, underwoods, commons, and common of paſture, feedings, fiſhings, fiſhing places, eaſements, privileges, profits, commodities, emoluments, advantages, hereditaments and appurtenances whatſoever to the ſaid Plantation and lands, or any part thereof, belonging or in any wiſe appertaining, or therewith or to, or with any part or parcel thereof uſually held, occupied, poſſeſſed or enjoyed or accepted, reputed, deemed, taken, or known as part, parcel or member thereof, or of any part thereof. AND alſo all and every the Negro and other Slaves now upon and belonging to the ſaid Plantation, and particularly mentioned and ſet down in the ſchedule hereunder written (being in number ninety-eight) and the reverſion and reverſions, remainder and remainders, rents, iſſues and profits of the ſaid Plantation and Sugar Work, lands, tenements,

ments, Slaves, and hereditaments, and of every part and parcel thereof. TO HAVE AND TO HOLD the ſaid Plantation and Sugar Work, lands, tenements, Slaves, hereditaments, and all other the premiſes mentioned or intended to be hereby bargained and ſold, with their and every of their iſſue, increaſe, rights, members and appurtenances unto the ſaid J—— M—— and T—— S——, their executors, adminiſtrators and aſſigns, from the day next before the day of the date of theſe preſents, for and during and unto the full end and term of one whole year, from thence next enſuing, and fully to be complete and ended, yielding and paying therefore at the end of the ſaid term the rent of one pepper-corn, if the ſame ſhall be lawfully demanded. TO THE INTENT, That by virtue of theſe preſents, and of the Statute for transferring uſes into poſſeſſion, they the ſaid J—— M—— and T—— S—— may be in the actual poſſeſſion of the ſaid Plantation, Sugar Work, lands, tenements, Slaves, hereditaments, and all and ſingular other the premiſes mentioned or intended to be hereby bargained and ſold, with their and every of their iſſue and increaſe, rights, members and appurtenances, and thereby be enabled to accept and take a grant and releaſe of the reverſion and inheritance thereof to them, their heirs and aſſigns, in ſuch ſort, manner and form as ſhall be declared in an Indenture of releaſe intended to bear date the day next after the day of the date hereof, and made or mentioned to be made between the ſame parties as are parties to theſe preſents. In witneſs whereof the ſaid parties to theſe preſents have hereunto ſet their hands and ſeals the day and year firſt above written.

The

The ſchedule to which the above Indenture refers: Men, 1. Antigua, Eſſex, Quamin (and fifty-five more named in the ſchedule under the deed). Boys, Little Thomas (and three more named in the ſchedule under the deed). Women, Nancy, Senia (and twenty-four more named in the ſchedule under the deed).

J—— N—— (L. S.)

Sealed and delivered (being firſt duly ſtampt) in the preſence of

R— C— L—.
J— B—.

The RELEASE.

THIS INDENTURE made the fourteenth day of November, in the ſeventeenth year of the reign of our Sovereign Lord George the Third, by the Grace of God of Great Britain, France and Ireland King, Defender of the Faith, &c. and in the year of our Lord one thouſand ſeven hundred and ſeventy-ſix, between J—— N—— of the pariſh of T———, in the Iſland of Jamaica, Eſq; but now in London, and A——— his wife, of the one part, and J —— M—— and T—— S—— of the City of London, merchants, of the other part, witneſſeth, That for and in conſideration of the ſum of four thouſand pounds of good and lawful money of Great Britain, to the ſaid J—— N—— in hand well and truly paid by the ſaid J—— M—— and T—— S——, at or before the ſealing and delivery of theſe preſents, the receipt whereof the ſaid J—— N—— doth hereby acknowledge, and thereof and of and from every part and parcel thereof, doth acquit,

quit, release and discharge the said J—— M—— and T—— S——, their executors, administrators, and every of them, for ever; by these presents, they the said J—— N—— and A—— his wife have, and each of them hath, granted, bargained, sold, aliened, released, conveyed and confirmed, and by these presents do, and each of them doth, grant, bargain, sell, aliene, release, convey and confirm unto the said J—— M—— and T—— S——, in their actual possession now being, by virtue of a bargain and sale to them thereof made by the said J—— N——, in consideration of five shillings, by Indenture bearing date the day next before the day of the date of these presents, for one whole year, commencing from the day next before the day of the date of the said Indenture of bargain and sale, and by force of the Statute made for transferring of uses into possession, and to their heirs and assigns, All that Plantation and Sugar Work commonly called and known by the name of R———, situate, lying and being at or near M———, in the said parish of T———, in the Island of Jamaica, containing by estimation five hundred acres (be the same more or less) butting and bounding easterly on W——— Plantation, belonging to the heirs of J—— D——, deceased, westerly on the heirs of J—— L——, deceased, northerly on P——— Plantation, belonging to J——— C———, and southerly on S——— Plantation, belonging to the heirs of B——— B———, deceased, and all messuages, mills, mill-houses, boiling-houses, curing-houses, still-houses, and all other houses, out-houses, edifices, erections and buildings on the said Plantation and lands, or any part thereof, erected or built, and all ways, paths, passages, waters, water-courses, woods, underwoods, common,

mon, and common of paſture, feedings, fiſhings, fiſhing-places, eaſements, privileges, profits, commodities, emoluments, advantages, hereditaments and appurtenances whatſoever to the ſaid Plantation and lands, or any part thereof belonging, or in any wiſe appertaining, or therewith or to, or with any part or parcel thereof, uſually held, occupied, poſſeſſed or enjoyed, or accepted, reputed, deemed, taken or known as part, parcel, or member thereof, or of any part thereof; and alſo all and every the Negro and other Slaves now upon, or belonging to, the ſaid Plantation, and particularly mentioned and ſet down in the ſchedule hereunder written (being in number ninety-eight) and the reverſion and reverſions, remainder and remainders, rents, iſſues and profits of the ſaid Plantation and Sugar Work, lands, tenements, Slaves and hereditaments, and of every part and parcel thereof; and alſo all and every the mules, ſteers, neat cattle, and other live ſtock upon or belonging to the ſaid Plantation, and mentioned and ſet down in the ſaid ſchedule hereunder written, and all coppers, ſtills, worms, worm-tubs, ladles, ſkimmers, drips, pots, pans, Plantation utenſils and implements of planting, upon or belonging to the ſaid Plantation, and alſo all the eſtate, right, title, intereſt, property, inheritance, claim, and demand whatſoever, both at law and in equity, of them the ſaid J—— N——, and A— his wife, of, in, and to the ſaid plantation and ſugar-work, lands, tenements, ſlaves, hereditaments, and other the premiſes herein before granted and releaſed, or intended ſo to be, and every part and parcel thereof, and all deeds, evidences, letters patent, muniments and writings touching or concerning the ſaid hereditaments and premiſes, or any part or parcel thereof, of, TO HAVE AND TO HOLD the ſaid plantation and ſugar-work, lands, tenements, ſlaves, hereditaments, mules, ſteers, neat cattle, and other live ſtock, and all other the premiſes mentioned, or intended to be hereby granted and releaſed with their and every of their iſſue and increaſe, rights, members, and appurtenances unto the ſaid J—— M—— and T—— S——, their heirs, executors, adminiſtrators and aſſigns, to the only proper uſe and behoof of the ſaid J—— M—— and T—— S——, their heirs, executors, adminiſtrators and aſſigns reſpectively for ever, according to the nature and quality of the ſame premiſes reſpectively, ſubject always nevertheleſs, to ſuch proviſo of redemption as is herein-after contained, that is to ſay, PROVIDED ALWAYS, and it is hereby declared and agreed by and between the ſaid parties hereto, and it is the true intent and meaning of theſe preſents, that if the ſaid J—— N——, his heirs, executors or adminiſtrators, or any of them, do and ſhall well and truly pay, or cauſe to be paid unto the ſaid J—— M—— and T—— S——, their executors, adminiſtrators or aſſigns, at or upon the Royal Exchange of the City of London, the ſaid ſum of four thouſand pounds of good and lawful money of Great Britain, together with intereſt thereon, at and after the rate of ſix pounds for every one hundred pounds by the year, on or before the fourteenth day of November, in the year of our Lord one thouſand ſeven hundred and ſeventy-eight, and that without any deduction, defalcation or abatement out of the ſame, or any part thereof, for or in reſpect of any taxes, charges, aſſeſſments or impoſitions whatſoever, taxed, charged, or impoſed, or to be taxed, charged or impoſed upon the ſaid plantations, ſugar-work, lands, tenements,

tenements, ſlaves, hereditaments, and premiſes, or any part thereof, or upon the ſaid J—— M—— and T—— S——, their heirs, executors, adminiſtrators or aſſigns in reſpect thereof by any power or authority whatſoever, or for and in reſpect of any other matter, cauſe, or thing whatſoever; then and in ſuch caſe, and at all times thereafter this preſent Indenture, and every matter, cauſe, and thing herein contained, ſhall ceaſe, determine, and be utterly void to all intents and purpoſes, any thing herein contained to the contrary thereof, in any wiſe notwithſtanding. AND the ſaid J—— N—— for himſelf, his heirs, executors and adminiſtrators, and for the ſaid A—— his wife, DOTH hereby covenant, promiſe, grant, and agree to and with the ſaid J—— M—— and T—— S——, their heirs, executors, adminiſtrators, and aſſigns, in manner following: that is to ſay, That he the ſaid J—— N——, his heirs, executors or adminiſtrators, or ſome or one of them, ſhall and will well and truly pay, or cauſe to be paid unto the ſaid J—— M——, and T—— S—— their executors, adminiſtrators, or aſſigns, the ſaid ſum of four thouſand pounds, together with intereſt thereon as aforeſaid, at ſuch place and time, and in manner and form as herein before appointed, for payment thereof, without any deduction, defalcation, or abatement as aforeſaid, according to the purport of the aforeſaid proviſo, and the true intent and meaning of theſe preſents. AND ALSO, That they the ſaid J—— N—— and A—— his wife, at the time of the ſealing and delivery of theſe preſents, are, or one of them is lawfully and rightfully ſeiſed of and in the ſaid plantations and ſugar-work, lands, tenements, ſlaves, and hereditaments, and other the premiſes hereby granted

granted and releaſed, or intended ſo to be with their iſſue and appurtenances, of a good, ſure, perfect, abſolute, and indefeaſible eſtate of inheritance in fee ſimple in poſſeſſion, without any manner of condition, power of revocation, limitation of uſe or uſes, or other matter, cauſe or thing whatſoever, to alter, change, charge, defeat or determine the ſame, except as herein after is mentioned. AND ALSO, That they the ſaid J—— N—— and A—— his wife, have in themſelves, or one of them hath in himſelf or herſelf, at the time of the ſealing and delivery of theſe preſents, good right, full power, and lawful and abſolute authority to grant, bargain, ſell, releaſe and confirm the ſaid plantation and ſugar-work, lands, tenements, ſlaves, hereditaments and premiſes hereby granted and releaſed, or intended ſo to be, with their iſſue and appurtenances unto the ſaid J—— M—— and T—— S——, their executors, adminiſtrators, and aſſigns, in manner aforeſaid, and according to the purport, true intent and meaning of theſe preſents; and alſo that from and after default ſhall happen of or in payment of the ſaid ſum of four thouſand pounds, or any part thereof, or of the intereſt thereof contrary to the form and effect of the aforeſaid proviſo and covenant for payment of the ſame, and the true intent and meaning of theſe preſents, it ſhall and may be lawful to and for the ſaid J— M—, and T— S—, their heirs, executors, adminiſtrators, and aſſigns, peaceably and quietly to enter into, have, hold, uſe, occupy, poſſeſs, and enjoy the ſaid plantation and ſugar-work, lands, tenements, ſlaves, hereditaments and premiſes hereby granted and releaſed, or intended ſo to be, and to receive and take the rents, iſſues, and profits thereof, and of every part and parcel

thereof

thereof to their own proper uſe and benefit, without the lawful let, ſuit, trouble, denial, eviction, moleſtation, or interruption of or by the ſaid J—— N—— and A—— his wife, or either of them, his heirs or aſſigns, or of or by any other perſon or perſons whomſoever (other than and except the perſons claiming, or to claim by, from, or under the prior incumbrance herein after mentioned), and that free and clear, and freely and clearly acquitted, exonerated and diſcharged, or otherwiſe by the ſaid J—— N——, his heirs, executors, or adminiſtrators, well and ſufficiently ſaved, defended, kept harmleſs, and indemnified of, from, and againſt all and all manner of former and other gifts, grants, bargains, ſales, leaſes, mortgages, jointures, dowers, titles of dower, uſes, truſts, wills, intails, ſtatutes, recognizances, judgments, executions, extents, rent, arrears of rent, and all other titles, charges, and incumbrances whatſoever, other than and except a certain indenture of mortgage from the ſaid J— N—, and A— his wife, to the ſaid J— M—, bearing date on or about the thirty-firſt day of December, in the year of our Lord, one thouſand ſeven hundred and ſixty-ſeven, and alſo except the quit-rents thenceforth to become due and payable to his Majeſty, his heirs and ſucceſſors, for and in reſpect of the ſaid lands hereby granted and releaſed. AND FURTHER, That they the ſaid J—N—, and A— his wife, and his heirs, and all and every other perſon and perſons, having, or lawfully claiming, or who ſhall or may have or lawfully claim, any eſtate, right, title, intereſt of, in, to, or out of the ſaid plantation and ſugar-work, lands, tenements, ſlaves, hereditaments, and premiſes, mentioned, or intended

tended to be hereby granted and releaſed, or any part thereof, by, from, or under, or in truſt for her, them, or any of them, ſhall and will, from time to time, and at all times, from and after default ſhall happen to be made of or in payment of the ſaid ſum of four thouſand pounds, or any part thereof, or of the intereſt thereof, contrary to the form and effect of the aforeſaid proviſo and covenant for payment of the ſame, and the true intent and meaning of theſe preſents, upon the reaſonable requeſt of the ſaid J— M— and T— S—, their heirs, executors, adminiſtrators, or aſſigns, and at the proper coſts and charges in the law of the ſaid J— N—, his heirs or aſſigns, make, do, acknowledge, levy, ſuffer, and execute, or cauſe or procure to be made, done, acknowledged, levied, ſuffered, and executed, all and every other lawful and reaſonable act and acts, thing and things, devices, coveyances, and aſſurances in the law whatſoever, for the further, better, more perfect, and abſolute granting, conveying, aſſuring, and confirming the ſaid Plantation and ſugar-work, lands, tenements, ſlaves, hereditaments, and premiſes, mentioned, or intended to be hereby granted and releaſed, with their iſſue and appurtenances, unto and to the uſe of the ſaid J— M— and T— S—, their heirs, executors, adminiſtrators, and aſſigns for ever, according to the nature and quality of the ſaid premiſes reſpectively, freed and abſolutely diſcharged of and from the aforeſaid proviſo or agreement for redemption, and all equity thereupon, as by the ſaid J— M— and T— S—, their executors, adminiſtrators, or aſſigns, or their or any of their council learned in the law, ſhall be reaſonably adviſed or deviſed and required. AND IT IS hereby

hereby declared and agreed, by and between the ſaid parties to theſe preſents, that, in the mean time, and until default ſhall happen to be made of or in payment of the ſaid ſum of four thouſand pounds, or ſome part thereof, or of the intereſt thereof, contrary to the form and effect of the aforeſaid proviſo and covenant for payment of the ſame, and the true intent and meaning of theſe preſents, it ſhall and may be lawful to and for the ſaid J— N—, his heirs and aſſigns, peaceably and quietly to have, hold, uſe, occupy, poſſeſs, and enjoy the ſaid plantation and ſugar-work, lands, tenements, ſlaves, hereditaments, and premiſes, mentioned or intended to be hereby granted and releaſed, and to receive and take the rents, iſſues, and profits thereof, and of every part and parcel thereof, to his and their own proper uſe and benefit, without the lawful let, ſuit, trouble, denial, eviction, moleſtation, or interruption, of or by the ſaid J— M— and T— S—, or either of them, their or either of their heirs, executors, adminiſtrators, or aſſigns; or of or by any other perſon or perſons lawfully claiming, or to claim, by, from, or under, or in truſt for them or any of them. In witneſs whereof, the ſaid parties to theſe preſents have hereunto ſet their hands and ſeals, the day and year firſt above written.

The SCHEDULE *to which the above* INDENTURE *refers.*

Men: Antigua, Eſſex, Quamin (and 55 more named in the ſchedule under the deed). Boys: Little Thomas (and 3 more named in the ſchedule under the deed), Women: Nancy, Senia (and 24 more named in the ſchedule under the deed).

deed). Stock: 20 mules, and 40 head of black cattle.

J— N—. (L. S.)
Sealed and delivered (being A— N—. (L. S.)
first duly stampt) in the J— M—. (L. S.)
presence of T— S—. (L. S.)
R— C— L—.
J— B—.

RECEIVED the day and year first within written, of and from the within named J——— M——— and T——— S——— the sum of four thousand pounds of good and lawful money of Great Britain, being the consideration money within mentioned, to be by them paid to me,

J—— N——.

Witness, R— C— L—
J— B—.

BE IT REMEMBERED, That on the thirtieth day of November 1776, J——— N———, Esq; and A——— his wife, parties to the within Indenture, personally came and appeared before me Sir Thomas Hallifax, Knight, Lord Mayor of the city of London, and acknowledged that they severally signed, sealed, and as their respective act and deed delivered the within Indenture: AND the said J——— N——— also acknowledged, that he signed the receipt hereon indorsed; and likewise that he signed, sealed, and as his act and deed delivered, the Indenture of Lease mentioned in and referred to by the within Indenture: AND the said A—— N——— being by me privately examined separate and apart from her said husband, declared, That she executed the within Indenture of her own free will and accord, without any

any force, threats, compulsion, or coercion of or from her said husband.

THOMAS HALLIFAX, Mayor.

TO ALL TO WHOM THESE PRESENTS shall come, I Sir Thomas Hallifax, Knight, Lord Mayor of the City of London, in pursuance of an Act of Parliament made and passed in the fifth year of the reign of his late Majesty King George the Second, intituled, " An Act for the " more easy Recovery of Debts in his Majesty's " Plantations and Colonies in America,". DO HEREBY CERTIFY, That on the day of the date hereof personally came and appeared before me J——— B——— the Deponent named in the Affidavit hereunto annexed, being a person well known, and worthy of good credit; and by solemn oath, which the said Deponent then took before me upon the Holy Evangelists of Almighty God, did solemnly and sincerely declare, testify, and depose to be true the several matters and things mentioned and contained in the said annexed Affidavit: And I the said Lord Mayor, DO HEREBY FURTHER CERTIFY, That on the day of the date hereof also personally came and appeared before me J——— N———, Esq; and A— his wife, parties to the annexed indenture of Release, and acknowledged that they severally signed, sealed, and as their respective act and deed delivered the same: AND the said J——— N——— also acknowledged, That he signed the receipt thereon indorsed, and likewise that he signed, sealed, and as his act and deed, delivered the Indenture of Lease hereunto also annexed: AND the said A——— N——— being by me privately examined separate and apart from her said husband, declared, that she executed

cuted the ſaid Indenture of Releaſe, of her own free will and accord, without any force, threats, compulſion, or coercion of or from her ſaid huſband.

LORD MAYOR'S SEAL.

IN FAITH and teſtimony whereof, I the ſaid Lord Mayor have not only ſigned the acknowledgement indorſed on the ſaid Indenture of Releaſe, but have alſo cauſed the Seal of the Office of Mayoralty of the ſaid City of London to be hereunto put and affixed, dated in London the thirtieth day of November, in the year of our Lord one thouſand ſeven hundred and ſeventy-ſix.

BEACH.

LONDON to wit,

J—— B—— of the pariſh of Saint Giles in the Fields, in the County of Middleſex, Gentleman, being duly ſworn upon the Holy Evangeliſts, maketh oath and ſaith, That he this Deponent, together with R—— C—— L——, did ſee J—— N——, Eſquire, ſign, ſeal, and as his reſpective act and deed deliver, the Indentures of Leaſe and Releaſe hereunto annexed, bearing date reſpectively the thirteenth and fourteenth days of this inſtant November, the Releaſe made or mentioned to be made between the ſaid J—— N—— and A—— his wife, of the one part, and J—— M—— and T—— S——, Merchnts, of the other part: And this Deponent, together with the ſaid R—— C—— L——, did alſo ſee the ſaid J—— N—— ſign the receipt indorſed upon the ſaid Indenture of Releaſe: and this Deponent further ſaith, That he, together with the ſaid

R——

R—— C—— L—— did ſee the ſaid A—— N——, J—— M——, and T—— S——, ſeverally ſign, ſeal, and as their reſpective act and deed deliver, the ſaid Indenture of Releaſe; and that the name J—— N——, ſet to the ſaid Indenture of Leaſes and Releaſe, and alſo to the ſaid Receipt indorſed upon the ſaid Indenture of Releaſe, and the names A—— N—— J—— M——, and T—— S——, ſet to the ſaid Indenture of Releaſe, are of the reſpective proper hands-writing of them the ſaid J—— N——, A—— N——, J—— M——, and T—— S—— parties thereto, and that the names R—— C—— L—— and J—— B——, ſubſcribed as witneſſes to the execution of the ſaid Indentures of Leaſe and Releaſe, are of the reſpective proper hands-writing of the ſaid R—— C—— L——, and this Deponent; and further this Deponent ſaith not.

J—— B——.

Sworn the 30th day of November 1776, before me,

THOMAS HALLIFAX, Mayor.

Enrolled in the chief Office of Enrollments in Jamaica, this 8th March 1777, lib. 282. fol. 37.

Extur.

R. LEWING, Sec.

APPEN-

APPENDIX.

THREE orders of the King in Council (relative to the trade between the subjects of his Majesty's dominions, and the inhabitants of the United States of America) made in pursuance of the powers given to his Majesty by 23 Geo. III. c. 39. which was passed the 12th of May 1783, two of which orders were made since this work went to the press, vid. the Act, *antea*, page 41.

At the Court at St. James's, the 14th of May 1783.

PRESENT,

The KING's most Excellent Majesty in Council.

WHEREAS, by an Act of Parliament passed this Session, intituled, "An Act for preventing "certain instruments from being required from "ships belonging to the United States of Ame-"rica, and to give to his Majesty, for a limited "time, certain powers for the better carrying on "trade and commerce between the subjects of his "Majesty's dominions, and the inhabitants of the "said United States," it is, amongst other things, enacted, That during the continuance of the said Act, it shall and may be lawful for his Majesty in Council, by order or orders to be issued and published from time to time, to give such directions, and to make such regulations with respect to duties, drawbacks, or otherwise, for carrying on the trade and commerce between the people and territories belonging to the Crown of Great Britain, and the people and territories of the

the ſaid United States, as to his Majeſty in Council ſhall appear moſt expedient and ſalutary; any law, uſage, or cuſtom to the contrary notwithſtanding. His Majeſty doth therefore, by and with the advice of his Privy Council, hereby order and direct, That any oil, or any unmanufactured goods or merchandiſes, being the growth or production of any of the territories of the ſaid United States of America, may (until further order) be imported directly from thence into any of the ports of this kingdom, either in Britiſh or American ſhips by Britiſh ſubjects, or by any of the people inhabiting in and belonging to the ſaid United States, or any of them; and ſuch goods or merchandiſe ſhall and may be entered and landed in any port in this kingdom, upon payment of the ſame duties as the like ſort of goods or merchandiſe are, or may be ſubject and liable to, if imported by Britiſh ſubjects in Britiſh ſhips from any Britiſh Iſland or Plantation in America, and no other; notwithſtanding ſuch goods or merchandiſe, or the ſhips in which the ſame may be brought, may not be accompanied with the certificates or other documents heretofore required by law. And it is hereby further ordered and directed, That there ſhall be the ſame drawbacks, exemptions, and bounties on merchandiſes and goods exported from Great Britain into the territories of the ſaid United States of America, or any of them, as are allowed upon the exportation of the like goods and merchandiſe to any of the Iſlands, Plantations, or Colonies belonging to the Crown of Great Britain in America. And it is hereby further ordered and directed, That all American ſhips and veſſels which ſhall have voluntarily come into any port of Great Britain ſince the 20th of January 1783, ſhall be admitted

to

to an entry; and, after such entry made, shall be intitled, together with the goods and merchandises on board the same ships and vessels, to the full benefit of this order. And the Right Honourable the Lords Commissioners of his Majesty's Treasury, and the Lords Commissioners of the Admiralty, are to give the necessary directions herein, as to them may respectively appertain.

W. FAWKENER.

At the Court at St. James's, the 6th of June 1783.

PRESENT,

The King's most Excellent Majesty in Council.

WHEREAS by an Act of Parliament passed this Session, intituled, "An Act for preventing "certain instruments from being required from "ships belonging to the United States of America, and to give to his Majesty, for a limited "time, certain powers for the better carrying on "trade and commerce between the subjects of "his Majesty's dominions, and the inhabitants of "the said United States," it is amongst other things enacted, That during the continuance of the said Act, it shall and may be lawful for his Majesty in Council, by order or orders to be issued and published, from time to time, to give such directions, and to make such regulations with respect to duties, drawbacks, or otherwise, for carrying on the trade and commerce between the people and territories belonging to the Crown

of

of Great Britain, and the people and territories of the ſaid United States, as to his Majeſty in Council ſhall appear moſt expedient and ſalutary; any law, uſage, or cuſtom to the contrary notwithſtanding: His Majeſty doth therefore, by and with the advice of his Privy Council, hereby order and direct, That pitch, tar, turpentine, indigo, maſts, yards, and bowſprits, being the growth or production of any of the United States of America, may (until further order) be imported directly from thence into any of the ports of this Kingdom, either in Britiſh or American ſhips, by Britiſh ſubjects, or by any of the people inhabiting in and belonging to the ſaid United States, or any of them; and that the Articles above recited ſhall and may be entered and landed in any port of this Kingdom, upon payment of the ſame duties as the ſame are or may be ſubject and liable to, if imported by Britiſh ſubjects in Britiſh ſhips, from any Britiſh Iſland or Plantation in America, and no other, notwithſtanding ſuch pitch, tar, turpentine, indigo, maſts, yards, and bowſprits, or the ſhips in which the ſame may be brought, may not be accompanied with the certificates or other documents heretofore required by law: and his Majeſty is hereby further pleaſed, by and with the advice aforeſaid, to order and direct, That any tobacco, being the growth or production of any of the territories of the ſaid United States of America, may likewiſe (until further order) be imported directly from thence, in manner above mentioned, and may be landed in this Kingdom; and upon the importer's paying down in ready money the duty commonly called the old ſubſidy, ſuch tobacco may be warehouſed under his Majeſty's locks, upon the importer's own bond for payment of all the further duties due for ſuch tobacco, within the time limited

mited by law, according to the net weight and quantity of ſuch tobacco, at the time it ſhall be ſo landed, with the ſame allowances for the payment of ſuch farther duties, and under the like reſtrictions and regulations in all other reſpects, not altered by this order, as ſuch tobacco is and may be warehouſed, by virtue of any Act or Acts of Parliament in force. — And the Right Honourable the Lords Commiſſioners of his Majeſty's Treaſury, and the Lords Commiſſioners of the Admiralty, are to give the neceſſary directions herein, as to them may reſpectively appertain.

STEPH. COTTRELL.

At the Court at St. James's, the 2d of July 1783.

P R E S E N T,

The KING'S Moſt Excellent Majeſty in Council.

WHEREAS, by an Act of Parliament paſſed this Seſſion, intituled, "An Act for preventing "certain Inſtruments from being required from "ſhips belonging to the United States of America, "and to give to his Majeſty, for a limited time, "certain powers for the better carrying on trade "and commerce between the ſubjects of his Ma"jeſty's dominions, and the inhabitants of the "ſaid United States," it is amongſt other things enacted, That during the continuance of the ſaid Act, it ſhall and may be lawful for his Majeſty in Council, by order or orders to be iſſued and publiſhed from time to time, to give ſuch directions, and to make ſuch regulations with reſpect to duties, drawbacks, or otherwiſe, for carrying on the trade and commerce between the people and territories belonging to the Crown of Great Britain, and the people and territories of the ſaid United

United States, as to his Majeſty in Council ſhall appear moſt expedient and ſalutary; any law, uſage, or cuſtom to the contrary notwithſtanding; his Majeſty doth therefore, by and with the advice of his Privy Council, hereby order and direct, That pitch, tar, turpentine, hemp, and flax, maſts, yards, and bowſprits, ſtaves, heading, boards, timber, ſhingles, and all other ſpecies of lumber; horſes, neat cattle, ſheep, hogs, poultry, and all other ſpecies of live ſtock and live proviſions; peas, beans, potatoes, wheat, flour, bread, biſcuit, rice, oats, barley, and all other ſpecies of grain, being the growth or production of any of the United States of America, may (until further order) be imported by Britiſh ſubjects in Britiſh built ſhips, owned by his Majeſty's ſubjects, and navigated according to law, from any port of the United States of America, to any of his Majeſty's Weſt India Iſlands; and that rum, ſugar, molaſſes, coffee, cocoa nuts, ginger, and pimento, may, until further order, be exported by Britiſh ſubjects, in Britiſh-built ſhips, owned by his Majeſty's ſubjects, and navigated according to law, from any of his Majeſty's Weſt India Iſlands, to any port or place within the ſaid United States, upon payment of the ſame duties on exportation, and ſubject to the like rules, regulations, ſecurities, and reſtrictions, as the ſame articles by law are or may be ſubject and liable to, if exported to any Britiſh Colony or Plantation in America.——— And the Right Honourable the Lords Commiſſioners of his Majeſty's Treaſury, and the Lords Commiſſioners of the Admiralty, are to give the neceſſary directions herein, as to them may reſpectively appertain.

STEPH. COTTRELL.

F I N I S.

E R R A T A.

The Reader is desired to correct the following mistakes.

Page 11. l. 34. *after* Lord, *read* Chief.
—— 13. l. 17. *dele* clearly.
—— 140. l. 9. *for* that, *read* who.
—— 148. l. 16. *for* hurted, *read* hurt.
—— 256. l. 28. *for* twenty, *read* twenty-five.
—— 262. l. 2. *dele* superior.
—— 447. l. 7. *for* theretofore, *read* thentofore; l. 28. *after* be, *add* therein.
—— 448. l. 2. *for* as any, *read* as if any; l. 4. *for* his, *read* her.

INDEX